T0381410

From me
to you:

THE
TAPESTRY
OF LIFE
AND ITS
SECRETS

"I wanted to leave a gift
here on this planet and
let others discover earlier
certain things that took
me years to learn, which
could change the way
they see the world and
enhance their life."

- Author Lily Foyster

LILY FOYSTER

BALBOA.
PRESS

A DIVISION OF HAY HOUSE

Balboa Press books may be ordered through booksellers or by contacting:

Balboa Press
A Division of Hay House
1663 Liberty Drive
Bloomington, IN 47403
www.balboapress.com.au
1-(877) 407-4847

ISBN: 978-1-4525-1171-9 (sc)
ISBN: 978-1-4525-1172-6 (e)

Printed in the United States of America

Balboa Press rev. date: 11/26/2013

Contents

Contents

DEDICATION

I would like to dedicate this book to my sons, Dominic and Daniel, who have heard all that I am saying in this book in one form or another, most of their lives. I love you both very much and am very thankful to have you both in my life. I wish for you that you will continue to learn, grow and develop and achieve your full potential. I hope that The Tapestry of Life somehow reminds you of some of the wisdom that I have tried to share with you and that it encourages you to take appropriate actions whenever necessary. Be the best that you can be. Dominic you have a beautiful soul and I am proud of you and of the talented man that you are. Dan, you just "crack me up!" Your sense of humour is legendary! I am just as proud of the man you are, with your own talents, strength and resilience. You are both a great gift in my life.

I would like to dedicate this book to my husband, Leigh, who has had to put up with me spending a lot of time locked away in the computer room. You are the love of my life and I thank you for who you are and for everything you do. Thank you for your thoughtfulness and all the wonderful dinners.

This book is also dedicated to Tracey and Annie as well as Jamie and Maya, who I love very much and are all very special to me. I pray, Jamie and Maya that as you grow up this book will help you to discover wisdom that will guide and help you navigate the sometimes treacherous terrain of life. I wish for you that you live a full and happy life, expressing gratitude for everything that you have and that you achieve what you are meant to in life by avoiding many of the pitfalls that can sometimes trip you up. I will love you always and will always be there for you. Choose to live well and be happy.

In addition, I would like to dedicate this book to all the young people in my family, whom I hold very dear to my heart, wishing them the very best that life can offer. Thank you Manuel for your feedback and encouragement; I appreciate it. I hope that you are all able to gain some insight and help from The Tapestry of Life to help you achieve your full potential and live a full and happy life without regrets.

I dedicate this book to my clients, past and present (including those in the UK), from whom I have learnt so much. It has been my privilege to get to know you, care for you and help you; in particular, Catherine, Marina and Laura (UK) as well as Candice, Deanne, Angie, Heather and Nadia (Australia). Thank you for nominating me Australian of the Year 2013. I am humbled and appreciate this great honour.

I also wish to dedicate this book to my wonderful neighbours and friends, Winnefred, Steyn, the beautiful Win-Marié and the gorgeous Petrie. Thank you so much Winnefred for all your help with the editing of this book. I very much appreciate it and am extremely grateful.

Last but not least I would like to thank my mother for the wonderful mother that she has been to all of us. She is a living example of what "an attitude of gratitude" is. I wouldn't be where I am today if it wasn't for you. *Merci Maman, tu es adorable*! I would also like to thank my wonderful father, who sadly is no longer with us. I simply cannot miss to dedicate my book to my 7 sisters and my brother. They are a constant source of love, inspiration, fun and an absolute pleasure to be with. Thank you so much for all your kindness, caring, enthusiasm and encouragement. You are my best friends. I can go on and on about every single one of you as you all have very special gifts and talents, but I would especially like to thank my sister Christiane for her constant caring, kindness, selflessness, help, encouragement, optimism and marvellous sense of fun. Your giggle is the best thing that anyone can hear to uplift them at any time, whatever the situation. I thank you for all that you do for the family and for the truly amazing person you really are. You are an example to all who knows you. I must also thank my sister Josette, a true woman of substance, who has literally kissed the Blarney stone. She is responsible for the flash of inspiration that provided me with the title of this book. You are all my very special people in my life and I love you all so much. Thank you for helping me to be the person that I am today. I am eternally grateful for the family that we have and the love and unity that we share.

God bless every single one of you abundantly!

INTRODUCTION

What I like about a good author is not what he says, but what he whispers.
—Logan Pearsall Smith

I aim to whisper many secrets from me to you about the tapestry of life, in the hope that they help you avoid some pitfalls along life's bumpy road; secrets to help you triumph and succeed in the game of life and secrets to assist you and guide you to reach your full potential.

The aim of this book is to help you understand some of the secrets of life so that once you understand them, can help you shed your limiting beliefs and enhance your life while successfully changing the direction of your life for the better.

One thing for sure is that we do make mistakes, and hopefully we will learn by them. However, if we become knowledgeable about a lot of life's skills that can be learnt through other people's experiences, our lives can be improved a hundred fold with less anguish.

As this life is no dress rehearsal, the more pointless mistakes we can avoid, the happier we can be.

My reason for writing this book is that I wanted to pass on to others the wisdom I acquired during my lifetime, especially throughout my work. My wish is to contribute and make a difference in this world. I want to leave a gift to my children and grandchildren, to the young people in my family, to my clients past and present who have taught me so much and to the world, in the hope that it will continue to inspire people even when I am no longer here.

I was mainly motivated by my clients, by my sons and other young members of my family. I wanted to teach them earlier in life what took me a lifetime to learn. I believe that you can gain years of wisdom by learning from other people's experiences, and having good role models to follow.

What are the things that you need to know, to give you an edge in life—without having to go through mistake after mistake and heartache after heartache, before you get the answers you're looking for? Maybe you have made the mistakes and had the heartaches and need to start over—but how?

I have thought of some of the most important life lessons, and put them together in this book, so that you, my dear readers, can get that edge. You may find that I repeat myself at times; however, I believe that when we see things again and again, it tends to stick in our brain. They say that repetition is the mother of all skills.

Life is a skill we need to learn to acquire. We come into this life without a Life Manual to tell us how to play this enigmatic game, we just need to learn and discover the rules as we go along. The quicker we learn the rules, the more skilled we get, the easier life becomes and the more we can achieve what we want.

We can just about learn anything—if we want to and are open to learning.

Sometimes, the truth of the matter is that you may really be trying to do your best in life but you keep coming up against stumbling blocks; however the problem is that you don't know how to turn things around even if you want to. The fact is that you can't know what you don't know. If you knew it, you could do something to change your life. I do hope that you find the answers amongst the following pages.

When all is said and done, The Secrets of the Tapestry of life is directed to anyone who may not have discovered these secrets earlier in their life or it may serve as a reminder of the secrets we may have forgotten. It is never too late to learn and to make positive changes in life.

My story

My background is in Advanced Nursing. I always had a passion for helping and caring for people since I was a little girl. I remember bossing my two younger sisters with my caring attitude by lining them in front of me and enthusiastically tucking their shirt or blouse into their skirts, and making sure their hair was nicely combed, as of course, I was much more capable than them, being an experienced five year old bigger sister. Thank goodness, in a large family, you don't learn to complain much; you just have to fit in. So they fitted in with my need to care for them!

My first experience of being a home nurse was when I was probably about seven years old, and I caught the measles first and recovered; but as I was into sharing I very generously gave the virus to my poor unsuspected mother and the rest of my siblings. Of course, by the time they caught the virus, I was well on my way to recovery, as there was a two week incubation period. I enjoyed being the nurse helping my dad to take care of my mum and my sisters. Perhaps, that's where my love for nursing started after I was able to practice on my own family. I'm sure I was overbearing with my attention, but no one probably had the heart to tell me so.

I worked in most areas of nursing, but specialized in working in the Emergency Rooms as well as in Intensive Care, after being the Nurse in Charge of a Surgical Unit and an Orthopaedic Unit. I then moved on to Community Nursing, which stimulated my love for life-long learning. I loved and enjoyed my work as a Health Visitor, and qualified as a Specialist Practice Teacher to teach Health Visitors in the UK for very many years. For over 20 years I was a Post-natal Depression (PND) Specialist as part of my job, and gained much experience dealing with anxiety, depression, Parenting issues and Relationships too. I conducted courses and enjoyed teaching, which led me to become a speaker. I have spent years learning and I particularly enjoyed anything related to Counselling and Behavioural Psychology. I have a Bachelor of Science (Hons) Degree in Health Studies, and, worked for nearly 9 years as a Qualified Nurse Practitioner, in a GP surgery, in the UK two evenings a week. A Nurse Practitioner in the UK can assess the patient's health, diagnose, order the necessary investigations, prescribe treatment and/or refer to other agencies if appropriate. I found this work very satisfying and loved it. At the same time, I continued being a PND Specialist, Team Leader/Manager and continued with my Health Visiting and Teaching duties. In between, I indulged in my great passion for Self-development.

I often wonder now how I fitted it all in. I believed and still believe that where there's a will, there's always a way! Life was busy but stimulating and enjoyable. Sometimes the more you have to do, the better organized you become at managing your life.

I had a zeal for helping mothers with Post-natal Depression (PND). It was my enthusiasm for improving the lives of mothers suffering from this debilitating syndrome that led me to become a Personal Development addict. While I wanted to be able to help them as much as I could, it also stimulated my thirst for knowledge about alternative therapies and nutrition. I finally culminated my passion by formally training to be a Life Coach in Perth, Western Australia. Today my medical knowledge is a great asset to my Life Coaching practice, especially as I identified another interest of mine to be Brain functioning and Nutrition. I believe that professional coaching can enhance the life of anyone. You do not have to have a problem; you may just want to do better or enhance your life.

The marvellous thing about Coaching is that it doesn't have the stigma that other helping professions may carry. Anyone can access a Coach, even when they are doing well. If they wish to achieve a certain goal, a Coach is the ideal person to raise awareness, identify what you want and walk with you until you achieve your goals. Coaches are professionals who hold high standards and are committed to help you achieve your goals in a non-judgmental and safe environment. It is a sure way of achieving what you want instead of struggling to do so and never really managing to get there. In the same way, that if you want to lose weight or get fit, you may access a Personal Trainer at a gym to push you to achieve your goal, a Life Coach would do the same thing for you in achieving your life's goals and teach you life's skills.

When I was working as a Post Natal Depression Specialist, I had set up my own PND group as well as other PND groups in several areas of the Borough, which were then manned by a Health Visitor and a Mental Health Practitioner or a Psychologist. I soon realized how quickly my own clients improved compared to the other PND groups.

My clients not only recovered quicker but were motivated to go on to achieve what they had dreamt of all along but had previously thought that they were incapable of achieving. For instance, one client trained as a teacher, another who had always dreamt of opening her own garden nursery went ahead and opened one and became quite successful at it; another client who had always wanted to train as a nurse, changed career and went ahead on her nurse training; another client was very good at writing, so she was encouraged to start by writing short stories and getting them published; to-day she has written her own book on Post-natal Depression, which has now been published. Another beautiful and charming young woman was, Laura, who has now obtained her degree in Anthropology; the hilariously funny, kind and incomparable Marina, used the experience to further her art career and eventually trained to become an art teacher, which had always been her dream, and many more achieved so much more than they ever thought possible.

The clients were always encouraged to see their illness as a catalyst to change their lives, which they will never regret as they would learn so much from it, and to use the experience to grow and develop beyond their wildest imagination. Many came back and said so.

I started to ask myself why my clients did so much better than the other groups. Their illness time was shorter and they were very motivated in changing their lives and improving themselves and their relationships. Sometimes, that also meant having the courage to separate, if the relationship was toxic.

Then it dawned on me that the reason why they did so well was because I was actually coaching them rather than going down the traditional mental health route. They were in fact gaining valuable life lessons, which inspired and motivated them to put these into practice, whether that was on a personal level or in their relationships. They were encouraged to cultivate optimism, enthusiasm and positive thinking. That way of normalizing their illness and seeing the positive side of life seemed to really resonate with them and they thrived on it. A supportive group environment was ideal for the optimism bug to spread.

The main thing was that as they learnt life skills and got the support of the group, they were in point of fact rewiring their brains which in turn changed their perceptions and their emotions. Consequently improved their usual negative pattern of thinking and as a result enhanced how they felt. This in turn produced better mental and physical health, and ultimately changed their lives. They developed a kindred spirit of togetherness and eagerness when they met each Wednesday and looked forward to see each other. The support they got from each other was exceptional. Their demise was also the catalyst to open opportunities for them. Their focus had changed, from concentrating on their PND and all that was wrong in their lives to one where they looked forward to the future and being the best mother that they could be, as they learned to believe that good things could be round the corner instead of the doom and gloom that was so familiar to them. They developed an eagerness to become the best parent that they could be. As they made progress their relationships too improved. I studied nutrition to see what else could help them and realized the value and role of Magnesium, Zinc, vitamin D, Vitamin Bs and the essential role of Omega 3 (bearing in mind that 60% of the brain is made up of omega 3); and iron for those who suffered with anaemia. They all got their thyroid levels checked too, as it can have a big impact on PND.

It became a matter of Belief! If they thought they would get better and do something positive with their lives, they did. The key was to change their focus, beliefs and their perceptions for an improved one.

If you think you can, you can. If you think you can't you're probably right.

—*Henry Ford*

My passion for helping people was given a major boost and I became very excited as I identified my long-term goal of becoming a REAL Life Coach. I avidly devoured anything to do with personal development books; I couldn't pass one without reading it. I tried to learn as much as I could a very long time prior to formalizing my learning to becoming a Life Coach. When the time was right I formalized my goal by taking on the Life Coaching training, and since have not stopped to develop myself and increase my skills so that I can give a full range of services to my clients, and help make a difference in their lives.

I am very passionate about coaching my clients, as I was with helping the mothers with PND. I am particularly fond of using certain techniques like Emotional Freedom Techniques (EFT) and Neuro-Linguistic Programming (NLP), as I believe that they are wonderful techniques which produce amazing, and miraculously fast and lasting results.

As much as I do some mentoring and counselling, I chose Life Coaching instead of any of the other helping professions because Life Coaching is future-based, whereas, often many of the other helping professions are past-oriented. Understanding the past is very helpful, but once you've understood why you are as you are, you need to do something about doing different in the future. I believe that Coaching is the answer. In Coaching, it doesn't matter how you got to where you are; this is what you have to work with; we raise awareness and identify where you want to be; we help you to bridge the gap and walk with you to get you where you want to be.

I am completely dedicated to helping my clients and have learned a lot from them. I get my reward when my clients do well and become who they choose to be and have the life they want for themselves. I am very grateful for the work that I do with them and was very surprised this year when they nominated me to be Australian of the year 2013. I would like to thank them for this honour for which I am entirely appreciative.

A Life Coach helps you with life skills to win in life as a Sports Coach would do for an athlete to give them the edge to win. Working as a Speaker and Life Coach made me realize that one of my most important values was the value of contribution, and making a difference in the world. This is where the idea of writing this book sprung from. In my enthusiasm for Coaching and my passion for helping people, I wanted to leave a gift here on this planet and let others discover earlier certain things that took me years to learn, which could change the way they see the world and enhance their life.

So, From Me to You, I do hope that you enjoy the Secrets that are revealed about The Tapestry of Life, in this book.

ENJOY!

With Love
Lily

CHAPTER ONE

Some Secrets Revealed
To Help You Create Your Life

Life isn't about finding yourself. Life is about creating yourself.
—*George Bernard Shaw*

Life's Too Short

There is nothing new in telling you the well-known secret that Life's too short. People often say that *Life's too short* as a cliché. It is often a phrase that gets bandied about without much thought put into it, without really thinking about the significance of these three small words. Yes, we do know that life is too short to waste it. However the reality is that life is happening when we are busy making a living or wasting it getting upset or hurt over trivial things. If we put our aspirations on hold without a time frame because we are too busy on the wrong things, we may never get where we want to end up.

When we are young we think that there's plenty of time to do what we want to do. Before we know it the time has passed and unless we have a plan and stay on target, we may end up not achieving any of our goals as time has quickly passed us by, without us even having noticed it.

Think about where you were at, 10 years ago! How fast did that go? Well, the next ten years will gallop just as fast! If you are now 20 years old, ten years ago you were a child of only ten years old. It is now already too late to wish that you had applied yourself better at school so that you wouldn't find it such a struggle to get a good job now. In the next ten years you would be thirty years old. How much of that time would you remember or waste? What have you learnt in the last ten years? What would you do differently if you knew better then? In another ten years you would be forty and looking at middle age fast! One minute you're a child, the next you have lived more days than you have left! And all of it feels just like yesterday! Scary? . . . Yes! . . . . So there's no time to waste!

This is how you will feel all your life. Days become weeks; weeks become months and before you know it, years have gone by! The years will race on and one day you will wake up and you may be forty, fifty, or sixty and beyond in no time, and still think: where did that time go?

The only thing is that your brain and your feelings and emotions will not age as fast.

When you are fifty, you will still feel like you are twenty or thirty inside. Some of us may wish we could do things differently if we were given another chance. Problem is we can never go back again. We get one chance and one chance only to go through this life. So we better use our time wisely. If we want to be happy and reach our full potential we best get it right the first time; or at least for most of the time! So let's live the best life we can without wasting any of it, and if the secrets revealed in this book can stop you from wasting a good life and make it great instead, all the better.

The past is over and done and cannot be changed. This is the only moment we can experience.
—Louise Hay

Life really is too short not to live it meaningfully. You have to do the best you can and live your life to the full without wasting time on unimportant things, as Father Time is constantly ticking and doesn't miss a second. Don't squander valuable energy getting upset and bearing grudges. Don't live a life of addiction that can spell nothing but trouble, under the pretense that you're young and having a good time. Life honestly is too short for that!

> *So the first secret to learn is to: Respect time and respect life and use them both wisely, as life is too short to waste it and not live it well.*

The next secret is to:

Plan and Create Your Life

If we want to reach our full potential or if we want something, we need to plan and create, otherwise it just doesn't happen, as we have no direction to aim towards. It is like being at sea without a compass or going somewhere without a map or satellite navigation (GPS) to get us there. We have no starting point and no destination, how can we achieve our goal of getting there? We need a direction for our lives to work towards. We can't leave something as important as our destiny to fate, to others or to whatever else.

When we plan and create, we have a direction to work towards, and that gives us confidence.

You may have your own reasons for wanting to change your life, but one of the main reasons may be that you are not happy with certain aspects of your life as it is and you want to improve on them or change them altogether.

Plan your life. If you don't, you will always be reacting to what someone else is deciding for your life, which can be the reason why you may feel insignificant and unhappy. You are giving the control of your life to others to do as they please with you. Decide where you want to be. What do you need to do to get there?

Decide where you want your life to be in 5 years from now. Then, where will you be in ten years? If you want to be in a certain place, you may need to work steadily towards your long term goal. This may mean that you have to do certain things to be able to achieve your goal. This may well mean extra training.

> *Secret: Plan and create your life.*

A Secret about Learning

The fact is you picked up this book because you want to learn something. It doesn't matter how old you are, you can improve your life at any stage. Learning is for everyone, young, not so young and old alike. Being open to life-long learning is an asset that you can capitalize on throughout your life, at any given time. It probably is the next secret that you should become aware of:

> *Never stop learning as you go through life.*

Human beings have a natural need to learn, grow and develop. We are all natural born learners. Learning enhances our life enormously. If we stop, we become stuck and unable to move on.

It isn't the responsibility of others to teach you. It is your responsibility to seek to learn and improve. None of this: No one ever taught me how to do this, is valid. It is down to you to seek how to progress, it is not anyone else's responsibility.

People who love to learn are more confident, enjoy life more and are more satisfied in life.

People who hate to learn have linked a lot of pain with learning.

People who love to learn link a lot of pleasure with gaining knowledge.

Knowledge helps you to make informed choices. Knowledge translated into action is power! Power gives you freedom of choice. Freedom of choice can help you to make better decisions. Better decisions send you in the direction of the path that you wish to follow and hence have a huge impact on creating your life.

There is a misconception that misleads many people to believe that to make a change in their life can take a very long time or that they need to do something extreme like changing their job or career, move house or city or go abroad even; or that they need lots of money otherwise any change is impossible. That usually is hopeless negative talk when people really want to change but don't know how to. Many people incorrectly make this assumption, because they don't feel empowered and they don't know what to do and do not know the secret to help them make the necessary changes in their life.

The reality, however, can be quite different. Changes in our lives can manifest themselves incredibly fast at times; contrary to the belief that changes can take a very long time and that you need certain resources to make them happen.

Some may rely on their will power. Now, we all know what happens when we put our faith in our will power? When we fail, we give up as we realise our effort is unattainable, therefore lose confidence in ourselves and in our goals.

> *The secret to this is that it is important to have the understanding about giving "a different meaning to things" for you to be able to see them in a completely different light.*

The actions you then decide on can be very different from the ones you might have taken had you not had the correct understanding and meaning in the first place. Acquiring the necessary knowledge and meaning can make all the difference.

With Neuro-Linguistic programming, (NLP) changes can be lasting and immediate.

NLP is an effective collection of techniques which helps us to run our own brain. NLP: Neuro (nervous system) Linguistic (the use of language to communicate with ourselves) Programming (installing a new program). The techniques of NLP are incredibly valuable and can help you make instant changes by using our neurology, (our central nervous system) and the movies we make in our minds (the images and sounds we make in our heads) including using our physiology (our body). You need to research these further should you be interested in them, as they are beyond the limitations of this book.

Simply put, it is like taking out the faulty software in your computer (brain) and installing new software (program: new belief or new behaviour). If you put in the new software, changes are often instantaneous; just like removing a DVD and putting in another one.

Once you know how to do things a better way, you would never go back to your old ways, would you? Of course not! You now know better!

There are many Life Coaches who use NLP to help make positive changes in their clients' lives, and I use them with much success in my Life Coaching practice.

The secret of pain and pleasure

All of us are dictated to by two domineering rulers: **Pain and Pleasure**. We are all the same, no matter who we are and what we say, without exception. We all search pleasure in life and seek to avoid pain. It is said that we are all hedonistic by nature; this means that as human beings we are programmed to avoid pain and to seek pleasure.

Think about it: Whatever you do, you do it because you like to or want to; in other words, it either brings you some pleasure doing something or you want to avoid experiencing some sort of pain by doing it or not doing it. Even if you do your job under duress and do not enjoy it, you still do it, because you can avoid the pain of not having a job. The job gives you money which provides for your needs which can bring pleasure.

Procrastination

We procrastinate because we connect more pain with doing something than not doing it. When it becomes more painful to avoid doing something than doing it, then we end the procrastination and get on with it.

> *In fact what we need to do is to associate a lot of pleasure with doing the task and then it becomes easier to execute.*

This principle doesn't only affect some of us and not others; it affects us all! As a human being we all react this way. Ask yourself why you do some things and why you don't do others? In fact the main reason behind all our behaviours is that we do everything we can so that we can avoid pain and acquire pleasure.

This is an important thing to know, because it actually means that we can use pain and pleasure to help us achieve what we desire and to alter unwanted behaviours.

> *We need to attach as much pain as possible with what we don't want in our life and we have to connect as much pleasure as possible with what we do want.*

If we do this we can make the changes that we want to achieve a lot easier. If for instance, you don't like to learn, and you associate pain with education then you must link as much pleasure as you can to learning; make your learning environment exciting and fun, become really enthusiastic about it; reward yourself afterwards, or study with a good friend and make it fun.

Keep in the front of your mind what it will be like when you would have achieved your goal. Link a lot of pleasure to the end result. You will find that pretty soon learning will be associated with fun and you will find learning fun, easier, stimulating and exciting.

When we gain pleasure from doing something, we become keen to repeat it and really enjoy it. And before you know it, your newly acquired knowledge has the ability to produce the change you desire.

For instance, if you want to stop smoking, you would have to associate a lot of pain with the smoking and a lot of pleasure with stopping. You could really watch, (instead of switching off the channel or avoiding them) the shocking advertisements about quitting smoking on TV, which depicts someone who had his tongue cut off because of oral cancer and is dying due to cigarette smoking; see the sufferings that the person and his relatives go through; or watch the struggle that patients with Chronic Obstructive Pulmonary Disease go through just to take ONE breath, having to have their tank of oxygen close-by at all times, due to the effects of smoking; thereby linking a lot of pain to smoking. Also remember how smoking can prematurely age your skin and give you wrinkles? That's not a great thing, especially for us girls, right? Your thinking can change very quickly. The pain you get from this will make it very difficult for you to take pleasure in lighting up again. You will want to avoid the pain that smoking can create in you.

You can keep kidding yourself that these things won't happen to you and yes, you will stop one day, but you are not ready yet! . . . . that's called kidding yourself! That way, you will never be ready as there is always . . . . Tomorrow . . . . so you think! The reality is that bad health problems do happen to those who smoke. Living in denial doesn't stop you getting a nasty diagnosis. Think, what will it feel like to get a diagnosis of cancer when you are 35? 40? 45? 50? How would that feel like? What would you say to your wife? Husband? Children? Mother or father? Brother or sister? Grandparents? Nieces or nephews? (All these people will be affected by what happens to you!) Knowing you could have stopped that happening to you and your family had you taken appropriate action years earlier. Does that feel like pain to you? . . . . undeniably!

This may sound dramatic (and I know, you will hate reading this if this applies to you) but we all know what damage cigarettes can do to us. However unless you are confronted with the reality of life, you may never do something to help yourself. Life is truly too short to waste it. You may think that at some point you will give up because you do know how bad it is for your health, but you can only think about your instant gratification for now; you may think: One day, I will give up, but I am still young enough and will quit before any damage happens. But, as we said, life's too short to take bad risks! Time goes by very quickly and you find yourself with your same anti-social habit, frowned upon by your family and friends. Nowadays, there are no excuses. You can see your doctor and get some help to stop or else there is always hypnotherapy or the many quit lines. They will only work, if you access them and want it to work.

The problem is that you are kidding yourself thinking that it won't happen to you. Living in denial has been shown to kill or have dire consequences.

Really bad health problems happen to young people who take risks with their health. Don't kid yourself thinking that it's for others or older people and not you!

It does happen to somebody! Why couldn't that be you? Why do you think that you are immune? What makes you so special?

The fact is that none of us know when it is our turn to get a dreadful diagnosis, and what damage has already been done.

The good thing is if you quit, you can slowly start to repair the damage. However the longer you leave it, the worse the damage you are causing to your health.

Does that mean that there's no point giving up as you have already caused damage? Absolutely not! Whenever you give up, the lungs slowly start to recover and repair the damage. So, it is never too late!

Please do not kid yourself anymore. It is unintelligent to live in denial for the pleasure of instant gratification. At the back of your mind you do know that your luck may not last forever and that you are only waiting for the day that a shocking diagnosis comes knocking at your door. That's not pleasure that's pain!

A friend of mine had spent years chain smoking; then one day another friend told her that she couldn't understand how she could still put a cigarette to her lips, knowing that someday, may be soon, she may be diagnosed with lung cancer, and that her two daughters will be left without a mother to grow up. From that day on, she never ever lit another cigarette ever again. Her good friend helped her link more pain with smoking than the instant pleasure she got from lighting up.

If this is you, then I hope that you have a true friend to help you link pain with smoking or whatever your addiction is.

Deep down, we all know that addiction to anything is not a good thing!

The other side to this coin is that you can start getting excited about all the money that you will be saving and plan what you will do with that extra money. Think how far that money will go towards your next holiday, or you could give yourself regular mini-breaks with the money you would be saving or maybe you can now afford something that you have been wanting for a while, but felt you didn't have the money for it before! Does that sound like pleasure to you? It sure does!

You can even save the money and give it away to a good cause close to your big heart. Let it go to feed some children or help give clean water to a village in Africa, or help immunize some children in India! Or sponsor a child's education with that money. Think how good you would feel about that! And you would link much pleasure with stopping to smoke. You would have contributed to improve somebody less fortunate's life somewhere in the world!

It's not for everybody, I agree! You would rather spend the money on yourself? Well, why not? Of course you deserve that week-end away! You gave up smoking didn't you? What about those regular cheap deals that you couldn't previously afford? Celebrate your victory in an invigorating way! That is pleasure!

In this way you would have associated a lot of pain with smoking and a lot of pleasure with quitting smoking. Smoking becomes more and more painful and quitting becomes more and more desirable.

This principle works for any negative habit you want to stop.

Try associating a lot of pleasure with what you want to achieve and a lot of pain with what you want to give up. Promise! It works! I didn't invent this, that's just the way things are.

Reinforcement

> *The secret to maintaining the changes is that once you make a change, you need to reinforce it straight away by taking action towards it. Therefore you need to condition the new behaviour in a way that it will become natural for you.*

For instance, you can start planning a piggy bank where you would save the money that you would otherwise have been spent buying cigarettes; start looking at which holiday you would like to go on; get some brochures in and start to plan when you will be able to do it or research which charity you would like to invest your money in. Do some investigations into your new addiction free future. These will reinforce the fact that you are truly determined to give up smoking. Clean up your environment. Tell all your friends that you quit and they can no longer smoke in your house, and if they are good friends, they will support you. If they are not, they may sabotage you.

You have to keep using the new behaviour to condition yourself that you have now adopted a new way of being; otherwise you would revert back to the old behaviour. For instance, keep reinforcing your new behaviour by keeping your environment clean: no cigarettes in the house, in the car or anywhere, no ashtrays, no lighters or matches and not allowing any visitors to the house to light up; keep your clothes washed and fresh. Your house is definitely a smoke-free zone. Burn some aromatic oil in the house to change the usual overpowering smell of cigarettes. Avoid smoking places. Enjoy rattling your piggy bank to check how much money you have saved to date, and plan how you will spend your savings. Even open a special bank account for those savings.

Now, you have another dilemma: you need to pick your friends and associates to support you not to harm you.

> **Not only do you need to reinforce the new behaviour, you need to reinforce the associated behaviours as well.**

You have to condition not only giving up smoking but also the associated behaviours you had when you smoked. If you want to give up smoking, for example, and your usual time to smoke is associated with meeting friends and having a drink with them, you need to change these associated behaviours which accompanied smoking. Change your usual routine.

Make sure that you replace the smoking behaviour and the associated behaviours with other positive ones, for example, going for a walk with your partner or a non-smoking friend or chewing gum at the time that you would want a cigarette. Do something different with your hands. Play table tennis, squash, or any other game. Replace your negative habit with a new positive behaviour. Draw, paint, exercise, play a musical instrument or knit whatever takes your fancy, but use your hands to do something different than to put it to your mouth! You need to do something that will bring you pleasure. Practice the new behaviour until you are completely conditioned, like you once were when you were smoking.

Curious things, habits. People themselves never knew they had them.

—*Agatha Christie*

Stressful Family Patterns

People often react to stress in a family pattern. What I mean by this is that if a mother is normally anxious, she can often pass this anxiety down to her children. The children can become affected just by watching and observing their mother's reaction to every day events. You may find that the grandmother and her other siblings all react in a similar vein when something stressful or uncertain happens.

Self-awareness and insight into your behaviour are essential. Someone who has had a very difficult childhood may be caught up in a lifetrap. This is a long-term pattern which is deeply ingrained, originating in childhood, which is repeated over and over again throughout life, keeping the person trapped in their own self-destructive or self-sabotaging behaviours. Lifetraps can be hard to change, and may require a good therapist.

Perception

An age old secret is that:

There is no such thing as reality, there is only perception.

- Our perception is our reality -

One of life's secrets that changes all aspects of your life when you understand it is: **PERCEPTION.** This is a truth well accepted by all for a very long time. Reality as we see it can be very different to different people.

Our reality is our own, but it is not reality itself.

Have you ever had one of those 'Aha' moments, like suddenly a light bulb lit up over your head and you understood something you couldn't get before? What happened is that in that flash, your perception of something changed. Instead of seeing it the way you used to, you now have another way of seeing it. In that moment your reality changed.

Once your perception of something changes you cannot go back to believing what you did before.

Remember what it was like when you found out that there was no Father Christmas or Tooth Fairy? Once you know it, you can't go back to believing in this magical white bearded jolly old man we call Father Christmas, who can fly his reindeers all over the world in one night, squeezing his fat belly down everyone's chimneys, drinking milk and eating mince pies left for him in almost every household all over the world (no wonder he is fat!) and who delivers presents to all little boys and girls worldwide. Never again can you believe that the mysterious creature we call, The Tooth Fairy who knows exactly when every child loses a tooth and slips quietly through a window in the middle of the night to put some money under your pillow. No! You will never fall for that one again! Once you know that Father Christmas and the tooth fairy don't exist, try as you may to believe in them again, you will not be able to; because you now know different! Your perception has changed.

It is the same when you change your perception of anything. You cannot go back to believing what you did before, because by now your perception has changed.

It is only my perception of things means that *I choose to give a certain meaning to an experience or event that is my reality.* Others, however, may have the same experience or witness the same event and may give it a completely different meaning. That is their perception, their reality of how this experience or event is defined for them. It doesn't make me right and others wrong or the other way round.

Now, my husband and I have very different views on whom we find attractive or beautiful. It doesn't make him right and me wrong or vice versa. Beauty is in the eye of the beholder explains this phenomenon very well. What you may find beautiful may not look very pretty to someone else. The subject is the same but how people see it is different for everyone. The perception of every new mother of their new offspring is that they are just the most beautiful baby ever, even though they may look like Winston Churchill (without the cigar!) or Buddha! That is their perception! It's not right and it's not wrong. It is not true and it is not false. It is their perception of their baby. Their perception is their reality.

With perception, there is no right or wrong. I truly believe that there were never any babies as gorgeous as my sons when they were born. This was reinforced by lots of people: *my* husband, *my* mother, *my* father, *my* sisters etc.! (Our perceptions of course! Not everybody else's! But we enjoyed believing that.) This perception, however, changed for my sisters when they had their own babies!

Our perception is unique to each one of us as we are all individual human beings with very different backgrounds, childhoods and life experiences.

The way we see the world influences what interpretation we put on an event or an experience.

> **Each one of us sees the world through our own unique filters.**

What we call reality is subjective to each one of us. In other words, it is only our reality, the way we choose to see and interpret the world.

Each one of us may see things completely differently from another, depending on which filters we see the world through. This depends on our background, our upbringing, our life influences, education and our life experiences.

Our reality is our own. It is exclusive to each one of us, no matter how like someone else we may think we are.

So, reality to the same events can be entirely different to different people experiencing the same thing, especially as we come from different points of view and have had different experiences and influences in our lives. That's why it may be pointless to force your point of view on someone else, as they are not looking at life through the same filters as you.

It would be as if two people are looking through a window at the world outside. They are looking at the exact same scenery. The first person is looking through a window which has a green tint on the glass, and the other person is looking at the same scene outside but through a window which has a pink tint on it. The two people would be seeing the same thing but the fact that they are looking through different filters, will make a difference in how they interpret what they see. It would not be wrong if one says that everything has a green tint and it would not be wrong either if the other says that everything doesn't have a green tint but a pink one. They are seeing things from their perspective.

If we change our perception of something, we no longer see it the way we used to and as a result we would no longer feel the way we used to feel.

> **When we change our perception of something, we also change how we feel.**

If you want to change your life, the change that needs to happen is often a change in perception.

For instance if you believe that no matter what happens in life, I am doomed to have bad luck! and the next morning you discover that by chance you've won the lottery and you also find out that the one you have fallen in love with, is absolutely smitten with you, I think that your perception of I am doomed to have bad luck would suddenly change. Your perception may now be: Things are looking up, good things do happen! Or maybe: I'm the luckiest person alive!

This change in perception changes everything in the world around you.

What you were once certain of, what you once fully understood and believed in, no longer has the same meaning. Your attitude changes totally.

To change our perception we need to change the meaning that we give to things.

Nothing has any meaning until we decide what meaning we choose to give it.

It is us who decide what meaning we want to give to any event or experience. If you have given a negative meaning to an experience or event that troubles you, you can ask yourself if there can be possibly a more positive meaning to give it. Keep asking yourself this until you come up with a better explanation and you will immediately start to feel better about it.

> *The meaning that we give to things can put us in a positive emotional state or a negative emotional state. It is up to us to make that decision.*

We choose the significance of any event or experience in our life. Therefore we should aim as much as possible to give an experience or event a positive meaning, as it has an effect on how we feel.

Whatever meaning we give to things, will determine whether we are happy or not. Emotionally, if all we do is to change the meaning that we have given to some specific experience or event, and find a better explanation for it, we will feel so much better. What we all value is to feel better. We do not enjoy negative feelings and emotions.

> *Our aim is to get out of pain and get into pleasure.*

For instance: If the news breaks that Anthony Murray has beaten Roger Federer in the finals in the tennis tournament; is that good or bad? Or if you hear that the American housing market has crashed again, what would you think? Is this dreadful news? Is it great news that President Obama has defeated Mick Romney in the latest US elections?

Your reaction will depend whether you support Anthony Murray or Roger Federer; it may even depend on what nationality you are and where your support lies. It is good news for some and definitely bad news for others. The meaning you will give to the US electoral results will also depend again on where your allegiance lies too or maybe you couldn't care less.

> *The meaning you give to any information is what makes it good or bad, positive or negative, happy or sad.*

The adults of this world may interpret the crash of the American housing market as dreadful news because the meaning we give it, is that the crash of the American market affects our shares and house prices and ultimately our lifestyle; so definitely bad news. But if you are a young person still dependent upon your parents, with no financial portfolio or understanding of the financial world situation, it would mean that this is just news, with maybe no negative or positive feelings associated to that news. They may see it as neither good nor bad, and see America as a long way away and unable to affect their lives.

Why? Because this is what perception is; it depends what meaning you give to any news. In other words it is not good or bad news. It is what it is: News!

It is what meaning you give to anything that makes it positive or negative, good or bad. So it is your perception that makes it good or bad news.

> *In fact there is no reality, only perception. Your reality is your perception.*
> *Your perception is your reality.*

Reality is merely an illusion, albeit a very persistent one

—*Albert Einstein*

If you don't like the meaning that you have given to some things in your life, you can change that meaning to a more acceptable reality for you.

If you have chosen to fall out with someone in your life because of the meaning you have given to something that they have said or done, now is the time to think again! Ask yourself: What else could they have meant? Is there another way of seeing this? Were they just trying to meet their own needs instead of doing things to intentionally hurt you? Or did you jump too quickly to the wrong conclusion? Were you reacting to your present or your past? Could it be that you were too sensitive or that it might be a pure misunderstanding or coincidence?

Now, think again! Then do the right thing, whatever that may be for you.

When you change the meaning you give to things, you can change your perception of the world around you. Think, what else could you see differently, had you given it another meaning? Life could start looking up! It can open many opportunities that you hadn't realized before.

When we see things negatively, we can only see obstacles; we do not see the opportunities that are looking at us; however, when we give positive meanings to things, suddenly we see opportunities that we were unable to see before even with both eyes wide open.

Often when events happen in life, we react to it like a knee-jerk reaction, and get carried away with our negative emotions; we get blinded by anger and become overemotional.

> *The secret is to take time to think first before we jump to negative conclusions.*

Ask yourself whether the meaning that you have given to the event or experience is fair or not; if not keep asking yourself if there is another way of interpreting this event or experience until you come up with a more positive meaning.

The problem is that very often we do not react to the present; instead we remember a similar experience from our past and react to it in its place; therefore we are not reacting to what is happening in the here and now; we're reacting to our past instead.

Most of the time, we very nearly always react to an event from our past not our present. We search our memory bank from our past experiences and see if we have encountered a similar situation, and use this experience to guide us on how to react. Consequently we do not react to what's happening in the present moment in time, we react to what we know happened in our past. We need to learn to live in the present; in the here and now, not in the past.

What is happening in the present may resemble a past experience but in reality it is a completely new one, which deserves to be assessed on its own merits.

If for instance, if we believe that someone has done us wrong, and we harbour negative thoughts towards that person; the fact that we are harbouring those pessimistic thoughts, has a physiological effect on us and makes us feel very unhappy in ourselves. If a similar thing happens to us at a later date, we remember that occasion and are more likely to give this new event a similar meaning, which end up producing similar psychological and physiological effects on us. Hence we feel as unhappy as we did before with that similar (but different) situation.

Our brain links the two similar situations together and we jump to the conclusion that this situation too is negative, without giving it a fair chance. We are not being fair to the present situation as we are not responding to what in fact happened in the present, but to something negative from our past.

However, we can make a decision to see things from another perspective, and ask ourselves *what else could this possibly have meant*? And if we come up with an empowering meaning we can change our perception and how we feel. We can decide to see that that person was not deliberately trying to hurt us, but he or she was only trying to meet their own needs. We just happened to be a casualty in the process. We gave this incident our own negative interpretation, according to our personal filters, with the corresponding emotional effects on us. If we question ourselves, we could change our perception of how we now view things and help us avoid pain and get into pleasure.

What others say and do is a projection of their reality

—*Don Miguel Ruiz*

Sometimes we tend to personalize things that really have nothing to do with us; however, it is more frequently not about us at all. We jump to conclusions far too soon.

Most people often do things because they are trying to get what they want, not because they are calculatingly trying to harm you. You may get hurt in the process, but that wasn't their aim. Their plan was to do what they thought best for themselves.

Some people tend to think that others deliberately plan things against or say things about them. They would be very amazed to know that other people seldom think about them. People are more concerned with themselves than with you.

> *Assume that every action has a positive intention initially behind it.*

It is just that sometimes in getting this positive intention met, they have given little thought to other people and others can get hurt as a result; but the original intention wasn't about hurting them or trampling over their feelings; it was about meeting their own needs. When we understand this, it becomes easier to forgive and move on.

It is a fact that some people happen to get hurt by other people's actions through the pursuit of getting their own needs met.

When we feel hurt, we get upset and angry and feel the need to blame the other person. Unfortunately, we live in a blaming society. If something goes wrong, someone has to be blamed for it! We don't stop long enough to think rationally.

> *Anger has the nasty habit of confusing our thinking and of making us put negative meanings where they do not belong.*

Whether we feel good or bad, will depend upon the meaning we choose to give to things. If we decide to put negative meanings onto things and fall out with others because of some negative meaning "we" have decided on, we can only spread misery and unhappiness that could have been easily avoided had we taken the time to give what was happening a more resourceful meaning.

If throughout your life you find that you keep falling out with family and friends, or other people, then make sure that the meaning you are putting on your life's events and experiences is not working against you.

If this is a recurring theme for you, you have to know that it can't always be others at fault. Look for the common denominator. Get real!

Don't live in denial. Face things and be prepared to take responsibility for your own actions and reactions. You can't improve your life until you are authentic with yourself and look at things as they are, not that the way you want them to be.

There is absolutely no shame in admitting that you were wrong; in fact it is a brave thing to do and people appreciate honesty and respect that. Be humble enough to admit that this time you are wrong. You didn't know any better; but when you know better, you can get better results in your life. It will stop you from going from crisis to crisis. We all get things wrong some time.

When we examine the meaning we give to things, it is easier to change our perception; sometimes it helps to see the things that we feel hurt about, in the third person. In other words you see it from another person's point of view.

Think of someone you admire and respect, and ask yourself, how would that person react to this particular event? It will make it easier to let go and move on. It will make you a lot happier in the long run.

If you see your glass as half full instead of half empty, you are more positive and tend to have a better experience of the world. If your glass is half empty, you have a negative experience of the world which leads to wild imagination and destructive thinking, which in turn gives you a poor quality of life. Those whose glass is half empty, are more likely to put negative meanings to what happens to them and to others around them.

> *Whether our perception is real or imagined, it is up to us what meaning we choose to give to our experiences in life.*

If you want to change your perception, you need to be conscious of your thoughts and try and not follow negative thoughts and scenarios through.

Exercise to reprogram your mind

- For every negative thought that you have: make a point of giving it an alternative positive thought. Even if you don't believe it at first, keep persisting. Positive thoughts lead to positive results.
- Write it down in a journal. Read it again and again. When your eyes see the positive statements written down, it is more likely to stay in your subconscious and you will end up believing it and becoming more positive. In this way you are reprogramming your thoughts.
- If you do this for seven consecutive days, it will begin to become a new habit.

Whatever you do consistently for seven days, will end up by becoming a habit after seven days.

So if you change every negative thought that comes to your mind into a positive one for seven consecutive days; by the eighth day, you should be getting into the habit of thinking more positive thoughts naturally.

This, my friends, is the secret of Perception!

Everything we hear is an opinion, not a fact. Everything we see is a perspective, not the truth.
—*Marcus Aurelius*

For us to understand how we can change our thinking, it is useful to understand a little about the human mind and its principles. The next chapter will be dedicated to explain in simple language the principles of the human mind.

Our greatest battles are that with our own minds.

—*Jameson Frank*

Notes: What have you learnt?

CHAPTER TWO

Well-known Secrets About The Magic of Our Brain

Your mind is a tool you can choose to use any way you wish
—Louise Hay

Our Brain, a Divine Gift,
its Functions . . . . and Much More

Our brain is a miraculous gift from God. It is a magnificent goal-oriented, thinking, all-singing, all-dancing and problem-solving machine of which the capabilities are hard to believe—so incredible, that we haven't begun to discover its unique ability as yet. It is even smarter than the most sophisticated computer ever invented! It is truly remarkable what our brain is capable of, although the information we have about it today may only be the tip of the iceberg.

Its power is so colossal that researchers are only just beginning to understand a little of its gargantuan potential. It is said that we use only about 10% of our brain; some probably a lot more and some a lot less. In fact I believe that Einstein said that we only use 5% of our brain. If we live for over one hundred years, we would never run out of neurons as we can never make complete use of all the nerve cells that so generously inhabit our 1.5 kg brain.

The learning principle of the human mind is to: Generalize, Delete and Distort.

How Does The Mind Generalize?

It is very simple the way that the mind generalizes. We learn one thing then we generalize it to everything else related to it.

For example: When we are about 12 to 18 months old, our parents teach us about parts of our body; that we have eyes, a nose, a mouth etc. We then generalize this principle by learning that mummy and daddy and grandma and grand dad, in fact just about everybody too have eyes, a nose, mouth etc. etc. We are not the only privileged ones to have eyes, a nose and mouth etc. When the baby sees other people, the baby's brain has generalized that all human beings have the same parts of the body that they have (well, almost!).

In the same way, when we are children we learn the principle of how a door can open and close; so when we see other doors, we presume that they too open and close. The mind has generalized this principle to all doors.

Do you notice how small children are fascinated by opening and closing doors, and even using any key they may have, to try and open a door? Their brain has generalized the principle that not only do doors open and close but keys can open doors too. As they get a little older, they learn that there are electric doors that open and close as you approach them. That's the reason little children become fascinated that certain doors can open and close by themselves and they want to keep opening and closing them by stepping near them. Clever little people, children . . . . Or is it clever little brains . . ? The only problem is that they probably believe that they are doing the opening and closing themselves without realizing the electronics behind it!

Toddlers too are captivated with light switches; they love to turn them on and off; so when they are somewhere else and they see a light switch, they know that if they put it down, that the light will go on and if they were to do the opposite, the light will go off. Again, their brains generalized this principle to all switches.

It is the same principle that teaches us when we touch a hot oven that it is hot and that we may burn our hand if we touch it. By our brain generalizing this principle, we learn to be careful of hot ovens or else we may get burnt.

How Does The Brain Delete Information?

The next principle is that the mind deletes information that it thinks is irrelevant or unnecessary. So if sometimes you are told that you already had some information that you probably didn't want to hear, however you have absolutely no recollection of it, your brain may have just deleted it because it suited you; we only hear what we want to hear. If it's not good news some can conveniently delete it if they don't want to hear it.

If our brain took on board every bit of information that it was flooded with that come through our five senses we would go crazy, as it will lead to information overload and completely overwhelm us. Consequently the mind is clever enough to create a short cut, just like a computer: it keeps the information it thinks it needs and presses the delete button for superfluous information.

As a *pro* the mind quickly checks the information and if it thinks that the information is unnecessary, it simply gets rid of it, leaving the important information that the brain needs and can cope with.

How Does The Brain Distort Information?

The third principle of the brain is to distort information, if it suits.

Have you ever heard of someone who caught a fish which was approximately six inches-long, and yet when relating the story of their fishing exploits to their friends, the fish is now six foot-long? The brain distorts this information, because it suits the situation. Truth is that fishermen like to brag about their fishing; that's what we do when we want to impress our friends, right? **It can also easily distort other information if it thinks that it is to our advantage too.**

> *We distort information if it suits us or we can distort information if the truth is too painful and we would rather not hear it.*

This is exactly what we do with our experiences in life. We generalize things and if it suits us, we delete useless information or what we don't want to see or hear; and if it suits we also distort things.

This has a lot of repercussions on how we relate to other people. This principle can sometimes lead to misunderstandings that can cause us and others pain. Understanding this principle helps us to reflect before we take offence by choosing negative meanings to experiences or events. We can learn to be more forgiving when we understand this.

For example, if someone came into work late for 2 consecutive days in a month, never having been late before, he or she may be known for always coming in late. Two occasions has turned into always. Have you ever heard people say things like: you always say that! Or you always do that? You may have said it once or done it twice, but their mind has distorted the information. Once or twice has turned into always. If this happens to you, you can calmly understand that their mind is generalizing and distorting information.

When an event happens we make a representation of it in our brain; which means that we represent the information, that we have taken in, from our five senses to our brain once again; the mind may then generalize, delete or distort it, as it thinks necessary.

This principle is the same whether the experiences are good, bad or indifferent, helpful or painful, negative or positive. This is the way the brain works for all of us. It is not different for some and not for others. We all operate this way.

The benefit of understanding and becoming aware of this principle is that all the negative (distorted) beliefs we have collected about life as a child or even as an adult, can now be reprogrammed into positive ones.

> *You can now give a different meaning to some of your previously painful experiences which may have been generalized, distorted or exaggerated or deleted in the past.*

If for instance you have been told as a child that you are stupid or useless, you now know that you can reprogram your brain to reflect a more positive reality for you. If you were told as a child to shut up, and not to be stupid every time you said something, your brain may generalize this information and distort it even as an adult; so when you need to speak up, maybe in a meeting, with friends, at work or during an interview and say what you think, you keep quiet, believing that someone else may know better than you. We sometimes can make false Neuro-associations because of this principle of generalizing, deleting and distorting which can lead to avoidance behaviours or phobias.

This can lead you to have a limiting belief in yourself that you need to reprogram with some good positive affirmations. If you use affirmations with intent and discipline and repeat them regularly, you can reprogram your brain. For instance:

—I believe in myself.
—I trust myself.
—I am just as capable as everyone else.
—What I think and what I have to say is valuable.
—I can do whatever I choose to.
—I have the right to express what I think.

Add some of your own to these.

So by understanding how our brain has generalized certain information we can then change our perceptions. Consequently we can reprogram our brain and our world can change almost in a few minutes—almost in the time it took you to read this! You can have one of your lightbulb moments.

To be able to understand how we do this, it is useful to understand a little more about the functions of our amazing super duper computer and how we can use this information to our advantage.

> *As a human being, you are irreplaceable, unique and priceless. As such you are of greatest value.*
> *—Julie Fuimano*

The Amazing Anatomy of the Human Brain

Sometimes people call other people **nuts** if they don't like them. I wonder if that's because they know that the brain is a **walnut-like** structure? The brain weighs approximately 1.5kgs. The brain is made up of gray matter and white matter. It consists of 78% water, 10% fat and around 8% protein. Our brain represents about 2% of our total bodyweight, but uses 20% of our calories.

From each breath that we take our brain consumes 25% of our total oxygen intake. For being such a small organ, it is very demanding and has numerous parts, each with its own specific role and function. It is extremely sophisticated and has unbelievable power.

Although researchers still have a whole lot more to discover about our brain, they do now know that our brain is soft-wired by our environment and our life experiences.

If we keep doing the same things, we strengthen the corresponding neural pathways in our brain, and it becomes easy to keep doing them. However, if we stop doing those same things we would find it harder to do or may even completely forget how to do them. If we use the neural pathways, we keep them; if we don't use them, we lose them.

> **As with everything else in our body, the brain too is constantly changing**.

We now know that we can generate new brain cells, something we never realized before 1998. In fact our brain can respond to our environment and to novel experiences by growing new brain cells. Isn't that just a miracle?

Sometimes we can have excessive ways of responding to our life situations, because some parts of the brain have not been trained and kept under control. This can cause preventable emotional tension, stress and anxiety. These are the times we find ourselves in crisis, overreacting and end up making poor life decisions.

Understanding a little about its functions helps us to keep these parts under control.

The top part of the brain, the cortex, contains the gray matter. It is soft and is covered by a thin membrane. It is a convoluted mass of nerve cells or neurons with folds and flaps and is found within the skull. The subcortex is the lower part of the brain. Both regions of the brain have very different roles to play, but they are integrated so that both parts can work in sync with each other.

The white matter connects different parts of the brain and is found more deeply within the brain, beneath the cortex. White matter helps the passing of information and insulates nerve cells and nerve tracts.

Most of our cerebral processes like thinking, memory, speech, planning, concept formation, problem-solving, spatial representation, auditory and visual processing, mood and personality as well as any muscular movement are found in the cortex.

This processing takes place on a conscious and deliberate level.

The left cortex deals with academic activities in most people, such as logic, words, lists, numbers, linearity, analysis etc. The right cortex is used more for imagination, special awareness, behaviour, rhythm, colour, daydreaming and dimension.

The cortex is divided into 4 primary regions or lobes:

The Frontal Lobe
The Temporal Lobes
The Parietal Lobes
The Occipital Lobe

If you place your left hand on your forehead, you are in the region of your prefrontal lobe, the frontal lobe is just a little bit higher; if you use your right hand and touch the back of your head, you are in the region of your occipital lobe, putting both hands either side of your head, will indicate the region of your parietal lobes, and if you put both hands either side of your face, your temporal lobes will be situated under your fingers.

Each of these 4 Lobes has their own specific functions in their region.

The frontal lobe is involved in executing and organizing behaviour, planning, conceptualizing, maintaining flexibility and stabilizing mood.

The left frontal lobe promotes positive feelings and the ability to take action. A time for this will be when you feel driven to achieve something (like finishing this book). The right frontal lobe promotes passivity and negative emotions. Procrastination lives there.

It is said that our personality is lodged in the frontal region of our brain. This has grave implications if our frontal region is affected by trauma, disease or drugs.

Now you understand why people's personality change when they are under the influence of drugs or alcohol and it is definitely not for the better. People with major trauma to their frontal lobe also suffer a change in their personality.

The temporal lobes are where you find your auditory brain, memory, new learning and language. Damage to the temporal lobe will seriously affect the functioning of these areas resulting in amnesia, learning difficulties and speech difficulties.

It is an age-old adage that women are better at talking than men. That is not new but do you know that there is a scientific reason for that? It is because women have a greater density of neurons in the temporal lobe than men, which specialize in language.

Women are born this way! So if we talk too much, that's not our fault, we are programmed to! We are only taking advantage of our gift and turning it into our talent!

The parietal lobes are responsible for spatial orientation, memory, reading, writing, mathematics and an appreciation of right versus left.

Now, if men are better at finding their way and reading maps, well, they are born this way too!

The occipital lobes' job is to help us see, perceive and discriminate what we see.

The subcortex sits under the cortex and on top of the ascending brain stem. Its primary function is to process rote skills and procedures. Most of this process is subconscious. Many skills such as driving a car, getting dressed, brushing your teeth, computer work, anything involving rote skills are done at a subconscious level, therefore by the subcortex.

Your brain is a magical piece of equipment where everything has its proper place, and each part has its proper role and function and each knows exactly what to do and when to do it. It is all designed to work like a clock in synchronized harmony with one another.

When disease strikes, this harmony is interfered with and depending on the severity of the disease, confusion may dominate until the right treatment is given and equilibrium is eventually restored.

The brain is divided into two hemispheres: The left and the right hemisphere.

The two hemispheres are bridged by a kind of cable, the Corpus Callosum, which contains more than 250 million nerve fibres and plays an important role.

The Corpus Callosum ensures good communication between the two parts of the brain.

> *Research shows that if we work on developing a certain area of our brain which we consider to be weak, we also improve on all areas of the brain, as we can't strengthen one part of the brain without the other areas benefitting from it.*

Some highly intelligent people can use both sides of their brains equally. Others tend to use their dominant side more than the non-dominant side.

It is said that geniuses like Einstein, Leonardo Da Vinci or Picasso were actually whole brain thinkers. They were able to develop their left and right hemispheres equally. The advantage they had as whole brain thinkers created their genius to develop a huge amount of talents in numerous fields.

Similarly, if you went to the gym to work just on your core strength, at the end of three months training, you wouldn't only benefit on your core strength, but other muscle groups would also have benefitted and improved their performance too. It's the same with the brain, when you strengthen one part of the brain other parts improve too.

Men and Women

Females process information differently from males as they have a larger corpus callosum. So when your partner doesn't think like you do, there is a very good reason for it. We are actually physically wired differently. Having this understanding helps your communication with your partner and helps you understand why sometimes they can think very differently to you; just because they don't think like you, doesn't mean that they no longer love you or care about you or that they are stupid. Women tend to use both sides of their brains to process information, whereas men rely mainly on their dominant hemisphere.

(I wonder! . . . Does that mean that women are actually the cleverer ones?) . . . . Okay, Okay, you men! It's a JOKE!

The Brain's Physiology

The brain consists of approximately a billion neurons or nerve cells, which are specialized structures which receive and pass on information. These neurons can transmit sensory and motor signals in all parts of the body. Each neuron can communicate with as many as 100,000 other neurons.

Information is passed on from one neuron to the other through the process of neurotransmission. Neurons communicate with one another by sending chemical messengers called neurotransmitters.

We have more than 60 types of neurotransmitters. Some of these neurotransmitters calm us down, whereas others excite us and can get us in trouble in times of stress.

Neurons work by transmitting electrical impulses called synapse between neurons. These form interconnected circuits to communicate with one another.

There are 2 neurotransmitters that represent 80% of the brain activity:

- Glutamate, which is excitory and hypes up brain activity. The more times this neurotransmitter is fired between two neurons, the stronger the wiring between these neurons.

The more times you repeat certain actions, these neurons are strengthened and they wire together; as a result these actions become easier and easier to perform. This is when habits are formed.

- Gamma-Aminobutyric acid (GABA) inhibits activity and keeps you calm when you need it. Approximately 40% of the brain's neurons use this neurotransmitter.

The GABA receptors are part of the Benzodiazepine system, because this is the system that benzodiazepines influence.

The Benzodiazepines are a type of medications which were introduced in the 1960s such as Diazepam, Alprozolam or Clonazepam. These drugs were popular in the treatment of anxiety. However, their well-known side effect is that they are highly addictive. They increase and prolong the effects of GABA, the brain's antianxiety neurotransmitter.

Research tells us that people with anxiety disorders have fewer benzodiazepine receptors than non-anxious people.

Neurotransmission takes place in the space between the nerve ending and the dendrites of the next cell, called the synaptic gap. The connection between two neurons is a synaptic connection.

The amount of synaptic connections we have linked with specific information, will determine the accuracy of our memory.

In other words the more connections i.e., the more neurons that are fired up when we are storing specific information, the higher the probability we have to recall it in future.

So if you want to remember something accurately, live in the present and be consciously aware that this information is being stored so that you fire up the right neurons.

Neurons consist of 3 main parts:

A single Cell body, one Axon and numerous Dendrites.

The Axon is the extension of the nerve cell from the cell body. It is covered with a protective myelin sheath and sends signals to other neurons.

Certain diseases, such as multiple sclerosis, affect the myelin sheath, which explains why, signals from the brain to the muscles can be interrupted, affecting the person's ability to move their arms or legs as they wish.

Dendrites are found at the end of the neurons and are branches which are highly complex structures. These dendrites receive information and initiate contacts with other neurons, which allow the transmission of electrical impulses. They are involved in the process of receiving and integrating information gathered by our five senses.

It is only in the last fifteen years that neuroscientists have proved that the brain has plasticity. They proved that the brain is dynamic and that it continues to be shaped and develop as we age, by our experiences of life and our environment, and that we can regenerate brain cells!

How cool is that? As such it shows that there are no limitations to anyone's brain power. The sky's the limit!

We can work at improving our intelligences as we age. Our brain continues to be shaped by environmental input from before we were born right throughout our life till the day we die! Even if we thought that we were dull, we have the hope of increasing our intelligence with our novel life experiences and our changing environment.

The more we learn and the more we have novel experiences, we reduce our likelihood of being affected by diseases like Al Zeihmer's or Dementia.

The Hippocampus

I love the Hippocampi as they can generate new brain cells!

The Hippocampus sits in the middle of each of your temporal lobes, which lie under your temples on each side of your head. You have two hippocampi, one in each hemisphere. Its role is to take in new information.

New brain cell development can continue to happen at any age, known as neurogenesis in the Hippocampi. Our brain continues to be influenced by our environment no matter what age we are.

If we experience joy or grief or any other emotion, the chemistry of our brain is altered accordingly and therefore, has an effect on our brain function. If we understand this basic fact, we can ensure that our brain has the right influence and environment for improved health.

Neurochemicals changes have an influence on our moods and behaviour.

There are three popular neurotransmitters which have been particularly researched, as they all have a direct effect on our moods: Serotonin, Noradrenaline, and Dopamine.

These neurotransmitters alter the sensitivity of receptors. They make a neuron more efficient or let the neuron know that it needs to make more Glutamate.

Serotonin is an important neurotransmitter as far as mood is concerned. It plays an important part in regulating our moods and many of our emotional responses. It helps to keep the brain activity under control. Low serotonin levels are often attributed as the cause of anxiety, depression or even obsessive compulsive disorder.

Serotonin is more widely distributed in the brain, however, it can be found in many of the same areas as Noradrenaline such as in the cortex, the Amygdalla and the hippocampus. The brain has specific serotonin receptors, some of which can increase anxiety, whilst others decrease anxiety. The 5-HT Re-uptake Inhibitors antidepressants, such as Fluoxetine (Prozac) are used to raise Serotonin levels, which in turn helps depression.

Noradrenaline is produced by the two Adrenal glands, which sit on top of our kidneys. They produce Adrenaline and Noradrenaline, as well as Cortisol, our stress hormones. Noradrenaline is the major chemical in the brain that deals specifically with fear.

About 90% of the brain's Noradrenaline is found in the small Locus Ceruleus, the brain's alarm centre. This centre is connected to the neurons that manage emotions, including the Prefrontal Cortex, the Amygdalla and the Hippocampus.

When you are scared, this system swings into action and produces changes in the brain and throughout the body, hence you have the physical reactions of the fight or flight response.

Noradrenaline magnifies the connections that influence perception, arousal and motivation. Like Serotonin, Noradrenaline too has been involved with altered mood and depression. Noradrenaline is often one of the main ingredients used in antidepressants just like Serotonin.

Dopamine drives us, sharpens and focuses our attention. It is associated with learning, reward and movement, and is known to be the pleasure neurotransmitter. Dopamine activates the pleasure centre in the brain when we see something we are excited about.

Consequently our dopamine levels have major repercussions for drug abuse, gambling, smoking, alcohol abuse and other addictive behaviours. When this centre is constantly triggered, it becomes very difficult to stop the behaviours that activate it, which is why it is so difficult to change addictive behaviours, such as drug abuse or gambling. Dopamine is very similar to the Endorphins, the brain's own pleasure-producing chemicals.

Like Serotonin and Noradrenaline, Dopamine too has a role to play in anxiety especially social anxiety disorders. Widespread release of dopamine in the brain is triggered by acute stress.

Finally apart from the Hippocampus there is another structure deep inside the brain that is involved with memory and fear:

The Amygdalla

The Amygdalla is an almond-shaped organ, situated deep inside the Temporal lobe of the brain, adjacent to the Hippocampus. It is a Limbic System structure that is involved in many of our emotions and motivations, particularly those that are related to our survival.

The functions of the Amygdalla include arousal, autonomic responses associated with fear, emotional responses, hormonal secretions, and controlling memory. A faulty Amygdalla may be to blame when one suffers from anxiety disorders or panic attacks.

The Amygdalla controls our emotions and our reactions to fear and anxiety.

As a metaphor, I like to explain this by imagining a weather-fire warning board which predicts the risks of fire for the day. This board looks like a half moon board and has a needle that predicts the severity of fire risk for the day. Basically the needle travels between zero and 180 degrees. It is divided into different coloured sections indicating Mild, Moderate, High, Severe or Catastrophic conditions. So the needle is set on zero, mild, moderate, high or catastrophic depending on the fire risk for the day.

If that was a board representing how your Amygdalla responds to fear, then your needle should be set at zero (no fire risk) for basically no fear.

However, if you have a little anxiety, the needle rises to mild and then resets itself back to zero. If the fear is moderate, the needle will rise to the section pointing to Moderate. When the fear or anxiety passes the needle resets itself back to zero, and so on.

The problem arises when people who have a long history of fear and anxiety, often stemming from their past, which keeps their (fear scale) needle stuck on moderate or high at all times. All that is needed is a little extra anxiety or fear to send their needle in the High, severe or Catastrophic range. This is when you see people over reacting emotionally or experiencing panic attacks leaving others puzzled at their behaviour. Professional help may be needed to reset their emotional needle back to zero.

Dysfunction of the Amygdalla is responsible for the inappropriate response to emotions of fear and anxiety.

The Amygdalla is triggered by intense emotional states like fear. It can stir anxiety in you to help you in a dangerous situation; however, it can also make you oversensitive to certain things, which can make you overreact fearfully.

The problem arises when it becomes unnecessarily activated when you don't need to be fearful.

It is just like having a faulty switch. It switches itself on for the wrong reasons, so you experience fear and anxiety when there is absolutely no reason to. When this happens it may be necessary to see a Therapist to reset your switch if your own personal efforts are not enough.

We now turn to your conscious and unconscious mind. This understanding leads you to better appreciate how your conscious and subconscious mind affect you, and you will be able to use this knowledge to make better informed choices.

Life is full of obstacle illusions.

—*Grant Frazier*

The Conscious and Subconscious Mind—
How they affect our lives

Research tells us that as human beings we consist of 3 major components: the conscious mind, the subconscious mind and the physiology.

The human mind comprises of two different functional parts namely the conscious—and subconscious mind.

Each part of the mind has an array of varied incredible talents, functions and qualities which work in unbelievable synchronization when required.

The Conscious Mind

The conscious mind helps us on a daily basis to make decisions. Our conscious awareness is needed in new situations to decide what we need to do, when and where.

The conscious mind takes action and solves problems.

Our Conscious mind deals with our rational and logical thinking. That's where our rational decisions come from and where we do our active thinking.

This is important to know because when you are under the influence of drugs or alcohol, you are not able to fully access your conscious mind and think rationally, and make informed choices. The choices you make then may have serious repercussions on the rest of your life. For instance, that is the reason why there are laws concerning drugs and drink driving.

Decisions you make when your conscious mind is altered may have serious long-lasting life effects not only on yourself but on others too.

Recently a policeman, who was on duty, was attacked by a drunken man in a brawl; he has now got to spend the rest of his life severely handicapped because of someone else's irresponsible action because his consciousness level was altered by substance abuse at the time. His action doesn't only affect that policeman, it also affects his wife, children, his parents, siblings, family, colleagues, friends and the list goes on.

Our conscious mind forms part of our immediate awareness of the world around us, our decision-making process, including what we choose to think.

The voice we speak to ourselves with and the images and movies we create in our mind are all the products of our conscious mind.

Our conscious mind creates the meaning we give to events or experiences as well as creating our awareness of our world.

As our conscious mind creates meaning, it is up to us to create positive meaning rather than negative meaning for us to feel happy and content.

There are two processes of our conscious mind:

Our Consciousness is our awareness. We create meaning in our conscious mind—in other words it is there that we choose to interpret any event or experience.

Our awareness helps us make sense of the world. Our understanding of what we see and hear only makes sense to us when we put a meaning to it.

Any information that we take in through our 5 senses is presented once again to our conscious mind, where we decide what that experience or event means to us.

Now that you understand this, it is up to you what meaning you choose to give to the things in your life.

Choose a positive meaning and life looks up but choose a negative meaning and you suffer the negative consequences in how you feel.

> *You have a choice about the perspective you take on life.*
> *See tragedy and the world is tragic.*
> *See beauty and the world is beautiful.*
>
> —*Jonathan Lockwood Huie*

So, if you decide to give an event or experience in your life a negative meaning, you soon know it because you will have the negative physiological reaction in your body. If you are not feeling good, you better think again and find a better way of explaining things to yourself. Remember, nothing has any meaning until you choose to give it meaning.

Let's the meaning you decide on be as positive as you can.

The subconscious mind

The Subconscious Mind is the larger and much more sophisticated part of the mind. It is there 24/7 with you, listening to what you are saying to yourself or to what you are thinking. It is the spy within which works relentlessly even when you are asleep to get you what it thinks you want and to prove you right.

The subconscious never sleeps. If, what you are saying to yourself isn't very nice, be careful! It is eave's dropping! It will remember even if you don't.

It is your internal undercover agent! However, it doesn't understand the negatives like no or don't. If you say to yourself: I don't want to be poor, it will interpret it as I want to be poor and strive to get you what you want. So, it is wiser to say I want to be rich or wealthy or abundant.

If when you look into the mirror, and you start to put yourself down and think that you are fat and ugly, your subconscious mind, will listen and strive to make you fatter and uglier because it will believe that's what you want. So watch out! When you look in the mirror, you'd better be thinking Hello you gorgeous creature!

The subconscious mind forms part of our memory, our thinking and mental activities which occurs on an unconscious level.

Our subconscious mind deals with any automatic behaviour that we use to live our lives. Repetitions and learnt behaviour are dealt with by the subconscious mind.

For example, once we've learned to drive a car, we no longer have to consciously have to go through all the steps of driving to be able to drive the car. Usually we put the key in the ignition (these days, we may just press a button) and the subconscious mind takes over. We don't have to think, now let's make sure that our seat is in the correct position, look into our mirror, think how to put the car in first gear etc. etc. No! We do all these things, but it comes automatically and we are not fully conscious that we are actually going through all these steps. Our subconscious mind which deals with automatic and learnt behaviours helps us out.

Habits

Habits are learned behaviours that we all have, such as getting up, brushing our teeth, getting ready for work, eating our breakfast, finding our way to work or school etc. These are all habits—actions that we perform every day, without having to do any active thinking. We do them automatically thanks to our subconscious mind.

Our habits enable us to do literally thousands of tasks every day, without consciously having to think about them. Once we've learned how to cook, we do not have to get the recipe book each time to prepare those regular dishes. Our subconscious mind becomes the cook. Imagine if we had to get the cookery book out every time we want bacon and eggs! Once we are trained and competent in our jobs, we no longer need to get a policy or procedure book out every day, because our training has been stored in our subconscious mind.

However, as the subconscious is part of our memory, we may have problems recalling events correctly when we feel emotionally disturbed.

One of the functions of our subconscious mind is to store the habits that we have learnt. It links the habits that we have and that we do together, automatically. It becomes our short-cut to doing things quickly and not waste valuable time. The subconscious use our habits to allow us to be more efficient and do things faster than if we had to consciously think about each task. It is actually our autopilot.

Many a time we hear people say: *I'm on autopilot.* They are spot on! In other words they are not actively thinking or consciously using their conscious awareness to do what they are doing; the subconscious mind has taken over and is doing it for them, as it is by now an expert in using our habits to help us.

Our subconscious mind helps us to drive to work and back again, whilst we can think about our children or the meeting that we are going into or about what we will be cooking for dinner. Our auto pilot watches the road for us, but should there be any signs of danger on the road, it brings us right back to consciousness and we are consciously ready to take appropriate action as need be. We can focus our full attention back on the road and our conscious mind takes over, helping us to take rational decisions and avoid any risky situations.

When we understand how these things work, we can use our brain more efficiently. Our subconscious mind remembers when we do things together, and if we keep doing them together, very soon the first action triggers the second action and so on. We have built neural pathways to support doing all these actions together and in sequence therefore it becomes easier and quicker for us to perform.

For example, if we usually have a drink at 6pm, then light up a cigarette. Soon drinking becomes associated with having a cigarette at 6pm and it becomes an automatic act of our subconscious mind, whether we consciously want a drink or a cigarette or not—hence the unconscious habit of many smokers lighting up without even thinking whether they really wanted that cigarette or not.

Habits and the Role of the Subconscious Mind

Our Subconscious mind soon makes bigger habits out of lots of unconscious ones all joined together for instance when we hear the alarm clock, jump out of bed, brush our teeth, shower, make a cup of tea, have breakfast, get dressed, put our makeup on (us girls! then again maybe not only the girls!) These habits play a vital part as it allows our conscious mind to think about other essential things. We could be rehearsing our presentation or the morning meeting or thinking about our first client in our conscious mind while our subconscious takes care of brushing our teeth or doing our hair.

On the other hand, there are some unconscious habits that we need to consciously change, if they do not serve us well. Unconsciously getting stuck into the biscuit tin for instance is not a helpful habit if we want to keep trim.

How many of us remember as children that we were not allowed to leave the table until our plate was empty, even if we were absolutely full and not at all hungry?

> *Habits acquired as children become deeply ingrained and are often very difficult to break unless our conscious mind takes charge of them.*

Many of us adults carry on with this habit of eating everything on our plate whether we are hungry or not, automatically, with no idea where this habit stemmed from. What is worse is that we pass it on to our children unaware that it can be detrimental to their health too and as a consequence end up with unwanted extra weight on. If we do not want to carry excess baggage on our hips (and elsewhere), it is one habit we really need to consciously reconsider.

Have you ever watched people, who do not have a weight problem eat? They don't finish everything on their plate if they've had enough. They don't eat fast. They chew well. They are not in a hurry to put the next forkful in their mouths. They rest their knives and forks on their plates in between mouthfuls and they take their time. They stop as soon as they are satisfied, no matter what is left on their plate, whether they are enjoying it or not. Everything is done slowly and with ease and more often than not, they leave something on their plate. If we do not want excess baggage, we can use them as role models. It is better for our health and certainly better for our digestion and our clothes.

Have you also watched some overweight people eat? They shovel their food in as if there is no tomorrow and as if they hadn't had anything to eat for the last month! The forkfuls are really quick in between, with hardly any break; they hardly chew anything and before you know it, the whole plateful has vanished in the blink of an eye. With not a scrap left on the plate!

What are you like? Do you stop when you've had enough? Or must you finish everything on your plate? Realize that it is an old program which makes you do that! It is time to change it now! We need to reprogram ourselves to stop when we've had enough, even though there is still food on our plate . . . . Yes! Even if we are enjoying it! We have to get over that business of not liking to waste food, which is a legacy from the world wars passed on from our mothers and grandmothers. The wars have been over for decades, almost a century ago!! If you eat when you are not hungry, it means that your waist line will just keep expanding! Looking at portion control is also helpful. This may be hard to understand, but it is important to do so if you do not wish to carry excess weight. (I have to tell you that I do feel a bit of a hypocrite here, especially at times when I don't do what I preach! But, honestly, what I am saying is true; sometimes putting theory into practice can be hard! But I aim to improve . . . . as they say: it is work in progress!)

Another bad habit that some mothers often have is that they often feel compelled to finish their children's leftover food because they do not like to waste food. (Guilty!!! Again!!! I've done that too at times, when my children were little!) The consequence is those love handles that nobody loves, least of all me!

SO LET ALL OF US STOP THIS NOW!

Conditioning

A conditioned response is one by which you have strengthened certain neural pathways to certain behaviours, for instance like finishing all the food on your plate whether you're hungry or not.

Some conditioned behaviours are harmless such a greeting rituals, however, others can be very destructive such as comfort-eating, drinking or smoking when you feel sad or stressed. When you feel down, the automatic reaction is associated with the biscuit tin, cigarettes or the booze cabinet! **STOP THAT TOO!**

The good news is that conditioning also works the other way round too. We can consciously uncondition ourselves to bad habits.

The good thing is that we can undo our conditioning to bad habits and retrain to condition ourselves to good habits and get rid of the bad ones.

Do this little experiment, for fun, to change your neural pathways:

(Assuming you use your hand, if you don't, maybe you use a glass, then, change the hand you hold the glass in):

If you use your hand to rinse your mouth out after brushing your teeth, try using your non-dominant hand to rinse your mouth out in the morning. Initially it will feel odd, but if you keep doing it, you will find that after a while it will become easier and easier and eventually it will feel normal, just like your dominant hand now feels. What you would have done would be to build a new neural pathway in your brain and rewire your nerve cells to a new way of rinsing your mouth. Admittedly this will not happen overnight, but as you keep doing it, it will feel more and more comfortable.

If you can change this simple habit that easily, you can also change other habits that do not serve you well by rewiring your brain. You can try doing that with other things and before you know it, you may become whole brain thinkers, like Einstein or Leonardo Da Vinci.

Imagination

A very powerful way to install positive behaviours to help us feel better is to use habits and imagination. The human body responds extremely positively to the use of vivid imagination.

> *The mind cannot distinguish between something that is real and something that has been vividly imagined.*

Exercise to help you relax and fool your mind

Do the following exercise:
- Close your eyes
- Imagine yourself on your favourite beach; visualize the words RELAX; now let the words LET GO flash through your mind. Now feel the heat of the sun on your skin; enjoy the feel of lying in the sand; bask into the sun and take in through your eyes the clear aqua blue sea.
- Vividly feel the warmth of the sun all over your body, feel how relaxed you are, see what you see, see yourself in your favourite swim gear and see other people on the sand, in the sea. Hear what you can hear, people enjoying themselves, the sound of the waves. Maybe add some relaxing music in this movie of your mind if you prefer.
- Vividly feel (in your body) that relaxed content feeling. Let that relaxed feeling run from the top of your head to the soles of your feet and back again . . . slowly. Now make the sounds louder and what you see brighter. Intensify the colours and intensify the good feelings of relaxation and contentment in your body. Relax your facial muscles and let all the tension leave your body. Feel your facial muscles smooth out. See what you see, hear what you hear, feel what you feel. Now, intensify those feelings again. Double their intensity. Stay with this feeling for a while.
- When you are ready, open your eyes, keeping the positive, wonderful feelings of relaxation with you.

By the time you have finished this exercise your body will feel like you have just had a little holiday, because:

Your mind isn't able to distinguish between something that is real and something that you have vividly imagined.

So if you are vividly imagining what you say to yourself, again that better be good! Watch what you say to yourself.

If what you are imagining in your mind is making you feel bad, you need to change the images or movies you are playing in your mind.

You can set yourself up to win or to lose; to fail or to succeed; to be happy or to be miserable, just by the thoughts that you choose to continually entertain in your mind.

Whatever you repeat over and over again in your mind conditions you.

You are programming your mind with whatever you focus on.

If you have got negative messages going round and round in your head, you are conditioning yourself to these negative messages. If you are worrying about something, chances are that you are rehearsing what you fear might happen, instead of what you would like to happen. This only serves to make you panic and be fearful.

You can reverse this by deliberately focusing on positive messages to condition yourself to positive new behaviours. It doesn't matter if you originally don't believe what you are saying to yourself, but by continuously repeating it, you will condition yourself to your new positive message.

What you focus on enters your subconscious mind and stays.

Athletes often visualize winning over and over again in their mind, to be successful. They condition themselves to success. A successful athlete never entertains the thought of failure or anything less than a winning outcome. I'm sure that we would never hear Roger Federer ever doubting that he could win at tennis. He plays to win. You too need to play to win at the game of life.

One of my clients, who is an amazing golfer, visualizes every stroke, every put, every movement and every part of the course including the weather conditions; she rehearses winning in her mind over and over again prior to her game. In other words, she conditions her mind to success. Is it any wonder that she is a fantastic golfer, who is the envy of her club? No! She wins, because she is focused on winning and does her homework. She uses her mind to prepare her to win, way before she sets foot on the golf course.

By focusing over and over again in their mind and visualizing every action as well as the environment they are in, successful athletes, condition their neural pathways to success.

The way we feel affects what we do.

The above denotes the close link between the mind/body connection, and the resulting behaviours. Our breathing or muscle tension influence our emotional states.

All our behaviours depend on the emotional state we are in at any given time.

We will talk more about this later, when we discuss our emotions.

The garden of our mind

The mind has long been compared to a garden metaphorically. Now, let's think of our mind as a garden and we are the gardener in charge. Our job to constantly plant seeds in our garden. Similarly we are continually planting seeds of thoughts in our subconscious mind. As the seeds are based on our habitual thinking, we are not even aware of doing it most of the time.

Whatever we sow in the garden of our mind (subconscious mind), we reap in our body and in our environment as it creates the results we enjoy or not in our life today.

In other words we always reap what we sow.

Whatever seed we choose to sow, we will harvest later on. Whatever thoughts we choose to allow in our subconscious, we feel the outcome of these thoughts in our physiology (our body) and its results in the quality of life that we enjoy or not as the case may be.

One of life's secrets to keep in your mind is:

> *You get more of what you focus on. Whatever you focus on grows; it becomes bigger and stronger.*

Focus on good and you enjoy the good. Focus on bad and you experience the misery of bad. Either way, whatever your focus is on, you will get more of.

If you focus on positive thoughts, your life is filled with joy and happiness; however, if you focus on negative thoughts, you suffer the consequences of negativity in your life as it affects the quality of your life.

In other words, focus on good and you attract good things in your life; focus on bad and you attract more of that into your life too. It's that simple!

The definition of insanity is to keep doing the same things over and over again and expect a different result.

—*Einstein*

Imagine your subconscious mind as dark rich productive soil, just ready to be planted and cultivated. This luxuriant soil is begging to cultivate whatever seeds you choose to sow in it.

If you want roses you need to sow rose seeds and you can reap a garden full of roses. In the same way, if you cultivate positive thoughts in the garden of your mind, you benefit from blooms of positivity and enjoy the rewards of an enjoyable life.

If you sow weeds, your garden will be full of overgrown weeds. The same thing happens in the garden of your mind. If you entertain negative thoughts or feed your mind with horror books, horror and dark occult or scary movies and such like, which are likely to distort your thinking and your perceptions, you reap the effects of these negative actions in your mind, emotions and in your body, which result in an anxious and disturbed life. You have sown weeds in the garden of your mind to torture you.

However, if you do not sow anything, you also reap the negative effects, just as if you did not tend to your garden by not sowing anything beautiful, the weeds overtake the garden, because it hasn't been cared for. You need to look after your garden, water it, feed it and maintain it if you want a beautiful garden.

Likewise you must feed your mind with the right kind of thoughts, literature, auditory and visuals, for a healthy and positive mind.

If you entertain negative thoughts, thinking the worst or do not feed your mind with positive and empowering thoughts, negativity and fear will rule your life. So it is very important what kind of seeds you allow to grow in the garden of your mind, and what kind of seeds you allow to flourish or contaminate your garden.

If you only want blooms, you only allow positive thoughts in; however, if you are not sure what you want in the garden of your mind and you are not as selective as to what you sow in your garden, consequently you'll reap whatever comes up.

You can choose: Blooms or weeds? Your choice!

If you choose blooms, it means that you must consciously feed your mind with the right thoughts, literature, or any other visual or auditory positive stimulants.

Otherwise, if you choose weeds, you feed your mind with dark thoughts, crazy, horror, violent or zombies' movies or literature and other negative visual or auditory stimulants, which trust me, never fail to leave their disastrous effects on you to disturb your peace. You may well ask yourself why you are suffering from fear, anxiety and depression or panic attacks! Impressionable minds are very easily influenced!

Yet, you may say that this is all a lot of rubbish, because you like these things and find them exciting and would rather not give them up, which of course you can if you choose! But if you don't suffer from anxiety now, how can you be sure that you won't in the future? Ask anyone you know who suffer from anxiety, if that is something that they enjoy and wish to keep in their life.

It is so simple but not something that most of us deliberately think about. Cultivate high-quality thoughts and you have positive results; focus on unresourceful thoughts and the results can be disastrous. We don't do it because deep down we can't believe that it can be that simple and that's how things work, or we just choose not to believe it. We often refuse to believe it because we want instant gratification. We want what we like, now! We just react to life, instead of using our brain.

As a result there are a lot of unnecessary sufferings from troubled lives and troubled minds, because very little thought is given to understanding our mind.

If you just don't believe it, try it for a while at least. You have nothing to lose and you will see the benefits that you will attract in your life if you change your focus; it will change your experience of life.

So feed your mind with superior thoughts, positive literature, uplifting CD's, inspiring movies and spiritual and motivational books. Behave in a positive way, towards your family, friends, colleagues and anyone whom you have the pleasure to meet. See the best in people and your life takes a turn for the better.

The mind is made up of 60% of Omega 3, and if we are depleted in Omega3, it affects the quality of our thoughts. So, supplements of Omega three is helpful. Some people think that just because something awful has happened to them that they have the right to feel the way they do. They reason it out by saying that anyone else would feel this way, given what has happened to them. Yes, perhaps it is understandable that things haven't worked out well for them, through no fault of their own, but that doesn't mean that they have to stay in this place. An understandable excuse is no reason to continue with negative thinking and toxic thoughts. This is the stuff of self-pity that keeps you stuck and reacting as a victim.

> *There is never any point in wallowing in negative thoughts and self-pity, because one has an understandable excuse.*

Remember, life changes constantly. Bad times always have a beginning but they do always have an end.

You've been through bad times before and you got over it! This time too, won't last forever and better times are ahead!

You now have the past experience of knowing that when bad times hit, it is not forever, even though it may feel like it at the time.

So when you are going through a bad patch, think that this bad time won't last, and better times are just round the corner; times will change and good things are on their way! In fact there may well be very exciting times on their way to you! Keep this at the forefront of your mind and repeat it to yourself constantly, until the good times arrive. Adopt this as a new belief.

Other people close to you should not suffer just because you do; neither should you have to continue to! It means that you can choose not to be negative as negativity only increases your misery and tortures your mind. Use your knowledge of your mind to get yourself out of your negative cycle

Trying to find a positive in any situation helps you to feel empowered and gets you out of the troubled spot you find yourself in. Do this and you will inspire others too.

It helps you to feel a lot happier instead of wasting life being miserable and feeling victimized. Remember, there is very often something good which happens as the result of a bad experience. Because we can't see the bigger picture, we torment ourselves unnecessarily sometimes however, if you keep this in mind, it will help you to deal with your challenges in a more positive way.

Whatever the situation you always have a choice.

You can choose to be positive and find a solution or you can struggle in feeling sorry for yourself.

Sometimes it is easy to feel like you're powerless in certain situations because when bad things happen to you, it saps your energy and you can end up feeling bombarded by negative thoughts. Lack of sleep compounds tiredness and depression which can lead you to feeling powerless.

This is when you need to put all your energy in filtering what you will allow in your mind and on what your focus will be.

Write things down so that you can be clear on what you choose to concentrate on.

If you write things down, it serves as a reminder and helps you to refocus when your concentration wanders. Keep things to give attention to in the forefront of your mind. Then you can control the negative thoughts. The more you read and re-read what you've written, the more your subconscious mind will take it in and remind you to be more positive when you feel low.

Powerlessness is often a matter of perception.

Very often, an experience is not a fact. It is just the way we are seeing things in that moment. To change the perception of powerlessness, we need to change the meaning we have given to our experience into a more positive reality for us.

Important points that are really significant to our well-being are: the choices we decide to take, our problem-solving ability, our thoughts, our memory, our concentration, worry and more. I will expand on some of these later.

Choices

In all things we do have a choice on how we behave or how we react.

All of our choices have consequences, some good, some not so good, some bad, but nevertheless they all carry consequences.

That's why it is essential for us to realize that whatever choices we decide on in life, we are going to have to enjoy or suffer their consequences.

The choices that we made yesterday are the results that we have in our lives to-day. The choices that we make to-day will be the results we will have in the future, and these altogether shape our destiny.

The choices we make send us down the paths we call our life, good and bad. We wrote the blueprint for it. The consequences are all our own exact design.

Often people say: But, honestly, I had no choice. Although we might often believe that we had no choice, what we actually mean is that we don't really like the choices we had. We always have a choice. It may not be a very favourable one, but we still have that choice. Even when we choose not to choose, we are making a choice.

Being consciously aware of making the right choices for our future is what matters. It can send us down a straight path or it can send us along a tortuous road full of obstacles.

When you tell yourself that you have no choice, you are adding to your sense of powerlessness and it contributes to feelings of hopelessness and depression. These feelings instead of being helpful cause you to act in destructive ways, like resorting to comfort eating, drinking, smoking or drugs, rather than using your energy to seek a positive solution to the problem or situation. It is worth just asking yourself some specific questions about the situation you find yourself in; and if you keep asking eventually your subconscious will provide you with the answers.

Problems

When you have a problem, try not to look at the problem as a whole. When you break any puzzle down to the small pieces from the very beginning, they become much more manageable.

> **Whatever problem you have, break it down in small pieces and you will then find it easier to find a solution.**

Ask yourself, what is the next step that you need to take? Then what's the next step, after that, what else do you need to do and so on and so on. Before you know it, you have the answer to your problem.

> **Try to drop the emotions, as you can find better solutions when you are in a resourceful state. So, keep calm!**

Remember that your subconscious is like a missile that is searching for its target; whatever question you ask of it, it will find a way of giving you the answer. But if you want better-quality answers, then you must ask better-quality questions. The important thing is to ask empowering questions and it will give you empowering answers. Of course if you ask preposterous questions, would you be surprised that you get bizarre answers?

Your subconscious mind never sleeps; it is working for you 24 hours a day. It may be your spy within, but it is a hard-working one! It sees itself as your ally. It works hard to get you what it thinks you want. If you keep asking, you will get the answer. It will come to you, maybe when you are least expecting it.

Have you ever looked for the answer to a question, and could not get it all day and then suddenly at two o'clock in the morning, the answer came to you in your sleep? That's the reason why! When you were relaxed and sleeping, your subconscious mind was faithfully busy looking for the answer going through all the filing cabinets of your mind and—Bingo! There was the answer! (In that file tucked right at the back!) Watch out! Your friend will not thank you for giving them the answer that you were looking for if you call them at 2 a.m.

Concentrate on what you do want

You can direct your thoughts to concentrate on what you do want instead of what you don't want. Whenever I ask my clients what they want, they often talk about what they don't want. The problem is that we have a good idea of what we don't want; but we are very muddy about what we do want.

If we are not clear about what we do want, how can we get it? How will we know when we have it?

It is important to think and know what it is you do want; if you don't know what you want, you will not get the results that you are looking for; but, if you know what you want you have a direction to lead you towards what you really want. It makes all the difference to what path your life will take and where you will end up.

Exercise to find out what you want

Ask yourself:

- What do I want in my life?
- What would make me happy?
- What do I want to happen so that I can have what I want?
- What do I need to do?
- What will it cost me if I don't do it?
- What will I gain if I do?
- What's the worst that can happen?
- What's the best that can happen?
- How could this change my life for the better?
  Now write this all down.

Sow the right thoughts in the garden of your mind, and take action right away towards it. Taking action gathers energy. Even if it is something small, it will get you on your way. The secret now is to stick to your plan until you get there. Even if you don't get the answers straight away, if you keep asking yourself these questions consistently, you will gain impetus, you will feel empowered and your life will gradually begin to improve. The important thing here is not to get angry or upset, fed up nor to give up. Be patient and know that the answer will come when the time is right.

> *There is a time for everything! If you don't get what you want straight away, develop the belief that it may be for a very good reason.*

Waiting can test your spirit but you can prove to yourself that you do have strength of character. Take small steps and do not let stress get you down. Be patient.

Another Secret to commit to memory:

> *You always choose your behaviour and you always choose your attitude.*

Yet if you can't alter your situation immediately, at least you have the power to choose your behaviour, your attitude and how you react to what is happening to you.

How you react to any situation and what attitude to take is always your choice.

You can choose depression and destructive behaviours or you can choose to be constructive, have a positive attitude and to be resourceful, and to find a solution to your problem and be happy.

Good and Bad Situations

When you come across a difficult or negative situation in life, remember:

You can choose how you react and you can choose the attitude that you will take.

You can make a bad situation worse by feeling depressed and negative or you can keep trying to find a positive solution to your problem and you can choose a positive way of reacting, which can only help how you feel and make you more resourceful.

If you choose to feel depressed because you find yourself in a difficult situation, what happens as a result is that you have a difficult situation and depression as well! It is all a matter of what you feed your subconscious with.

If you choose a positive attitude to your difficult situation by knowing that you have previously encountered difficult situations and that you got yourself out of it that time, then know that you will do it again this time too.

This time, you may have a difficult situation but you also have hope that you will get out of trouble, and that things will change, because you've been there before, done it, seen the movie and are probably wearing the T-shirt as you read this! In yourself you will feel a hundred times better because you know that you have trust in you to find a solution, whatever your problem. When bad things happen, you dust yourself down and keep going and do what it takes until you find a solution.

No one is immune from bad things happening to them. It happens to each one of us at different times. No one, but no one escapes the ups and downs of life, no matter what we may look like to the outside world. We all have good and bad times.

It is how we react and behave that matter and this has a big influence on how we get out of the bad times.

We can lie down and die and feel sorry for ourselves, or we can straighten our back bone and tell ourselves that we are not going to be beaten and that we will find the right solution. We can choose to enjoy the free time that we have in between difficult situations, knowing that when trouble strikes, that in a month, three months, six months or a year from now we will be in a very different situation. Like the song says: Mama told me there'd be days like this.

Develop the belief that:

Whatever bad times you go through it is only for a while, and these times will go away soon enough. Bad times just as good times are never forever!

After winter, spring is eager to burst forth. Know that the next season always comes! When you are in the depth of sorrow, despite its heartbreak, there often can be something special about it and life's lessons to be learnt. It may be times shared together with special people in your lives that you might not have had otherwise or strength gained from family and friends! From every situation we become more resilient, a value which may prove very useful in the future. A bad diagnosis may bring you closer than ever to your family and help you find special times with them.

The old saying: *what doesn't kill you makes you stronger* demonstrates just that.

> *Develop resilience. Difficult situations enable us to become more and more resilient, which is an advantage when we hit problems in the future.*

If you do have faith, exercise the muscle of your faith, pray! You will feel one thousand times better. If you don't and wish you did, explore it, you may gain great spiritual strength which will help you cope with trials and tribulations. After all, we are mind-body-and-spirit! That is not even in dispute.

If not, use relaxation CDs and breathing exercises. We have talked about feeding our mind with the right thoughts; we know that we need to keep our bodies healthy by eating the right things and having plenty of exercise and rest. We need to feed our spirit too with what is right for us, to have an accomplished life.

Remember, you do not have to feel bad just because you think that everyone else would do so given your situation. You can choose to prove everyone else wrong and choose to be in control instead of giving in to despair and depression.

> *Choose to be your own champion. You can do it!*
> *Choose your behaviour. Choose your attitude.*
> *Choose how you react. Choose to be positive.*

Suddenly you will see solutions that you were unable to see before when you followed negative, depressed thoughts. When you are depressed and negative, you can't see the woods for the trees. For every solution offered to you, you can find something wrong with it. You may say: Yes, but . . . . and find a reason why things won't work. It only serves to make your situation worse, makes you feel even more powerless and encourage depression to flourish!

Know that you do have a choice! It is a matter of believing and looking for the right one, till you find it. Never ever give up!

To start with, if you do the right thing, no one can criticize you for that! Even if you think that you are letting others win. If that is so, you are still thinking negatively and have the wrong thinking and attitude. You need to change this fast! It is not about others winning or losing over you; it is about doing the right things for you! You shouldn't care if others win or lose, that's their look out.

What's the worst that anyone can say? She/he did the right thing! What's so awful about that? If you know in yourself that you have done the right thing for you, you will be able to act calmly and it will give you a confidence you didn't have before.

You don't have to overreact; you can choose to stay calm and level-headed. You will be more open to suggestions made to you and the solution will come to you in a clearer fashion. Even if the solution takes a while to come to you, there may be a good reason for that. Maybe there are life's lessons for you to learn in the meantime.

Thoughts

Our thought life mainly takes place in our subconscious mind while our conscious mind is used for decision-making. Every thought we have is a cause, and every condition is an effect. This is the reason why it is so vital to take charge of our thoughts.

> *Thoughts are not reality and they do not accurately reflect reality either.*

Some may believe that it is impossible to change our thoughts. This belief is wrong! It is possible to change our thoughts by changing what we choose to focus on; we just need to know how. We need to be willing to, and believe that we can. We have to make a decision that we can change our thoughts. By changing our thoughts we can bring about desirable outcomes instead of disastrous ones. There are many techniques to help you control your thoughts. Using NLP and EFT are very useful.

We do have the power to control our thoughts.

We do not have a little alien controlling our thoughts in our head. We are in the driving seat. We have this power. We do not need to entertain negative and destructive thoughts, unless we choose to. We can choose which thoughts we follow through as we (our conscious minds) decide which thoughts to go with. When we get anxious, we are focusing on negative thoughts. We are following a scenario through and we're letting fear dominate us. The only problem is that when we start thinking negatively, we get scared and trapped by those thoughts which stop us to see the positive side of things.

> *As we have the ability to focus on the negative, we also have the power to focus on the positive.*
> *It is a matter which we decide to select.*

We need to concentrate on positive thoughts and choose to let any negative thoughts we have go; see them leaving our mind just like balloons in the breeze.

Thoughts are composed of a mixture of words, sentences, symbols, mental images and sensations. They can sometimes be very disturbing and unwelcomed intruders. Intrusive thoughts can be very alarming. They often catch us out of the blue and these thoughts trigger a whole psychological and physiological process. It may even make us feel like we are losing our mind. These are usually the negative thoughts that come into our heads without our conscious awareness that they're there.

> *If we become fused with our thoughts, in other words if we fixate on our thoughts, we become at one with our thoughts, and they determine how we feel.*

If our thoughts are positive, we will as a result feel great, but if they are negative, we trigger very unpleasant emotions and feelings within us. When we allow ourselves to become fused with our negative thoughts, we effectively are building a prison of our own and we become hostage to our thoughts. We are at their mercy and turn into a victim of our own thinking.

We have given away our power to our thoughts and they master us. Considering that thoughts are not reality there's a lot scope for disasters to be fabricated by wild imaginations. The power our thoughts have over us depends on the degree of importance that we give to them.

Before we realize that we are in control of our thoughts, we tend to go with the flow; whatever thoughts and scenario that enter our heads, we just follow and suffer the consequences of these negative thoughts. We can become confused and do not know what to do for the best.

> *When we learn that we can control our thoughts, we then can become selective and decide to choose which thoughts that we follow through with and which thoughts that we choose to dump.*

Thoughts and Physiology

Every thought has a corresponding electrochemical effect in our brain.

Our hormones travel throughout our body in intricate electrochemical feedback loops such as Serotonin, Dopamine, Adrenaline and others.

Scientists tell us that at any given time our brain performs about 400 billion activities; however, we are only aware of approximately 2000 of them. Each of this regulated activity has an electrical and chemical component responsible for triggering our emotions.

Endorphins or feel good chemicals are naturally produced by the body after exercising. They are produced by our brain's ability to release specific neurotransmitters; and as a result these specific chemicals help us to feel happy or high on feeling good. However, when we feel sad, angry or hurt, our brain releases other different types of chemicals which can damage our health if prolonged.

> *The brain produces different types of chemicals depending on what kind of emotion we are experiencing at the time.*

According to how we are feeling, our brain will release the appropriate chemicals for the emotions we are experiencing at the time. Depending on the meaning we give our thoughts and the words we choose to talk to ourselves with, will depend whether these chemicals are toxic to our body or not. They will either help us to feel good or will harm us.

If thoughts are harmful, they can create mental or physical problems or both. This becomes manifest in the mind or in the body or in both.

Negative emotions such as, unforgiveness, hatred, anger, jealousy, resentment, revenge, fear, anxiety, guilt or even excessive grief can release an explosion of very damaging chemicals throughout the body and can seriously affect an individual's quality of life.

Research confirms that our thoughts are responsible for 87% of all illnesses. 13% are attributed to our diet and genetics. Many studies reveal that negative emotions and lifestyle are the culprits for a lot of common chronic diseases. For instance they are the cause of hypertension, diabetes, cancers, migraines, strokes, allergies, immune system illnesses such as Lupus, arthritis, infections and many others. Studies point out the correlation between fear, anxiety, and heart palpitations, irritable bowel syndrome, tension headaches, and heart problems.

If you allow other people's negative emotions to get to your core, you too, can become affected. It is helpful to be a good friend or listener, but not at all healthy to let their problems become your problems. You are no help to them if you allow yourself to get sick, because of their issues. You need to have strong boundaries. You can empathise with others but don't take on their problems as your own. This is not healthy.

Research proves that what we think affect our emotional and physical state.

> *Think good thoughts and you feel good. Think bad thoughts and you feel bad. It is virtually impossible to feel bad thinking good thoughts; equally it is impossible to feel good thinking bad thoughts.*

The mind/body connection has long been recognized. Negative reinforcement releases negative chemicals and positive reinforcement releases positive chemicals, and therefore they influence how we feel emotionally.

If you are feeling bad, you can change it in an instant by changing what you're thinking and what you are focusing on.

For instance if I told you that when you wake up to-morrow morning, that you will win $30 million. How would you feel? . . . . Hum . . . . Yep! I can see the smile on your face already!

However, if I was to tell you that one of your loved ones has been involved in a really bad accident, how would you feel now? . . . . Hum . . . . Yep! I can already see the tears in your eyes!

This only shows how what we think affects how we feel, and the scary part about it is that it is not even reality, yet our mind and body react to what words are said and what we are thinking.

In general if you are focusing on negative things, you need to change your perception. You have a choice which thoughts you choose to follow. When you feel you have no control over your thoughts you feel powerless.

Empower yourself to find alternative positive thoughts rather than feeling powerless. Write them down.

Powerlessness leads to despair, panic attacks and hopelessness. Choosing the right thoughts can lift anxiety and depression.

Your thoughts can make you feel happy, contented and de-stress you, make you feel calm or in control or it can do the exact opposite. Catastrophic thinking is at the base of anxiety, panic attacks, anger, fear, frustration or depression. It looks for someone else or the circumstances to blame instead of looking at yourself and your attitude.

The Hypothalamus

When we first start to develop a thought by building a memory, it activates the Hypothalamus. The Hypothalamus is the heart of the Endocrine or Hormonal system, which responds to our thoughts.

When we feel a negative emotion, stress hormones such as ACTH (adreno-cortico-tropin hormone), Cortisol and Adrenaline are released, which can play havoc in us. Continuous large amounts of Cortisol and Adrenaline throughout the body can cause an array of diseases such as, cancers, cardiovascular disease, hypertension, heart arrhythmias, aneurysms, or strokes, not to mention their attacks on our immune system.

Stress hormone releasing Cortisol has a huge effect on our memories, creativity and our ability to remember; which is why we forget a lot of things when we're under constant stress. Prolonged release of cortisol due to stress can lead to Adrenal fatigue. This in turn leads to other health problems such as chronic fatigue syndrome.

The hypothalamus responds to our emotional state.

It is the reason why a toxic emotional thought life affects our physical state.

> *It is very important to control our thoughts to be able to lead an emotionally happy and physically balanced and healthy lifestyle.*

Thoughts have long been compared to trees with branches. A thought is like a tree with many branches in our brain. The more branches there are the more accessible the thought will be. We have numerous of these thought trees. Each thought tree is made up of neurons. Those excitable cells make up the trees of our mind including our memory.

We have around 100 trillion of these thought trees and each one is capable of growing 70,000 branches. It is said that we have approximately 3 million years worth of storage space for information in our brain; no matter how old we live to or how clever we are, unless we live 3 million years, we will never be able to make use of all our amazing brain's capacity. Our brain's ability is so vast that no one can use it all up in a human being's lifetime . . . . yes, not even Einstein, Michael Angelo or Leonardo Da Vinci! It is truly a generous divine gift!

The brain builds a double memory of every thought, on the left side and one on the right side of the brain. The more focused and aware of our thinking we are, the stronger the memory we will build, and the easier the recollection.

To keep focused on positive thoughts and on the present, it helps from time to time to ask yourself: *What am I thinking now?* This helps to keep you focused and your memory strong. It brings us back to the here and now instead of focusing on the past that has gone or worrying about future events that haven't happened yet. All we have is now.

> *It is a drain of energy to focus on past events or worry about what may happen in the future.*
> *Focus on the here and now.*

If we focus our energies on past or future thoughts, we become incapable of dealing with the present due to poor energy levels. If we give poor attention to our thoughts, our thinking is weak. The memory we build is weak and soon pruned by glial cells.

Glial cells are essential to brain functioning and act like little vacuum cleaners, which gobble up our poor memory connections while we sleep. They are our brain's night janitors. When we are unable to recall certain memories, it can be that the memory we built was weak in the first place and was easily wiped out by glial cells in the night. We have 100 billion or more neurons but we have 50 times more glial cells. Without them neurons would be unable to function properly. They provide all the support, resources and back up including the nourishment and protection our neurons need to receive; they analyze process and store information. Glial cells sort out our thinking but they can't do a good job unless we cooperate and think clearly.

Toxic Thoughts

Negative or toxic thoughts interfere with these important electrochemical processes of the brain. When toxic wastes build up through negative thoughts, they diminish the quality of the stored memories. This is when we fail to remember things accurately; our memories become distorted, and as a result we can become confused. Whilst they do not stop us from building memories, the memory we build is distorted and harmful. We give unresourceful meanings to events and experiences, because of the already negative thoughts that occupy our brain.

When the neurons are able to work properly by thinking appropriately, they build healthy memory.

> *Keeping our thoughts under control is vital to our emotional health.*

In any given day, we have 90,000 thoughts going through our mind; and 60,000 of those are repetitive thoughts. Now, if only our 60,000 repetitive thoughts are toxic, we are doing ourselves a lot of harm, and setting ourselves up for disease.

Memory

The brain's neural pathway of each idea or memory is being strengthened every time we recall something. Whenever we have an experience which carries a strong emotion, we record it in our nervous system as a memory of the sequence of the behaviour that led to it.

For instance, if one time when you had to take a tablet, you had a thought that you were going to choke and as result you ended up choking followed by a full blown panic attack; your nervous system will record taking a tablet with the fear of choking and having a panic attack. From that time on you would have made a false Neuro-association when taking a tablet; you would have linked it with the thought of choking which can then induce a panic attack, unless you actively seek to disassociate yourself with the sequence of the behaviour. Otherwise you may find taking medication very difficult.

Any new experience creates a new neural pathway, so that we can access it when we want to. Each time we repeat this behaviour we strengthen the neural pathway for that behaviour. Research shows that the neural pathways actually get physically larger through repetitive behaviours. Therefore the repetitive behaviour becomes quickly accessible.

The act of memorizing encourages brain cells to make more connections and create new neural pathways in which the new memories can be stored and easily recalled.

Often it is not that you suffer from a poor memory, but it can be that you are out of practice retrieving your stored memories, as you have not practiced retrieving them. So, story-telling about your positive experiences is a great thing! It gives you the chance to relive your happy memories, feel good, strengthen your neural pathways, and keeps your memory alive.

> *Like a lot of other parts of the body, memory is like a muscle. Use it or lose it. Exercise it and it gets stronger and fitter. Don't use it and you will lose it.*

The more you practice memorizing information, the easier it is to recall stored information from the memory bank. Do you notice how older people enjoy telling you the same stories over and over? One good reason for it is that every time they have to recall a memory to tell others about it, they are keeping these memories alive in their mind, and we all know that long-term memory gets better as we age and short-term memory gets worse. They find pleasure in recalling the good old times but there is little pleasure in recalling what you had for dinner yesterday or for breakfast this morning!

> *Having a poor diet, being depleted in Omega3, poor health or being stressed can affect the quality of our memories and our ability to recall information.*

Supplements of Omega 3 can help.

Concentration

Research shows that concentration is a good exercise for the brain. Brain scan images demonstrate immediate increases in blood flow whenever the mind is stimulated. This stimulation has been proven to encourage growth density and efficiency of the axons and dendrites, the dense tree-like branches that link the brain cells.

The ability to concentrate can make our life a lot easier, especially for school children and people in the work force.

We need to concentrate when we are studying, working or socially. Life is so difficult for those whose powers of concentration are impaired, for example for those afflicted with ADD or ADHD. If we can improve our ability to concentrate it can help us avoid various problems, misunderstandings and disappointments.

> **Concentration gives us focus; focus gives us power and power gives us an edge.**

Focusing helps us to live in the here and now, and improves our memory. It is essential to practice using our memory from the time we are still quite young and throughout our lives. If our memory becomes affected, as we age, with Alzheimer's or Dementia, these diseases steal from us, who we are, and our life story, which die prematurely with our brain cells, as no one else can know what we have lived. Our life story is unique to us. No one else can relate stories from our past like we can, as they are not privy to all that we have lived.

How sad will it be if we can't tell our grand children the story of our life just because we can't remember, or if we can't pass on any little bit of wisdom to them, that may be able to enhance their life?

So as children are little adults in training, we start there, by improving their focus, their concentration and their memory and by giving them healthy habits.

It is good to start young however age is irrelevant, because it is never too late to help improve our focus, concentration and our memory at any time in our life. We now know that we can regenerate brain cells, with the right stimulation and the right environment.

Grandparents have a crucial role to play in their grand children's lives and it would be such a pity to let preventable brain disease to stop them from telling their grand children tales and events from their life story. It is part of their folklore and culture.

If you are still young and reading this and feel that this doesn't apply to you, think again! Life travels at such a fast rate and before you can even blink and before you know it, your tiny children would have finished university and having children of their own. Besides, concentration and memory exercises should start as soon as we become aware of how easy it is to lose them.

You may be still young enough but if you haven't got any memory, you will not be able to enjoy life the way you should and reach your full potential.

The morale of this story is that we must all work hard to keep our neurons healthy and in good working order so that our brain cells are not attacked by premature disease.

These days, Alzheimer's and Dementia have been known to affect people earlier and earlier. When our memory is affected by brain disease it is too late! We need to practice taking good care of our memory and doing brain exercises all our life, starting when we are still young.

Research in Neuroplasticity tells us that novel and different experiences including exercise can help manufacture new brain cells enhance our intelligence and prevent brain disease.

Exercise to Preserve our Brain:

- Taking very good care of our brain health is essential at all ages, for instance by doing some brain gym, Sudoku, crosswords, puzzles or memory exercises precisely to use it so that we don't lose it. Supplements of Omega 3 are always useful, as a great part of our brain is made up mainly of Omega 3.
- Practice using your concentration and memory everyday by living in the here and now and every night make a point of recalling all the events of the day and remember them. Try to memorize dates, places, events, the times tables, anything that you think can enhance your memory.
- Keep a journal as an aide-memoire and once you have jogged your memory, make a conscious effort to remember it.

Often we hear people say things like: *I've got a head like a sieve; If my head wasn't attached to my shoulders I'd forget that too!* They say it as if it's a virtue and a nice little joke, ah, ah! . . . . NO! It isn't a joke! It is no laughing matter! Especially if you are young enough and not really functioning and asking the same question over and over again because you couldn't remember saying it before due to your lack of concentration! Work towards improving your memory.

The onset of Alzheimer's and Dementia can be prevented or at least delayed if we take our brain health seriously, and this starts when we are still young.

Anxiety, negative thoughts, worries and fears can very often interfere with our powers of concentration; but we now know that it is possible for us to control our thoughts and change the way we feel.

Exercise: What to do when you are feeling unresourceful:

- Exercise is always good for the mind. Go for a brisk walk or put on a dance CD and dance to it. Zumba is very popular these days. Go to the Gym, if you belong to one. If not, there are plenty of exercises that you can do that do not need equipment, like Jumping jacks, jogging, skipping.
- Change your physiology. If you change what you do with your body, it will alter your emotional state, i.e. your mood or how you feel.
- Vacuum the house. Vacuuming is a type of physical exercise. Decide to change the furniture in your house around, either in your lounge or bedroom for instance. There is nothing like a bit of hard work to energize you and help improve your concentration.

- Concentrate on doing something you have promised yourself to do for a long time but never found the time, like that herb garden you promised yourself or like sorting out your wardrobe; get rid of anything that you haven't worn in the past 12 months (I need to take some of my own medicine here!). The charity shops could do with them, instead of cluttering your wardrobe.
- Have you got a stack of photos left in boxes for years? Sort out your old photographs. Isn't that something you have been meaning to do for ages? Get some albums. You will feel so good afterwards.
- Get busy. Think how good you will feel afterwards.
- Yoga or Pilates are good for the body but also for the mind. How about joining a boxing class? That is sure to lift your spirits.
- Concentrate on tackling your housework; attack the house a little bit at a time; start with a corner of a room, then go to the next bit, then the next until you finish one room, then you can start attacking the next room; or decide to change the beds or clean your bathroom from top to bottom. Let your favourite music entertain you whilst doing it.
- If you are troubled by problems: whilst you are busy doing these physical things, imagine writing each of your problems on separate sheets of paper.
- Mentally pick up each sheet, rip it up, mentally watch yourself walk to your front door and throw the pieces away in the wind, and watch them fly away (in the movie of your mind of course; I wouldn't want you to be arrested for littering!). Once you've done that, let go of any negative thinking.
- Change your focus and concentrate on all that is good in your life. In other words count your blessings not your woes. Write them down and keep them where you can see them. Make some flashcards write down a few of the greatest blessings in your life.
- Keep a gratitude journal.
- Think about the precious people and things you have in your life, that make your life worth living. Give thanks for them.
- Every day before you get out of bed, lie in a comfortable position and concentrate for the next 5-10 minutes on any positive moods (such as joy, cheerfulness, enthusiasm or optimism) you want to create for the day—then, get up and concentrate and live these positive moods throughout your day; reminding yourself frequently that to-day what you are concentrating on, for instance, feeling joyful or cheerful or optimistic or whatever feeling you want to create for the day.
- Release any suppressed feelings as they cause bad attitudes, and interfere with your concentration. So it is essential to release these negative feelings. You need to find a healthy way of releasing your pent up emotions, whether it is through meditation, EFT, relaxation, prayer, exercise, have a good cry, line dancing or rock n rolling.
- Go for a lovely walk in the woods or if you are lucky enough to live near the beach, take a beautiful walk in the sand.
- It is not healthy to keep negative emotions festering. Festering emotions are very toxic emotions and are very destructive to your mind, body and relationships. They underpin a lot of diseases. You may end up snapping the head off some poor innocent person, if you keep them pent up. Release them!
- Learn to just be and accept what is. Stop fighting with yourself. Regularly practice relaxation.

Sometimes you can catch yourself not concentrating and believe it or not, when this happens you can do or say some silly things you never intended to. You may be lost in your own thoughts, but are not consciously aware of them. This happens when you are not living in the present. You are not present now. Try to be present now! Repeat: **Be present now!**

Repetitive Thoughts

If you try hard to get rid of a repetitive negative thought it can be very difficult for you to achieve it. Accept that you have this thought and that it is what it is: just a thought. Don't fight it, just surrender to it and accept that is what you are thinking now, but then you can redirect your focus on a happy memory or event and tag this to your thought process so that you can concentrate on the positive and end the negative thought with something positive. So the next time the same thought comes to mind, you will accept that is what you are thinking, but now, your mind will link it automatically to the positive memory or event and your repetitive thought will end up with the happy memory.

When you are trying not to think about something, your mind becomes occupied with that same repetitive thought—and you cannot concentrate. It becomes automatic. The more you try not to think about it the worse it becomes. Your mind becomes preoccupied with fighting the thought and failing to do so, makes you lose faith in your ability to control your thoughts. Instead you spend a whole lot of energy fighting with yourself. End the fight now! Just accept what is. That is what you are thinking but . . . now you are thinking of your happy memory (make a point of recalling your happy memory, including the happy feelings that go together). So each time the repetitive thought comes back, you know that it will be linked to a happy ending and you haven't wasted your time feeling distressed and fighting yourself. Adding another positive thought or memory at the end can start to change your focus, as you always end up with the happy memory.

Exercise to get rid of repetitive thoughts

- Take five minutes to sit quietly with your eyes closed. Just let the thoughts go in and out of your mind; become your observer and observe your thoughts; just notice them dipping in and out of your mind; just like cars on the Freeway, knowing another one will soon come along; do this calmly and without judgment; just observe them.
- When you want to let go of a thought, see it float away like a balloon in the gentle wind. If another thought comes in to bother you again, watch it drift away without judgment. Then return to the here and now.
- Let yourself just be. Repeat to yourself: Be present now.

If you stress and think that you can't get rid of that thought, you will get yourself so worked up that you won't be able to. You need to be really quiet and calm, and then you will be able to redirect your thoughts and be present again.

If you go through a negative experience, it is important not to fight it with your mind; it will only hype you up. You can choose to *let it be*. If the sounds of building works, dogs barking, road works, traffic, noisy neighbours or crying children, especially (if you are on a flight or in a restaurant) are bothering you, you can repeat in your mind, Let it be, instead of getting cranky and wishing them away. If you focus on how irritating these noises are the worse you will feel; however, if your focus is on accepting what is, you will feel a whole lot better!

Then return to the here and now and concentrate on repeating: Be present now and return to what you want to do or just enjoy being peaceful. When you are unable to have any influence on your environment, it is better to just let it be, otherwise you are setting yourself up for a stressful time.

Letting something negative over which you have no control, irritate you only serves to make you feel worse. It stops you from concentrating and you then allow it to ruin your day or night.

There's a time for everything; there's even a time for Worry.

If worry is an issue for you, some have found it useful to set aside a Worry time. Yes! Strange I know! But it does work well for some! Not all, I must admit, but if it works for you, great!

Choose a specific time just for worrying, for instance let's say between 7pm and 7.30pm, it will free your mind during the day and you will be able to concentrate better on what you have to do in the here and now, knowing that you will be able to concentrate fully later on what is worrying you. If the subject of your worry creeps into your mind during the day, you will be more comfortable to let it go, knowing you have a set time to concentrate on it later. Let the thought go just like the balloon in the gentle wind or the cars on the freeway. This may not work for all of you, but it is very effective for those who can manage it. At least they can go through their day, worry free. It is worth a try!

Studies have shown that people, who have a regular special worry time, tend to worry less.

Still, I also live in this world and realize that not everyone can be that disciplined. This can be quite a hard thing to do, but if you can try it and find that it does work, it can really benefit you.

You can choose which time is convenient to you; it may be first thing in the morning or early evening, however don't do it before bedtime, as your worries are more likely to stay in your subconscious all night and stop you sleeping. So setting a special worry time each day can be very helpful, so long as it is not the last thing at night.

You have to plan an appointment with yourself every day. It is important not to forget your worry time or not to put it off. You must be disciplined about it, otherwise it won't work. Do your worrying at your appointed time whatever happens; but when the time is up, that's it! No more worrying until the next day, same time, same place. The rest of the day, be fully present and concentrate on what you want to achieve.

All too often we worry about things that may never happen. For instance we can worry about hearing a small noise coming from the car on the way to work, and worry that we may have an accident; and if we have an accident, who will look after the children, and how will your husband cope without your help; what if you die? How dreadful would it be for him and the children at your funeral, how would they cope? Will there be donations or flowers? Etc.etc.

A small noise from the car, which may be nothing at all, has turned into your husband losing his wife, your children losing their mother, and seeing them at your funeral wondering whether there would be donations to charity or flowers and who would attend! This is the result of a wild imagination unchecked!

This is what happens when you don't keep your thoughts under control. This kind of thinking is called Catastrophysing! You now know that when you start to follow a negative scenario through to stop it at the very beginning and say NO to yourself that you are not going down that road! This is indulging in negative thinking.

> *Don't worry about tomorrow for tomorrow will bring its own worries. To-day's trouble is enough for to-day.*
>
> —*Mat 6: 33-34*

Let's not waste valuable time and energy worrying about to-morrow, and about things that may never happen. Let's live in the present.

Now that we understand a little about how our brain works and how we can control our focus and our thoughts; and how we can enhance our memory and concentration, it is a good time to look at our **ATTITUDE.**

> *Your life is what your thoughts make it.*
>
> —*Marcus Aurelius*

Notes: What have you learnt?

ATTITUDE

Attitude, to me, is more important than facts.
It is more important than the past, than education, than money, than
circumstances, than failures, than success, than appearance,
Giftedness or skill.
It will make or break a company . . . . a home . . . . a relationship.
The remarkable thing is, we have a choice every day regarding the attitude
we will embrace for that day. We cannot change our past.
We cannot change the inevitable.
The only thing we can do is play on the one string we have, and that is
Our attitude.
I am convinced that life is 10% what happens to me, and 90%
How I react to it.

—Charles Swindoll

CHAPTER THREE

Secrets About Attitude

Our attitude towards life determines life's attitude towards us.
—Earl Nightingale

I want now to dedicate a little time to talk to you about our attitude and how it can turn our life from disaster to success or from success to disaster. Our attitude of approach is actually everything!

If you have the wrong attitude it won't matter how many life's secrets you learn about, you still won't get it right. If you want to convince someone but you do it with a chip on your shoulders, you will not have a successful outcome.

> *Learning how to approach life with the right attitude is a skill that we should all endeavour to master, as life is a skill in itself.*

Observe some people who are very successful as they glide through any situation with charm and ease. Their attitude is never one of contradiction, aggression or forcefulness. They always manage to get what they want with graciousness and charisma. There is no resentment or blame.

Being aggressive and forceful is not an attitude that enhances our life; being calm, relaxed and able to put a point across with openness, good manners and charm, will get us everywhere.

Winston Churchill once said that attitude is a small thing that makes a big difference. The right attitude can help us to influence, negotiate, collaborate and persuade others. The wrong attitude can lead to conflict, unresolved issues, emotional upsets, poor behaviour and regrettable outcomes.

> **If you change your attitude of approach, the benefits can be huge. The difference may be changing from being unhappy and powerless to being happy, empowered and successful.**

> *Our attitude of approach to any situation determines whether we are happy or unhappy; it influences whether we are a winner or a loser, a success or a failure. It even decides whether we are sick or healthy, slim or fat, helpful or unhelpful, resourceful or unresourceful.*

The world always reacts to us by the way we treat ourselves and others.

If we see everything in life as a problem, we notice every single little obstacle in the way. However, if we are prepared to face life with a positive and honest attitude and expect things to work out for us, we then notice every single little opportunity that presents itself.

When we see life as one problem after another, we are not aware of any opportunities as we are not looking for them. They could hit us in the face and we do not see anything. On the other hand we emphasize every obstacle as we are looking for them. We often hear some people say things like: I don't know! It's just one thing after another! These people would not notice any opportunity presented to them if they tripped over them. They can only see problems as their focus is on problems! They are so busy counting all the bad things coming their way and in the meantime, have probably passed on several opportunities that could have opened themselves to them. They didn't see them or notice them as they were not looking for them.

We only see or hear what we expect to see or hear.

Search for the good and you find it, but look for the bad and you will certainly find that too. Negativity spreads like a virus!

Winston Churchill once defined a pessimist as one who makes difficulties of opportunities, and an optimist as one who makes opportunities of difficulties.

What's the difference? . . . . their **ATTITUDE!**

A positive attitude gives us positive outcomes and a negative attitude, can lead us to failure, disaster and without doubt leaves us feeling miserable and sorry for ourselves.

A negative attitude comes from entertaining negative thoughts; you cannot be happy thinking bad thoughts. However, you can be happy entertaining positive and empowering thoughts.

We will now look at a few attitudes that can play havoc in our lives, starting with a jealous attitude:

Jealousy: that dragon which slays love under the pretense of keeping it alive.
—*Havelock Ellis*

Jealous Attitude

Far too often, people ruin their lives and other people's because of their jealous attitude. They are jealous about anything and everything! If someone has a better job, more money, more fun, better house, better car, better relationships, better education, better childhood, better holidays, better family, better neighbours! You name it! They just need to keep up with the Jones's at all costs. They cannot be happy for someone else because they want it; not only do they want it, but they want it BETTER and BIGGER than others. But then when they push themselves to keep up with the Jones's because of their jealous attitude, the problem is that there is always someone else who has something better than they have. It is never ending because the jealous person can never feed that green eye monster enough. It is insatiable! It becomes a vicious circle. Hence, the jealous person is an unhappy person, always on the lookout for what others are doing and for what they have.

It is all a matter of degree! Many people who suffer from jealousy end up in constant conflict within their own family, let alone with others; often one member not talking to another for weeks, may be months and sometimes years. The stupidity of it is that they may not even remember why they stopped talking in the first place. A jealous person cannot be happy if some good fortune falls upon someone else and not to them.

If that is you: if you suffer from jealousy, do everything you can to get rid of this curse. It is like a cancer that invades you. It gnaws at your soul, and only brings misery. You cannot be truly happy if you suffer from jealousy. It makes you suspicious of everything and it seriously affects the quality of your life and relationships.

If you can't by your own means, then get professional help; but do something! Do not entertain this fiend and think that you can't help it! You can never be happy until you kill this green-eyed monster, otherwise it will keep raising its ugly head to haunt you, and make you and the people around you miserable.

> *To cure jealousy is to see it for what it is, a dissatisfaction with self.*
>
> —*Joan Didion*

May be you think that being jealous is normal and that the others are wrong, and you justify yourself that way. Deep down you know what you are doing or feeling isn't right. May be you think that you are misunderstood; but you're not happy neither are those close to you. In fact you are wracked with the pain of your jealousy and others are suffering because of you.

> *Whenever a friend succeeds, a little something in me dies.*
>
> —*Gore Vidal*

> *It is not normal to feel wracked by pangs of jealousy most of your life! Unless you do some work on yourself or get help, it will plague you for the rest of your life and affect all areas of your life.*

Jealousy affects your relationships. You are jealous when you feel the need to possess another person and control what they do.

> *Jealousy has nothing to do with love.*

Often a jealous person will say: *I do this because I love you so much.* Well, I have news for you! It's not true! *Not at all*! I repeat: **Jealousy has nothing to do with love**. It is just your excuse and you know it!

Love is freedom; Love is not control!

The jealous person does it because they want to possess and control you because their jealousy dictates to them how they should treat you. It is their pathetic distorted ego that feels the need to get the undivided attention of their partner or of others. Their partner becomes the person who should shower them with love around the clock, and the jealous person is only happy when this happens, but even then, this is not enough! It is never enough!

On the other hand the victim of the jealous person feels constant fear and is wary where they tread, should anyone, heaven help them, show them any unrequested attention, whilst at the same time dreading their partner's reaction. They walk on egg shells. Consequently their partners suffer with very low self-esteem and tend to react as victims.

Jealousy is very selfish. Jea-lousy is exactly that: lousy!

It doesn't really care about the needs or well being of the other person. The jealous person thinks they care and love their partner, but the way they act has very little to do with caring and loving. Jealousy sufferers are always, suspicious. Hence the need to know where their partner is going, what he or she is up to, who they speak to and what was said and who was on the phone, and who sent this email and who wrote you this letter or that text, who phoned you, and what time will you be home, who did you meet? What did they say? Where have you been? What have you been doing all this time? Why did you take so long? Etc.etc.

Trust

Trust is almost non-existent in the relationship! Surprise, surprise! There is very little trust, if any! If trust doesn't exist in a relationship, it becomes a very low-grade relationship—not one where the partners are happy and relaxed with each other and live a quality life; the kind of relationship one should aim for.

> *Jealousy, like sulking, can be emotional torture for the other partner.*

Jealousy is all the fun you think they had . . . .

—*Erica Jong*

Sometimes, jealousy can lead to obsessions, where they believe that their partner will find someone better, someone more attractive than them and leave them, and they are scared of confirming their own suspicions. The jealous person's self-esteem is low, because underneath everything, they know that what they are doing is just not right. It is common for them to check their partner's clothes for clues of their betrayal, check their phones for strange numbers, texts or messages, check their receipts, their briefcase, their purse or handbag, their mail, emails etc. At worst, they may even employ a private detective to satisfy themselves, which either way can never put to rest their unquenchable suspicion.

People with a jealous attitude more often than not suffer from a destructive inferiority complex; in addition their self-esteem is usually at rock bottom; they cannot quite believe for themselves that their partner would want to stay with them, for themselves. It doesn't matter how much they are reassured of their partner's loyalty and how much attention they get, they are like a bottomless pit. They can never be reassured! They can never be filled!

Did you see the movie: *Sleeping with the Enemy, the movie with Julia Roberts and Kelvin Kline?* This was about an abusive, jealous husband.

> *Please do not stay in an abusive relationship for years and years in the hope that it will improve! It will never happen unless the offender has insight into their destructive behaviour and decides to do something about it, SERIOUSLY!*

Controlling and Abusive Attitude

With jealousy, there is always control. The jealous person controls what you do, where you go, even where you work sometimes.

If he or she lays a finger on you, walk straight out of that door!

Better still get rid of them, never go back, unless they've had some therapy and can **prove** that they've truly changed. That happens as often as we have an eclipse of the sun! Do not waste years and years feeling trapped, hoping that somehow a miracle will happen and sort your life out.

Heaven helps those who help themselves.

Unless you are prepared to do something about your relationship, this abuse will continue. People don't just change like that, because you want it to happen. You need to take some action for things to change.

Nowadays there is a lot of help out there provided by private companies and the government. All you have to do is ask and make some enquiries. Talk to different people. The internet is a good place to start. The police have a department specifically for this problem and usually are very helpful and very informative.

> *Every day that you stay in an abusive relationship is a day wasted. By accepting the abuse in the first place, even if it is because you don't know what to do, you have taught your partner, that it is okay to abuse you.*

Worst of all your children are observing and learning, as their parents are their first couple role models. Don't be surprised if they do not become carbon copies of you. They may turn out to be bullies or door mats and victims with very deflated self-esteem.

Life with a controlling and jealous person can be camouflaged as a happy couple or family to the outside world, but in private it can be hell on earth.

Do not allow anyone to abuse you whatever their excuses.

Do not allow anyone to control you either.

> *We are all free spirits, born with our own God-given free will, to make our own decisions.*

If you want a normal healthy relationship, you need to decide what you have to do. This does not happen if you are living with a jealous or controlling partner. If you need to walk away from a destructive relationship, then so be it! Your safety is paramount. Taking care of your mental health is essential and your human right.

> *Remember, abuse need not be only physical. Abuse comes in many forms, physical, mental, emotional, financial or psychological.*

You need to have a healthy attitude towards yourself, and have a healthy self-respect and good self-esteem. This doesn't happen when you are in a relationship with someone with a jealous attitude. Make sure that if you were to leave that you could keep yourself and if you have children, *safe first of all from any reprisals.* Get the law on your side. Get some support from the right people around you.

Jealous or controlling partners can prove to be very vengeful.

Make sure that you have some back up. Remember also that they may try to disempower you by telling you that you have no money and that you wouldn't be able to survive without them, that no one would want you, or try and make you feel that you are losing your mind. See it for what it is! That is sheer manipulation! That's a controlling way to overpower you.

> *There is always a way; if you search for it, you will find it!*

Talk to the right people; find out what you can. Get as much information and ammunition as you can, arm yourself; then take action! You may be poorer but you will feel empowered and will have peace of mind.

You can do and achieve anything you want to do, if you put your mind to it! There is always a way. Search until you find it. Okay, so they've said they are sorry! However, if it ever happens again and again, you know that it is not true and that nothing is going to change. It can be the start of a cycle of abuse, then I'm sorry; it will never happen again, until the next time, when it starts all over again! You deserve peace of mind!

> *If you stay with an abusive partner, male or female, you will suffer from low self-esteem and will behave as a victim, which gives the jealous, abusive person more power to abuse you again. It will become harder and harder to leave the relationship.*

The later you decide to leave, the more traumas you would have endured; the lower your self-esteem would be and the more you will see yourself as a victim; the more self-pity you will suffer from. The harder it will be to take action and leave. The more you and your children would become contaminated by dysfunctional ways and distorted views of life. The more difficult it will be for you to seek help and the longer it will take for you to become functional again; except, that it may be too late for your children who may look for the same kind of man or woman for their future partner and replicate the cycle of abuse they so hated in their childhood.

> *If you need to leave a destructive relationship, leave sooner rather than later. Do not stay for the sake of the children and do not stay hoping that things will improve when it has already gone too far!*

The sad thing is, that even though their partner started by loving the jealous and controlling person, they end up by pushing them away. Even if they do stay because they don't have what it takes to leave, they will never know how their partner really feels about them. They reap what they sow! Their partner feels that they are damned if they do and damned if they don't. So sadly, often their suspicions end up by being true. So if you now have an affair and are accused of it then at least it is true!

> *In a relationship where jealousy and control reign, there is no trust, least of all respect.*

When there is no trust or respect in a relationship, then there is nothing else. The point is you may have to face that you need to move on. Jealousy and controlling attitudes are a sure way of at least destroying any relationship whether it is an intimate one or whether it is a family relationship, neighbourly, work relationship or friendship.

A Jealous attitude is a poisonous, ugly one which you must not entertain and must do your best to get rid of it; avoid it like the plague!

If you bring jealousy into a relationship, however good it is, it has a destructive influence on the relationship. Of course, jealousy doesn't only affect couples; it can affect others like mothers, fathers, brothers, sisters, mother-in-laws, sister-in-laws, brother-in-laws, daughter-in-laws, son-in-laws, siblings, friends, other family relations, neighbours, work colleagues and many others.

Whoever is afflicted by jealousy, it's never good news. Often the relationships end up breaking down and the non-afflicted party move on when they realize that they no longer have to put up with such destructive behaviours. However, this may happen after many years of pain caused by pernicious jealousy.

> *Jealousy is a noxious disease. It does not only damage your personality and who you are, but your innocent partner's too, including your children if you have any.*

If not treated, jealousy spreads and contaminates the rest of you. Of course if you suffer from jealousy, you probably won't only be jealous of your partner. It spills into all your relationships and other areas of your life; you are very destructive and a great energy drain to your friends, neighbours, work colleagues and other relationships too.

> *If you suffer from jealousy, you must make every effort to work on yourself and get rid of it, if you are to live a quality life. If you can't, get help from a good Therapist or Coach.*

Exercise to Change Your Emotional State:

- Like any emotional state, if you want to change your state, you need to change your focus first. That means changing what you think; what you do with your body; and choosing what you focus on.
- Choose what thoughts you decide to focus on. Choose what words you use to talk with yourself and choose what subject you pour your attention on.
- For every jealous thought that comes into your awareness, change it to one with a healthier meaning for you, whether you initially believe it or not. Write them down.
- It is important to keep a daily journal and write your thoughts and affirmations down.
- Keep a journal of gratitude. Concentrate of all the good things in your life that you need to be grateful for. When you flood yourself with gratitude, it becomes harder for jealousy to intrude your thoughts.
- Instead of focusing on the subject of your jealousy, focus on something positive like helping someone else; help a more vulnerable member of your family, community or become a volunteer.
- Repeat appropriate positive affirmations until you start to believe them.

Affirmations

- I choose to love and be loved.
- I enjoy good relationships with everyone.
- I am fully satisfied with my relationships.

- I choose to be happy.
- I am happy for the good in other people's lives.
- I choose to be positive in my relationships.
- I respect myself and my relationships.
- I choose to trust my partner.
- I am happy that others are successful.
- I choose harmony and reject jealousy.
- Jealousy has no place in my life.
- The only person I choose to control is me.

Make a decision and a commitment that from now on that you will no longer entertain a jealous attitude and behave accordingly.

Monitor your own behaviour and thoughts very closely. Write them down as a record, where you can check on yourself. Engage a good friend to help you monitor your behaviour.

Thirdly use your physiology; when you feel slight feelings of jealousy coming up, kill the monster while it's still little. Stop it the minute you feel the slightest pang of jealousy. Use your body in a different way. If jealousy gives you a certain expression on your face, change it; put a relaxed smile on your face and change the way you move your body; change your intonation. Change your words. That is where your focus goes instead of focusing on your jealous feelings. Go and do something positive for someone else.

Exercise is always a good distraction when you are trying to avoid something negative. It releases endorphins. Walking, Jogging or skipping are great exercises for changing your emotional state. Go for a power walk and clear your head from any negative thoughts. Breathe fresh air. Concentrate on your environment. Get close to nature. Constantly reconfirm to yourself the decision and commitment you made to yourself. Keep the end goal in mind. That is, that once you get rid of the green eye monster that you will be able to have an easy going, pleasurable relationship, peace of mind without the torture of jealousy. How good would you feel not being tormented by these habitual jealous thoughts?

> *Important Secret: We all create our own experience of life, good or bad.*

By our own attitude to life, by our own behaviour, our actions and our thoughts, we create the results we enjoy or not to-day.

It is a cop out to say: *That's what I'm like I'm jealous, that's just how I am, and I can't help it.* NO! It isn't just how you are! You are choosing to be this way!

> *Whatever your past experiences, as an adult, you are choosing your own attitude and your own behaviour, today, yesterday and tomorrow.*

You choose these feelings, by the thoughts you choose to entertain and the actions you decide to take. You choose these behaviours by the thoughts you choose to focus on. When you are jealous, you are making a choice. That makes you responsible for how you are and what you do.

You are choosing to create the experience of jealousy in your life. You are choosing to entertain the feelings of jealousy instead of seeing what feelings you could choose to be constructive.

Choose a better attitude, so you can feel better. You will behave better and can have better.

By saying: *That's what I'm like,* you are making excuses for yourself, and you are not taking responsibility for yourself and for your behaviour.

> **Love doesn't claim possession, but gives freedom.**
>
> —*Rabindranath Tagore*

When all is said and done, we are all accountable for ourselves and for the results we have in our life; by the consistent actions we take daily, we create our own experience of life and our world as we know it.

We are all responsible for our own behaviours and attitude. We are all responsible for where we are at, whether it's good or whether it's bad. Our choices can send us down the right path or they take us down in the ditch. If we choose a better attitude we get better results.

Everything we experience in our life to-day is the product of what we have created ourselves by the consistent decisions, choices and actions we took in the past.

> **It is not weak to ask for help; it is the smart and sensible thing to do. If you need help and are too proud to access it, that's weak and pathetic! Don't let pride get in the way of your happiness. Humility is a virtue!**

The buck stops here! We can't blame anyone else. If it's great, pat yourself on the back; if it's not so great, promise yourself to work on it or get some help if you can't do it alone, so that you can have a quality life to take pleasure in and be proud of.

Otherwise nothing will change; and then one day you wake up at forty or fifty or even sixty, full of regrets as you realize that life has passed you by because you chose certain negative attitudes and beliefs or you were too proud to ask for help.

It has everything to do with your attitude. It is no good, playing the victim or living in denial. So whatever your life is like to-day, it is a consequence of what you consistently did yesterday. Whatever your life will look like tomorrow will be a result of what you consistently do to-day.

The results you have now and in the future is always a consequence of the efforts or lack of them that you put in, in the past and in the present. No one else is doing it for you. That is the honest truth.

> **Your life is the sum result of all the choices you make, both consciously and unconsciously. If you can control the process of choosing, you can control all aspects of your life. You can find freedom that comes from being in charge of yourself.**
>
> —*Robert Foster Bennett*

> *In life we get back what we put in. To-day you are getting back what you put in yesterday.*

Put in a lot and you get a lot out. Put in little and that's exactly what you reap. Life doesn't short-change you.

If you are not happy, there's only one person who can change things and that's you—not your partner, not others, just you! Before you do anything else, it is your attitude of approach that needs to be looked at first. It's great to be able to understand that you need to do different if you want different results but you have to take appropriate action. It is never too late!

A serious change of attitude can work magic! Believe it or not, that's not a bad thing!

> *You can't control others, but you can control you and what you do.*

Anytime you realize that you are on the wrong track it is better than not realizing it at all; or knowing it and pretending that things will sort themselves out with time and continue to live in denial.

> *Time doesn't change anything. What creates the change is what you do with that time.*

This is not something new! This law has always existed; that's the law of life. We are all responsible for our lives and have always been; only you didn't know it before and were not aware of it. But now, there is no excuse, you know it! So it's up to you: take responsibility or continue with a less than satisfactory life. Don't sell yourself short.

This is not about blaming, or pointing the finger or making you feel bad or guilty if things aren't right; it is about learning, growing and developing through life so that you lead an empowered life, in order that you can be happy and proud of who you are and who you have become.

Age has no importance here. Some people are early developers and others take a little longer to get there. Just a fact of life, pure and simple! Sometimes it takes a while for some to realize this. This is about facing things as they are and finding ways to improve, whatever stage of life that you are at. Anything else will not get you moving and you will maintain the status quo.

Before you can do anything about change you have to come to the realization of what you truly are doing to get the results that you are getting. Don't feel down about it, instead feel excited that you can do something now to change and improve the quality of your life.

> *Think: Five years from now, who and where will you be? If you start creating now,*
> *what can you achieve?*

Wherever and whatever you are at to-day, is down to you. Some of you may be congratulating yourselves, others may be feeling depressed. If you are not happy where you are, the good news is that things can only get better as you can change them. Get excited! That's within your power!

It just means you've got some work ahead of you, and you can look forward to some exciting times to come; get energized, as you go towards discovering the amazing new you.

Negative Attitude

There are a whole load of negative people in this world. Are you one of them?

People with a negative attitude often imagine the worst instead of evaluating a situation with a clear mind. Negative people always find the worst case scenario to focus on. However, as you know, in life you get more of what you focus on.

Whenever you focus on the negative, you become a magnet for attracting negative events and experiences. On the other hand the opposite is also true.

> *What we think about we create in our world.*

Successful people, never waste their valuable time focusing on negative outcomes. They concentrate on what can go right and they too are a magnet but to positive things coming their way. What they focus on, they create in their world. We all create what we focus on.

Generally, people with a negative attitude are usually not the successful ones in life. If you are serious about winning in the game of life, your attitude is the first thing that you need to pay attention to. Someone once said that life is a game; the only problem is that it doesn't come with the Rules manual. We have to work out what the rules are as we go along.

The rule number one needs to be, to approach life with a positive and resourceful attitude.

If you catch yourself being negative, do something to change these thoughts immediately to a more positive reality for you. Nothing good comes out of a negative attitude in life. It blocks any opportunity that might have otherwise presented itself to you. Fake it till you make it if you have to.

Learn to be enthusiastic and cultivate optimism.

When you are enthusiastic and optimistic, there is no room for negativity to intrude on you. Decide that you will live these two values every day and that will be your attitude towards whatever you have to deal with every day. Embark upon anything that comes your way with enthusiasm and optimism. Do this consistently for seven days and you will be well on your way to acquiring a new habit. In the end, you will no longer have to fake it; it will come naturally.

The bonus is that you will be infecting others with your newly acquired virtues of enthusiasm and optimism, as these values carry positive energy and are very contagious. They will lift your spirit and that of others; you will be contributing to making the world a much happier place.

Difficult Attitude

Some people can turn anything, any place, anywhere, into their personal battle station. These people are prickly and aggressive towards life; however they are incensed when others mirror their behaviour when interacting with them. We all have mirror neurons. Well? They do fire together enabling us to reflect each other's behaviours.

Some people are precious whereas others can be *touchy*, but both can make anything simple become as complicated and as complex as the Geneva Convention!

Isn't it much nicer to have an easy ride in life than to have to struggle for everything? If you want life to be peaceful and more pleasant, you need to look at your attitude.

When you treat the world with love and respect, the world responds back to you in a similar vein. Yet, the opposite is equally true.

Make a decision and choose that you will treat others with love and respect and not look to complicate things because of your attitude. When your attitude changes, your world too becomes easier and more pleasant. You will soon realize that there is less conflict in your life and your world is much simpler. Oh, joy! May that day come to you very soon!

Entitlement Attitude

There are others who have an attitude of Entitlement; they behave as if the world owes them something. Research shows that when children are brought up with praise only and not enough constructive criticism, they end up believing that they are just marvellous and that everyone else should treat them as *someone special* because they are *entitled* and of course, no question about it! They are always right. When the world doesn't, because they are no more special than you and I, they are horrified and act up. They can become aggressive, bullies and demanding; or they can become depressed or very difficult or even abuse their parents or anyone else they are in a relationship with. If they hurt someone in the process, that's not their problem! Honestly? They truly don't care. They lack empathy.

If you recognize yourself here, how does that feel to think that you may be a bully or an abuser? Not nice, huh? Though, the good news is that it is never too late to make amends. Parents can be amazingly forgiving to their children. Others too may be willing to forgive you if you have a sincere change of heart and attitude.

When parents or guardians give in to their children for an easy ride after the child has demanded something for a while, the children learn that if they whine, yell and scream, they will get what they want in the end. This attitude can continue into adulthood, and this is when you see adults creating as much fuss as they can, becoming aggressive until they get what they want, whether it is in the work place, in relationships or in the public arena. They have never learned that sometimes you need to wait to get what you want or to work for it; or it may just be impossible to get what you want because what you want may not be the right thing or may not be appropriate. What they want is instant gratification because they are entitled to it.

Now, don't you read this and think of a friend or someone else you know! Are there any truths here about YOU? Is it time to get real with yourself, if this applies to you?

We all need insight into our behaviour; we also have to be honest with ourselves. It is never too late to change what doesn't serve us well.

If you like the way things are, even if you recognize that you do have an attitude of entitlement, then, you are not living a quality life. The problem with an attitude of entitlement is that on some level, it works for you, because you end up getting what you want; so it is difficult for you to see why you should change it. Still, you do know that it doesn't make you a very nice person, if it is at the expense of others. Having what you want in an honest and polite fashion is what you aim for. At times, we have to wait for what we desire.

Your attitude of entitlement may be working for you, but what kind of human being does that make you? You can never live a quality life that way. Going through life trampling on other people's feelings so that you can get your own way is a horrible way to be. Not caring if you hurt others so long as you get what you want is shameful.

However, if you do have an attitude of entitlement but have enough insight to recognize it, you have the power to do something about it! You do not have to accept what you don't want; and if you want a worthy life, then you need to make quality decisions followed by superior actions.

Make a commitment to abolish your attitude of entitlement and stick with it.

Make a commitment that from now on that you will live the life you choose, by putting in the effort and not walk on others. What can you do straight away, towards your commitment? Do something! Anything! Even the smallest thing towards it, will start to gain momentum.

It is important to take action straight away, when you make a commitment towards a new goal, otherwise you lose momentum and making changes become too difficult.

That means:

- Writing down your new goals about how you will eliminate your attitude of entitlement.
- Find out your options and your opportunities. What can you do to keep it in check? Engage a good friend if possible to keep you on tract.
- Check if your goals are realistic.
- Decide what steps you need to take. Keep a record of what you do and how it is changing your attitude of entitlement.
- How will you measure your change in behaviour?
- Plan your way forward.

Make sure that you follow-up what you promise yourself and put your decisions into action.

Victim Attitude

Many believe that they have nothing to do with the results that they are producing; they believe that it is just what life throws at them or just their luck; some prefer to play the victim and blame others or circumstances instead. The blaming game is a fool's game. It's called living in denial or in cloud coucou land! It is shifting the blame from you to someone else or something else so that you don't have to deal with it. It's just pretending when deep down you know that the reality is much different, but it's too hard to take the responsibility for yourself.

Even if there had been extenuating circumstances or other people have done things to you that were unfair, you still played a part in it; your reaction is your own, no one else's. You are the one who chose how you reacted.

Own your responsibility, so that you can change things for the better. Unless this happens, there will be no change.

As we are not into blaming, it doesn't really matter whose fault it is, does it? What matters is that your life takes a turn for the better.

Another important life's secret to remember:

> **We all do the best we can with the resources we have at the time.**

It means that you did the best you could with the knowledge you had at the time. But because you didn't know any better, you got the results you are struggling with to-day. When you know better, you can do better and consequently get better results. Right?

You do have a choice on how you react to any event or circumstance.

You can choose how you react to any event or circumstance. You don't have to follow the crowd. You can make your own decisions. Be honest with yourself; at least, then you can improve things and get better results. If you persist in thinking it's not my fault, I'm the victim here! then you stay at an impasse; that is reacting as a victim and nothing changes for you other than you will indulge more in your own self-pity. The choice is yours! Become victim-wise, not a victim!

Having a victim attitude stops you from learning from your mistakes, and entices you to repeat them again and again.

Sometimes mistakes are blessings in disguise; they are there to teach us valuable lessons if we are prepared to learn from them.

At times, you may really believe that you don't have a choice. What you mean is that you don't like the choices that you have. But that's different from not having any choice at all. When you say that you have no choice, all it does is that it contributes to a sense of powerlessness; this attitude causes you to react as a victim, rather than seeking a more proactive solution.

- When you feel you have no choice, brain storm on a piece of paper and write down all the options or opportunities that are open to you.

- Be bold and don't make any judgment; be creative. Write everything down, even if it sounds impossible and far-fetched. Think that you are finding the best solution you can for your best friend.

Then look at all the options that you have written down; now check them out one by one, until you find a solution that you are happy with.

Even if you are unable to physically alter a situation, you at least have the choice of choosing your viewpoint, your attitude and your reaction to the things that happen to you. You really do not have to react as a victim.

Life is 10% what happens to me and 90% how I react to it.

—*Charles Swindoll*

If you approach life as a victim, you never grow, never move on or never get anywhere.

Self-pity is your drug; you can't get enough of it! Not only do you feel sorry for yourself but you also **crave** for others to feel sorry for you. You **thrive** on other people's pity.

If someone casually asks you how you are, rather than say I'm feeling very well, thank you; you, suddenly, seize the opportunity for someone to feel sorry for you, so you reply: *I have been bette*r! Which then begs the next question: *Oh, haven't you been well? . . .* Now, you have a captive audience ready to listen to your sad tale! . . . . And you relish in telling them all your woes! All they wanted to hear was; *I'm fine, thanks and move on.* After all, they were just being polite! Right? They didn't really want to hear the ins and outs of your health or relationship disasters! . . . . whether your last operation was a lot of problem or that your husband or wife has left you or is having an affair etc. By the time they leave you, you have sapped all their energy!

It may be that you have learned that this is the only way that you can get attention or love from others. However, feeling sorry for yourself, and getting others to do the same, does not move you forward towards a quality life. In fact it keeps you stuck and paralyzed into inaction with your self-esteem dragging on the floor.

You may look at other people and say: *It's okay for them, they have money, or they have a good family, or had a good upbringing or a good education, better job, better luck, but it isn't like that for me.*

This attitude screams: *I'm a Victim!*

It's making excuses for yourself for all your failings, and not being honest enough to look at the truth face on and take responsibility for yourself. The past is the past and we can't go back and make it better; all we have is the present so that we can improve the future. So, let's see things as they are, not as we wish they were; that way, we can take appropriate action. Making people feel sorry for us, achieves ZILCH! It only makes us feel worse and confirms our sorry state of affairs to ourselves.

Many have said that you are not responsible for the hand you were dealt with at birth, but as an adult you are certainly responsible for how you play that hand. Some have privileged backgrounds, whereas others struggle from the time they are delivered on this planet. If you choose to play the poor me, ain't it awful you continue to feel sorry for yourself, and as such you remain trapped in your situation. Nothing changes and you continue to obtain inferior results as a consequence. If you want to lead the quality life that you deserve, you need to change that attitude. Pronto!

Grab life with both hands and be serious about what you want to change, and don't stop until you have got the results you want. Be consistent in your approach and work steadily towards getting the results you do want.

The truth of the matter is: you are not a victim! Whatever your circumstance! No one is! You are only a victim, if you choose to be one and if you choose to worship self-pity.

> *Self-pity is a nasty habit, to which some people are addicted to, and loathe giving up.*

Self-pity is a destructive game that victims play so that others give them attention and sympathy. Playing the victim is a very negative way to be, is very manipulative, and consequently adds no benefit to anybody's life. When you play the victim, your partner, children and family do not have the best of you.

We all know that some people have had poor life experiences, and I am not making it light of it, far from it; as a consequence there are some who learn to manipulate or squash or bully others to meet their needs or for their survival. They find a way to rationalize it to themselves, to justify themselves and end up believing that they are the victim so that they can live with themselves. They have not learnt another more resourceful way of coping.

This is not the stuff that a superior quality of life or happiness is made of.

Victims are never truly successful and satisfied because other people are always taking advantage of them or they are being bullied, and of course it wasn't their fault! That is the story of their life! There is always a sad tale or two to tell . . . . You won't believe what happened to me . . . .

They see themselves as a victim and this behaviour becomes their way of life, by now not consciously realizing what they are doing. They rationalize it by saying that that they are right in their attitude because no one has helped them in the past, and bad things have happened to them. Some often hurt people before others hurt them, or reject others before they reject them; as if two wrongs could ever make a right! That's the way they make themselves feel better.

As a result, these people live their lives most of the time on the defensive and often in isolation, because they cannot allow people to get close to them as they do not trust anyone. All the time that you believe that you are a victim of other people's actions you can never be happy or live a quality life, as you have no control over other people.

Wherever victims go, they come across problems; they often fall out with others, but never question their attitude as to why this is always happening to them. It's not their fault!

Victims repeat the same mistakes over and over again and create conflict around them; however the sad thing is that they never make the connection, that *they* are the common denominator.

Victims need to change their attitude first before others change towards them.

When you read this and before you start thinking about someone else you know who behaves this way: Examine yourself. Can this be you? Be honest with yourself! You have plenty to gain if you get real with yourself.

> *Remember, the way you react to the world is the way that the world responds to you.*
> *You get back what you give out.*

If your attitude is less than amiable, chances are that others will respond to you in the same vein. If you treat yourself as a victim and behave as one, others will treat you in that same way.

Victims believe that there is always someone somewhere to do something ghastly to them or that they can be the object of someone else's cruelty at any given time. Consequently they have the weight of the world on their shoulders, because they know that things won't work out for them.

It is just their luck! They do not see themselves as captain of their ship or master of their destiny, as they believe that it is outside of their control. If you want to know how someone will behave in the future, take a minute to see what their past behaviour was like.

> *Your past behaviour predicts how you will behave in the future.*

As a life secret that's a given. The tragic thing about it is that victims do not seem to have any insight into their own behaviour. If they did they wouldn't want to know it. You only have to look at someone's past behaviour and you have a pretty good idea of how they will behave in the future.

Listen now! I am telling you! If you think any of this applies to you, look at your past behaviour straight in the face; examine your past relationships; Take a frank look at your current relationships; Did you fall out with many different people, like your mother, father, brothers and sisters, mother-in-law, father-in-law, sister-in-law, brother-in-law, aunts, uncles, friends, neighbours or any other relationships, and have done so for years? But you have always justified it by telling yourself that the people you fell out with were dreadfully awful to you and it was all their fault and you had nothing to do with it? Some may well have been awful, but if you learn to be generous and pass on silly things, you will prevent yourself from a lot of unnecessary hassles—however is it a regular pattern for you? You have a role to play in how you react to any situation no matter what others do. Soooo! Start seriously looking at your own behaviour. As a life secret, this is an important one!

If you want to know the answer to your problems, look inside not outside of you. If you look outside you are not going to find any answer because you are not looking in the right place!

Always look inside of you and you will get the answers you need.

Is it possible that the common denominator is YOU?

If you keep falling out with lots of people, even when you move and come across new people, new situations, start to ask yourself what it is that YOU are doing or what role did YOU play in these situations? Look at the honest truth, however ugly it is. It is okay, because then, you can begin to improve your life, and model a better behaviour for your children.

Your children are the adults of to-morrow who model their lives on yours. If you want theirs to be better, then, start by being better with yourself and dump that victim attitude.

Find out what meaning YOU are giving to your life experiences that makes you fall out with other people like this! You may be saying to yourself that it is normal that lots of people fall out with their families and friends and others, as your family and friends are not like everybody else's; the fact is:

No! It is not normal to fall out with lots of people *all the time*, and believe that everyone else is dreadful except you!

Those bad things do not only happen to you, because you have bad luck. They happen to you, because you are behaving in a very unresourceful and dysfunctional way. You may not have fallen out with some others, not because you didn't try but because these others were kind to you and avoided to conflict with you, for your sake or for theirs.

First face things so that you can do something about it. Unless you make a decision to be 100% honest with yourself, you will never change. You must be truthful with yourself if you are genuine about wanting a better quality of life. Until now, you may legitimately believe that you had a lot of bad luck in relationships with partners, friends, family etc. By now, you may seriously avoid people. Now is the time for you to get real and be really honest with yourself. Unless you actually genuinely realize that you had a big role to play in the past, you will never be able to change your future.

Who have you fallen out with? What about your family? How many members of your family do you not speak with? What about friends? Do you keep losing friends? What about work colleagues? What about neighbours? What about school friends or those related to the school life? At University? What about people in your clubs, gym or church? Anyone else?

The good news is that if you are honest with yourself you can move on and transform your life. You will never regret this decision. This is for you! Heal your life, and all that goes with it, starting with a healthy attitude. Happiness is waiting for you.

Denial

Some people live in denial with what is happening in their lives and pretend all is well, when confusion is king around them. This is a way of lying to yourself, as you look at life through rose coloured glasses instead of accepting what is. For some when they feel that reality is too hard to take, they go into denial as they would rather live in a pretend world rather than face some harsh reality.

Living in denial keeps you trapped in a fake world and can have very grave consequences. It stops you from seeing things as they are. You end up believing what you pretend to yourself. For instance you refuse to see that someone close to you has a drinking or drug issue or that your partner is being unfaithful. Denying that you have a lump in your breast or testicle can shorten your life considerably. By the same token denying any illness because you cannot stomach what it would mean to you until it's too late and the inevitable happens is too pointless and tragic. Living in denial is lying to yourself and others too. You are being dishonest with yourself and with those close to you. You are not living with integrity. There are others who blame other people or circumstances instead of looking inside. They pretend that everything is Honki Dore on the outside, even if their whole world is crashing down around them.

The husband of a client of mine whose marriage is falling apart because of his incessant abuse to his wife, professes his undying support in a social media for other women from all corners of the world: to give the vote or freedom to the women of Egypt or Syria, to end domestic violence or support the *Medecins sans frontieres, Amnesty International, The red Cross* etc. Yet, he is a wife beater and a mental, emotional, and psychological abuser of his own wife! He is a cowardly phoney who would rather live in denial than face the ugly truth about him. The thought that charity begins at home first never crosses his mind as he is too busy lying to himself and others. It doesn't occur to him that he must take care of his own responsibilities before preaching to others. As far as he thinks, the world believes that he is a gentle kind man who defends down-trodden women. He lives in denial in the hope that others cannot see his true personality by advocating for everything that he isn't and doesn't do. That is called deliberately lying to oneself and to others and not being real. On the other hand, it can also be a deliberate ploy to mask his real narcissistic personality in the hope that others don't find out who he really is. Living in denial and pretending to the world that he is someone he really isn't, by fooling himself that he can successfully manipulate other people to see him as a really good person. But, you know what? People are not stupid! They can read between the lines. He may live in denial, but others do not!

You know why? It's because he sees himself as a victim instead of looking at what he really is: an abuser! A wife-beater! He would rather continue to live in denial instead of looking at how he is really behaving in his marriage. He would rather believe that his life is where it is at because of what his wife and others have done to him instead of what he is doing to his wife and his marriage.

Self-pity is a terrible place to hide in!

Self-pity ruins not only his life but the lives of those closest to him, his wife and children. So, consequently nothing will change for him, unless he decides to be honest with himself first and stops the denial and the lies.

If you have a problem, be brave, acknowledge it. If you are unhappy, be honest with yourself, and then you can do something about it; choose to see things as they are, not as you pretend they are. If your life is not where you want it to be, look at it squarely in the face; don't pretend or live in denial. Nothing will ever get better if you live in denial.

If you don't come clean with yourself, you cannot change anything. You remain caught up in misery with the usual poor outcomes to cry over. It remains the same old dramas.

To be able to make changes in your life, you need to acknowledge that you do have a problem first. Without this first step, nothing changes. The day you decide that you will no longer live in denial, is the day you can start to turn things around in your life.

If you are not being supported by your partner or your family, then get to grip with it and admit it. If you're the destructive influence in your relationship, time has come to own up, because you can never be happy otherwise. If you think you have a health problem, denying it may land you in dire circumstances. If you are addicted to any substance that is detrimental to your health, acknowledge it before you do further damage to your health. Denial is not your friend. Basking in the sun after the removals of cancerous moles and telling yourself that a tan is more important, is the essence of denial. If anything else is wrong, admit it! That way, you can begin to heal and improve your life.

> **Denial can deny you life!**

Go on, face it! It's only then that things can begin to look up.

Have a Self-Reliant Attitude

If you know that you can rely on you, then you know that you won't be let down or be disappointed. You do not need to live in denial or as a victim, if you are self-reliant.

If you are self-reliant, you will have resilience, confidence in your abilities, trust and belief in yourself. You have all the resources you need already inside of you. All you have to do is to reach out to them.

Being self-reliant is the opposite of having a victim attitude and the opposite of living in denial. It is looking at things as they are. It's calling a spade a spade.

When you behave as victim, your partner or family may not be supporting you, maybe they even take advantage of you, use and abuse you, because they know that you are predictable; that you will continue to play the victim because your needs will take over; cry and do nothing about anything afterwards; still be the same self-sacrificing martyr who will still serve them when they snap their fingers, because you are too scared that you will not be loved by them! When you behave like this, it is not very smart or kind or caring or anything

No one will thank you. Your so-called kindness is seen as weakness! It is plain dumb!

Whether it is your husband or wife or your children or anyone else, they just take your victim-like attitude for granted and will continue to use you and abuse you, as you have become used to expect, for as long as you tolerate it. They justify it by saying but she or he likes it this way; or he or she's used to it. When you behave like this, you give away your power; therefore other people continue to take advantage of you and do not appreciate you. You are enabling them to continue to manipulate you.

Not clever! Not clever at all! In fact too sad for words! Give them the shock of their life! Stand up for yourself; show them that you are worth much more than their poor treatment of you, and that you are no longer prepared to live in fear of not being loved; that you deserve better than the way that you are being treated. Show them that you believe in yourself.

Show them that you are self-reliant; that you respect yourself; that you are as important as they are; your needs too are as important as theirs. Show them that you have a life as much as they have one.

Please do not prescribe to martyrdom!

Show them that you know that you have confidence in counting on yourself and you do not need to go begging for some attention from others. Be proud to be able to rely on you.

If you have to leave so be it; but at least, you will no longer be bullied or abused emotionally, or just taken for granted, you then can stand a real chance of happiness; and having a life worth living with good self-respect instead of being the usual door mat; it may be difficult for you to see that now. But comes a time when enough is enough!

Chances are, if you stand up for yourself, others will be so shocked that they will start treating you with much more respect. It may have never occurred to them that you too have a life, as you never made it a priority before.

When you behave as a victim, you get treated as one. When you do not show yourself much respect, others will not show you much respect either. Treat yourself with respect and become self-reliant, then others will respect you.

When you no longer behave as a victim, you take back your power and your life; ultimately you take your destiny in your own hands, instead of leaving it in the hands of others. Once you do that, you feel empowered and strong and are able to take appropriate action and you command respect.

When you show the world that the opinion that matters to you is how you feel about yourself, you no longer worry about whether you are loved or not because you love you. When you love you the world loves you back.

The fact is because you show yourself self-respect you automatically think the best of yourself. When you think the best of yourself, you love yourself, and you believe in yourself and when you believe in yourself, you become self-reliant.

Come on! Claim back your power! Show yourself some respect! You certainly deserve it.

- Ask yourself: how did I get here? What role did I play in getting where I am to-day?
- Be willing to see yourself, warts and all. Then take action.

One fact is sure that you are the only one who got you to where you are to-day. Others may have contributed, but you were the one who accepted it and acted on it. Despite any advice you may have received, you were the one who made the decisions for yourself.

Choose not to have a culture of blame. It isn't about blaming! It is what it is, without any opinions or judgment. It is about being honest and self-reliant so that you can move on with your life and take responsibility. We all create the results we have to-day. You created the results you're having by the actions you consistently took. You have always done it. You did it in the past, you are doing it now and you will be writing on your slate what happens to you in the future too.

If you are unhappy in your relationship, when it comes to deciding on a partner, getting married, to divorce or to separate, you have to stand up and be counted and understand that you are the only one who took these decisions; no one else. May be you played the victim by allowing your partner to belittle you and to put you down; nevertheless you played a key role in the way things are to-day by your attitude. Be frank and see things the way they are; not how you have been telling yourself that they are. Take responsibility for yourself.

Heal Your Life

When it comes to your difficult relationships, what role did you play there? Then, what are you prepared to do to change? If you are not happy in your job, well, what are you going to do about it? If you are not talking to your parents or children or friends, look at what you did instead of trying to blame others. Then, act. Restore your life; anything else is far too hard!

Even if all of it isn't entirely your fault, understand that you still had a role to play in creating your experience. You were the only one who chose your reactions.

Did you allow other people to bully you or were you the bully? As dreadfully sad as it is if you are suffering from the consequences of an illness because you ignored it until you could no longer do so, you are responsible for what is happening. Acknowledge it, and then you can move forward; perhaps you can now heal and be at peace.

Did you spend years abusing your health knowing full well that one day it will catch up with you when you hear the news that you have been dreading? Sadly that day comes much sooner than you think! Denial never pays! GET REAL!

Or are you the spoilt brat with an entitlement attitude who should know better instead of trampling on others to get what you want?

Do you recognize any of these scenarios? Well . . . Then? . . .

No! No! No! No more! You need to face what's going on before it is too late; stop kidding yourself and pretending that everything is alright or that you are enjoying yourself, when you know that the truth is far from that.

Time has come to grow up and face things! You do not need to receive a terrible diagnosis before you do something about your attitude to life! You do not need to spend years in misery before you do something about your relationships! You do not need to be abused by anyone or abuse anyone anymore before you decide to take action! You do not want to waste valuable time getting upset and angry and not speaking to your family or other people for futile reasons! Enough is truly enough! Life really is truly too short!

Your moment is right now! Take stock of your life now!

Now is your time for action! Come on!

No one else is responsible for where you are at but you. It is pointless blaming others or circumstances. It doesn't get you anywhere. So if you are have a great attitude, fantastic! If not there is no one else to look for! This is it! We can all do with improving something in life!

> *Look for the answers inside of you. The answers are not out there. They are within you. You have all you need inside of you.*

For every down side there is an upside: it is never too late to do something about it. Perhaps the realization that you do not have to continually blame other people or circumstances is a great moment of revelation for you. It doesn't matter what others think; what matters is that you are honest with yourself. It gives you more power to take charge of your life and to think hard before making the right decisions for you.

It all comes down to your **ATTITUDE.**

You didn't know any better before, but now there is no excuse! You now know better. Get excited, because you now realize this, things can only get better. Things will start looking up now! You must take action, and most of all, be honest with yourself. If there is something that you should have done or that you must do: well? What are you waiting for?

Do it now! There is no time like the present.

Blaming other people for the problems you have in your life is a cop out. Feeling sorry for yourself and making others feel sorry for you because others are mean to you and not doing anything about it, is pathetic. You don't want to play the victim anymore; you are now victim-savvy! Not falling for this again!

If others agree with you when you are a victim, then they are not helping you by confirming to you that you are a victim. It only serves to make you feel more hard done by and stay the same old poor me, while others walk away enjoying their lives.

If your partner agrees with you, it is only for a quiet life or in a false attempt at protecting you, not because he or she really believes it; or because it is the best course of action for you, but because it can be quite confronting to tell the hard truth to someone, especially if it is someone close to you as they don't want to upset you. Friends may facilitate your victim status because they don't want to hurt you either, but it is not helpful.

Pointing you onto the right path would be the appropriate action, even though you may not appreciate it at first. However, you must be open to listen! What you need to do is to face it, so that you understand what role you played in your own unhappiness by your attitude and the decisions you made in the past so that you can change what you don't want. It is only then, that you can have a constructive solution to your problems. Only then, will you stand a chance of getting where you want to be.

When you can see things as they are, warts and all, in complete honesty, you can begin to work towards a better future. If you think that it is too hard to do it alone, get professional help; but get help!

If you are full of resentment, bitterness and revenge, you can pretend to yourself that you are happy for a while, but your soul will know that it's only pretend; and when you are alone with yourself, you will feel the deep unhappiness and emptiness that you alone recognize.

In relationships as well as in other areas of your life, the attitude with which you approach things is as important as to what you actually do. You can do all the right things, but if your attitude is wrong, it will not bring you fulfilment.

> *Your attitude can escalade something small into something enormous or your attitude can instantly dissolve a conflict by the way you handle it.*

If you need to make someone else feel bad for you to be happy, not only is it unkind but you are being a bully as well. You will find it hard to lead a quality life and be truly happy. If you can't get yourself out of this hole, get professional help.

Being grateful in life can change any negative attitude into a positive one.

Stubborn Attitude

If you ever thought that being stubborn was something special for you, get it out of your head right now! Stubbornness like denial are two naughty cousins. They are not on your side! Stubbornness for the sake of it is a very undesirable feature whenever it raises its ugly head; however, people sometimes *boast* about their stubbornness as if it is something to value or to treasure!

I am telling you: to be stubborn for the sake of it is not good for you or for those around you!

Typically stubbornness is a reaction to other underlying emotional issues, such as a lack of self-worth and self-esteem. Focus on this, and you can realize the effects of the disadvantage of this attitude; then you can start improving your life and the lives of those close to you.

People often stay stubborn because there is this mistaken innate need to protect themselves and save face, sometimes at all costs. Being stubborn for the sake of it is an unappealing characteristic. Stubborn people are people with Ego issues; the more egoistic they are the less emotional stability they have. Their ego gets in the way of being able to back down and see the whole picture. They see it as losing or being made to feel small, or feeling less than instead of genuinely being able to see someone else's point of view.

If they feel that way, remember, that these are the thoughts they have in their head, but not reality per se. This is only their perception of things. The meaning they give to things is that if they back down, it means that other people are better than them. They see other people having *one* over them and that will never do! Didn't I tell you there is an *Ego* issue here? . . . Hum, yep!

Very often anger, bitterness and resentment are involved, especially if they feel the loser. Some would rather go through the whole emotional upheaval that stubbornness can cause, maybe by not speaking to their husbands and wives or friends for days or weeks at a time, rather than graciously back down and admit that on this occasion, maybe their opponent had a point! They would rather ignore the truth and continue their inflexible train of thoughts, and as a consequence their thinking is very blurred. Their ability to think things through and to remember is affected.

Of course as you may have noticed with stubborn people there is a bit of a power struggle going on. One needs to be the Top dog and get others into submission.

Due to their emotional attitude of needing to be dominant and their fear of being controlled, these individuals often misread other people's intentions and reactions towards them, causing much emotional misunderstandings and pain. On the other hand what they do not realize is that their power isn't really true power. It is simply their illusion! This attitude often makes them passive-aggressive in their behaviours, which can result in anger, and resentment towards them.

This is wide generalization but stubborn people often can hold on to their grudges! You may find that they are very closely related to the Sulkers! They just often can't let it go! But they don't like it when others remind them of what they once did! Sadly this obstinate attitude transports them towards much more emotional pain.

The problem is that when they are in this mood, they want to wallow in it and stay with their resentment, because of course in their head they are RIGHT! The silly thing is if they dropped that pigheaded attitude and really realized that they are no more diminished, no more of a loser, and that their winning isn't really winning, and that their power isn't real power either, they would spare themselves and others a heck of a lot of emotional trauma.

We do not have to win every argument we have! Take the attitude that we win some, we lose some, and that's okay.

No! Honestly, we don't have to win every argument! We can learn to agree to disagree. Sometimes we can get it wrong! It is okay, it's human! Others will respect you for recognizing this minor detail. In fact when we get things wrong, it is an opportunity for us to learn something new. If we get things right all the time, there is nothing to learn and we cannot grow and develop.

And if you find that someone else has a point, be gracious and acknowledge it! . . . . Now! That's attractive! It does the soul good sometimes to admit that others are right and that we are wrong. Humility is an understated virtue!

The problem with being stubborn is that it can really ruin your life and that of your partner's and children. It can bring a lot of pointless misery in any relationship.

It is important to know when to stand your ground and when not to. If it is to compromise your beliefs and values, you can stand your ground.

When you refuse point blank to see another's point of view, you need to remember to give yourself a reality check. Look at what effects your attitude has on those around you. If you can, put yourself in their shoes, you will change that attitude, I promise.

Compromise is a good friend to call upon in times of conflict, and we mustn't forget its cousins **Cooperation and Collaboration**. These friends can get you out of a lot of trouble at times, especially if they are used in your relationships.

One time that it pays to be stubborn is the one time when someone, be it a teacher or someone in authority or anyone else, tells you that *you are useless* or that *you would never amount to anything in life.*

Now is your time to show them how stubborn you can be and work REALLY hard as to prove them wrong! Decide that you can do whatever you set your mind to do.

Another time when stubbornness works for you is when you have been told that you cannot do something because something happened to your health at some point in your life; now! You can be as stubborn as you like until you prove to yourself that you can do it. If you fail a hundred or a thousand times, stubbornness can be your friend, if it helps to improve your quality of life.

Did I already say that no one is perfect or right all the time? We are not perfect and we do not need to win every time. As they say: *You win some, you lose some.* Choose to be a winner by losing if it is the right thing to do; live and let live! By compromising, cooperating and collaborating when need be.

> *When a person doesn't have gratitude something is missing in his or her humanity. A person can almost be defined by his or her attitude toward gratitude.*
>
> —*Elie Weisel*

Develop an Attitude of Gratitude

No client of mine gets away with not keeping a gratitude journal. I believe that when you have an attitude of gratitude, there is very little room for negative feelings such as anger, jealousy, bitterness, resentment, vengefulness, anxiety or depression to come into your life. The positives crowd out the negatives.

Everyone, without exception needs to develop an attitude of gratitude, even the Queen! Where would she be if her people didn't want her as head of country? With an attitude of gratitude you will not be tempted to flirt with revenge, bitterness, self-pity or other unresourceful feelings.

Gratitude overcomes every negative feeling, if you are genuine.

This is an appeal to all mothers of young children: Teach your children gratitude from a very young age. It's a great natural gift that you can easily give to your children. It costs nothing and your children will reap the benefits ALL their lives. In fact it is your duty to do so!

> *Remember that your children are little adults in training. You are not bringing up children, but you are bringing up future adults. Whatever you do with them when they are little, will remain part of their lives forever.*

Teach them gratitude and they will be grateful to you and others all their lives. Can it be that you can avoid teenage problems if you teach them gratitude from an early age?

If someone gives them something, make a huge point of making them appreciate the gift and say thank you. Teach them to phone the person and coach them to say thank you as soon as they start to learn to comprehend and to talk. When they can write teach them to write little notes of thanks.

It doesn't matter that the other person may not expect all this but it will do your children a lot of good and give them a good basis for their future. If you teach your children gratitude from a very young age, you are giving them a very precious gift which will stay with them the rest of their life, and in turn they too will teach their children to have an attitude of gratitude. The fact that they have learnt to be grateful from a very young age will help them throughout their lives, not to have an attitude of entitlement, as if the world owes them something. They will become much more balanced individuals.

Recently, I forgot to stock up on children's treats and had completely forgotten that it was Trick or Treat night. Some children came knocking at my door and as I don't generally keep sweet things in the house (It removes temptation) I didn't have anything to give to the children. Horror of horrors! What do I do??? I had even run out of fruits! So I decided to give the first three of them some money in their bags. (I know, I know, fruits would have been better!!!! Sorry! Didn't even have any!!!) Well! They were so indignant!!!! And all three spat out: "What???? Money?????" You should have seen their disgust! It was appalling! I explained that I was very sorry and had forgotten all about Trick or Treat and that I didn't have any treats, but it was the best that I could do. These children went away disgusted! Not a word of gratitude uttered!! The father was there and never said a word either! (He probably was just as disgusted!) Well!! Now it was my turn to be appalled as I thought that these children knew absolutely nothing about gratitude and least of all about manners and being gracious!! Talk about an attitude of entitlement! What on earth are these parents teaching them? After that I put a notice on the front door saying: *This household sincerely apologizes to all children as they forgot to stock up on treats because they do not have small children in the family. They have completely forgotten that it was Trick or Treat night. We do hope that you have a good time.* After that I was left in peace. But instead of getting some money, they got nothing! ***A treat is not an entitlement! It is a gift!***

Unfortunately, this society is a **ME** society and we tend to have so much and expect so much too. People tend to forget the basics of politeness of thanking someone who offers them a gift. All too often it is taken for granted as they get given too much. I do not, however, forget that many others do not have much at all. In their case I would be surprised to see them with an attitude of entitlement. When you don't have much and you get given a small thing, you overflow with gratitude.

If this is you: make a decision that from now on you will express gratitude for anything that comes your way; and for everything that is already your way and for everything that has been your way and will go your way in the future.

You need to make a decision to feel gratitude for everything in your life. Starting with your eyes that see, your nose that can breathe clean air, your ears that hear, your heart that never misses a beat, your brain with which you can think and do so many wonderful things with, your mouth that can speak and nourish you, your God-given talents and gifts etc.etc. Then start with your family, your friends, other relationships that you have, your environment, the country you live in, the place where you live, the job you do, your church, your clubs etc. etc. Do you get what I'm talking about? We must all do this. If your heart becomes full of gratitude for everything that you have in your life, it will leave little room for harmful feelings to come in and damage your life.

It is impossible to feel negative when your heart is bursting with gratitude. The catch is that you need to be sincere and really feel the gratitude in your heart. If it doesn't come naturally, fake it till you make it.

> *Gratitude unlocks the fullness of life. It turns denial into acceptance, chaos to order, confusion to clarity. It can turn a meal into a feast, a house into a home, a stranger into a friend. Gratitude makes sense of our past, brings peace for to-day, and creates a vision for to-morrow.*
> —*Melodie Beattie*

Decide to do express gratitude first thing every morning, while you're brushing your teeth or having a shower, if you don't have much time. Then it will set you up for a great day. When you approach everything with an attitude of gratitude, negativity fades into insignificance.

The best way to keep this attitude of gratitude is to write it down in your journal, so you never forget, and you can keep reminding yourself how grateful you really are for everything that's in your life.

When you think good things, opportunities present themselves to you that you never expected.

Why should you be grateful and develop a positive attitude?

If you are grateful and become positive in your thinking, it changes your whole outlook and attitude in life, and then miracles start to happen.

Remember the world reacts to your attitude of approach to life. It helps you to be happier, more relaxed, have better relationships with others and even healthier! And you have more fun in life.

Besides if you learn to be more positive, you are able to access your resources to draw on positive energy, when you come across a difficult patch. An attitude of gratitude opens up opportunities for you that you wouldn't even notice if you were feeling negative.

An attitude of gratitude leads to a positive attitude. A positive attitude leads to better relationships and you become more successful in life. People seek you out and you are more popular. The other side of this coin is that you rub off on other people and you can be an example or role model to others, enabling them to live a better quality life.

Exercise to change your thinking:

1. Reframing

You can learn to re-frame, that means finding more resourceful meanings for your experiences. When someone or something upsets you, you can try not jumping to conclusions and avoid representing it to yourself in a negative way; this includes not using any negative words to describe what you feel. It means changing the meaning you give to something into a more positive acceptable reality for you.

Get into the habit of never saying anything negative. Find the positive way of describing anything, however insignificant. If you find it hard, at least say the minimum negative statement about it that would still be true. If you choose to do this, you will see that things that used to bother you no longer have that power over you.

Get into the habit of thinking the most positive option instead of the worst case scenario. You can choose to find a positive meaning to things rather than get carried away with the negative meaning.

If the meaning you have given to things does not make you feel good, then change it to something more acceptable to you.

2. Words

Watch your language and the words you choose to speak to yourself with. Make them positive and words of gratitude.

Be conscious of the type of words that come out of your mouth.

For example: if you say: *I hate this,* try saying: I don't like this or I prefer something else.

Change the words you use that carry a lot of emotions, for example: like hate, furious, detest, evil, livid or vile; change them for a milder version. Instead of saying: I'm furious, try saying: I'm irritated or annoyed or frustrated; instead of detest or hate try saying I don't like or as one of my son says: It's not my favourite. When you change those words for ones that carry a lot less emotions, you will find that you will feel a lot better and not be so hyped up by the negative emotions that these words carry.

3. Focus
Put your focus on the positive and resourceful rather than the negative and unresourceful.
Remember:

You get more of what you focus on.
What you focus on becomes bigger and stronger.
What you focus on, you create.

If you find something good, say it. If you focus on good, you feel good, and find the best in what you are looking for.

If you focus on bad, you always find bad and with it, feel bad; that focus brings to you the worst that you were dreading.

You always get more of what you focus on and of what you concentrate your energies on. Focus on the positives and you get more good things coming into your life; focus on the negatives and you get more of that too.

So, to bring good things into your life, have an open attitude, find the good in life, and show gratitude; you make others feel good too. Look for the good in others instead of looking for what's not so good. If someone does a good job, tell them so, and make their day.

Someone once said that life is like a boomerang: What you give out always comes back to you.

4. Affirmations
Use affirmations, especially true ones.

For example: repeat with commitment and intention:

All's well
I choose to focus on the good in my life.
I choose to be grateful.
I have all the time I need.
I am resourceful.
I have unlimited resources inside of me.

If you are going through a challenging period, you can say: I've been through bad times before and they went away; this too will soon go away.

Challenging times have a beginning but they certainly have an end too. Remember the sun comes after the rain; after winter, the spring is waiting to burst forth; nothing lasts forever. Remind yourself of anything that you feel will lift your spirits and improve your mood. You've been through bad times before and you know that things tend to get better after a while. So, this time too things will get better. This is what you keep in mind when times are tough.

Should

Avoid the word should. When you say: you should . . . . you patronize the other person, assuming that you know better than them. Instead of using words like I should substitute them with: I'm going to or I have to. When you say the word should it implies a reproach or that you didn't do something that you ought to have done, or that you know best; whereas if you say: I'm going to, there is no reproach there or judgment; it's just something that you are going to do, without any feelings of blame or judgment.

Humour

Humour tends to get us out of many awkward or difficult situations. Use humour to change your attitude and your emotional state.

Hang around people who are up-beat; positive people. Even better, hang around people who are funny and make you laugh, especially people who have an infectious laugh (just like my second sister!—(I have to specify as I have seven of them)—She has a special gift! Everyone seeks her company; I just wish you could meet her! She is hilarious and makes you laugh with one of her famous infectious giggle!)

Practicing humour can even make you find the funny side of yourself, and discover that you too can be funny! Can that be one of your new-found talents? I sometimes purposely tell my sister a funny story, so that I can hear her infectious giggle, knowing that I will end up having a good laugh; this way, I reap the benefit of feeling good and uplifted too.

Another way to help you acquire positive energy is to watch funny movies, comedies and sitcoms. It is a sure way to alter your mood. Any English people will know all about *Only Fools and Horses, Fawlty Towers, Keeping up appearances or The Vicar of Dibley and Allo, Allo* amongst many others light hearted comedies that can tickle you pink!

Keep a book of funny jokes, and relate them to your family or friends or when you're in company or at a social gathering. It lightens up the atmosphere and is contagious; I must confess rehearsing some special jokes for my grandson Jamie and my granddaughter Maya.

The best way to cheer yourself up is to try to cheer someone else up.

—Mark Twain

Have you noticed how people love a story teller? (My husband is a great one for this!) Story tellers are always popular and other people enjoy their company because they know that a story teller is either funny or will have something interesting to relate. Watch their style and copy it if you like it. You will find that others want to share their jokes and stories with you too. Something as simple as this can make a big change in your attitude to life; it can help to lift your mood and help you enjoy life better.

Research has shown that smiling and laughter have great health benefits and can even ease pain.

Laughter and smiling, release Serotonin, one of your feel-good hormones. It can even lower your blood pressure. So practice smiling! Smile at yourself in the mirror when you first wake up, then smile at your partner or children or the next person you meet; but keep the smile never far from your lips. As you smile, keep smiling knowing that you are building your feel-good hormones. You will find that your attitude will be more positive, and that you feel happier too.

It is said that we should make a point of smiling as many times as we can during our day and laughing at least 20 times a day.

It is up to you. All you have to do is to make a decision to lead a more positive life.

> *Your attitude in life is everything. It can determine whether you are happy or miserable.*

Ah! I forgot to say: Avoid the doomsday energy-drainers at all costs! They will do nothing to help improve your attitude! Those who relish telling you how the stock market is bound to crash AGAIN! (Even more than it already has!) And we will all lose all our money, and besides it is so scary this global warming business, and they say it's only going to get a lot worse! Healthwise, they are doing dreadfully! Clearly the end is nigh and we are all going to lose everything or go through a dreadful time through unbearable temperatures before we die of some ghastly disease, and what's worse is that we will all die poor!!! Etc. etc....

Run, Run, Run .... the other way! Completely in the opposite direction if possible when you see them coming!

They will undo all the good that you have been trying to do in a couple of sentences! You will go home in deep depression!

What they need is a serious change of **ATTITUDE!**

We have seen how our attitudes can change our lives, now we will look at how our **emotions** affect our lives.

> *If you want to feel rich, just count all the things that you have that money can't buy.*
> —*Anonymous*

Notes: What have you learnt?

CHAPTER FOUR

Secrets About Emotions

Emotions are the force of life.
—Anthony Robbins

The way we are feeling to-day in our body, whether, we are thin or fat, fit or unfit, happy or sad is the result of what we ate and whether we exercised or not, or what kind of thoughts we have allowed in our minds in our past. Likewise, it is the same story with our emotions. The way we feel emotionally to-day is the result of what happened to us in the past.

Every single emotion is a product of the thoughts that we entertain. It is a state of mind. Every emotion has a direct physiological reaction in our body and carries some information to help us, either to protect us physically or emotionally, or to help us to take some action.

Each emotion results in an attitude and a behaviour. An attitude is also a state of mind, which produces a direct physiological reaction followed by certain behaviours.

All negative emotions are fear-based.

Positive emotions such as love, joy, happiness, forgiveness, self-control, promote positive attitudes and therefore we benefit from the resourceful resulting behaviours and the ensuing good physiological reactions in the body.

Consciously cultivating positive emotions is an excellent habit which contributes to our happiness. An attitude of gratitude generates positive emotions in the body and contributes to our happiness too.

Fear can help us or hinder us.

Fear can be our friend as it can save our lives, but irrational fear can be an evil enemy as it can make our daily lives a living hell and can be a major contributor to poor mental health.

Fear, worry and anxiety automatically put the body on high alert and in a stress state, resulting in negative physiological reactions in the body. We all know the symptoms of fear or anxiety, as no one escapes feeling anxious or worried at some point in our lives. Those tummy butterflies don't feel good, do they?

What about those sweaty palms? Or that feeling of a racing heart? Not pleasant, huh? So, the idea is to try and avoid being triggered by unnecessary, irrational and irrelevant worries.

Negative emotions based on fear, such as anger, hatred, unforgiveness, resentment, and aggression cause a lot of stress, even anguish and frustration to other people, but most of all, they affect the one who chooses to entertain these destructive emotions: YOU!

For example, if you choose to hate someone; that someone, may have absolutely no idea how you are feeling and how they are being hated and would go along their own sweet way completely unaware that your life is totally screwed up with your feelings of hate and anger towards them. So, who's the one hurting? YOU!

On the other hand, YOU, are being consumed by your hatred, and suffer mentally, emotionally and physically and can't move on. So, who is it affecting? YOU!

The answer to this is:

Choose never to hate anyone.

Hate emotions affect only the person who hates not the hated one. Hate can literally damage your health. You can dislike someone but avoid hating anyone.

Steer clear of using the word hate, as words like this hype up the intensity of your negative emotions, and you pay a high price for it in your emotions and in your body. Choose not to hate anyone! They may not be your favourite people, but you do not have to hate them.

The special word is: **Choose;** the reason for that is when we hate someone, we are choosing to do so. No one forces us to hate anyone, even if they have done us the most despicable of acts. It is us who decide, no matter what the other person does to us. We can choose to dislike them, and have nothing to do with them, but we don't have to hate them. If someone has done something unspeakable to you, find a more resourceful way of dealing with it. I agree it can be very hard!

There is no rule that says that if someone has caused you harm, that you must hate them. You hate them because YOU choose to. This person may have been trying to meet his or her needs, and you may have got hurt as a result. Even if they deliberately did you some harm, you can choose to move on with your life. An eye for an eye is not a good way to deal with hurt feelings. Ignoring someone you dislike is a lot healthier than hating them.

You don't have to love everyone but try to keep away from hate, as hatred carries destructive chemicals that can damage the health of the one who hates, not the one being hated.

I have never been in a position where someone has taken the life of my child or done some such heinous act. I would like to think that I would have it in me to forgive, but unless one is faced with that situation, it is difficult to tell. These are extreme situations; I am talking about more common everyday situations. However, there are wonderful forgiving people that you sometimes see on the television, who forgive those who have killed their child in a drink and drive accident or some other ghastly situation. You can only be humbled by such humanity and generosity of spirit. Nonetheless, that is a healthy way of coping with something as enormous as that. They often get their strength from a Higher Spiritual Being. These people make a choice of finding a positive way of dealing with their tragedy. Their compassion is overwhelming.

On the other hand, you can choose the word hate to give yourself leverage to get rid of bad habits. For example: *I hate smoking.* It motivates you to get rid of your smoking habits, instead of saying I want to give up smoking. No! You don't just want to give up, you absolutely hate it! It gives more intensity to your feelings, and motivates you to do something about it.

By the same token when you say I hate my boss or I hate my work; this *hypes up* how you feel about your boss and your work, when in fact he may just not be your favourite person, and your work may just not be stimulating you.

The problem with using words that intensify your negative feelings is that you feel the corresponding negative feelings in your body.

Instead, you could try saying: *I don't like my boss or my work isn't as stimulating as it could be* then the effects in your body will be kinder on you. Your body will not be secreting as much Cortisol which can cause you harm.

Our nine emotional needs

Dr Mark Atkinson teaches us that we have nine emotional needs which need to be met for us to be emotionally satisfied. These are:

- Giving positive attention
- Receiving positive attention
- Connection with a wider community
- An intimate close relationship with at least one other person
- Autonomy
- Status
- Competence
- Privacy
- Meaning and purpose

It is important to identify any of our unmet emotional needs, so that we can work towards meeting those unmet needs. Nature has equipped us with all the necessary resources for us to meet our own emotional needs. It is a natural instinct that we have to give and receive positive attention. Emotionally, it brings warmth to our hearts and fulfils a need in us when we give to others and when we receive from others. As human beings we have the ability to make connections with other people. We are able to empathize with others and build relationships. Women are instinctively better at that than men as we are wired differently.

Curiosity

We all have the intrinsic gift of being curious.

All of us have a certain curiosity that we can use to our advantage. Curiosity is also linked with intelligence. It enables us to grow, learn and acquire new knowledge and insight. Yet, when I was growing up, I thought that curiosity was a negative thing, as one of my teachers constantly repeated to me: Lily, you are so curious, that one day, you will be the sort of woman, who will go to your neighbour and lift the saucepan lid to see what she is cooking! I never fail to smile and think of him if I ever feel tempted! However, he failed to recognize that curiosity is a God-given natural gift linked with being smart!

What can we achieve without imagination?

Our imagination is a precious God-given gift. With imagination, however, we are able to think, problem-solve, develop new ideas, and plan our future. Our imagination makes use of our subconscious mind to distort painful memories in order to protect us. Everything that has ever been created started in the imagination of someone first, for example, the chair you're sitting on; the dinner plate you're eating from, to the paint brush or pencil you use. We have discussed the amazing resource of our conscious mind, which can rationalize, take decisions, plan the future and control our emotions. Besides we are the only beings on this planet with the innate gift of imagination.

We also have the wonderful gift of intuition.

Again only us, human beings, have this ability sometimes just to know something or to have a gut feeling about something, although we may not be able sometimes to explain why. Our intuition is an amazing tool that can give us unspeakable advantages or get us out of trouble. This amazing talent helps us to understand the world unconsciously by using metaphors. Our intuition is a privilege and a divine gift bestowed only upon us human beings.

We also have the unique ability to be our own observer.

Homo sapiens are also the only living beings who have the skill of being able to step back and observe our emotions and thoughts. This ability of self-observation helps us in getting emotional insight. It is yet another ability that distinguishes us from our furry friends.

Why do we dream?

We have been given the sensational gift of being able to dream. This ability to dream is a natural way of relieving stress, giving us a break from ourselves, develop ideas or use our subconscious to work things out for us. Sometimes our ability to dream helps us in relieving unresourceful emotional states, and sometimes our dreams inspire us to access resourceful states to create what we desire or to give us an answer that we have been searching for.

Have you any idea how blessed we are as human beings, to have all these gifts naturally, inside of us? All we have to do is to reach inside and claim them. We need to take full advantage of what we have been given in order to meet all our emotional needs.

What happens when we fail to meet our emotional needs?

Failing to meet our emotional needs can lead to psychological stress, such as anxiety, depression and in those who are predisposed to mental illness, neurosis or even psychosis.

Continuous unmet emotional needs can lead to toxic emotions, which, in the long-term can prove very detrimental to our health.

Toxic emotions produce feelings which produce toxic physiological reactions which in turn produce toxic attitudes, and toxic behaviours which is no recipe for a happy and stress-free life. If you choose toxic emotions, you trigger a chain reaction which ends up making you feel pretty awful mentally, physically and hijack you psychologically and emotionally, and help you behave in such a way that can only lead you to pain.

Anxiety which belongs to the same group of emotions as worry and fear can still be troublesome years well after the initial problem has long stopped or been forgotten. People, who have been abused in their childhood, still suffer from the negative effects of their abuse in their 30s, 40s, 50s, 60s and more; some never recover. As for one client of mine, an incident of being bullied at school when he was 10 years old continue to affect his life causing anxiety and depression at the age of 24, compiling the problem with the use of Cannabis, and comfort-eating, many years after the original bullying had ceased.

Emotions are contagious, good or bad.

Toxic emotions can grow very quickly in abundance. It is our job to keep our emotions in check. Research shows that negative emotions literally demand more physical space in the brain, therefore, leaving very little room for positive emotions. They crowd the brain and don't allow space for positive thoughts and emotions to take place, which is why you can feel overwhelmed by your negative thoughts and emotions. They keep you caught up, paralyzed, unable to take any positive action. They are insidious and are the result of your own thoughts.

However, positive emotions are also contagious. Have you ever seen some people having a wonderful fit of the giggles? Before too long many surrounding people are also laughing. Laughter contaminates you. They are not really sure why they are laughing but they laugh all the same because others are laughing heartily. This often happens with my seven sisters. Two of us may start and before long all of us are laughing, often not really knowing why! But it feels great and lifts our spirits.

There are now laughter clubs to help induce good feelings and positive emotions in their members. When you laugh you release feel-good chemicals, which make you feel great and happy. So, laugh, laugh, and laugh as much as you can! In fact make a point of laughing at least 20 times a day. You will change your life. Laugh even if you have nothing to laugh about, especially if you have nothing to laugh about! In fact that's the more reason to laugh and build those feel-good chemicals.

Laughter has the power to change your blood chemistry.

Electrochemical reactions

As previously stated, our thoughts, whether negative or positive are communicated in the body by electrochemical reactions. Our body is made up of a chemical system—the endocrine system, (hormones)—and the other electrical system—the nervous system.

Physiology

We have talked about the Conscious mind and the Subconscious mind. Now, the third component to a human being is the physiology, the body.

As we have seen, every thought has a direct physiological reaction on the body. In other words with every thought that we have, we feel a chemical reaction in the body.

For instance, if you are walking down a dark alley at night time, suddenly you hear footsteps behind you—you think that those footsteps are following you; you start to panic and your heart starts to beat faster and faster; so hard that you feel that it will come out of your chest, your palms sweat, your throat is dry, you skin is so pale that you look like a ghost!—You get the picture? And yet nothing really happened, other than you heard footsteps behind you; however, it was the thought that you may be in danger that caused the physiological reaction of your heart beating so fast, your palms sweating etc, in your body.

This is the fight or flight response, which puts your body on alert and tells you that you may be in danger and that you, may have to take action to protect yourself. You are ready to run away or fight for your life. In this case this fear emotion is a positive one. It serves to warn you that you may be in danger, so that you can save your life.

The autonomic nervous system is the body's own intelligence.

The heart pumps approximately 2000 gallons of blood a day and beats about 100,000 beats a day. It is your autonomic nervous system that regulates your heart; it also regulates your breathing and your muscles, making sure your cells are oxygenated. It regulates your digestive system and your cycle of sleep and wakefulness (your circadian cycle) as well as the fight or flight response; this is the body's way to survival without having to go through the conscious mind. It is in fact a short-cut. This autonomic nervous system response happens automatically, without us having to use our rational thinking (which would take too long) to take any action.

Not only some, but all our mental and emotional states have a corresponding component in our body. Research shows that our thoughts and behaviour correspond to the same patterns of activity in the brain called neural pathways.

Sometimes we *attach* to some thoughts more than others. The more we repeat the same thought and behaviour, the more we strengthen the corresponding neural pathways. It hard-wires us to the same thoughts and behaviours.

All the time we practice the behaviour, we literally make a bigger neural pathway for that behaviour in our mind; however, when we choose to no longer practice the behaviour, the neural pathway weakens and we lose it. That neural pathway eventually disappears, and the memory of that behaviour dies away with it. If that neural pathway carries positive emotions, we feel good; however, if it carries negative emotions, we feel unresourceful.

I like to explain this by comparing a neural pathway to a brand new field, where no one has ever walked on before, as a metaphor. You need to get from one side of the field to the other side of the field. The first time you walk across the field, there is no path, but only your tiny footsteps. By the time you have done this 100 times, there is now the start of a small tract; but by the time you walk the same path 1000th times you definitely have a real path by then.

This is exactly what happens in our brain. The first time we think a thought there is a tiny path in our neural pathway, but by the time we've had the same thought or behaviour for the 100th time, or 1000th time, we now really have an established pathway, which means that we have the exact same brain wave or pattern for the corresponding thought or behaviour. This can happen very quickly. This neural pathway can lead us to think or do things a lot quicker, which include the corresponding emotions which accompany the behaviour.

What happens in the conscious or subconscious mind directly influence what happens in the body—the mind/body connection. The thoughts that you entertain in your minds have a direct physiological result in your body. This can make you feel good or bad. Every thought that you harbour in your mind has the potential to change how you feel.

For instance, if your husband is late home from work, and you think: Oh, he is very busy at work and probably will be home in an hour; or you could think: He's not normally late; he must have had an accident! Or, why is he late? Is he having an affair?

How different do you think you are going to feel in the first, second or third scenario? The first scenario may keep you relaxed in the anticipation that he will soon be home. The second will stir feelings of anxiety and fear; and the third scenario may bring feelings of anger and suspicion. For each of these thoughts you will have a bodily reaction to them which will guide how you feel emotionally, psychologically and physically.

How we feel in our body has a direct effect on the state of our conscious mind and as the mind influences the body, the body too influences the mind.

If we carry physical tension, we also carry emotional tension as a result. Since what we do with our body affects what goes on in our mind, it means that if we make physical changes, we can alter how we feel and therefore change our emotional state.

These three aspects of the human being, the conscious mind, the subconscious mind and the physiology exist together and are consistent. None of them can function independently without affecting the others. They influence each other. Any change in one alters the others and therefore changes how the whole person thinks and feels. Our emotions affect all three systems.

We often react to our past and to our anticipation of what may happen in the future rather than to the present.

Our memory of something that happened in the past and what we anticipate may happen in the future is able to affect how we feel about present or future events. Albeit that all this occurs unconsciously. This has a lot of repercussion if you have had poor childhood experiences. Understanding this may help you not to let your past dictate your future.

Sometimes we jump the gun and guess about what is going to happen rather than wait and see what develops in the present. When we do this, we are reacting to our past, not our present. The state that our body is in, affects how we react emotionally. Being physically unwell or how we use our body can affect how we react emotionally.

If you adopt a depressed state, looking down, sad expression, shoulders down etc., you will pretty soon actually start to feel down. Equally, if you change this physical state by looking upwards, smiling, taking a relaxed stance, or start to hip hop or rock and roll to music or sing you will soon start to feel uplifted.

If you are feeling low, you need to change what you do with your body, if you want to feel better. If you are feeling down, and give in to those miserable feelings and decide to vegetate on the couch or in bed, just you and your negative thoughts, with the remote control for company flicking in between channels, you end up feeling more depressed. If you are feeling low, and decide to go for a run or do some exercises, listen and dance to some upbeat music, you will feel much more optimistic when you've finished. You may even forget that you started the day feeling sad.

So, what you do with your body matters!

Stress

As the mind can influence the body, the body in turn can influence the mind.

Finding ways to release stress, either through physical exercise, music, meditation, prayer, relaxation or by any other means, help the body to feel more relaxed, calmer and in turn affect how we feel emotionally.

All of these help our emotions to calm down, improve our focus, help us feel more relaxed, and enable us to sleep much better.

Research has consistently shown that regular physical exercise improves depression.

Now that you understand how your conscious and subconscious mind work, and how your emotional state can affect your physiology, and vice versa, let's look at other influences that can affect your emotions and ultimately the quality of your life.

Our Emotional State

An easy way to think of our emotional state is to see it as the way we feel at any moment in time. There is a good reason for all our emotions. That is because all emotions serve a purpose. In fact as much as I am calling some emotions either toxic or negative, in reality those emotions too are there to give us a message for us to heed, therefore they too serve a function.

Every so-called negative emotion is a warning to let us know that we need to take some kind of action; like changing or doing something else. We can change how we feel by changing what we focus on; in other words, by changing our thoughts—by becoming consciously aware of what we are thinking. We can also change how we feel by changing our physiology—in other words by changing what we do with our body.

Our Emotional State Affects Our Experience Of Life.

Have you ever heard of two people who witness the same accident or event, and yet their recollection of the event couldn't be further apart? Their experience could not be more different if they tried? Have you ever wondered why their perception of what happened is so different? Is one of them lying, or both? How can two people see the same thing at the same time and have very different views of what they saw?

The answer to this puzzle is that that neither of them is lying; but it is their perception based on the emotional state they were in at the time. The meaning they give to the event depends on how they were feeling at that particular time, including their own filters through which they see the world; these factors influence what interpretation they choose to give to the event.

Our filters

We all see the world through different filters, depending on our past experience of life. It is as if there are three people, all looking at the world through their window. One is looking through clear glass; the second looking through green-tinted glass, and the third looking through pink-tinted glass. All three are looking at the same scenery, but the way they will be seeing the world would have different nuances.

These nuances are the filters through which we see the world. They are influenced by our past experiences.

If we are witnessing a motorcycle accident against a car; I have a son who rides a motorbike; I understand and am aware of the problems that motorcyclists face on the road, and usually am very conscious of them on the road. Therefore, I may perhaps be inclined to be more compassionate towards the motorcyclist than the man in the car (even though the rest of us are car drivers! That's a mother's heart for you!) whereas another car driver who is exasperated with motorcyclists weaving in and out of the traffic, will perhaps see it from the point of view of the car driver.

The difference comes from the emotional state that the witnesses are in at the time including the filters through which they see the world. Our emotional state can vary frequently during any one day. We are constantly experiencing various emotional states all day long.

We may wake up feeling relaxed, a little later getting stressed going through the traffic to work, then getting angry with something that happens at work which results in a lack of confidence, but feeling touched by something a colleague does or says, then we go back home feeling affectionate towards our family, and then we can be sad and compassionate whilst watching a heart-wrenching movie. We may feel loving, happy, fearful, angry, and interested, irritated, or lack confidence all in the one day. These emotional states are unique to each and everyone one of us, because we are all unique individuals, with our own personal past experiences, background, education, situations and reactions.

These are our personal filters which affect our emotional states individually. They are unique to us as no one else can have the experience that we have. We can have a sibling who goes through similar experiences that we have but they may interpret their experiences completely differently to us.

Our emotional state is basically the mood that we are in at any given time.

Most of us have experienced feelings of love, enthusiasm, optimism, cheerfulness, joy, determination or confidence. These are positive and resourceful emotional states. On the other hand, we also know that we can feel anger, hate, jealousy, anxiety, depression, distress, to name but a few. These are negative and unresourceful states.

Understanding the importance of our emotional state is crucial, because it can influence the course of our lives, in fact to be precise, our future.

Our emotional state is important not only because of how we feel but also because it affects what we do. In other words our behaviours are the result of how we feel at any given moment in time. The way we feel affects our actions and our behaviour. Put simply: the way we feel affect what we do and how we behave.

Our emotional state not only influences what actions we take but also as a result affect what choices we make. Daily, we react to events happening in our lives. It may appear that the way we feel is due to what is happening outside of us—i.e. that things that happen beyond our control. In fact when something happens, there is actually a development that takes place inside of us, i.e. internally in our bodies, in between what is happening and our reaction to it.

As we saw earlier the way we use our bodies affect our emotional state. So, if we change our breathing, our posture, our muscle tension and facial expression, looking up instead of looking down, all of these influence how we feel and our reaction to an event. If we are tensed and are not aware of our physiology, we could tend to over react to the same event. On the other hand, if we use our body differently, our experience can be completely different. We can feel very different emotionally after a relaxation exercise than we did before the relaxation exercise. Our posture, our breathing, or muscle tension all influence how we feel; in other words they too affect our emotional state.

Exercise

So, if you are feeling stressed, change first of all what you do with your body; if you are standing, sit down; in fact sit up straight, shoulders back, looking straight ahead; take some deep breaths; tense then relax all your muscles in your body, one after the other slowly; breathe in between each tension and relaxation of each muscle group. You would end up feeling very much better and more positive. It is as simple as that, but you have to do it, instead of disbelieving the simplicity of it and telling yourself that it won't work. It simply works!

This is an exercise recommended by Dr Mark Atkinson in his book on True Happiness:

Breathing Exercise

Take a deep breath in on the count of four, and slowly exhale on the count of seven. Exhale longer than you've breathed in. This is often enough to change the way you feel in the moment.

Do this for 5 or 10 minutes and you will feel much calmer, ready to deal with what you have to cope with.

Exercise to stay calm

If you want to calm down quickly, try alternate nostril breathing. Block your right nostril, and take a deep breath in. Now block your left nostril and take a deep breath in.

Breathe normally.

Now block the right nostril and take a deep breath . . . . and so on for the next five minutes. This is a really quick calming exercise.

When you are stressed your body produces very different chemicals than when you are relaxed, calm or happy. Basically when you are relaxed, you build up good chemicals, such as Dopamine or Serotonin; and when you are stressed you build up bad chemicals, such as Cortisol or Adrenaline in your body. These chemicals are trapped in your body and don't have an outlet, so the only way you cope with it is by the feelings they give you which is to be stressed, anxious, angry, depressed or rave and rant. Therefore, depending on which state you are in, you will feel differently and think different thoughts.

Movies of the Mind

When an event or experience happens, we immediately represent it by making a movie of it in our mind. We all do this naturally all the time. We experience this event again in our mind in images or picture form.

The pictures we make in our imagination and what we say to ourselves affect how we interpret that experience or event. This movie of the mind affects how we feel and it also affects the meaning we give to the event. Consequently it influences what we do about it. How we feel affects what meaning we give to things and what actions we take.

How we feel have consequences on the actions we decide to take and the behaviours we choose at the time.

These internal representations are unique to us and it is our reality, our perception—not that of reality itself or anyone else's reality.

This is our own personal way of seeing the world (our personal filter)—not anybody else's. This is like our map of the world, our way of viewing the world. The problem with that is that maps are not faultless or detailed; they include generalizations, deletions and distortions, aided by our faithful subconscious mind. Hence, this is another reason why two people can witness the same event and yet experience it completely differently, like with the motorcycle accident. The problem with that is because each of us makes our own interpretation of life, it is open to misunderstandings between us. Having a clear appreciation of our perceptions, our filters, our emotional states allow us to be more generous when communication problems occur.

The movies of our mind and the internal voice we talk to ourselves with, contribute to influence our emotional state.

We choose the quality of our thoughts and the movie that we make in our mind, therefore it is our responsibility. It isn't something we can't control as it is our choice. So, watch what you say to yourselves and how you say it, together with how you use your body, as they all reflect on the way you feel and what you do.

You have a choice to how you feel in any situation. You also have a choice of how you react to any given situation.

For example, if you have some negative thoughts about someone or something, you could try to reframe this by asking yourself: Is there another explanation? What else could explain this? If you keep asking, you will eventually come up with a more positive truth for you. Sometimes we jump to conclusions far too quickly which may not necessarily be the way it actually is.

People most of the time, do things to meet their own needs, rather than to intentionally cause us harm.

Even if they did, giving them the benefit of the doubt is much more constructive; you may move them and they may, by this, be encouraged to do the right thing or what they should have done in the first place.

When you happen to get hurt because of something someone said or did, you would more than likely find that they did it for themselves, because they were trying to get something to make themselves feel better or to do something so that they would feel better—rather than doing something because they deliberately meant to harm you. You may just be a victim who happened to be in their path . . . . Yes! Yes! I agree, it may be selfish, but they may know no different; but you do! You can rise above and choose not to take issue with certain things. It is much healthier for your own mental health.

The problem arises because we all carry emotional baggage with us; our past plays a role in the meaning we put on an event or experience. Consequently, we put negative meaning onto things before we give positive meaning to them, and end up catastrophysing. The way we talk to ourselves is very important and has a massive impact on our emotional state.

The thoughts and feelings that we choose have a direct correlation to the biochemical activity in our brain. Simply put:

Our thoughts affect the chemistry of our brain.

As previously mentioned, Dopamine and Serotonin are two feel good neurotransmitters which play an important role in how we feel and they affect our behaviour. Dopamine is our pleasure neurotransmitter which drives us to get what we want. Serotonin is the one which make us feel good when we have what we want. These chemicals affect our feelings and emotions, just as our feelings and emotions affect these Neurochemicals.

Lacking Dopamine can make us experience feelings of craving, whilst having low Serotonin levels is the villain responsible for feelings of depression.

The movies we choose to entertain in our mind and the meaning we choose affect how we react to events around us. I repeat that it is important to remember that we always have a choice on how we react. What we represent in our mind (our movie) has an effect on our emotional state; and what we think, in turn has an effect on our Neurochemicals. These Neurochemicals have the subsequent effects on our body. This process has an effect on how we react.

An understanding of this process can help us in representing things more positively to ourselves and to choose our thoughts carefully, if we want resourceful emotional states.

Our emotions form part of our intelligence. We have our Intelligence Quotient (IQ) which is to do with how smart we are or how academic we are; but our Emotional Quotient (EQ) is to do with our Emotional Intelligence; how smart we are emotionally. It is much more beneficial to have a high EQ and an average IQ, than to have a low emotional EQ and a high IQ.

Our emotions serve an essential purpose.

Emotions are our subconscious mind's way of letting us know that we need to concentrate on something that is important. Our emotions exist so that they can give us the message that they want to bring to our attention. It may be quite unwise to ignore what our emotions are trying to tell us, as their message can literally save our lives or help us avoid trouble along the way.

It may help to ask ourselves:

—*What am I feeling? What is this emotion trying to tell me? Take a few moments to try and feel what you are feeling and define it. Then ask yourself what message, that feeling, this emotion wants you to understand.*

Sometimes we try to ignore our emotions, but when we do that, have you noticed that they don't go away? They keep on upsetting us more or making us feel more and more uneasy until we have no other choice but to take notice of them, and heed the message that they are desperately trying for us to get.

There is a good reason for our emotions; otherwise we would be no different from our furry friends from the animal kingdom. Our emotions exist so that we can do something to help ourselves or take appropriate action. As human beings we are very good at playing the blame game. We can even blame our emotions or somehow make them wrong. This is seriously, pointless. As we frantically search for someone else or something else to blame, instead of finding out what we need to do, we then, choose to behave as a victim.

Silence is Golden

When we want to hear what someone is saying, we have to be quiet and listen. It is the same with your emotions, if you want to know what they are trying to tell you, you need to listen to them. Use silence to listen to what message that your emotions are trying to give you. This becomes easier as you practice being calm and quiet and really get to know you, see yourselves warts and all. Teach yourself to love you as you are, and like your own company. You do not need noise around you all the time. In the still of silence the message that you are looking for is able to speak to you.

We have to stop that business that many of us do so well, by feeling sorry for ourselves and for it being just our bad luck; but really take a good look at ourselves and take responsibility for who we are and realize that WE are in control of your emotions, not the other way around. But, if we want to hear, we need to listen and we can find out what our emotions are telling us.

Just because you are not happy with your circumstances doesn't mean that you should allow yourselves to get depressed, because things are not going the way you want them to. Rise above it and keep looking for a solution. If a solution isn't quickly available, you keep on and on and on until you find the solution you're happy with. Use your energy to search for that solution, instead of giving in to your depressed feelings; do not waste precious energy to feed all your negative thoughts and emotions, as this is just a recipe to keep you static where you are. Negative energy can quickly gather momentum.

Actively work towards not giving in to depression because if you do, you end up with **A** problem **AND** depression as well; instead of just having the one problem, you now have two! Depression only serves to keep you stuck, paralyzes you and makes you too stressed to find the right solution for your circumstances. You cannot have healthy constructive thoughts when you are depressed. When you do not have healthy constructive thoughts, you do not have healthy, constructive emotions; you can keep looking but you will not find the right solution. It becomes a vicious circle. Put all your energy into finding your solution instead.

The time to realize this is as soon as you feel yourself feeling down. You need to change what you do with your body and actively work towards changing your thoughts and be proactive in looking for a solution to your problem. Do not follow negative scenarios through. It only helps to panic you.

The way you feel at any time is the direct result of the way you are using your physiology. In other words what you do with your body affects how you feel.

If you are feeling down you need to right away change what you're doing physically. Do some form of exercise if only for five minutes at a time. It will change how you feel. If you're sitting down, get up; if you're walking, run; if you're reading, get up and dance to your favourite music; but change what you do with your body.

Here are some of the most common emotions and the message that they try to tell us:

Anger

It is normal to feel angry when something or someone violates one of our personal rules. It is usually the degree to which it affects us that makes it healthy or not. In fact it is very unhealthy not to ever express anger or to repress it. The problem is "how" we express anger that matters. Anger is an emotion that is very common to most people. We have all been there at some point in our lives. It is one that can cause a lot of people a lot of grief, as they have never learned the right way to express their anger and heed the message that this emotion is giving them.

Some people have repressed anger, because of the way they grew up, but that doesn't mean that they do not feel anger, it just means that they turn the anger onto themselves.

Anger, if not expressed in a healthy way can turn to disease or illness.

Some people tend to accumulate their feelings and do not express their anger at the time but instead they keep storing it; the problem with that is that this anger eventually finds an outlet.

It eventually explodes at the wrong time, in the wrong place with the wrong people.

Other people still get into strife because they express their anger too much; these are people with a lot of issues that need addressing, preferably with a good Therapist.

Anger can cause very erratic or aggressive behaviour, can make you lose your job or can land you in jail; can put you on bad terms with your nearest and dearest or other people in your life. We all live our lives by our own specific self-imposed rules. When our rules are infringed either by ourselves or by others, we often experience anger as a result. If expressed in a controlled way, anger is a very healthy and normal emotion to experience.

Anger is often a result of hurt feelings. Anger is usually hurt in camouflage clothes.

The message is either that we need to stand up for what we consider is right; or in some cases, the message is that we need to have the wisdom to accept the things that we cannot change and be wise enough to learn to accept it. It may also mean that sometimes we need to be big enough to let go of some things, pass on them and move on.

Fear

Fear, anxiety and worry belong to the same family. Too many people's lives are plagued by fear, anxiety and worry. It can be pervasive and progress to panic attacks, or an anxiety disorder, which can be crippling. Living in fear can become a state of being after a while. Some can be almost shaky most of the time. Fear per se is not a terrible thing. It can in fact be very useful and save us from problems.

The message of fear is to be prepared as you could be in danger or that something bad could happen. Fear warns us against physical danger. This is a very useful message as it can either save our life or make sure that we are prepared to tackle an imminent danger. It means you have to prepare and get ready. If you are fearful because you have to give a presentation, the message is to get prepared. Prepare, rehearse and prepare again until you are confident about your presentation. If you have prepared well, the fear will disappear as your confidence increases. If you are going for an interview, recognize that it is normal to feel anxious; so the message is to be well prepared and your nervousness will become less and less. Interviewers are well aware of this phenomenon, and usually make some allowance for this.

If you are fearful that something may happen to you in other areas of life, it means that you need to prepare yourself and be ready to do whatever is needed. Keeping it real is very important. If you are very often easily fearful for no reason, you may have long term underlying issues and the message that it is trying to tell you is that you need to get some professional help to control it. If you suffer from excessive, irrational fear or panic attacks, that is something else; the message is that you need to access professional help, so that you can keep things in perspective, and work out the difference between irrational fear and when it is normal to be fearful.

Guilt

You may suffer from guilt because you feel that you have let yourself or someone else down; you may have acted below what you think are reasonable standards. You have acted in a way that is unacceptable to your own conscience and your moral code. You have broken your own personal rules.

The message of guilt is not to do it again and you need to do what needs to be done to put things right again. If you need to apologize or do something to do the right thing, then do it as soon as you can. But do it!

If you suffer from guilt, you have to tell yourself if there is something that you can do to make amends, then you need to do it; however, if there is nothing you can do, then promise yourself never to do this again and move on. You cannot go back and fix the past; you have to let go of the past, however, you can make the future better. For now you only have the present in which to do what needs to be done.

It is most unhealthy to continue to live in excessive guilt, perhaps because someone has passed away; truly it serves no purpose to man or beast, least of all to the person you are missing. It is sometimes something that some people indulge in, because they have the belief that it is the right thing to do or what is expected of them, maybe culturally, or sometimes, it is a type of self-punishment; either way, it is not healthy.

Someone who has passed away will not want you to live in constant guilt because of something you did or didn't do, or even because you are here and they are gone. Please try to give their passing a positive meaning and remember the good things about them; believe that they are now in a better place, free from worries and pain, and they are at peace now. So, help them to remain at peace, let it go! Move on and keep the good memories. This doesn't mean forgetting them; never! Let them rest in peace, knowing that you too are at peace with yourself. It's the healthy thing to do. Seriously, think: the person who is no longer here would not want to condemn you to a life of guilt, especially as there is no recourse of making things better. That person would want the best for you; so it is safe, it is the right thing to do; let it go and move on, with a clear conscience. Absolve yourself. Guilt in this situation serves absolutely no purpose to keep punishing yourself and torturing yourself uselessly. You have to remember that guilt also forms part of the stages of grief. However, it is not healthy to stay stuck there. You really need to move on, with a clear conscience, knowing it's the right thing to do.

Some people feel guilty for the slightest little thing, due to the way they grew up; it is now time to be grown up and realize that feeling guilty for the slightest thing is unnecessary and is unproductive; and it is not the grown-up way to be. You too need to move on!

Sadness

Who hasn't felt sad in this world? Everyone has been there at one time or another. If you haven't you are not from this planet! Welcome to Planet Earth! We often feel sad because we have lost something, or feel like we have. Sadness results from a feeling of loss. Something is either missing from our lives or may be lost or we've lost someone or lost touch with someone or something that matters to us.

The message of sadness is to accept and appreciate the loss, especially if the loss is permanent. Acceptance brings relief from the sadness. Once you accept the loss, it becomes easier to move on with your life. However, in some cases it may mean, you may have to take some action and fight to get it back. If you believe that you have lost someone or something that's important to you, you may have to put yourself out of your comfort zone to try and get it back. Go for it!

Frustration

Now frustration! Isn't frustration SOOO frustrating? Even this word is frustrating!!! You know exactly what I mean when I say the word, frustration. We can all do frustration, can't we? It means that we are dissatisfied with the upshot that we think we can achieve within a given time frame, and believe that we can do better or that someone else can do better. Or that we are disappointed that we haven't got the results that we want to achieve in a certain situation or with someone. We can be frustrated because we associate more pain to doing something more than the pleasure we associate with it once it's done.

The message of frustration is to get going and do something about the situation in which we are frustrated. We need to associate as much pleasure with the end result and very little pain with doing it. All we need do is START; if we do that, we can start to gain momentum. We may then find that it is not half as hard as we, originally thought. We may need to work harder and do whatever needs to be done to achieve it.

> *Angry and happy don't mix.*
> *Flush out the angry, and the happy has a place to put down roots.*
>
> —*Jonathan Lockwood Huie*

We have seen how our thoughts can influence our emotions and our physiology and vice versa; and how we have emotions about the pictures or the movies that we have in our heads or about the voice we use to talk to ourselves with. So we have emotions about our internal movies and about what we say to ourselves. The problem is that often we do not react to what is happening in the moment but to what happened in the past.

Emotionally we react to our past experiences and we respond to memories or usual thought patterns we have been having.

These are the emotional baggage we carry with us throughout our lives. We learn a lot of our values and belief system during our childhood from our parents or guardians who are our main role models; depending on our role models, we may have inherited ingrained negative thought patterns from them. These patterns tend to repeat themselves automatically throughout our life without our conscious awareness.

Negative messages, such as: *Don't trust anybody; the world is a dangerous place; it's dog eat dog out there; everyone for themselves; people are out to get you; big boys don't cry; An eye for an eye; Shut up, don't be stupid* can all lead to limiting beliefs.

These are limiting beliefs that we grow up with which we inherited from our parents and guardians, teachers, friends and others, and as we become adults, we do not know or realize, that they have a huge influence on our emotions. These values and beliefs are outdated and no longer help us; we need to update them. The advantage of this is that these beliefs can be re-examined and broken down and rebuilt into positive ones.

We can choose to update our values and beliefs to take on more useful and resourceful ones; however, we must respect and listen to our emotions and heed their message or warning. Now is the time for us to examine how our belief system affects our lives.

> *To-day is your day to dance lightly with life,*
> *Sing wild songs of adventure,*
> *Invite rainbows and butterflies out to play.*
> *Soar your spirit, and unfurl your joy.*

—*Jonathan Lockwood Huie*

Notes: What have you learnt?

IF

If you think you are beaten, you are
If you think you dare not, you don't
If you'd like to win, but think you can't
It's almost certain you won't.
If you think you'll lose, you've lost
For out of the world we find
Success begins with a fellows will—
It's all in the state of mind.
If you think you're outclassed, you are
You've got to think high to rise
You've got to be sure of yourself before
You can ever win a prize.
Life's battles don't always go
To the stronger or faster man
But sooner or later the man who wins
Is the one who THINKS he can.

—Walter D. Wintle

CHAPTER FIVE

Secrets About Our Belief System

I would rather have a mind opened by wonder than one closed by belief.
—Gerry Spence

The secret why we do what we do and why we make the choices we make time and again are all down to our belief system. Our beliefs control all our thoughts and actions, including the reasons why our life is where it's at to-day.

Our beliefs have massive power over our daily decisions and over our behaviours. They dictate why we behave the way we do on a regular basis. Our belief system helps us to make sense of the world around us. We make decisions every day based on that same belief system.

If we are unhappy with the decisions that we regularly make, then we must examine what we believe in, as it is our belief system that guides those decisions.

To have a belief in something is to have complete conviction in that thing. We are 100% certain that it is so. We do not have any doubt about it at all and do not question it any longer. As far as we are concerned, it is a fact and that's how we treat it. Once we believe that something is in fact true, we believe it as much as we believe that we have two eyes and a nose in our face. We would never dream of questioning it or even doubting it. To believe in something is to have a feeling of absolute certainty about what that something means. We then treat that belief as a fact, which we never question or have to think about it when we need to make decisions, because we have complete faith that's the way it is. It is our belief in ourselves which conclude whether we can or can't do something.

If you think you can, you can. If you think you can't, you're probably right.

—Henry Ford

Where do we get our beliefs from?

Like a lot of other things, our beliefs originate from our past life experiences, especially our childhood. As children we take on the beliefs of our parents and carers.

Parents or carers come out with a lot of expressions during our childhood; these expressions often describe perfectly what they believe in. However, these expressions and beliefs do not fall on deaf ears, as children eagerly copy what their parents or carers do and say, but most of all what they believe in.

Our parents may have said things like: *You're stupid* or *You're useless* or *Big boys don't cry,* or *If someone hits you, you turn the other cheek* but then again they may have said things like *If someone hits you, you hit them twice as hard, or work hard, and stick at it no matter what* or they may even have repeatedly told you that *You would never amount to anything* or maybe they said *you can be whatever you want to be* or *you can achieve whatever you want to achieve* depending on their beliefs and values at the time. In an effort to teach you to be resilient they may have repeatedly told you: *If at first you don't succeed try, try, try again!* Well, if they did, lucky you! If they didn't, it's never too late to adopt a new belief!

All these beliefs that our parents or carers, maybe unconsciously have, we end up taking on board as children, and they end up becoming our beliefs too, as our parents or initial carers are our very first teachers. As we grow up, we continue with the same belief system, adding some more beliefs gathered from other influential sources on us such as school, friends or the media; until we become enlightened enough to think for ourselves and make a conscious effort to update certain beliefs, if we realize that they no longer serve us well.

> *Beliefs need to be updated from time to time. What was relevant at one point in our life may no longer be relevant at another time as life is constantly changing.*

Can you think about what kind of things you were told repeatedly as a child?

Did your parents, guardians or teachers or family members ever say things like *You mustn't rise above your station* or *You're too big for your boots* or *You can never do anything right!* Or *you're not as clever as your brother or sister* or *you will never be any good at Maths* or *you're rubbish at sports* or maybe *who would want to employ you*? Or maybe something else which has now become one of your limiting beliefs?

Perhaps you can even hear the person's voice who said these things to you all these years back, in your head. All these negative things penetrate our beings and end up becoming our limiting beliefs in life. These limiting beliefs are the very things that keep us fixed in life; they stop us from reaching our true potential, and from becoming the person that we are meant to be.

Seen in another way, limiting beliefs steal from you the person you were intended to be. Who could you be if you got rid of the beliefs that are limiting you?

Often some of the things that our parents and carers say when we are children are quite unenlightened; they may not have meant it nastily, it could just be that they knew no better themselves; but unfortunately, when we're young, we do not discriminate and take them on board. When these things are consistently repeated these limiting beliefs become ingrained in us. They become part of us, and we innocently repeat this is who we are.

Sometimes, we have certain beliefs about ourselves, that we 100% believe to be true. Whatever those beliefs are, we have past experiences that we can recall confirming those beliefs, as they are supported by certain facts and reinforced by others.

For instance: if you believe that you are very smart; this belief didn't happen out of the blue! Since you were a child, your parents repeatedly praised you and told you that you were a clever boy or a clever girl; then when you went to school, your teachers reinforced that belief by praising you and maybe you consistently brought home good notes and good marks that reinforced that belief. Your friends maybe also reinforced that belief by telling you how smart you were and so on; and maybe when others were struggling to learn something, you found it easy, or you regularly came first in academic tests. Therefore you concluded that you are very smart. However, when you have a limiting belief, it works the same way too.

For instance if you were continually told that you were useless; that belief too was reinforced by your parents, maybe grandparents, other members of the family, the teachers, club leaders etc. You end up as an adult with a belief that it is true, that you are in fact useless; it was never true in the first place but it became true to you because it was reinforced so much that it became your reality.

Maybe you did something that didn't work out once, and you were told that you were useless; if you attempted to do other things, this time with a lack of confidence and failed, you reinforced to yourself and others that you were indeed useless. This confirmation and reinforcement then support this limiting belief and stopped you trying to do new things so that you don't appear so useless to yourself and others. That's how a limiting belief can start and end up preventing us from blossoming into who we are intended to be in life. However, it is never too late to change and achieve your full potential.

All you need to do is to make a decision that you will no longer let limiting beliefs stop you from being the person you are meant to be; go all out to destroy your limiting beliefs; take action towards dumping your limiting beliefs. If you are scared of failing, then keep trying new things until you start to get some success, and then keep building on that success. You will then develop a new belief that you can indeed succeed.

Your time is NOW!

Now is your time to reassess your limiting beliefs. If you do this, it can open endless opportunities for you that you never ever realized before. Think! Who do you want to become in life?

Well! YOU can be that person! But first you need to believe it fully!

So what is a limiting belief?

Any belief that does not let you progress in life is a limiting belief. Any belief which stops you from doing what you want in life is a limiting belief. Any belief which you feel ashamed of or feel that you have got to hide it from others is a limiting belief.

It is essential to make a conscious effort to rid yourself of your fixed or limiting beliefs, otherwise you will never be able to reach your full potential or be the person you are intended to be. Our first role models are our parents and carers; when we attend school, we get other input from our teachers, our peer group, the media, the clubs we attend, our church or the television; later our friends and colleagues also influence us; they all, contribute to form the belief system we have to-day; some good and maybe some not so good!

This does not happen on a conscious level; they almost creep up upon us, without us being aware of it at the time. The difficulty with a belief is that once it is established, we never ever think of questioning it or doubting it anymore; we believe and treat it as 100% fact, just like the sun rising every day. It is our truth, our reality.

This can work for the best as it can work for the worst, depending on the belief. If it is an empowering belief, one that will add to our life, we benefit from it; however, if it is a limiting belief, one that takes away from us or can hinder us, it can make our life miserable and keep us unable to move on.

Limiting beliefs are the main culprits behind some of our poor decision-making and some of our deplorable life choices in the past, including the reason why we are unable to move on with our life.

Empowering Beliefs V Limiting Beliefs

Any belief that adds value to our life is an empowering belief. Any belief that helps us to take action towards helping ourselves and moves us forward is an empowering belief. For example, if you have an empowering belief like: *There is nothing that I can't do*, it works in your favour and helps you to feel empowered in achieving things you would otherwise never have had the nerve to do. This belief encourages you to try new things instead of being scared of them. If this is your belief you will attempt anything that can get you what you want. The result is that your belief has empowered you to move forward and helped you achieve what you want. And when you get what you want in life, it goes a long way towards fulfilling your full potential and feeling satisfied whilst increasing your level of happiness.

However, others have limiting beliefs like: *I'm not very smart; I don't deserve it*; or *I don't deserve to be loved*; or *I'm not worth it*; or *There is no point in trying anything, I'm bound to fail*; or *I'm not good enough; knowing my luck, things are bound to go wrong.*

These beliefs can be very disempowering and crippling; they stop you from having a successful and happy life and stop you from reaching your full potential.

I understand that maybe some of you are already saying that this is rubbish, that you are *realists*. That is an excuse and you well know it! ***You are no more realist that the person who have empowering beliefs.*** The only difference is that the empowering beliefs will help them succeed, will help them to be positive, will help them to feel happy and emotionally balanced, will help them to get the results they want in their lives! Whilst your realistic limiting beliefs are still keeping you unhappy and unable to move forward!

The thing is, if you believe that you are no good or not worth it, you will never undertake anything much or try very half-heartedly so that you fail; that way you will never get what you really want, and will never achieve anything much either. You will settle for second-best or for something that you don't really want and will not feel satisfied in your relationships, in your work, in your health, in your finances, in your social life, or in your environment. Life passes you by; and as the saying goes: *Life is not a dress rehearsal*! You only get one chance at it! There is no second chance. No, I've messed up first time; I will try better next time! NO! None of us will pass this way again! This is it! Don't mess it up! Might as well make it the best you can be!

Some people can take ages before they get this, however, once they've got it, they can really make huge changes and achieve their full potential. Some people mature early in life; they get things quickly and can go on to achieve a lot throughout their lifetime and their life is enhanced because of it. Others mature later and can take forever to become emotionally and psychologically grown-up and it can take them years and years and years, before they get it; sadly, some never do get it! Limiting beliefs are not inconsequential.

I want you to get this as early as you can: you need to arm yourself with empowering beliefs and dump those limiting beliefs. However, if you are already older, it doesn't matter, as getting it is what matters. Once you understand that you have absolutely no use for any limiting beliefs in your life, your life will be enhanced and you will find a way to achieve your full potential. The world is your oyster! Now is your time to have many empowering beliefs to get you where you want to be.

How sad would that be if you get to the end of your life and you missed huge opportunities and now live in regret because you were paralyzed by your limiting beliefs, when all the time there were simple solutions to your limiting beliefs?

The thing is, what was important at one point in your life may no longer be an issue later on. I do not want you living in regrets of some beliefs which once mattered to you but no longer matters for who you are today and it's now too late to do anything about it. You didn't do anything about it, maybe because you were in denial or too proud to be truthful with yourself or with others? Or maybe you allowed some so-called friends to influence you to stubbornly support your limiting beliefs, because they were scared that you would move on and be better than them and leave them behind.

If you can't get past your limiting beliefs despite your best efforts, get yourself a good Coach who will help you. Your time is now!

Find your passion in life. Whatever your limiting beliefs are, don't put up with them any longer. Remember? **Life is too short**! Don't allow limiting beliefs to stop you! Become that person that you are always meant to be!

> *You have the power to do anything you want to do. You need to be willing to and to believe that you can.*

Commitment

Once you make a commitment all sorts of new opportunities will open up for you; but you need to make that firm commitment first. Instead of focusing on all the usual obstacles in your way, you will soon notice that opportunities present themselves out of nowhere. There is a saying that says: **Once the pupil is ready, the teacher will appear.** So make a commitment to yourself to change any limiting belief you have and when you're ready, the teacher will appear. Let this book be your teacher!

Whenever you make a commitment to something, wonderful things suddenly start to come your way. Providence moves to make things happen for you.

The great thing is that you can challenge any of your beliefs at any time, and turn them into empowering ones. That's really exciting! If you start to put doubt behind your limiting belief, it is possible to change these limiting beliefs. In other words you stop treating them as facts. If you actually doubt something, then you no longer believe that it is a 100% fact, which you would never question.

Begin to doubt whether there really is some truth behind the belief. For instance: *I'm useless*; you can start asking yourself: *who says that I'm useless? Where's the evidence?* Then start looking for some evidence when you achieved something, anything! You can subsequently start to doubt that this belief is indeed true! Because you now doubt whether you are really useless, you can attempt doing something that will prove this belief wrong. If at first you don't succeed, try, try and try until you do; then you will have proven to yourself that you are in fact *not useless*. You can turn this limiting belief into an empowering one.

Once you can succeed at one thing, you can afterwards venture to achieve another and when you succeed, make a fuss of yourself; reward yourself, tell others how clever you are. Next do something else, then try another and another and before you know it, you will have a repertoire of lots of little successes, which you must collect and reward yourself for. Keep a record in your journal of all your successes but keep your successes always at the forefront of your mind. This way you can eliminate that limiting belief for good.

Sometimes we don't succeed the first time round, because we may need to learn some lessons in life. But if we don't try again we miss the opportunity of learning other valuable life's lessons.

> **Anyone who has ever achieved anything has had to go through some failures first. Every failed attempt teaches us important lessons**.

> *Believe you are defeated, believe it long enough and it is likely to become a fact.*
> —*Norman Vincent Peale*

If for instance, you believe that there is no point in trying new things because you are bound to fail; start to doubt what you are telling yourself; instead start to think: *Supposing that's not true? What if I try? What have I got to lose? I can fail but then again I may be successful. But if I don't try, I will never succeed! There is a 50% chance that I can fail, but there is also a 50% chance that I can be successful. The only way to find out is to give it a go!*

If when you give things a go, you discover that you can succeed at certain things even though you may fail at others. It will alter that limiting belief into one that empowers you to try new things, because now you have references where you know that if you try, you may indeed succeed; and if you don't succeed, you would always have learnt something and you can have another go until you do succeed! However, if you never try, you may feel safer, but you will never succeed at anything, and you will stay fixed where you're at. You can do this with any limiting belief and take them apart bit by bit until you no longer entertain any limiting beliefs in your life.

Failure

Some people have limiting beliefs about being successful whilst others fear failure more.

The way you think about failure is how you will feel about it.

Instead of thinking of failure as shame or rejection or embarrassment, you can reframe failure as being a very important part of learning. It is often when you fail to achieve a certain goal that you get the opportunity to learn about other things, that you wouldn't have discovered had you got it the first time. Looking at your fear of failure this way can immediately change your fear of failure or rejection into an empowering one which can inspire you to learn, grow and develop.

You may not succeed at what you are trying to achieve, however, you may learn something on the way that may help you in other ways. A lot of new discoveries are found this way, such as toothpaste or penicillin.

Either way you got a result, maybe not the one you wanted on this occasion, but that result may save you a lot of grief in another situation, or may guide you to a better place. There is always a lesson to be learnt in any failed attempt, if we look for it and pay attention to it.

When we talk about failures, Thomas Edison is often quoted as a champion who never believed in failures. He had 10,000 attempts before he discovered the incandescent light; however he said that he was not discouraged as with every failed attempt, he moved one step forward. Edison like many other successful people knew one of life's secrets because he realized that:

> *There is no such thing as failure, there are only results.*

I didn't invent this! This fact is an empowering belief of many achievers throughout history. These old sayings are there because there is truth at the bottom of them. This is very much a belief that successful people adopt. They never let any amount of failed attempts dishearten them; and they never see their failed attempts as failure.

Any unsuccessful attempts are lessons for us to learn from.

Edison never gave his failed attempts the meaning that he was not succeeding or that he had failed; the meaning he gave to his failed attempts were that he got results, not the one he was looking for but nevertheless results, from which he learnt. Thomas Edison managed to give positive meaning to each failed attempt and turned them into empowering him to fuel his passion to continue his search, instead of being discouraged and giving up. He never once saw his numerous failed attempts as failure.

This is a new belief that you need to add to your belief system, especially if you do fear failure. If you know that you will get results one way or another, maybe not the one you are looking for, but whatever the outcome, you will be able to learn something from it, your fear will dissipate itself. The experience helps you to grow, learn and develop.

> *It is the meaning you give to failure that makes it empowering or disempowering.*

For instance, if you have had a fairly unsuccessful work history, and you translate it to yourself that you are a failure, you will suffer the consequences of depression, and you will be disempowered in finding the right job for you. However, if you see your past work history as essential lessons that you had to learn in life, it will spur you on to search and find where your niche in life is.

Become Creative and Resourceful

Feeling empowered develops creativity in you. Start to make a list of all your talents and gifts. Find out what your beliefs and values are; from that you will see where your passion in life is leaning towards. Then make a commitment to find the best job you can in that field and do not give up until you find it. If you have to retrain, then do it. You may not get the answer straight away, but if you stay committed you will find it!

Remember that once you make a commitment new opportunities open up.

Far too often we allow ourselves to be discouraged, telling ourselves we failed because something hasn't worked out for us. Instead we can use the results we get, to give ourselves leverage, may be alter our plans accordingly to carry on, until we get what we want.

It is the way you represent not being successful in your mind to yourself that matters. If you can language failure to yourself in a positive way, you can come out triumphant instead of feeling crushed.

Your beliefs have the power to help you create exceptionally amazing results or equally, they have the power to ruin you, and keep you trapped into a mediocre existence with a very poor emotional life.

It is vitally important to have a firm belief and trust in yourself, if you are to enjoy a happy and successful life. The first person you need to learn to trust is yourself. With limiting beliefs, you can never achieve your purpose.

How can you trust others if you have no trust in yourself? If you don't believe in yourself, why should others believe in you?

If you go for an interview for a job with very poor self-belief that you are indeed capable of getting the job, it will show on your face and in your demeanour! Then why should the boss give you the job, when you, yourself do not believe that you can do it? The fear of rejection at times stops you from being successful as it stops you trying in the first place. Being scared of failure or rejection stops you from trying new things; and if you don't try anything, how can you ever achieve anything? How can you learn, grow and develop? How can you move forward? How can you achieve your purpose? How can you become the person you were intended to be?

Our purpose here on planet earth, is to learn, to grow and to develop.

Fear of failure and fear of rejection do not allow you to evolve, learn, grow and develop, therefore will keep you living a less than satisfactory life, where you can never succeed at anything or feel satisfied. The way you think about yourself decides if you are successful or not. If you have no belief or trust in yourself, you are unable to achieve what you wish for in life.

For instance, I have to believe that I am capable of writing this book, to be able to write it. Without that belief, I am unable to do so. If you have no belief in yourself, you will not try anything much because your subconscious mind doesn't believe that you can achieve it. You will be reluctant to give anything a go, as you fear the worst. Then, because you don't try anything new, you will not achieve anything either. It becomes a self-fulfilling prophecy.

It is because you believe the way you do, that you will not take action to disprove your own limiting beliefs; therefore you bring about the very thing that you really didn't want in the first place, thus reinforcing your belief by proving to yourself that you were right all along. Beliefs work this way for most things in life.

> *Believe you can and you will; believe you can't and you won't. Your subconscious mind's mission is to prove itself right!*

It is a vicious circle—that started because you had a negative belief about yourself in the first place and your subconscious worked to prove to you that you were right. Therefore you conclude that your belief is right that there is absolutely no point in trying something new, as you would fail anyway; and as you are eager to avoid rejection, then, there is absolutely no point in trying. Q.E.D, problem solved! You do not try!

Only problem is that you haven't solved anything. You have only justified your limiting beliefs to yourself. Thus even though you may be unsuccessful at anything else, the one thing you are successful at is to fulfil your own prophecy!

If you believe something, your subconscious works to prove you right! Whatever you say to yourself in your deepest private moments, your subconscious is listening and acts to make it happen.

So the secret to note is:

> *Be conscious about what you believe about yourself and what you say to yourself. Your subconscious will not let you down. It will find a way to help you get what you are saying to yourself; whatever you are saying to yourself had better be good!*

Some adults have a firm belief that they are not very bright. This belief may have started as children when they were compared to their siblings or others. However, something that started so insidiously and crept upon them whilst they were growing up may now be controlling their life to-day. The only thing is they may be unaware of it, blaming circumstances or the environment or others for their troubles.

Let's look at Marie and her sister Ann:

When Marie and Ann were small children, Marie may have shown an aptitude for being quite smart, whereas, Ann may have been a natural Tom boy, who didn't show that she was particularly smart, quick witted or gifted. What can happen is that the parents and grandparents or others may have repeatedly said that Ann wouldn't amount to much, as she wasn't as clever as her sister Marie, who will do well in life.

Marie on the other end was constantly reinforced for being a clever girl; so she gave her best at school and did very well, went to university and afterwards ended up in a very good job. On the other hand, there were no expectations from Ann as her parents and grandparents had decided that she wasn't very bright anyway. Ann, on the other hand, who was constantly told how she wasn't very smart, did badly in school (as there were no expectations from her—why even bother trying? she would think, I would probably fail anyway!)—fulfilling the prophecy, confirming to Ann that she truly isn't very clever, certainly not like her sister, Marie!

This ends up being Ann's belief later on as an adult which she treats as a fact. Because of this limiting belief Ann has, she does not attempt anything challenging as she believes that it is beyond her capabilities. Therefore she has no particular ambition.

It could even have started that because Marie looked like her clever old granddad when she was born, that it was assumed that she would also be very clever, just like granddad, in life; therefore the parents and grandparents and maybe others reinforced the fact that Marie was indeed very smart, which clearly helped Marie to do well at school, and later on at University as she applied herself and eventually managed to get a very good job.

Yet, poor little Ann happens to look like that dodgy old Uncle Harry, who is as thick as two short planks! It may also have been assumed (wrongly) that poor little Ann, was going to be very dull in life, just like poor old Uncle Harry, who was clumsy and after all never achieved anything much! For that reason Ann was repeatedly reinforced on how clumsy and dull she was; the more it was repeated to her, the clumsier and duller she looked and became! She, therefore had no incentive in doing well in school as there were no expectations from her; forget about going to university and getting a good job! Fulfilling the prophecy!

Hence, Marie got positive reinforcement from the very start and Ann got negative reinforcement from the very start too. Ann was left to fight on in life with her limiting belief, whilst Marie was reinforced for every little success. As an adult Marie's self-esteem is very good, whereas Ann's self-esteem is sweeping the carpet!

It is not until something happens to disprove this limiting belief in herself that Ann is able to prove to herself that she can achieve as much as Marie, and maybe even more; Consequently, ridding herself of this limiting belief which was passed on to her by her parents, grandparents and others in the first instance.

When something is said repeatedly, we end up believing it, even though it is not true, and even if we don't agree with it in the first place.

It isn't something that is said once in a while that has this tremendous power over us; it is when the same thing is said over and over again day in and day out. We hear it so often that it becomes second nature to us. It stays in our heads and we feel it in our guts, in our beings and it becomes part of us, even way after it is no longer repeated to us.

Learned helplessness is something which you unconsciously learn as a child, but which is so deep inside of you, without actually being aware of what is happening at the time. You don't take up any new challenges because you are convinced deep inside that you are incapable of doing it; or if you attempt it, that you would fail. Why try something you know that you would fail at? There's no point at all.

If someone, whether it is your mother, your father, your husband or wife, your boyfriend or girlfriend, teachers or grandparents, again and again tell you that you are, for instance, useless, you end up believing that you are useless, and this becomes one of your limiting beliefs. To prove it to yourself you will not take up any new challenges because you believe that you are useless or you will make an inadequate attempt at something and fail to prove to yourself that you were right in the first place. From then on, that will be your limiting belief, because as far as you are concerned you have proved it to yourself.

Luckily we can reverse this belief. If this belief is so effective in a negative way, it also can be as effective in a positive way. If it works well for limiting beliefs, it can also work well for empowering beliefs.

The reason why you have limiting beliefs is because of the meaning you have given to some things that you heard or experienced in your past.

Keep in mind:

Nothing in life has any meaning until you decide what it means and you give it a meaning.

You have the power to give empowering meaning to your beliefs as you have the power to give them disempowering meaning.

When you become conscious that you have a limiting belief, you can then reverse this belief by giving an empowering meaning to what once limited you, by reframing its meaning.

Conditioning

Once you're able to do this, you need to use it regularly to condition your nervous system with this new meaning, so that your subconscious can truly believe your new empowering beliefs.

That may mean repeating positive affirmations regarding your beliefs over and over again. It helps to write them down; so that your eyes can see them and you can visualize these affirmations and create positive images in the movies of your mind.

Practice makes perfect.

Keep practicing your new empowering beliefs, so that it becomes established in your nervous system and becomes as automatic as you old limiting belief once was.

You have the power to choose what meaning you give to any experience. You can choose to be positive or you can choose to be negative.

Equally if the meanings you have given to certain beliefs do not serve you well, you have the power, in fact, even the duty, to question those beliefs and no longer treat them as truths, but doubt them, challenge them and replace them with beliefs that have much more empowering meaning for you.

> *If you start to doubt anything long enough, you will sooner or later not believe it and stop treating it as fact.*

There are many things you used to believe when you were younger or in the past; then one day the penny dropped, which made you doubt them and after that it was only a matter of time before you no longer believed them. Remember, believing in Father Christmas? Who hasn't?

For instance, If you are a confirmed Atheist, and one day you find yourself in front of the most amazing scenery, for example the Grand Canyon; you start to question yourself about the origins of the Grand Canyon; from further looking at the unbelievable scenery you come to realize that no human hands could have put this canyon together or no scientific explanation would satisfy you either. This almost spiritual experience is enough to start challenging your belief whether God exists or not. Astronaut Neil Armstrong had a similar spiritual experience when he first walked on the moon. An experience like this can completely change what you believe in.

Here I go again repeating myself! (When I do that, you keep learning): Remember how the mind works?

. . . It generalizes, distorts and deletes information if it suits us.

If any of you ever, had the unfortunate experience of being abused or assaulted by a man, your mind can generalize this to: all men are bad and they abuse you, which then becomes one of your limiting beliefs; this in turn stops you from having any kind of satisfying relationship with men in general. This limiting belief can affect your work life, your social life and your emotional life without mentioning your intimate life.

This can truly limit your potential, and influence your quality of life. At worst, it may mean that you never have any male friends, never marry or have children; you may find it difficult working with men or joining any kind of social group, or being treated by any male doctors; having nothing to do with your male neighbours; you may not be able to trust a male pilot or a male taxi driver or a male train driver to take you safely on holiday or work destination and the list goes on, as in life it is easier said than done if we were to limit our interactions to women only. For instance if you wanted to build a new house, it would be crazy to only choose a female work force. Most of the tradesmen are males. What about if you can't trust male policemen or firemen? Doctors or paramedics? This one belief can make one's life quite problematic! With this limiting belief, you may find that it encroaches on other areas too; for instance, it may stop you from going out after dark or interact with male waiters or sales assistants or enjoy male singers, the movies or theatre. Okay! Okay! I agree that this is a bit extreme, but you get what I mean, don't you? Nevertheless it can seriously affect the quality of your life all the same!

On the other hand, things don't always work that way. Some people may have had very poor life experiences in their past and strive to do their best to use those to do some good or contribute to the wider community, precisely because of what happened to them.

For example they may say to themselves: Because of what happened to me, I will do my best to help other women to feel empowered; Because of my poor childhood experience, I will make sure that I am the best mother my child can have and ensure her safety always. It's like the woman who was abused by her husband, and ended up establishing a chain of women's refuges for abused women in London.

Instead of letting our negative past experiences become limiting beliefs, we can use them to achieve positive outcomes for others.

David Peltzer is one such person who uses his abusive childhood to help others. He wrote his life story in A Child Called IT; The Lost Boy and A Man Named Dave. He was severely physically, mentally, psychologically and emotionally abused by an alcoholic, psychologically deranged mother, but to-day, he uses his experiences to help a lot of young Americans who have also been abused, and helps many young people in prison. He truly is an inspirational man who has managed to give positive meanings to his horrendous past and uses them creatively for the good of others and to make a difference in the world.

How else can limiting beliefs affect you?

Your limiting beliefs always have a negative impact on you. For instance: you may find it difficult to speak in public or dance in a social gathering, because you feel very self-conscious. Until now, you may have said to yourself: I will never be able to speak in public or do a public presentation, or I can't dance and I will not because I will make a fool of myself; you may have completely refused to do so and get very stressed out if you have to say anything in public maybe in a course that you attended or at a social gathering or avoid any situations where you would have to dance or talk publicly.

Be aware that these limiting beliefs restrict your potential. They are certainly not trivial.

Limiting beliefs can have social or career consequences.

Until now you may have told yourself that what you avoid have no real consequences; however that is not strictly true as for instance, it can hinder your choice of career or social enjoyment. You may have to miss out on promotions or different social settings only because you feel you can't keep up with others.

> *Whatever you avoid becomes a bigger and bigger limitation in your mind, and if at a later point you are confronted with it, you can find it crippling!*

Remember this!

Don't let irrational fears get hold of you and make you live a less than satisfying life or an incomplete life in bondage to your limiting beliefs.

You must fight irrational fears, tooth and nail. You must do what you can to overcome them. The fact that you can succeed in conquering one irrational fear, whatever it may be, can give you the confidence to get rid of other limiting beliefs; the result will be that you can achieve your full potential, and be who you are supposed to be without the hang ups.

The more you avoid things you don't like to do, the bigger they become in your head and in your body. The more stubborn you become about them, the worse things are for you.

It is only you who imposes a limiting belief upon yourself. It is only you who has convinced yourself of their accuracy, and allowed them to blackmail you and keep you in a self-imposed prison.

You have allowed negative thoughts to infiltrate your mind and they have become a belief that you are absolutely certain that you are not capable of doing certain things.

When you can't do something because of your limiting beliefs, it's different from choosing not to do something.

For instance: If you choose at times not to dance and choose when you want to dance, then that is fine. That's a choice, not a limiting belief. The problem arises when it becomes something that you can't do even if your life depends on it.

Think: **Your limiting beliefs are only negative thoughts in your head**. You're scared! So what? Give it a go and if you make a fool of yourself? Say to yourself: So what? Do you spend sleepless nights if others make a fool of themselves? I doubt it! And if they did, would you stress and die of shame because of it? . . . Then, why would you?

> *Never allow anyone to put any limitations on you.*

Allow yourself to be free and liberated. You may be awkward the first time you try something new and you may find it difficult to do; the second time it gets better; by the third time you will be so proud of yourself that you won't even care, as by then you would have broken down so many barriers!

Exercise To Free Yourself Of Limiting Beliefs:

It is useful to ask yourself: *What's the worst that can happen to me?* . . . . For instance: *if I say something in public? Or, if I dance at a party? Will anybody die? Will it make the newspapers to-morrow? Will I be arrested for embarrassment to the public?* The answer is absolutely not! On the other hand, you will feel proud of yourself for overcoming your limitations! Dance to celebrate!

Definitely, no one will die!—Not even you. To this day there are no recorded deaths from embarrassment.

Then, if the worst that can happen is that you may feel a little uncomfortable or embarrassed, what's the big deal about that? People get embarrassed all the time. We all do at times. It's not the end of the world. Embrace being embarrassed! Laugh about it! If you can laugh about yourself, others will laugh with you and respect you for it. You can give some people a bit of fun. Nothing major will really happen, other than you will be proud of yourself and eliminate one of your limiting beliefs forever! You will be empowered.

You may as well accept and embrace the idea that it is okay to feel embarrassed at times! Then when you feel embarrassed, say to yourself: *So what? Who really cares? Will it really make front page news to-morrow?* Very much doubt it! People are only bothered when it is them who are embarrassed but they soon forget it if someone else is uncomfortable or embarrassed.

And if people laugh at you? Laugh with them! Louder! Don't get hurt or upset! You are bigger than that! They will think you're fantastic for giving it a go, which may be a whole load better than what they can do! Like you used to be, they would wish that they could do what you can do . . . And if they gossip about you? They are not even worth listening to; to-morrow will be someone else's turn! . . . . Then, you don't even need to let that insignificant act trouble you! Don't stress about things that are not within your control!

The more you do something, the easier it becomes! People think about themselves, not about you! You would be amazed how little other people worry about what you're doing and what you're saying. Even if they say things about you to-day, to-morrow, it will be old news. No one will be interested.

The next thing you can ask yourself is what have you got to gain if you get rid of your limiting belief? If you can get rid of one limiting belief, what else can you do that you thought was beyond your capabilities?

Exercise the muscle of trying things you think you can't do. It will liberate you and you will feel loads lighter.

Accept the thought that it's normal to feel embarrassed sometime. You always get over it. Other people will join in with you and enjoy it, as they know that they too get embarrassed sometimes. It is okay to laugh at yourself sometimes! Join the others! It is really okay! Others would admire you to have the ability to be able to laugh at yourself. You will have gone a long way in making them feel comfortable. A lot worse things happen a lot of the time, than a little embarrassment.

For instance if fear of public speaking is your limiting belief, try saying a few sentences in a small public gathering when you're among friends, or when you're on a course, speak up! And if dancing in public is another one, when there's a party, try going round the floor with a partner. So what, if you're not the best dancer? Who is? Just look around the dance floor! Who cares? Haven't you ever seen some people gyrating on the dance floor, acting the fool and when you looked at them, did they care or drop dead with embarrassment? NO! They were having a ball! One of my little neighbours, Jenny, told my husband one time: *Oh Leigh, you're even more embarrassing than my dad!* when she saw him dance at a party once. Did he let that faze him? Absolutely not! (Okay Jenny! Maybe you had a point!) But I was proud of him for allowing himself to have a great time, instead of fading in the background feeling embarrassed and not enjoying the party. He had a fantastic time! The ones who do not join in because of their embarrassment are the losers, as the ones on the floor are having the time of their life! Their embarrassment makes them miss out! You may well find that they justify it to themselves by trying to convince themselves and others that their way is much better by being negative towards others.

On the other hand, if you do not dance, because you choose not to or because it doesn't do much for you, but not because you're embarrassed or limited in some way, then that's different! As long as you do not allow anything to limit who you are or who you can be.

Whatever you allow to limit you grows; first it may be just a small thing after that it spreads in other areas.

You just need to venture out and take a small step first, then do a bit more, then a bit more and before you know it you will be able to achieve your goal proving to yourself that if you can do that, there is nothing else that can stop you achieving anything else that you put your mind to.

This simple action may be the catalyst that helps you understand that if you can overcome this barrier, you can bring down other important barriers that may affect other areas of your life too. It just takes determination, willingness and practice of getting out of your comfort zone.

Now, if you can set yourself a goal and achieve it, what else can you achieve that you thought was impossible for you to do?

Why do some people get stuck and become unable to do some things whilst others are able to do it even though they may not be brilliant at it, and are not as smart as you are? This is because they have no limiting beliefs and they choose to have a go, instead of being restricted by their own self-imposed rules.

For instance, whilst those who don't dance because they feel embarrassed, are busy worrying about looking like a fool, to people they do not know and are not likely to see again, and definitely not enjoying themselves as much; the ones who did dance would have been busy building good hormones, having a wonderful time and feeling just great as a by-product.

Relax, enjoy yourself! So what if you feel a little embarrassed? Get over it! No one cares! Worse things happen! How important is it in the scale of life? In five years from now would you still feel the pain of the embarrassment? If it will not be important then, why waste energy worrying now?

> *Life is a lot happier for those who lighten up; are flexible and are not restricted by limiting beliefs.*

Dump your old disempowering beliefs similar to I can't speak in public or I don't dance or any other limiting beliefs that are keeping you restricted from living life to the full and being the best that you can be.

It is just a matter of free will and what you say to yourself. If what you say to yourself is not empowering you in life, then change it!

Adopt new empowering beliefs like:

> *There is nothing that I can't do or I can manage anything that comes my way.*

Then, live it and practice it every day. It will change your life.

You may even end up having a job, where you have to make regular presentations and enjoy it, and your new belief will have served you well.

Making a plan is crucial to success

If you do not like the results that you are getting in your life at present, it is time to plan to rid yourself of any fixed or limiting beliefs that are keeping you from growing and developing. Then you need to make a plan to create what you want in your life. Without a plan, you will fail to get to your destination as you will have no compass to direct you.

If you do not make a plan for your life, you are not in control of your life. You are giving the power to others to do as they please with your life; that way you just react to what others are planning for you. It leaves you entirely open to the mercy of others as they will plan your life for you instead. Rest assured that it won't be what you may have been thinking about. You will be lost and find yourself reacting to whatever life throws at you, as you will not know which direction you want to go, and where you want to end up. This can cause a lot of heartache and confusion. That is not the way to achieve your purpose on this planet. If you do not have a goal, you have nothing to work towards and you will not know which direction to choose.

Be aware of not letting some friends (who know no better and want you to stay trapped like them), influence you. Remember: if you change you may be showing them up! If they want to carry on being your friend, they either have to keep up with you and get out of their comfort zone or lose you as a friend. So, they may encourage you in your limiting belief and tell you that this is all a lot of rubbish or mumbo jumbo. They say that, because they do not have the courage or the intelligence or what it takes to change and enhance their own life. We will talk more about friends later.

You may even say to yourself as you read this: *This is a load of rubbish* because it is challenging you; but deep down inside you know it makes sense and what I am saying to you is true; you already knew it even but didn't want to acknowledge it, because it is uncomfortable and confronting! Right? . . . . hmm, of course! However, no pain, no gain!

Repeat affirmations:

For instance: *I can do anything I put my mind to*! Or *it's okay to feel embarrassed or uncomfortable* or *failure or rejection helps me to grow and learn* or any other affirmation to help any of your limiting beliefs whatever they may be. It will open doors for you, which until now have stayed firmly shut.

> *However difficult a situation we always have the choice of how we choose to react to any situation or experience.*

We can choose to let it crush us or we can choose to survive and we can use a negative experience to turn it into an experience which can benefit us and others. The people of Queensland are a prime example. Many after losing their homes and all their possessions in the recent floods and cyclones, could easily have given up, but many choose to believe that Queenslanders are strong and resilient people and that they will not be beaten and will rebuild again, instead of giving up and sinking into deep despair.

The secret is, that it is, the meaning we give to things that gives us the power to sink or swim, to do well and be happy or to be a victim and live a life of mediocrity and anxiety.

Another of life's secrets to consider is:

> *When things are tough and you do not know where to turn, think of others and do something for someone else, who is worse off than you.*

The mere fact that you concentrate on helping someone else will help you tremendously. When you constantly stay fixed on your own problem, you become overloaded and overwhelmed by them and can't see a solution even if it is staring you in the face. The minute you change your focus and redirect your thinking on helping someone else, suddenly things become clearer; you start to see solutions, you never even thought of previously, although they may have been blatant for anyone else to see. As a benefit you will raise your self-esteem and feel good about yourself, not to mention the benefit the others will receive by your helping hand.

One major problem with our beliefs is that none of us consciously choose them. They crept upon us; and often they are someone else's beliefs, which we have adopted without question and often without even realizing it.

> *Many of our limiting beliefs have been established because we misunderstood and misinterpreted our past experiences.*

If we give in to things because we have misunderstood and given it a negative meaning, the next time we are in a similar situation, it becomes more difficult; subsequently, we find it harder and harder to do until we are no longer able to do certain things. This is the stuff phobias are made of.

Never give in to your fears

It is important to challenge yourself if you find yourself in a situation that scares you or makes you feel uncomfortable. Consistently confront your fears instead of avoiding a situation. Don't give up until you've conquered your fears. Think how good you will feel if you can conquer something that really scares you.

The next time, it becomes easier and the time after that even better and so on. You feel empowered when you can conquer your fears. You will feel like you have climbed Mount Everest! If not, your fears conquer you. If you can't do it by yourself, make sure to get professional help.

Yes, you're absolutely right: It is not easy! In fact it can be darned difficult; but you now know that life isn't supposed to be easy and fair, right? But think: How good will you feel when you have proved to yourself that you can beat your fears?

You may say to yourself: It doesn't matter (for instance, if I can't use the elevator?), it's not hurting anyone, but believe me it does matter! It sure is hurting you! First it starts with one thing, but if you are of that mindset, it isn't just that one thing; it spills over in other areas too. So, if you are scared of taking the elevator, use it regularly. Whatever you do, do not avoid it.

Anything that puts limits on you is not good, and only gets worse with time.

Self-pity

Don't let self-pity grab hold of you. Its grip can be merciless. It is so easy to fall into this trap. Do not indulge in it, because it is not your friend, even though it may appear so at the time. Self-pity makes you feel sorry for yourself and paralyzes you into inaction.

Self-pity revolves around self-centeredness and results in misery and bitterness. You see everyone as better off than you in every way, which then encourages you to wallow in your own misery. Self-pity encourages a sense of powerlessness.

Self-pity robs you of your power. It steals from you and your family the person you are intended to be. Self-pity stops you being who you really are, who you should be or who you could have been.

Self-pity is a paralyzing agent.

For some people if they are told that there is a slim chance that something negative can happen, but there is also a 90% chance that it won't happen, the negative person concentrates on the slim chance that it may happen to them and lives their every moment in worry, fear and anticipation of when it will happen. They completely ignore the fact that there is the 90% chance that it is never going to happen. Instead, they indulge in feeling sorry for themselves; they waste most of their time in self-pity and can think of nothing else. Their imagination goes in overdrive. They imagine the worst case scenario over and over again, that they bring it into their world. They are so self-absorbed that they never give a thought, how difficult it is for those around them to have to live with their attitude, and the impact that their selfishness has on others.

For others if they are going through some emotional trauma such as a break-up of a relationship, self-pity can keep them incredibly busy 24 hours a day. They cannot wait to find any willing ears to listen so they can tell their tale of woe. They do not think of others, or of what problems they may be having to cope with. Those who suffer with self-pity feel compelled to tell their side of the story to anybody who stops long enough to say: *How are you?* I am not saying that it is not sad or even tragic what is happening to them, or that one shouldn't empathize with them; but we must choose whom we take as confidantes, not tell every Tom, Dick or Harriette. Once you have spoken about it, try to be more proactive in putting your life back on track instead of living in the past. Become solution-focused. Keep your dignity; you will need it when you are through with your problems. As you know, bad times have a beginning, but they also have an end.

On the other hand, for those addicted to self-pity, all the good it does is that it feeds their obsession for more and more self-pity. Like a drug, the more empathy they get the more they crave it. It reinforces to them how badly done by they are, not realizing that however bad they are, there are always others who are worse off than them.

It is not what happens to us that matter; it is how we choose to react to what happens to us. We can lie down and die or we can choose to react resourcefully and with dignity and self-respect.

> *Self-pity is addictive and like any addict you need more and more people to feel sorry for you so that you can get your "fix". Sadly, self-pity never fixes anything.*

Exercise to stop self-pity

- If you find yourself engulfed in thoughts of self-pity, immediately change what you are doing. Change what you do with your body; go for a walk; jog; skip; go to the gym; do some kind of physical exercise, and you will find that your self-pity thoughts will gradually evaporate. It changes your focus.
- Concentrate on the wonder of nature.
- When you exercise, your body releases Adrenaline. In turn this triggers a release of energy and lifts your spirits, enough to change your mood. After exercise you are rewarded by a natural release of endorphins which promotes a feeling of satisfaction and relaxation.
- Exercise is considered the best pick-me-up to rebalance your central nervous system and your body's chemistry. It rids your body from stress hormones and with it goes your self-pitying thoughts. Exercise restores homeostasis—in other words it brings equilibrium to the body. Repeat a mantra while exercising, such as: I have all I need to be happy or I am healthier, fitter and happier everyday; or I give thanks for all I have in my life. Or you can make your own.
- Repeat positive affirmations; pray or meditate.
- Read or listen or watch something uplifting, inspirational or motivational. Read inspirational quotes daily as a reminder to keep upbeat.
- Think of others. Anything you can do for anyone? Then do it! Whenever you are feeling down, the best remedy is to look at what you can do for someone else. When you concentrate on someone else, you are not feeling sorry for yourself. You stop feeling like a victim when you help someone less fortunate than yourself; on the upside, you increase your self-esteem. Count your blessings instead of your woes.

When you have thoughts of self-pity, you are rehearsing thoughts that encourage you to feel like a victim; and like a camel you ruminate on these *poor me* thoughts over and over again. It only encourages misery.

Express Gratitude

Even the worst amongst us, have things to be grateful for; If you look you will find. Even if it is only for the sun that shines, the country you live in, the air that you can breathe freely, a healthy body etc.

Instead of churning over self-destructing thoughts, rehearse and repeat continuously thoughts of gratitude. E.g. Thank you for my life, thank you for my eyes that can see, thank you for the country that I live in, thank you for my family, thank you for my work, thank you, thank you etc.

As I have said before: (but I do like to repeat myself; it's great for learning!), *negative thoughts physically take up more room in your brain leaving little room for positive thoughts to take root*. When you spend a lot of time in gratitude, it becomes harder and harder to be negative; therefore your positive thoughts can put up a really good fight for your brain space.

Ask yourself what you have to be grateful for, and keep rehearsing all that you have to be grateful for all day long.

Don't focus on getting rid of your negative thoughts; instead put your focus more and more on cultivating thoughts of gratitude.

Write your thoughts of gratitude down in your journal and keep looking and reading them.

When you achieve what you thought was once impossible to you, it has a snowballing effect as it makes you much more adventurous. You then become more and more able to achieve things beyond your wildest dreams.

Your success in many areas of life may depend upon your resilience. But it all starts there, with the small things first; so trust me:

It does matter! No more self-pity!

Fight phobias; they are not on your side.

If for instance, you have a limiting belief that you can't go out where there are lots of people; do not give in to your limiting belief and avoid going out somewhere crowded. Your small issue with crowded places takes on greater proportions and before you know it, you may be suffering from a serious phobia, unable to go anywhere where there are more than two persons present; and before you know it, years pass by and you are now crippled by your phobia.

This kind of thing can have a significant impact on your life. If this is the case for you, you must expose your fear and confront them. Get professional help if you can't do it alone. Practice the muscle of being in crowded places over and over again, little by little, and prove to yourself that really nothing much happens, except for the thoughts in your head. Do it regularly until it no longer becomes an issue for you. If you feel bad, it is because of what you are thinking not because something is happening to you.

The feelings of anxiety are only caused by the thoughts you are choosing to focus on at the time. However, if you are truly affected by this, it would be wise to seek professional help.

> **Whatever the situation is that you feel uncomfortable with, don't give in to it; do not avoid it. Whatever you avoid becomes a bigger problem later.**

Challenge yourself. Keep putting yourself in a position where you have to confront it. The more you do it the easier it becomes for you. Trust me, it's true! The more you avoid it, the more anxious you become and you are well on your way to developing a serious problem. Kill that dragon before it gets any bigger!

When you have confronted your fears many times, you find that you no longer are uncomfortable with them. You feel liberated and develop the belief that you can conquer any other fears that you may have. You will feel empowered and you would have taken your power back.

As previously mentioned, once we've adopted a belief, we no longer question it, until something happens which lets some doubt creep in and make us question it and turn it into something more empowering.

Or we may choose to stay stubborn and hang on to our limiting belief; then we remain fixed in the situation we're in and we become disempowered. Of course you can do that, but that is not living the best life you can. Remember, you only pass this way once! Only once! No second chances!

Our imagination

The other problem with our belief system is not only, what meaning we have put on our past experiences, but it has also to do with our imagination as well—often a wild one at that!

We often exaggerate or have delusions.

We can use our imagination to create references for things that we have never even experienced and end up believing what pie in the sky we have made up in our dreams or in our imagination, as factual.

> *The mind cannot distinguish between something that has been vividly imagined and something that is real.*

If we use our imagination to intensely imagine something, our mind then treats this as a fact, whether we have experienced it or whether we have only experienced it in our mind's eye. As a result we can confuse fiction with reality.

Instead of using our imagination to visualize catastrophic outcomes, why not use it to envisage positive ones? . . . As luck would have it, we absolutely can!

We can use this same principle to secure a positive result as well. If it works well for limiting beliefs, we can use the same principle and apply it to work on empowering beliefs too.

NLP uses the imagination and visualization a lot of the time to dismantle limiting beliefs. There are many other techniques, including EFT and affirmations that can be used to get rid of limiting beliefs.

Conflicting Beliefs

Our mind cannot cope with inconsistencies as its primary role is to prove itself right due to its needs to stay consistent. It cannot also deal with two conflicting beliefs; therefore it will try to prove itself right by staying consistent with what we believe in.

For example, you cannot become rich if you believe that all rich and successful people are villains or that they made their fortune by devious means or if you believe that only ruthless people get to the top or are successful, or if you believe that money is a dirty word which is the root of all evil—your subconscious who listens to what you say to yourself 24/7 will work hard to stop you from becoming one of those villains, devious, ruthless people whose money is at the root of all their evil ways. It will endeavour to do its best to keep you poor and unsuccessful so that you do not become one of them, because it holds itself way above being villains, ruthless and evil people who worship money.

As it happens, it is the love of money which is known as the root of all evil, not money per se. There is nothing wrong with having a lot of money providing you earned it legitimately and you do not allow money to become your god. There's a new belief for you, if you were one of those who despised money as being the source of all evil.

Equally, if you feel bitter and jealous of all successful people, your subconscious mind will stop you from becoming one of them too.

This is why it is so important to be aware of what your beliefs are; it is just as crucial to be aware of what you say to yourself when you talk to yourself. Don't believe for one minute, because you are only saying negative things in your mind only, that it is not hurting anyone!

You may be surprised to know that the main person that it may be harming is you. Sometimes, people have conflicting beliefs, one part of you wants something, but the other part of you resents it or even despises it.

If you have an aversion to all rich people and you get lucky and win the lottery or inherit a lot of money; you may find that some part of you is excited about the money whilst another part of you hates it, because it may turn you into one of those people you have spent years despising. One way or another you will find a way to end up losing the money because your subconscious needs to stay true to what it believes you want. This is the reason why you find people who have won a lot of money in the lottery, end up by losing it all and finish up in debt instead. Their beliefs became a major player in this scenario.

It would have been wiser to hire a Coach whilst they still had the money to get rid of their limiting beliefs first, so that they could find value in being rich, enjoy being rich and enjoy staying rich! There is nothing wrong with having money, providing you keep it in its proper place and do not value it above all else.

Self-Worth

It isn't only those who have had a deprived or abusive childhood that finish up with low self-worth. Wild imagination, drugs, and too much money too soon or fame, often can lead to low self-worth. In fact many celebrities suffer from self-destructive behaviours, due to low self-worth. We hear it almost every day on the news. We have all heard stories about Lindsay Lohan, Britney Spears, Charlie Sheen, Amy Winehouse and a whole host of others. In fact if you are a celebrity it is almost an essential accessory to have your own celebrity shrink or regularly go to rehab! That's actually not too fair on many of other celebrities who lead respectable, creative, empowering lives who also do a lot of good! To those, I sincerely apologize. Fortunately there are many others who are talented and enjoy good self-worth and good fortune.

> *How you feel about yourself, affects how other people feel about you and treat you.*

If you do not show respect for yourself, others won't either. In life we get what we think we deserve. No matter how many material things we have, they will not fill the gap, if we don't feel good about ourselves.

Our Belief System is crucial to our destiny.

The answer is to build up our empowering beliefs which can help us achieve our life purpose. We need to do everything we can to dismantle our limiting beliefs which can destroy us and keep us from a rewarding life.

We have seen how beliefs have a great influence on us, for better or for worse, but there are many other forces that exert additional influence on us without us realizing their incredible power over us, for example . . . . Our *Friends*!

Notes: What have you learnt?

CHAPTER SIX

Schhhh .... A Few Secrets About Friends, Persistence .... And More ...

My best friend is the one who brings out the best in me.
—Henry Ford

Our friends are phenomenal, amazing, brilliant, wonderful and invaluable! We looove them! Many of us can't live without them! We won't hear a bad word said against them! Some would much rather have friends than family! Many would risk their lives for their friends. Our friends can be the making of us or they can be our biggest downfall. Friends are not the only influence over us, but their power over us is an incredible strength to be reckoned with.

Our friends can make us winners or they can make us losers. They can make us happy or they can make us sad. They can enhance our lives or they can help us destroy our lives.

They are there in times of trouble or if they are not there, we soon learn who our real friends are! Some friends can be wonderful when everything is going great, but it is when we hit problems, that's when we soon learn if they are fair-weather friends or true friends.

For some who have very little family in this world, or have no family in close proximity, our good friends fill the gap that family can't. These good friends are to be treasured. They are your family.

All too often we are not consciously aware of our friends' enormous influence over us. When we are good friends with someone, we frequently end up seeing the world from their point of view. Their filters become our filters. When they are being destructive, we suddenly suffer from memory lapse and somehow cannot remember it for the life of us! We are only interested to keep the status quo as we like them the way they are. Should anyone venture to say something negative about our friends, we are the first to jump to their defence.

Have you ever noticed how many times you see friends who actually look like one another? Often they look physically alike, because they have a similar way of dressing, wear similar make-up, or have similar hairstyles or mannerisms, speak the same lingo, to the point that they are often thought to be sisters or brothers. Even the way and manner by which friends speak are often very alike. They even use the same vocabulary. Have you ever noticed that? Because they speak in the same way, they develop the same tiny facial muscles, which end up making them look like each other physically more and more.

I have this thing that I think I can guess some people's nationality before they even open their mouths because different languages use different tiny muscles in the face that gives a nationality a typical look. I can instantly tell a French or English person before they speak. Americans are different again.

The ways young people speak are very different to the way their parent's generations speak.... *You know what I mean like? I was like, oh my God!... etc etc.* Often when a young person speaks, they add a *like* in the middle or at the end of their sentence. Does it make sense? Not really! But most of them say it to stay popular and be like their group of friends, as they need to be the same, do the same things, act the same way, and speak the same way to keep their friends and to be part of the in-crowd. Friends tend to have certain codes to be part of the same club. Then, do they say that they want individuality? .... Hum! Really?? However, all these similarities demonstrate that we are very easily influenced by our friends, much more than we realize. They also illustrate the degree of importance we give to our friends in our lives.

Just as they speak the same jargon and tend to look alike physically, more importantly, friends very often share the same beliefs and have similar values.

The problem is that even if they were not your original values or beliefs, you end up sharing your friends' beliefs and values in the end. There is nothing more powerful than proximity and familiarity to exert an influence on you. That is great if your friends' values and beliefs are empowering, but if they are disempowering, they can significantly impact your life and those around you by making your life anxious and miserable, which can send you down a downward spiral.

Adapting to your friends' value and belief systems may be the cause of the conflict that you have with your parents, partners or other family members, even other friends and these may give very good cause for concern.

> *So, think! Are your beliefs your own, or someone else's influence over you? Are they empowering you or disempowering you?*

You choose your friends because you have a lot of things in common with them. If you find yourself criticizing them on a regular basis, you have to question your friendship, and ask yourself whether you should be friends with these people, as they are clearly doing something that goes against your true values.

The reason why you find yourself criticizing them is that your value system conflicts with theirs. If that is the case, be aware that if you continue with the friendship, before too long you may find yourself doing what you criticize your friends for doing now. Take note now!

> *If your friends have a negative pattern of thinking or are of dubious character, abuse drugs or alcohol, the chances of you being influenced negatively is very high.*

Don't think that you are so above it all and that you won't be affected, because according to you, you have a strong mind. If you do, you are deluding yourself.

When you are in close proximity of a negative behaviour and you see it regularly, it becomes the norm for you; you may find yourself making a thousand excuses for it. When you start to copy a negative behaviour, there is nothing stopping you from acting in the same manner you once criticized. What's worse is that you will, by then, see nothing wrong with it! What started by shocking you is now so familiar that you are no longer able to be objective about it.

You may protest and say that your friends may want to take on your good habits instead . . . . Yeah, right! History shows that it tends to work the other way around.

You are more likely to join the crowd, than the crowd to be influenced by your positive habits.

You are judged by the company you keep by everyone.

> *If you make friends with people who have dubious values and character, you will be judged by their standards and you will be tarred with that same brush.*

People are judged by the company they keep, rightly or wrongly. That's the way it is!

If your friends drink all afternoon into the evening until they can no longer keep their eyes open and you see nothing wrong with it, before too long, this will be you! Be warned! Even if you don't like this side of them and think that you will never do that; don't kid yourself! The more you are exposed to this behaviour, the more likely that you will see it as the norm, to replicate.

Things creep up on you so insidiously that you may not even notice that you actually are now where your friends used to be. . . . . May be it did cross your mind how easy it is to become an alcoholic or addicted to some other substance . . . . But you quickly dismissed it? . . . . This is the time to listen to your subconscious!

Your mind is busy making all sorts of excuses for you to carry on your self-destructive behaviours, because you do not want to lose your friends. You will come down very hard on those who dare criticize them. Chances are these friends are very charismatic and you really do enjoy their company; nevertheless if you want to achieve your full potential, you won't be able to, all the time you have friends like these to hold you back. Fast forward life a little . . . . Imagine what the future will bring! . . . . Could you end up in rehab? . . . . That is, if you're lucky!

All the same, once you go down the road of abusing substances, you are looking for trouble. You are ruining your health which may have more serious implications on your physical and mental health, your relationships, your work and so on. Your friends may be lucky but we all never know what kind of genetics we have inherited which can trigger other more serious mental or physical illnesses that we never bargained for.

The fact that the friends who abuse drugs, alcohol or cigarettes are relatively okay for the time being, can lead you into a false sense of security by making the mistake of thinking that you too will be okay.

The problem arises sometimes that some people become worse off than others due to their genetic make-ups. Some may be fortunate and get away with substance abuse for quite a while, but none of us can be certain if we do not have some predisposing genetic factors that can actually lead to long-term serious mental health illness like Schizophrenia or to a fatal outcome.

Recovery from alcoholism, drug or smoking addiction is a very long and arduous journey to have to embark on. This is best avoided by learning to do things in moderation. This includes cannabis, which should not be touched, not even every now and again.

I have seen the detrimental effects that Cannabis can have on a lot of young people through my work. It is a sure demotivator. It can alter their personality or bring on Schizophrenia or Paranoia if there is a genetic component there. People can make some very poor life choices under the influence of Cannabis, which later on can have serious repercussions on their relationships, their family, the work or career that they choose, where they live and so on.

The problem is that we will not know if we have some genetic predisposing factor that the use of cannabis can trigger a mental illness, until we actually use the drug. There are no such things as *recreational drugs*. If you play with fire, sooner or later you will get burnt.

Drugs are drugs and they are dangerous. They all affect the brain and are able to alter the brain's chemicals or brain patterns. They affect the prefrontal lobe, where our personality is situated.

Substance abuse impacts your social life far more than you can ever imagine. Think, just because you couldn't have alcohol in moderation, it may mean, not ever being able to meet friends at a place which serves alcohol. This can be rather restrictive as a lot of the pleasures in meeting friends and catching up can involve having a meal and a glass or two of wine together or a beer. Imagine the social impact on your life!

However, unless something changes drastically and you proactively take yourself in hand, you will be following that path. If you have friends who are into taking drugs or abusing alcohol, never make the mistake of thinking that you are immuned.

This can soon be you! Let this be your wake-up call!

You really are judged by the company you keep, even if you do not take on their destructive behaviours. This is the world we live in.

If you are not proud of the way your friends behave, know that others may be saying the same thing about you too.

If your friends very often disgrace themselves by being drunk or drugged or are aggressive when in company, you too will be tarred with that same brush as you will be seen to accept the very same low standards that your friends demonstrate.

So, as much as you may congratulate yourself than you can befriend anyone, it may not actually be a wise or smart thing to do, and you may not be doing yourself (or your children, if you have them) any favours.

You can have many acquaintances, but you must choose your friends sensibly. You can't choose your family but you can choose your friends.

We should all love our family and be there for them; however, it doesn't necessarily mean that all our family members are actually role models and exert a good influence. Nevertheless we must be prudent about those we choose as friends, as they have a great influence on the quality of our life and ultimately our destiny. If we have children, it is important that the people that they are in regular contact with are of good calibre, as they too, have the power to influence our children's value and belief systems including their moral values.

If you don't smoke, abuse alcohol and take drugs, or get involved in criminal activities, and you move in a circle of friends who do, it won't be long before you begin to justify that these behaviours are perfectly okay and that they are not harming anyone, however what happens next is that eventually to stay in that same circle of friends, you have to comprise your own values and join them.

If you are happy with where your life is at and about the influence your friends have over you and your children is a matter for you only to decide. If this makes you think deeper, you know what you have to do. That really doesn't mean cutting your friends off, but it is aimed at raising awareness at how easy it is to fall into negative behaviours when you are influenced by friends.

If your friends do not have a good influence on you, look for friends with a positive attitude in life and those who encourage you to grow and develop through life; those who will lift you up and see the best in everything and have an attitude of gratitude. Let their joyfulness, enthusiasm and optimism be the qualities that influence you. Remember, you will be tarred with the same brush!

You do not need to move in circles where everyone has the same level of education as you. Far from it! Many very successful people, like Richard Branson or Henry Ford have had very little formal education, and yet have done exceptionally well in life. The difference is that they also loved to learn albeit not in a formal way. These people are geniuses in their own ways, more than many other successful people who have their university degrees. However, they are also gifted with other gifts like enthusiasm, optimism, and they have a personal power and empowerment to be able to keep following their dreams until they achieve them.

If you are doing really well in life, that's wonderful! Brilliant! Fantastic! Congratulate yourselves. You probably have great positive friends. This is for those who need an acute awareness that negative influences in their lives may be hindering their life's journey.

A French proverb says: *Si jeunesse savait! Si viellesse pouvait!*
Literally translated, it means:
If youth only knew (had the knowledge); and if only the old only could! (Had the ability to)! I guess we would all do things differently!

The wonderful thing is that we can accelerate our learning when we are young by learning from past generations, which is why I am writing this book.

So, please do not wait till you are too old and live in sorrow that you didn't make the changes that you could do now just because you chose the wrong company at the time.

Do not waste your valuable young life with poor behaviours which you can only live to regret later on.

> *Youth doesn't last forever; but what you do in your youths may have very long term health or financial repercussions when you are older.*

You can change if you want to; you can do anything that you set your mind to do!

Does keeping friends present a challenge to you?

Making friends may not be a problem but keeping them as long-term friends can be a mystery to some; whilst others may have problems making friends and keeping them. They always find that this friend did something unspeakable to them, that friend was jealous, the other friend was sarcastic, someone else did something nasty to their child etc, etc. The upshot of it is that every friend that they have, something nasty happens that they end up falling out with the friend; and of course the next thing is that they then get dropped by those friends or they drop them. They justify it by saying to themselves that these friends were nasty or jealous or hypocritical, and they don't care if they are no longer friends. However, on the inside . . . . they hurt, they really hurt!

Does this seem familiar to you?

If this is you: the answer to this is *inside of you*. Look inside, not outside. If you look for an answer outside of you, you will never find it.

When you fall out with several people and it keeps happening, there is just one common denominator here: YOU!

You need to look at what you are doing and how you interact with people. Are you easily offended? Maybe you are misreading situations. If they have other friends and you are the only one that gets dropped each time, then look at what you are doing, how you react to others and what meaning you are giving to an experience together or event. How do you speak to people? Are you abrupt? Just because something is the truth, you do not have to say it if you are going to offend others unnecessarily.

Show love, compassion and kindness. Have no expectations and you will have disappointments. Learn to forgive the everyday little things. Forgive easily.

It could be that you have been affected by your past and you are still repeating those same patterns as an adult. Look at your behaviour closely. Do you have certain expectations from your friends? How do you talk to them? Is there pressure in your relationship? Are you kind? You may think that you are being kind, but do not realize that your words may hurt others. You may think that you are generous but you have expectations back. You give expecting something back in return; when this doesn't happen, you are deeply offended! You may live in denial or may have a spirit of criticism without even realizing it. Are you an energy drainer? Maybe you're a bit touchy? You may just think it's normal and that others think the same way too. (No! They may not!) Are you jealous of other friends' friends? If someone is your friend, can they also be friends with your other friends, or will you feel left out?

You may have very blurred boundaries with friends. You may expect things to be one way and they may not realize this. Some cultures are a bit more abrupt than others. Do you take offence at someone's mannerisms or manner of speaking because it's not your way? Do small things others do readily upset you? Are you thin-skinned and hurt at the drop of a hat or are you so thick-skinned that you are not aware that you are trampling on other people's feelings? Are you way over-protective about your own . . . . children? . . . . family? . . . . partner? . . . . Job? . . . . Do you have a naturally aggressive way of speaking? Are you a bit of a drama queen and make mountains out of mole hills? Or maybe you have always fallen in and out with friends since you were young and think that is the norm? Could you just be a tinsy weeny bit over-possessive or paranoid that others may want to hurt you and this causes you to overreact? . . . . Your children? . . . . Your husband? . . . . Your job? . . . . his job?

You may not realize what is *normal* for friends. You may not realize what acceptable behaviour is and what isn't. Maybe you read too much into someone's behaviour, and instead of clarifying the situation you just get hurt and drop them. So you don't give yourself the opportunity to learn. You may just think that you are being helpful, but in fact what you say may be quite offensive to your friends. Sometimes it isn't even what you say, but your tone of voice and your body language may betray you.

Ask yourself these questions:

- *Are you the perfect friend?*
- *Do you never do or say anything that others may misinterpret?*
- *Are you always perfect?*
- *Are you quick at criticizing or at passing judgements?*

Then give others some slack!

Role Model

Find a good role model. Someone, people just love being with. Become a good observer. See how they behave with their friends, and copy them. You cannot go wrong if you choose friends who have similar values to you, treat them with kindness and friendliness and show them love.

> *Smile easily and forgive even easier! When we learn to forgive the little things without difficulty, we become easier to love too.*

You cannot go wrong when you show, love, compassion, caring and kindness. Let this be your recipe for your new friendships. And if someone does something you do not like, pass on it, don't be too quick to judge, blame or criticize. Live and let live! You too do things that others don't like. You will not like everything that some people do, and they may not like everything that you do, but that doesn't mean that they are *bad*. We all have own gifts and talents and own ways of doing things.

Learn to be tolerant! There will be parts of some friends that we may not agree with but that doesn't mean that we still can't be friends with them; and it works the other way round too. You too will do things that others will disagree with, but that doesn't mean that you can't be friends, just because you do not think precisely like them. You can learn to agree to disagree! That's the mature way!

Add Tolerance to your values.

The Formula to Keep Good Friends

- Most of all, show kindness, compassion, caring and love and friends will come to you.
- If you want a good friend, you need to be a good friend yourself.
- Do not be easily hurt, angry or upset.
- Treat your friends with respect and expect them to treat you with respect.
- Abolish any judgment, criticism or blame.
- If you have a way of speaking that is offensive to others, change it.
- Never gossip, back-stab or tittle-tattle behind your friends' backs.
- Do not live in denial. Don't assume that everyone else is at fault except you.
- Laugh a lot and laugh easily. Smile even easier!
- Don't be sarcastic; show charm instead.
- If you can help, help without any expectations back.
- Never assume that others just want to take advantage of you.
- Assume the best instead of imagining the worst.
- Do not become an energy drainer by constantly telling them your sad tales. Friends need to feel energized when they leave you, for them to want to come back.
- Choose friends with similar values to you.
- Don't just drop friends because they did one thing that you didn't approve of. Your friends have their good and bad points (like you have) but who are we to judge them? If you can help them, help! You will have friends who will do things you don't like, but that doesn't make them bad because they did one thing that upset you.
- Have a balance between giving and taking.
- Always assume that behind their behaviour is a positive intention. Most of the time they are trying to meet their own needs, not trying to hurt you.
- Give positive meaning to your experience with them.
- Have a positive and grateful attitude. Give praise where praise is due; a genuine compliment is always appreciated.

However, if they have a destructive or have a negative influence on your life, drop them faster than you can say *friends*!

You would have found the formula to make good friends.

Persistence

Being persistent to achieve your goal will get you through.

If at first you don't succeed, keep going *until* you succeed.

We've all heard the saying that we have to try, try and try again since we were small children. It probably rings in our ears as we sing it! Our parents probably often said it to us, in an attempt to teach us to be resilient, when we attempted to do something that we found difficult.

Who can be more persistent than a toddler trying to walk? First babies crawl, then they pull up to standing, next they stand alone and finally they take a couple of steps. What happens then? They fall smack back on their bottom. They get up and try again; they fall down after a few steps, what do they do? Do they give up and think that this walking lark is not for them? No! They keep trying and trying *until* eventually they manage to walk unaided. Then what happens? They are not happy just to walk! They realize that they can run when they get to about 18 months. Now there is no stopping them; they run everywhere, they keep falling and bumping their heads this time! Does it stop them? No way! They will keep running until they get good at it! So if we were so persistent as a baby, what happens to us when we grow up?

If you need to achieve a goal, and feel that you haven't what it takes to keep going with it, just think at the process that you had to go through just to be able to walk and run; you clearly were persistent then. If you managed to do it when you were much younger, you can do it now, when you have so many more resources inside of you to resort to.

Thomas Edison is often quoted as an example of persistency. Had he not been persistent, I wonder how long it would have been before someone else thought about inventing the incandescent light! To-day, we are all very grateful and have been for centuries to Thomas Edison for his persistence, and for giving all his missed attempts a resourceful meaning. Thomas Edison had 10,000 attempts before he got it right. He realized that there is no such thing as failure; he said that each of his failed attempts brought him a step closer to his goal as he learnt something every time. Anyone who has ever achieved anything has experienced some failure of some sort before they got where they wanted to be.

Colonel Sanders at sixty-five years old decided to sell his special chicken recipe, which he knew that people loved. He was turned down 1009 times before someone decided to buy it. He told them that he didn't want any money for it but what he wanted was a proportion of the profit on every piece of chicken sold. To-day, Kentucky Fried Chicken is worldwide, thanks to Colonel Sanders' astuteness and *persistency*!

The problem with to-day's society, is that it is a *now* society and a *me* society. We want instant gratification; and when do we want it? . . . Now! And who is it about? . . . Me of course!

We no longer put in the effort to work at things like we ought to. We get married; we have a couple of arguments, we already decide to move on instead of working at things to make the marriage work, as divorce is now easily available. It seems that we no longer have any staying power. The problem with relationships is that it's not only about *me*! It is about two people (and the rest!). We can't just only consider *me*. There is someone else in the equation; and if that other person is also so concentrated on their *me*, then it's a catastrophe waiting to happen. One has to learn to give and take; not just take, take, take! Or give, give, give. The balance between giving and taking needs to be right. Often some people do not believe in being persistent and working through their problems. The attitude is that there are plenty more fish in the sea. Let's move on! The idea is if you get it wrong, be persistent in finding a solution and build on it each time.

We ought to all aim to have long, thriving relationships and try and work at it on a consistent basis. If we fail, we start again from afresh, and keep going and aim to get better and better at it. If we fall, we need to get up and try again and again and again until we get it right.

> **We need to learn the virtue of being persistent to get the life we desire.**

We do not only need to be persistent in relationships; we should aim to be persistent in all our life goals. Our aim is to keep trying until we get there and not let unsuccessful outcomes faze us. When we do not get what we want first time, or second or third time, we are learning. We may accidentally learn a lot of things because we didn't get it right first time. That knowledge may come in very handy at some point in your life.

On the other hand, there are always exceptions to any rule. There are others who through their persistency have managed great things, like 16 year old Jessica Watson who went on a solo voyage in her sailing boat around the world, against a lot of opposition. This year a nineteen year old Australian boy Ryan Campbell finally achieved to fly around the world stopping in fifteen countries, single-handedly after two years of preparation; or the Korean lady who passed her driving test in 2010 after her 960th attempt since 1999. That's persistence! You may well laugh, but she will not wake up one day in old age, saying: *I wish I could have been able to drive when I was capable to!* Good on her for being persistent!

Goals

To achieve our goals we need to be persistent. We must keep the end goal at the forefront of our minds and keep going until we achieve what we aimed for. Sometimes, we may have to look at the result we have and alter the course of our plan to meet our needs; if that is the case, then that's what we have to do.

If you make a decision about achieving a goal, keep focused, and persist long enough, and continually take action towards that goal; change direction if you have to, so that you keep on tract; then you will achieve your goal. You keep working towards your goal until you get the results you desire.

Choose persistence as a value to add to your repertoire of values. Do not allow the wrong outcomes to beat you down.

You need to be like a dog with a bone and not let go! At first you do not need to know the how of how you will achieve it. You just need to believe first of all that you will be able to achieve it. We do not need to know the intricacies of how electricity works to have electric power, however, we all firmly believe that if we press a switch the light will come on. We do not need to know how a fax machine works to know that if we send a fax one part of the world it will be received in another part of the world.

You need to have that same belief at first that you can achieve your goal, then start working towards your goal and keep focused; keep asking yourself empowering questions which will lead you in the right direction. You need to be flexible and keep the end result in your mind.

> **If you want something bad enough your subconscious will find a way.**

Ask yourself *what do I need to do? What is the next step that I need to take and the next and so on.* Persistence is the essential value you need to have.

As previously mentioned, there is no such thing as failure; there are only results. Like Thomas Edison and Colonel Sanders, failure was never on their agenda, they only saw results; just an outcome, not the one they were expecting on many occasions, but nevertheless, they had an outcome which taught them something. It was an empowering way of looking at things and motivating themselves to be persistent until they achieved their goals. You too, can achieve your goal if you are persistent and continually take the necessary actions towards your goal, only seeing any set back as an outcome, but carry on keeping focused. It may not be the answer you were looking for but nevertheless you have a result that you can interpret in a positive way.

Do not focus on failure but on outcomes or results; that way you are empowered to remain persistent. If you do not get the results you want initially, keep trying until you do.

Achieving anything begins first in the mind

Believe that you can do it first. By adopting this belief, it changes the way you see things. It gives you an empowering way of motivating yourself to achieve what you want. You will not be discouraged by seeing your attempts as failure.

I have always been fascinated by the life of Abraham Lincoln, and have recently seen the movie *Lincoln*, where the President fights to abolish slavery in the United States of America. Lincoln became President of the United States of America at 52 years old, after losing twice in business and being unsuccessful in a political contest; he became overcome by grief, suffered a nervous breakdown, lost two more congressional races, lost a senatorial battle, failed in an attempt to become Vice-President, and lost yet another Senatorial race at the age of 49.

It would be quite understandable if Lincoln had developed a belief that he would never ever be able to qualify to be in business or in politics, let alone, becoming the President of the United States, with a Resume like this!

Now, did Lincoln believe in being persistent? Absolutely!

Did he believe he could? Absolutely he did! Where did that belief start from? In his mind of course! He *believed* he could!

He probably was the first to invent the slogan:

Yes, we can.

Did he believe in himself despite the negative circumstances he found himself in? Absolutely!

Did he allow his circumstances to think of himself as a failure? Never! Did he give up, thinking he was bound to fail again and that there's no point in trying again? Never!

Lincoln showed us how persistency wins in the end and can achieve great things, if you keep focused on your goal and consistently take action towards your goal. But first he had to believe that he could, or else he wouldn't have been able to achieve the Presidency.

Every achievement starts in the mind first! Believe first that you can and your mind will find a way.

So, are you like Lincoln or do you give up when the going gets tough?

What do you do if you can't get what you want? Do you keep trying until you achieve what you want? Or do you give up and think that there's no point?

Now is your time to turn over a new leaf and learn the value of persistency.

Assertiveness

Another skill, apart from persistence, which helps you to get what you want, is that of assertiveness. Often times assertiveness is confused with aggressiveness. To be assertive is to know what you want and to state what you want in a calm and firm manner. It has nothing to do with being aggressive. When you are aggressive you are not being assertive.

It is helpful to know certain techniques to assist us in being assertive when we are being told what we don't want to hear or when we are not taken seriously by others.

In assertiveness training, the *broken record technique* is taught to help people to learn to achieve the result they want.

The broken record technique is a simple skill which entails repeating over and over again in an assertive and relaxed manner, what you want or need, until the other person either gives in or agrees to negotiate with you.

It is even more effective if you use it with a statement of understanding or empathy. This helps the other person to know that you have heard them and have considered their point of view and their feelings.

> *When people feel that they have been heard and that you have considered their feelings, they are more likely to listen to you and are more prepared to negotiate with you.*

It helps to rehearse what you want to say first. It gives you more confidence when you really need to say it.

Be clear and be concise. There's nothing worse than trying to decipher what you are trying to say because your sentences are packed up with irrelevant facts which has nothing to do with the issue that you are trying to discuss. Use a clear, concise sentence which outlines your needs.

Don't waffle or go off at a tangent. Stick to your point.

It helps to be relaxed, and speak clearly.

Breathe! Taking a deep breath is always helpful.

The broken record method can be very effective, but of course, like a lot of techniques, they are helpful but not perfect, as we have no control over other people's reactions. Life is full of a mixture of different personalities; some pretty inflexible and intransigent. There are those who believe that they are never wrong and are entitled. Those who believe they are right at all costs, and will not back down or do not care if anyone else is right. In which case, you may have to negotiate or compromise.

Tips for Negotiating

- Relax. Keep calm.
- Empathize; let the other person know that you have heard them and understood their position. Sometimes people get upset because they do not feel heard.
- Clarify the situation. Ask questions or for the information you need.
- Prepare; make sure you have all the facts and figures you require to support your argument.
- Be clear but concise; don't waffle or confuse the issue with something else.
- Keep to the point. Don't allow yourself to be directed elsewhere. Keep focused on the issue at hand. Use the broken record method. You may have to compromise; if so, offer a reasonable compromise. The other person may even be grateful for it.
- Always aim for a win-win conclusion.

Of course these things often depend on the beliefs and especially on the values of the people you are dealing with. As we talk about beliefs and values, let's see what *values* are and what role they play in our life.

> *The enlightened give thanks for what most people take for granted.*
>
> —*Michael Beckwith*

Notes: What have you learnt?

CHAPTER SEVEN

Secrets About Our Value System And Its Importance

Every sweet has its sour, every evil its good.
—Ralph Waldo Emerson

Our value system is crucial to our quality of life as every decision that we make in life is based on such a system. The nature of our daily experience is subjective to the values that we live our life by. The better our values are the better experience we enjoy and can benefit from.

Like our belief system, our values were placed in us a very long time ago and yet they still have enormous power over us to-day.

> *Like our Belief system, our value system needs constant updating so that we can live our life authentically for the person we are today.*

Our history often dictates our values depending on what kind of past we've had. Similar to our belief system, we inherited a lot of our values, from our parents or carers, peer groups, friends, teachers, clubs, organizations, Television, magazines, the media etc. It is said that by the time a child is three years old that they already have acquired all their values. Consequently, the values that we hold control the decisions that we take. The decisions we take determine, where we end up; in other words, our fate.

The trouble is that we could be making decisions on values that are not completely our own if they are not up to date. We may be making decisions on old-fashioned values that are no longer relevant for the person we have become. These out-of-date values were relevant to us at one point for the person we were then, but may be entirely wrong for who we have grown to be today. Consequently our decision making process becomes complex and conflict with what we value.

Our decisions define who we are, our life choices, our character, the path we choose to follow and ultimately affect the quality of our experience and our future.

Give me the child by the age of seven and I will give you the man.

—The Jesuits

It is important to get to know what your values are as you will then know why you regularly take the decisions that you do. If you do that, your vision becomes clearer and it will greatly enhance your life.

In fact if you keep making the same mistakes in your life, it may have a lot to do with your value system.

> *Your values in turn affect your behaviour. Identifying your values makes it easy for you to understand the rationale behind your behaviour.*

When you understand your values better, making decisions become easier and simpler. Some people make poor decisions because they are uncertain about what their true values are. It can be that you make decisions on whatever the trend is at the time or on what your friends suggest which can be contradictory to your true values. Consequently you remain discontented with a lot of the outcomes that you are getting, but don't understand why it is so.

When I ask some of my clients what their values are, they first of all look puzzled and they often struggle, because they are not consciously aware of what their principles or standards are, or what is behind their decision-making process. Most of them have never stopped to think what kind of attributes that they hold dear to them. Hence that's why many have problems making the right decisions for them, often are between two minds and make the wrong decisions for their lives.

Our values control our lives and our choices. Ultimately our values control where we end up.

In other words they control our future and what is called our destiny. They control the decisions which lead us to choose the paths that we take in life.

For us to be able to have equilibrium and live in harmony with ourselves, we must live by our values, even when the going gets tough and we find living challenging.

If we go against our values and our beliefs, those are the times when we struggle with inner conflict and find ourselves in difficult life situations, maybe suffering from guilt or resentment. We become confused because we feel pulled in different directions; our decision-making process becomes problematical, our boundaries become blurred and we are indecisive in making the right decisions for us.

Our value system guides us to take certain actions on *a regular basis*.

The results that we enjoy in our life to-day are the products of the consistent actions we took in the past. It is the decisions that we take over and over again which produce the results we have in our life to-day.

For example: If your morals are a bit dubious, and you end up in prison to-day as a result, it is because you have acted dishonestly on a consistent basis in the past.

If you have poor work ethics, you won't get up every morning come rain or shine to go to work. You will find any excuse to take a *sicky*. But if you value work and if you have good work ethics you will without fail wake up every morning and get yourself ready to go to work, whatever the weather, even when you don't feel like it. It may be that you would rather snuggle up in bed and have a lay-in instead; especially when it's cold and rainy, or when you're tired or when you don't like your work situation; even then, you would still get up and go to work, because of your ethical work values. According to your values you, regularly, will or will not get up to go to work.

As with our beliefs, our values were shaped when we were children.

It is worth repeating that every decision we take is based on our values and are influenced by our beliefs; bearing in mind that we may not even have deliberately chosen what these values are ourselves. You may be making decisions on values that other people laid down for you a long time ago, and you may not even be consciously aware of what these values really are.

It is amazing that we can even make some good decisions, when we don't know what we value. Is it any wonder that we make the wrong decisions sometimes? When we are not clear of our values, the decisions we make can be very hit or miss.

It is impossible to live by our values if we don't know what they are.

So, What Do We Mean By Values?

You value things that are important to you.

Anything that you hold dear to you is a value.

For example, some people value relationships, children, family, honesty, integrity, marriage, compassion, love, kindness, caring, or security, whereas some others value, education, money, freedom, adventure, hard work, success, contribution, pleasure and friends, as an example of values.

> **There are no right values and there are no wrong values.**

They are your personal preferences, based on your past experiences, how you were brought up, what kind of parents you had, the education and the influences you've had in your life.

As we are all unique individuals, our values are unique to us.

It is important for you to know what your values are. If you know what your top 10 values are in order of importance, it helps you to understand why you make certain decisions and why you do what you do. Some of values are more important to us than others.

Exercise To Discover Your Values

- Make a list of your 10 values which are more important to you than others: E.g. contribution, security, relationships, honesty, family, children, friends, freedom, love, integrity, trustworthiness, reliability, caring, kindness, adventure, money, hard work, education, pleasure, loyalty etc. etc.

- Now prioritize them. Write them in order of importance to you. Put the values that are most important to you in descending order 1-10. When you've done that, revise them again, making sure that your number one value is really the number one, nothing else is as important as that; then number two, then number three and so on.
- Write them on a flashcard in order of importance and put it in a place where you can see them every day. That way you can live these up-to-date values every day.

Keep your values at the forefront of your mind, and it will become easier for you to make future decisions.

Anytime you find it difficult to make a decision, it is because you are unsure of your true values.

May be your confidence level is low and you allow yourself to get swayed by other people's values; deep down they are not your true values. This is why you are never fully satisfied with the results you get, because you are acting on what someone else values, instead of being true to yourself.

Why do we need to know the order of our top values?

It is important to know the pecking order of our values, because they control the way we make decisions. That is we need to know our highest value first, then the second and the third and so on; otherwise we may make decisions that may meet some of our values but because they are not our top values we may not be fully satisfied with our decision, or it may be in conflict with another value that we hold dear to us, which can cause confusion or indecision. When we know what values we hold dear in priority, decision-making becomes easier and clearer, because we become consciously aware of what is most important to us.

Conflicting Values

Conflicting values are often the reason for disagreements. When our values are conflicting, they can cause us pain and confusion, and leave us feeling unsure and insecure. For instance, we may value freedom and adventure, but we may also value security and money highly. So, now we have a conflict! For example: Do we sell everything and go travelling (freedom and adventure) or do we buy a house and stay in our secure job and save the money (security and money)?

We may value security, so we may want to buy a house to feel secure that we won't end up without a roof over our heads; however, we also value freedom, which may mean that we may not want to be tied down by a mortgage. Now, this gives us a bit of a decision-making problem!

On the other hand, if you discover, that security is your number one value and freedom is your number nine value; it clarifies things for you, in that you will be living your highest value by buying the house as security rates far more than freedom. Your decision process becomes much easier to make.

Many of us have conflicting values, again because we didn't consciously decide on them ourselves at the beginning. We've allowed other people and our environment to influence us, however, it is never too late for us to change our values and upgrade them to better values.

Our values need to be updated regularly to make sure that we are living what we truly believe in for the person we have become.

We may have valued adventure when we were young, but as a more mature person we may value security more. Unless we update our values, this can cause confusion and insecurity. Some values may be appropriate for a certain time in our life, but when our circumstance change we may need to see whether these values still apply to-day as they once did.

For example: If your top value was to go clubbing with friends, drinking till all hours, dance all night and sleep all day at one point in your life, it doesn't mean that you would still value those to the same extent when you have children.

And if you do?—Now may be the right time to rethink these values!

Role Models

It is always helpful to look at people whom you admire, and who have achieved what you want to achieve in life. Use them as role models. (They've been there, done that!)

Think: *What would their values have had to be to achieve what they have?*

What would they have to value in order to do what they do?

These are the values that you need to move towards, if you want to achieve the same goals.

By the same token, there are some negative values that we may want to shed. There are some values that we hold that clearly cause us pain, such as anger, rejection, envy, jealousy, guilt, depression, procrastination, frustration, or humiliation.

You know by now that we are all pleasure-seeking beings; our philosophy is *to avoid pain and to seek pleasure*. However, sometimes it becomes much more important for us to avoid pain than to seek pleasure.

If we know that we would do anything to avoid feeling some specific emotions, then we can work out what our behaviour would be like in any given situation.

For instance, if we do not want to be humiliated, we would make sure that we behave in such a way to make sure that we steer clear of being humiliated.

To recap:

First, we need to gain an awareness of what our current values are in order of priority, so that we can understand why we do what we do.

Then, we have to make a conscious decision about what values we want to live by, what values we want to move towards and what values we want to move away from, in order to live the quality life that we desire.

Next we need to stay true to our values and live by them every day.

When couples or friends disagree it is often mainly because their values are in conflict.

> *If you find yourself in constant conflict with your life partner, or with a certain friend, it may be because the main values that you both hold dear to each of you clash.*

If one partner values money above all else and the other partner's values are about family, friends, caring, kindness, empathy, compassion, loyalty or integrity. There will be conflict. Not to say that if you value money, you can't value, family, friends, kindness, caring, empathy, compassion etc. or that valuing money is wrong. With values there are no right or wrong values. It is completely individual, however, if your main values are contradictory to your partner's main values, conflict will exist and you may not understand why each of you behave the way you do.

If money is your top value, and money doesn't figure on your partner's list and you will do anything to acquire it or save it, but, your partner does not understand why you are doing what you are doing or may not see the point of it, you will have conflict.

On the other hand, if both your top value is money, then, it may be a marriage made in heaven or in the bank, because you will both understand why each other put money first before anything else.

You may be working all hours when your wife is at home looking after the children and wanting you to be home at a time when you can give your children some quality time, as this is what is important to her. If your top value is to make as much money as you can, albeit that you justify it by being a good provider; but, your wife would be happy living in a mud hut, providing you give her and your children some quality time and show them love, you will both be battling with your values almost every night when you get home, and your poor children will be the ones paying the price for your clash of values.

This is the sort of thing that causes conflict, because neither party understands where the other is coming from. Neither of you understand each other's values and comprehend that your values are at the base of your conflict. Neither of you isn't just being difficult or nasty. You are both equally angry or outraged with each other and feeling completely justified in how you feel.

If you cannot see each other's point of view, then it is almost impossible to be able to compromise to keep each other happy.

On the other hand, if you do identify your top values, you may understand each other and find a way of reconciliating your differences, as well as respecting each other. It helps both of you to understand why you do what you do. If you are both aware of each other's top values, you can understand rather than get angry and think that the other doesn't care or is deliberately doing things to upset you. You are more prepared to compromise and find a solution rather than getting hooked up in your feelings.

This is a scenario I often come across with some clients. The man may feel aggrieved that he is working long hours to provide for his family as money is his first priority and family next; whereas, the woman will feel that it is much more important for her to see her husband and that the father should have a good relationship with his children and that the children should be enjoying some special time with their father, even if it means that she has less money. Neither one is right or wrong; it all depends what you value more in life. If you are in a relationship it just helps you to understand one another to identify and understand both your values and to work towards a solution for you both. You can both find a way of compromising but respecting each other's values all the same.

> **If we change our values, everything changes; our life changes too.**

For instance if we valued clubbing all night once, we now change our value to children and family values which then puts children and family first; our life will change as there will no longer be any *dance all night and sleep all day*, as there are now little mouths to be fed and needs to be taken care of.

Yet, we have to remember that we are not just our values; we are much more than that. Our intelligence has nothing to do with our values. The choices we make do not depend on how clever we are. Our choices depend on our values. Remember, as I've said before, most of our values were initially not consciously picked by us but by other people. That is the reason why they need regular updating.

Our values need to be our own conscious personal choices, not other people's leftovers.

Like the husband who values money above all else, may have come from a family where the value of money mattered above all else. Money is the currency that gave them importance in the family and in their social world. That's what he learnt: money is everything. If you have money, you have everything. You were someone important because you have money.

Or the father may not have been someone important because he had no money, but wished he could have had; therefore put that value in his son for him to be someone of importance one day by acquiring money above all else. As far as they are concerned to value yourself, to be somebody you "have" to have money. Sadly it is representing your self-worth by the amount of money you have!

He who is contented is rich.

—*Lao Tzu*

When you have conflicting values which affect your relationships it helps to move away from some of the values that are creating confusion in your life and move towards more positive values, for instance, such as joy, cheerfulness, optimism, enthusiasm, integrity, honesty, love, passion, health, and gratitude to enhance the quality of your life.

A lot of your values are the result of our conditioning when we were growing up, but they may very well be out of date for the person we have become today.

Time has come to update these values!

For example, if you choose to add joy and optimism to your values and decide that whatever happens to you, everyday you will stay faithful to those values. Okay, some of the time you may fail to feel joyful or optimistic, don't beat yourself over it; but if you try hard and make the effort to live these values every single day, can you imagine how this will change how you feel on an everyday basis? Instead of feeling low and moody, can you imagine how good you will feel?

Whatever comes your way choose to react with joy and optimism! The law of Reciprocity will dictate that other people will react to you in the same way and your joy and optimism becomes contagious! Try it! You'll see what happens! People will start seeking you out and you will become popular, as you spread a lot of joy and optimism in the world.

I have a colleague, who whenever you see her, her beaming smile and positive and optimistic demeanour immediately lifts you up. *Yes! It's you, Lisa!* No need to say that everyone is always happy to see her as she is a breath of fresh air. As she gets such positive feedback, she will continue to be this ray of sunshine to others and pleasantly work her magic on others.

Conditioning

Pavlov was a Russian scientist who did some experiments on dogs. Every time he fed his dogs, he would ring a bell. So the dogs knew that if they heard the bell that they would be fed. After a little while they started to salivate at the sound of the bell expecting that they would soon be fed. But the naughty Pavlov then decided to ring the bell without feeding them. So when the dogs heard the bell they would salivate even though they weren't being fed. The dogs had been conditioned to expect food when they heard the sound of the bell; they would then salivate when they heard the bell even though they were not being fed. This kind of process is called conditioning.

The same thing happens to us. When we were babies we got picked up when we cried; then as we got a bit bigger, our parents or carers rewarded us when we made them happy and punished us if we did something that they didn't approve of. We very quickly caught on to know what they liked and what they disliked. So we became conditioned to their likes and dislikes, just like Pavlov's dogs. The only problem is that our parents and carers are human beings who just did the best they knew how; however sometimes their best may not be the best for the person we are today.

> *As with your values the time is now to question your conditioning.*

What you need to ask yourself is:
- What values do I need so that I can plan the life that I want?
- What other values do I need to add to my values to be or have what I actually want?
- What values do I need to get rid of, for me to have the life that I really want?

Worry

> *Instead of worrying what other people say of you, why not spend time trying to accomplish something they will admire.*
>
> —*Dale Carnegie*

There are other values that even though we don't hold them dear to us, they can become part of our lives and have a negative influence on us. These are the kind of values, such as worry that we need to distance ourselves from.

Sorry to say, when we have a problem, what do we do? We worry! Now we have two problems instead of one! First the real problem; next the worry it causes! But the thing with worry is that it has a ghastly habit of interfering with our ability to think clearly.

Unless we can think clearly, we are unable to make the right synaptic connections in our brain. Worry interferes with our neurons and as such we make weak connections, which can easily be gobbled up by our Glial cells. The result being that we forget things or see things in a distorted way. This in itself can be a problem!

Worry only serves in blinding us and stopping us from thinking creatively and resourcefully. It can be so overwhelming that it overrides our rational mind. Worry causes us to be anxious and only helps to confuse us, keep us stuck, paralyzes us into inaction and makes us unresourceful.

The problem with worry is that we often react to worry in a familial pattern. If you have highly-strung parents, who are constantly stressed, chances are that they have passed that legacy onto you. Worry causes anxiety, which then can get passed down from generation to generation, which eventually becomes a way of life. It honestly doesn't have to be that way!

> *What worries you, masters you.*
>
> —*Haddon W. Robinson*

Remember: *We do get more of what we focus on! Whatever we focus on becomes bigger and stronger!*

Focusing on our worries only lead us to more unresourceful states.

Exercise To Live Your Values:

Now that you have written down your values in order of importance:

- Get to know your values thoroughly.
- Learn the values you want to get rid of.
- Learn the values that you want to adopt.
- Keep them within your line of vision whenever possible on a flashcard at home, in the office, where you can constantly and clearly see them, so that you can consciously live your values. You can put another card in your handbag, on your desk or in your car as a constant reminder.

If other members of your family or friends become aware of your cards, they will also act as a reminder and remind you to live by your values; or you can tell a friend or someone close to you what values you are trying to add to your repertoire, and what values you are trying to get rid of, so that they can act as a reminder to you when you slip up. If worry is one of the values you are trying to steer away from, others will act as a gentle aide memoire when you forget it.

If you commit to your new values and discard the old ones you've inherited (if they are no longer useful), you can use these as your new guide on which every decision that you make will be based on. If you do this, day in, day out, it will become second nature to you.

Whatever you do consecutively for seven days becomes a habit after that.

> **We are what we do repeatedly.**
>
> *—Aristotle*

When you become aware of your values and live by them, making the right decisions for you will no longer be a quandary, it will become a piece of cake!

Now that you understand what helps you to make the decisions you take on a consistent basis, let's look at how your self-image affects you.

> **Blessed is he who has learned to admire but not envy, to follow but not imitate, to praise but not flatter, and to lead but not manipulate.**
>
> *—William Arthur Ward*

Notes: What have you learnt?

CHAPTER EIGHT

Some Secrets About Our Self-Image

Feeling good about you is the key to success and happiness.
—Anne Hartley

Our self-image is how we see ourselves in our own mind's eye. It is how we talk about ourselves and how we describe ourselves. It is who we truly believe we are and what we imagine we are; in other words our self-image is our version of the kind of person we believe we are in our own eyes. It is the opinion we have of ourselves. It may not be reality per se, but it is who *we* believe we are.

People often say things like: *I'm not that sort of person* or *That's what I'm like*; *That's what I do*; what they are talking about is that's how they see themselves, not necessarily how they truly are; they are talking about the image they have of themselves in their mind's eye, and who they believe they are, and the opinion they hold of themselves. I'm not that sort of person means that they see themselves or their self-image differently in their own mind's eyes.

Whatever you think about yourself comes out in whatever comes out of your mouth. So, beware! When you speak, your words represent what and who you believe you are.

Your self-image is reflected in whatever you do and in whatever you believe in. It also affects how you feel at any given moment. In other words your self-image influences what you say including your behaviour, your beliefs and the way you feel.

> **Your outer world reflects your inner world as your inner world mirrors your outer world.**

Simply put: The world as you experience it is simply a representation of what is going on inside of you. Whatever you see on the outside is mirrored on the inside and vice versa.

If you look good and feel good, it will show in your appearance and in how you behave. If you feel bad, that too will be apparent to the outside world.

Whatever is going on the inside is reflected on the outside. Whatever you have inside your heart will reach the outside through your words and your actions.

Whatever you believe in, you find ways of justifying and supporting that belief to prove yourself right. Remember, our subconscious's job is to prove itself right.

For example if you believe that you are a failure, you will search for evidence to prove this: such as something a teacher once said to you, criticisms from others, family or work colleagues reminding you that you are not achieving your goals; comparing what you have in comparison with your friends and having a feeling of being inferior. You may use self-sabotaging behaviours to confirm your self-image of failure.

On the other hand, you ignore, and do not notice or make very little of the successes you've had or the compliments that are paid to you when you've done well or achieved something important.

In other words you emphasize your weaknesses and make little of any success that you do have. When you have a poor self-image you highlight the negatives and make little of the positives.

The reason why your self-image is important is that your behaviour is always in sync with your self-image. Consequently, you behave in such a way as to be congruent with what you believe your self-image and your inner world is like.

> *If you believe you are a failure, you act as a failure. If you believe you are a success, you also act as a success. You will behave according to what you believe your self-image is.*

Your self-image tells you how to behave and how you should act or react over and over again, in fact all the time; this keeps us in harmonization with the kind of person we believe we are. Unfortunately many of us are unaware of the importance of our self-image and the reflection it has on others.

How we think about ourselves affects how other people think about us and treat us.

You cannot be lonely, if you like the person you're alone with.

—*Wayne Dyer*

Sometimes parents are conflicting in the messages they give us as children. Mums and Dads may give different conflicting messages from each other. This is common; however this can be the cause of many children's and adults' confusion and insecurity.

It is good to know what triggered the way we feel by understanding our past; however, we don't want to dwell on the past too much or live there! Have your *Ah, hah* moment and let's move on!

Don't get stuck there, and give in to the negative feelings and please no pity party!

> *Focusing on the past stops us from moving forward.*

Our focus needs to be on the present and the future, to help us change our life and to help us reach our full potential. Understanding the past is helpful, but we mustn't linger there.

Exercise to discover where your self-image comes from

Think of 5 things that you learnt about yourself when you were a child, by the people who most influenced you as you were growing up.

For example:

Finish the sentences

From my mother I learnt that I........
From my father I learnt that I........
From my siblings I learnt that I........
From my teacher I learnt that I........
From my friends I learnt that I........

You may find that you repeat some of your answers. That's okay! But it will show you where the limiting beliefs that you have about yourself to-day came from and where your self-image sprung from. You may discover that some of these may be the reason why you are stuck to-day.

When you have finished this exercise, what you believe about yourself and where your limiting beliefs come from will become more obvious to you. This is about understanding, not about blame.

Understanding the origins of your self-image helps you to be able to shed some of your limiting beliefs for better ones.

Exercise

Friends are useful. We all need a good friend in life. It can be quite helpful if you can find a good friend who has a good listening ear to talk these things through with. You can ask them to inspire you to write down ways of how you can change some aspects of your self-image. Brain storm together. The good thing about involving a good friend is if they are involved they can help you to keep to your new resolutions too.

Now write a statement about the person that you want and choose to be from now on, and make a commitment to being that person from this day on and adopt your new self-image straight away.

Write it on a sheet of paper: From today (date) I choose to .... and you can sign and date it, just as if you are making a contract with yourself. You can get your friend to sign it as a witness and date it.

Now, keep it safe. This self contract will be a reminder that you need to fulfill your contract to yourself, and can be the catalyst in your change in behaviour.

Respect

If you do not show respect for yourself, others will not respect you either. On the other hand, if you treat yourself with respect, others will do so too.

People treat you the way you treat yourself. Treating yourself with respect demonstrates good self-esteem. Good self-esteem means good self-image. Our self-image isn't only about our behaviour it is also about what we say about ourselves.

We need to be genuine in what we say. To be congruent we need to mean what we say and say what we mean. What we say must match our body language. If we don't believe what we say, our body language will betray us; how are others supposed to believe us, if we don't believe what we are saying ourselves?

Whatever the situation, we always end up settling for what we think we're worth—No one will abuse us more than our own critical little inner voice. If we abuse ourselves even just in our thoughts, others will do so too, as our inside world reflects our outside world and vice versa. It is essential that we have power over that critical voice inside our head. No matter how many material things we have or how handsome or beautiful we are, it will never fill the gap if we don't like ourselves on the inside.

> *We need to do all we can to love ourselves first, before we can show love to others.*
> *We cannot give to others what we don't have ourselves.*

What Causes A Low Self-Image?

Research tells us that criticism is the main cause of low self-image. Growing up with criticism, gives us a very negative vision of the world. It makes us feel inferior and less than. We never feel good enough and worth it. Criticism eats away at our self-esteem. We notice the bad before we can see the good; we notice what's wrong before we can notice the amazing good there is. In a world where whatever we do or say is criticized, we learn not to trust and we end up with low self-esteem, poor self-worth and we are left feeling insecure as a result.

The tragedy that follows this scenario is that it doesn't only affect us when we are children; we grow up still feeling inferior and less than; never really being good enough and we really believe that we are not worth it. The problem is that these things do not improve as we grow up, they only get worse. We learn to distrust and blame as adults and too many end up hostile because of it. The misfortune is that it doesn't only affect how we feel, but it also affects our decisions and our behaviour and eventually where we end up in life. We learn not to put our trust in others and as far as we are concerned the world is a scary world out there.

What Can We Do To Raise Our Self-Image?

If we want to be a gymnast, we need to exercise and practice the sport on a very regular basis. If we want to be a great dancer, we need to learn to dance and put in the practice. If we want to be a great swimmer, we have to learn how to swim and put in the hard yards. All this doesn't happen overnight; it takes years to become expert at it. It is the same if we want to be good at anything: we have to learn and practice until we get good at it. It is the same with everything else in life. If you want a good memory, you do practical memory exercises to get better and better at remembering things. There is no quick fix! If there is one, you may well find that there is a catch somewhere.

If you want good self-esteem, it takes time and practice. It starts with loving yourself for who you are.

It is important to practice some exercises to raise your own self-esteem regularly like reminding yourself of what you have or can achieve; what good qualities you enjoy; what talents and gifts you are blessed with; what inner resources you possess; what you are good at, what you do to contribute to others etc.

> *Look to yourself to improve your self-esteem, not to others. Don't expect other people to take responsibility for your self-esteem. That's your job no matter how old you are!*

There is nothing like contributing towards others and doing something for someone else to help raise our self-esteem. Sometimes we are so concentrated on ourselves and fixated on our problems to think about other people. Getting out of our comfort zone and helping someone else, will go a long way in raising our self-esteem.

Some of you may be saying that you have enough troubles of your own to complicate your life with somebody else's problems. But I'm telling you, it is precisely when you have some issues that are engulfing you that you must stretch yourself and reach out to others and help someone else. Suddenly your problems will not appear so huge; your thinking will become clearer and your solutions that you couldn't think of before, will come to you; meanwhile you would be feeling great with yourself and would have really raised your own self-esteem. In fact the person shouldn't be thanking you; you should thank them!

Exercise To Raise Your Self-Esteem:

- Think about helping someone else or doing something for someone where you stand to reap absolutely *zilch* from them; there are always plenty of people less fortunate than you.
- Do some random act of kindness, for example help someone by giving them change to pay for their parking, or help to put your elderly neighbour's dustbins out for collection or you can offer to pay the fare of the car behind you on a toll road or give your time to someone who doesn't have many people in their life.
- Become a volunteer if you have any spare time for a worthwhile cause, for example, like the Red Cross, Mission Australia, Salvation Army, or become more active in your church or your sports club.

This is a great exercise in raising your self-esteem.

The duty of helping one's self in the highest sense involves helping one's neighbours.

—*Samuel Smiles*

Exercise To Get To Know Your Personal Gifts And Talents

- Make a list of all your qualities, gifts and talents; don't be humble here. This is a time when you can freely boast about yourself. Write about you as if you are a proud mother or father who wants to brag about their son or daughter to your friends.

Make a list of all your inner resources; for example: intelligent, resourceful, great organizational skills etc.

Now write a statement about all the qualities, gifts, talents and resources that you possess.

Write it down on a flash card, commit it to memory and keep it handy where you can see it every day as a reminder of the terrific person you are.

What you practice you become

Exercise to raise your self-esteem:

Think of 3 incidents in your life that have greatly impacted your life, where you had to use your inner resources and make new decisions.

Write down all the qualities and resources that you used at each occasion.

Again please do not be modest; write down every single quality or resource that you used, even the ones that you think do not matter much and that everyone else would have done it.

Again write as if you want to boast about someone you love very much (you) to their new boss. Tell him how much you think of her and what amazing talents and qualities she possesses, and what an asset she would be to him and his company.

Then write them on a flashcard and memorize them.

This is who you are! This is your new self-image.

Keep it at the forefront of your mind always and read it regularly to remind yourself every day of how many talents, qualities and resources that you indeed possess and what an amazing person you really are.

> **You need to look inside of you for what you need. All your resources are already inside of you.**

All you have to do is to reach out and grab them. They are there waiting for you to use them.

So, what exactly is Self-Esteem?

Our self-esteem depends on the thoughts that we have about ourselves! Yes! Our Self-esteem is the thoughts that we choose to think about us in our heads.

If you think good thoughts about you, you have good self-esteem.

If you think bad thoughts about who you are, then you have low self-esteem.

If those thoughts are not what you want to hear, it is definitely time to modify these thoughts. It is your responsibility to develop your own self-esteem; it is no one else's. So, it's no good just saying that you suffer with low self-esteem; it just means that you haven't taken good care of yourself. It is up to you to do something about it. You need to be proactive, to grow and mature, and work on yourself until you can feel good about yourself.

It's no good saying that you have a low self-esteem because you had a difficult childhood. If that is the case, you couldn't help what happened to you as a child, but as an adult today, you can choose to change it and make a difference and choose a quality life.

No one is born with low self-esteem. That is something you acquired as you were growing up. However, as an adult you can work on yourself to reverse that situation. It is pointless accepting the status quo, as you will never be able to get on and live a quality life otherwise.

I repeat: you already have all the resources you need inside of you. You need to believe this. You just have to reach out and take them. These are your God-given gifts at birth, and no one has the power to take them away from you, unless you let them. By the same token you have no right to neglect them or belittle them either!

You are as good as the next person and you matter just as much! You have been given the gift of imagination; use it.

Your job is to treasure your self-esteem and keep that *self-esteem tank* topped up all the time. Low-self-esteem isn't a mortal sin or disease; however, it makes you feel pretty lousy, saps your energy and demotivates you. It can make you make some dreadful choices in life because of it; consequently it can affect the path of your life; there is plenty you can do to help yourself.

It is not a virtue to keep your self-esteem low under the pretext that you are humble! That is not humility! That is stupidity! It starts with changing your thoughts and the meaning you give to things. In other words reframe what meaning you have given to certain events or life experiences about you and give them a new empowering meaning.

Reframing

To reframe is to change the meaning we have given to something. By re-framing the negative feelings you have about yourself into positive meanings about you, you can make a huge difference to the way you feel about you. To reframe something we need to change the meaning we once gave it, into a more acceptable positive reality for us. This takes awareness and practice.

You do have some awareness when you are feeling negative about yourself, because you do know when you don't feel good.

Exercise to help you reframe

- If for every negative thought that you become aware of, you search for a different meaning and do your best to change it into something that does not cause you to feel unresourceful, you will feel more positive and will be able to raise your self-esteem considerably. The result will be that you will be able to change how you feel about you for the better.

Remember, with every thought there is a physiological reaction. Your thoughts have the magical power of changing your biochemistry and alter how you feel. You will reflect those feelings in your mind and body. When your thoughts are negative you are unresourceful and you are building bad hormones in your body, but when your thoughts are positive, you are resourceful and building feel-good hormones in your body.

- Write your resourceful thoughts down, so that they stay in your mind and you can keep them in your awareness.
- Write and repeat positive affirmations about who you are everyday. And as you look at them, and take them through your eyes, and through repeating them with intention and discipline every day, you will start to believe what you are saying and what you are reading. Your subconscious takes it in and it becomes your new belief.
- You need to do this on a regular basis, for it to stick with you.

It takes discipline and it takes practice, conviction and certainly commitment to do this. You have to commit to doing this everyday consistently, for it to become a new habit. It raises your self-esteem, your self-worth and your self-image, and you will soon be able to act according to who you believe you are now and your life gradually starts to change.

If we understand our self-image, it helps us to understand ourselves; however, it is essential to understand that our belief and value system, as well as our self-image form part of our own **self-imposed laws or rules** which ultimately govern our life and determine our future.

We should try to be the parents of our future rather than the offspring of our past.
—*Miguel de Unamuno*

Notes: What have you learnt?

CHAPTER NINE

Secrets About Our Own Self-Imposed Set of Laws or Personal Rules

The Stone Age did not end because we ran out of stones. It ended
because it was time for a re-think about how we live.
—William Mc Donaugh

Now that you understand how our belief and value system were set up, including our self-image, it is important for us to realize that out of all of these we create our own rules or set of self-imposed laws. These are our personal set of laws or rules which manage our lives, and by which we live by.

Our own self-imposed set of laws or personal rules can liberate us, give us power or keep us locked in a prison of our own making for very many years. We all have some unconscious and conscious self-imposed set of laws or rules by which we live our lives. These rules control our lives often without our own conscious knowledge of them. Everyone you know, including yourself live by their rules or their own self-imposed set of laws. They affect all our lives.

Even though these rules are unwritten rules, they are our personal rules and they are nevertheless, as far as we are concerned set in stone and we obey them as we are slaves to them. We fully believe and live our lives being at the mercy of these rules.

If anyone violates or infringes our self-imposed set of laws or rules, we can get really offended, and that offender can even be us. These same set of laws that we live our lives by are very often behind much of the conflict we have with others. They are not necessarily full of common sense or even make sense sometimes but these rules are personal to each one of us. Like our beliefs and our values they are unique to us and equally there are no right rules or wrong rules or set of laws as we are unique individuals.

When you have a hard time forgiving someone, including yourself, you may find that under the hurt you feel, is a self-imposed unwritten rule that stops you. If forgiveness didn't come easily as you were growing up, you may well have taken it on board and as a result find it hard to forgive others including yourself. Those unwritten rules guide us about how we believe life should be; when either we or others don't abide by our set of laws, we can feel outraged, hurt, upset, disgusted or disappointed.

Different people have different rules according to the way they were brought up, their beliefs and values, their past life experiences and the influences in their lives.

We have rules about all sorts of things, for example about what we think we need to makes us happy, and what we think makes us sad; what gives us pain and what gives us pleasure, how we should bring up our children and what we expect in our relationships. Our rules also dictate what makes us experience other emotions such as anger, sadness, frustration or disappointment. In fact we have a rule about every emotion we experience.

Our reality is experienced by each of us individually; however, our reality is influenced by our beliefs and values, which control our experience of life. These unconsciously contribute to form our private set of laws or personal rules. In turn they influence our behaviour and our actions.

> *It is crucial to understand our own personal rules and where they stem from, as they in fact guide how we feel, how we behave and what we do and ultimately they predict our fate.*

These set of laws or personal rules we end up living our lives by, are the result of our life experiences, including our belief and value systems. We live by our own self-imposed rules because they help us to live a congruent life; otherwise we would be in permanent conflict with ourselves. Remember: our subconscious needs to be congruent with what we think, if not there will be inner conflict and we will not be congruent, resulting in inner turmoil.

What Does Happiness Depend On?

Some people believe that our happiness depends upon what someone else does; and if we're unhappy, that too is down to someone else. Unfortunately too many do believe that's how life works; but sadly that belief always end up with people struggling with lots of conflicts in their lives.

> *When your happiness depends on someone, it means that you are not in control of your feelings and of your life.*

A client told me that she had a big *ah hah* moment recently. She had been telling her partner what her needs were for her to be happy. This had caused a lot of conflict in the relationship. But suddenly, a light bulb lit up over her head! And she realized that it wasn't her partner's job to make her happy. That was her job! (Yes! Yes! She's got it!) However, they both can work together to help meet each other's emotional needs, as they are in a relationship. Well done! The penny finally dropped!

Important life's secret to memorize:

> *We are in control of our own happiness.*

We cannot allow our happiness to be in the control of someone else's whim. It is one of our powers to be able to choose how we feel. No one else controls whether we are happy or sad. That's our choice!

Others can try to make our life easier and more pleasant but they are not in charge of our happiness. It is not their job to make us happy. When we are happy we are choosing to feel happy, because we are following our rules that tell us that we should be happy when our personal criteria for happiness is met. It is not the responsibility of someone else to make us happy. Our happiness is our job; by the same token if we are unhappy it is no one else's responsibility but our own.

However, because we do have mirror neurons, we can be influenced by someone else's mood. Our mirror neurons can fire at the same time as theirs. The answer to this is to avoid being in the presence of an unhappy camper for a long time. It is best to do it in short bursts, and if you find that you are being negatively influenced, you need to change what you're doing and do something different.

In French, there is a little saying which says:

Qui s'assemble, se ressemble!

I believe the English translation is: *Birds of a feather flock together.*

So, if the mood of the flock isn't a happy one, try not to be around them too much or if the flock is doing something that goes against your personal rules, find another flock to hang out with.

We all hold different beliefs according to our individual rules. We all have our own personal criteria about what has to happen in any situation, so that we can feel happy.

The truth is that nothing has to happen in order for us to feel happy or sad. We always choose how we want to feel as we are in control of our emotions. We have some unwritten rule that says that when ". . . ." happens, and then we will feel happy. So when ". . . ." happens, we decide to release our happy hormones to make us feel good, as our criteria has been met! This criteria is made up of our personal rule.

Difficult concept to grasp, I know! But that's part of the rich tapestry of life.

We can all choose to feel good at any time for no reason at all. We just need to give an empowering meaning to any experience or event and it changes how we feel immediately.

Exercise To Help You Feel Good

- Now close your eyes and imagine as vividly as you can, that something really good is going to happen to you. Whatever your secret desire may be! To some it may mean winning the lottery; to others, it may mean that your prodigal son has returned home; to others it may mean something that you have been wishing for has finally materialized for you, then again to others it may mean being restored to good health.

- Go inside . . . . now deeper . . . . even deeper still . . . let go of everything that comes into your mind; don't attach yourself to any thought, just repeat let go . . . . think of the layers of the sea . . . . the top layer is full of movements . . . . the next layer is calmer, not so much movements going on . . . . then, you reach the third layer further down, where everything is completely calm. It's just like our brain, when we are consciously aware and active there are a lot of movements going on, but when we are relaxed, everything becomes still and calmer. Just stay there where it's calm and let your mind rest a while.

- Now think about what you would like to happen for you.
- Really believe that it is actually happening for you.
- Really visualize that this thing is happening and start to experience the feelings of joy that it brings to you. Feel that joy in your being; experience the physical sensation of that joy.
- See what you can see; hear what you can hear; feel what you can feel.
- Now make the colours of what you see brighter.
- Make things bigger, closer, and more colourful.
- Hear what you are hearing louder; if you can hear music hear it louder. Now increase the intensity of the wonderful feelings that you are experiencing and the joy of getting what you really want.
- Now intensify these feelings. Increase their intensity. Feel the incredible joy that comes with what is happening. Let your facial expression reflect your deep feelings. Feel any lines you may have smooth out, even the corners of your mouth go up.
- Let these feelings wash over your whole body, from the tip of your toes to the top of your head; and back again. Really feel these feelings in your nervous system.
- Magnify these feelings.
- Now, you are feeling really good. Hang on to these feelings in you as long as you can. Decide that you will not let anything spoil your intense feelings of joy.

And whenever you want to feel good like this again, you now know what to do.

When you are ready . . . . climb back from the third layer . . . . up to the second . . . . now you're up again. Open your eyes, keeping hold of these good feelings in your body and mind.

Now if you have done this exercise you will see that you managed to control your feelings. You did this exercise using your imagination that's all. You chose to feel good. Nothing else has changed otherwise. Yet, you were able to experience happy feelings of joy, just by imagining that something good that you really wanted was happening to you. In fact when you did this you were choosing to feel these feelings—therefore you were able to control how you felt; in other words you could control your emotional state.

This shows that you do have power over how you feel! You are in control of your emotions.

In the exercise you were able to decide how you wanted to feel; therefore you can do it at other times when you are feeling unresourceful or if you want to experience feeling good.

In 2010 there was a rock concert in Hyde Park, London, and Sir Paul Mac Cartney did his usual magic when singing Hey Jude; he got the guys singing nah, nah, nah, nah, nah, nah, nah; then the girls, then everyone together; everyone was very happy, laughing and singing heartily. They carried on Nah, nah, nah, nah, nah, nah for what seemed hours and hours. Yet what was happening was that everyone there was controlling their feelings; they chose to bring on these happy feelings. Their mirror neurons were having a field day!

The fact that everyone seemed happy doesn't mean that there were no miserable or no depressed people, in that concert; but it means that for those moments whilst the concert was on, the miserable or depressed people who also attended chose how they were feeling, and allowed themselves to release good hormones for them to feel good and happy. They chose to allow Sir Paul Mc Cartney to bring them joy, or even go back to some great memories from the past to make them feel good. The people loved it, swinging with the crowds, enjoying the concert and the atmosphere coming from hundreds and thousands of strangers that suddenly were united by their love of the music.

They have a rule that says that if you are at a rock concert, and you hear one of your favourite singers or songs, you allow yourself to be flooded with happy hormones and enjoy it; and that's exactly what happened that day. In that moment they were not focused on their misery or depression. The crowd was full of happy smiling faces. There wasn't one sad face to be seen anywhere!

On the other hand, can you see how they could control their emotions? If they were able to control their emotions then, they can control their emotions at other times too.

We all have control over our emotions! That is our God-given power! If we can control our happiness or sadness at times like this one, why can't we control our happiness or sadness at other times? The fact is: we can!

When you decide to feel happy, you also decide to release the happy hormones to help you feel it in your body. So your happiness doesn't depend upon anyone but you. You can feel happy anytime by choosing what you allow yourself to focus on.

We all decide what makes us happy, and what makes us sad or any other emotions for that matter. Our rules or our set of laws tell us when we are happy and when we feel other negative emotions. If somebody does us harm, our own personal rule dictates how we expect to feel about that and what we should do about it. Our rules decide how we react to it.

Very little is needed to make a happy life; it is all within yourself, in your way of thinking.
—*Marcus Aurelius*

> **Our happiness depends on us. We are the only ones responsible for our happiness. Not anyone else! We are however, not responsible for anyone else's happiness either. That's their job!**

Some people believe that it is only their husband, boyfriend, wife, girlfriend, or partner who can make them happy or sad. This is the stuff for novels, movies or magazines! However, we do feel happy when our significant other treats us well and unhappy when they don't. That's because we have our own personal rules about that.

The reason why we are unhappy isn't because it was their job to make us happy and they didn't; the reason why we may be unhappy is because they infringed one of our personal rules; we have our personal rules on how we like to be treated; we have a rule that says when he or she does this, we get hurt or upset; but when he or she does that we feel joyful or happy. In that case it is up to us to communicate what we want and not want in our relationships.

We are responsible for our own happiness. If we do not like what we see or hear or what is happening, it is our responsibility to change it or alter what meaning we have put on certain experiences to improve how we feel; it is not up to our partners to sort this out for us. Still, if they infringe our rules, it is also up to us to let them know and come up with some solution if not a compromise or may be some collaboration.

On the other hand, there are some rules that should not be compromised on; for example if you get hurt as a result of domestic violence, I have a rule that says that there is no compromise; give them their marching orders and never give them the chance to be able to repeat the experience a second time.

You may hold a belief that when you reach a certain salary or if you get the promotion that you are after in your company, or if you can afford to live in a certain type of house or address, or drive a certain car, then you will be happy. It is your rule that when you reach that certain salary or when you become manager that this is your measure when you will allow yourself to become happy. When these things happen then you will give yourself the permission to release your happy hormones in your body. These are your own personal self-inflicted rules or set of laws. As with your belief and value systems your personal rules too need to be updated for who you have become.

It is only when your criterion is met that you choose to feel good: you send a message to your brain which releases chemicals such as serotonin or dopamine in your body, which affect your emotions, your facial muscles as well as your breathing. These change your biochemistry and your nervous system allows you to enjoy the pleasure sensations of happy feelings.

In the meantime life is happening and you are missing out on living and on being happy. Happiness comes in moments. They do not come at the end of something when you achieve whatever you have in your head. If do that, you will never achieve happiness, because when you've achieved that goal there will be the next goal to achieve then the next, then the next and so on. In the meantime your life is on hold and one day you wake up, you are 40 . . . may be 50 . . . . may be more? And you haven't enjoyed life . . . . still waiting to be happy!!! Grab any moments of happiness you have with both hands, and be grateful and enjoy them the best you can.

Happiness doesn't happen when we win the lottery or when we reach a certain salary or a certain goal. That may be your self-imposed rule that says so, but not the rules of happiness itself.

Being happy is part of the emotions we experience every day, if we choose to. We go in and out of different emotional states at any time every day. We can have moments of happiness here and there and we can have moments when we feel sad or angry all in the same day. Equally depression like happiness isn't an everlasting state. Depression can be a very transient state or it can hang about for much longer.

You can feel depressed part of the day then you can experience moments of feeling joy and happiness, all in the same day. The problem is that we have these rules which tell us that we can't be happy until, something that we decided maybe a long time ago happens; hence we don't notice times when we could be happy throughout any day because as we have limiting beliefs, we also have limiting rules. When we don't capitalize on small moments of happiness throughout the day, we pass on them or pay no attention to them, and then we spend our lives in other unresourceful states as we are not focusing on being happy. To be happy you must profit from any moments of happiness that happens throughout the day. You can change your rules to make it fit your life to-day, in the here and now. If your rules are too complicated or if you have far too many rules that can easily cause you pain and you have a small number of rules for positive feelings, you seriously need to think again.

> **You need to make your personal rules work for you to be able to be resourceful and happy in life.**

Happiness isn't something that happens on the outside of your body. You, decide when you are happy, according to your own personal set of rules.

Happiness is an inside job! It comes from within.

We decide if and when we choose to release the right chemicals to make us feel happy or any other emotions too. If you choose to think that your happiness depends upon someone or something else that you cannot control, then prepare yourself to suffer the consequences, as you leave yourself at the mercy of someone else to pull your strings; yes! Just like a puppet! When you do this, you are leaving your happiness and future completely in the hands of other people and circumstances.

When you choose to believe that your happiness depends upon what someone else does, you are choosing to believe that you have no control over your future. You are in fact in the hands of others. This is a limiting belief. Watch out, this path leads to painful consequences.

The problem with happiness is that we don't learn how to be happy. There are no classes to teach us how to be happy. No one makes a concerted effort towards teaching us the path to happiness when we are children. If we are lucky enough to have had a happy childhood, then we are blessed and realize that life can be happy. However, many have had childhoods where they enjoyed very little happiness; so they rely on their experience of life to decide what happiness looks like for them. Their idea of happiness becomes very unrealistic. They look at what others have or look like on the outside or what some books or movies tell them about happiness to decide on their rules on happiness.

Happiness is never taught at home or in schools. We don't consciously grow up thinking *When I grow up, I want to be happy*. It's usually an astronaut, a nurse, a vet, a doctor etc. We tend to do what our first role models did; and if what they did wasn't inspiring, then we are in trouble. We either do what comes naturally, or go with the flow or copy others.

Often the thoughts we have about what makes us happy or not, are not objective; we follow our gut feelings, as our parents did before us; which can for some, let's face it be a big mistake which send them straight down the path of misery.

Stress

Mostly we react to stresses the way our original family did. We react perhaps as our mothers, fathers, grandmas, granddads, sisters or brothers did when we were growing up and carry on doing the same thing in our adult life, not realizing that these patterns are now way outdated, or are no longer valid in our lives as it is now.

If we do nothing about overreacting to stress, then, we are bound to continue to pass on that legacy onto our offsprings.

Over reacting to stress can cause us more problems than we had initially.

We have to think consciously and plan our rules so that we are in control of what gives us pain or pleasure and of what make us happy and of what make us unhappy; and not leave it to others to decide for us. What we must not do is to react to someone else's set of laws or rules or react in such a way to give us pain about something that isn't within our control.

For example: I will not enjoy holidaying in London if the weather is cold or rainy. The only way you allow yourself to have a good holiday in London, is if the weather warms up and the suns shines. Think about it! Can you control the weather? . . . . Hell! No! Why are you letting the rain or the sun or the temperature determine whether you have a good time or not? Why leave your happiness at the mercy of the elements? London is a wonderful city with amazing architecture, theatres, fashion, culture and much, much more than a bit of rain drizzle. The answer is to be prepared for all eventualities with the clothing that you decide to take with you. This rule is a disempowering one; a more empowering one is to decide that come rain or shine you are determined to have a good time in London. It is a very magnificent city, to be enjoyed on your holidays whatever the weather!

Your beliefs and your values are totally dependent upon your personal set of rules and vice versa.

As life is constantly changing, we need to update our beliefs and values to be able to adapt, grow and enjoy life; likewise your set of rules too need updating to keep up with who you are to-day.

Just as with our beliefs and values our self-imposed set of laws or rules are behind our behaviour and every action we take. Our rules tell us what to do whenever we meet a new situation. They guide our responses, our actions, our emotions, and become our moral code. They also influence the judgments we make.

Remember how we got our values and our beliefs? Our rules too are based on the same principle: reward and punishment. How we were rewarded us as a baby? Our mothers hurried to give us a cuddle when we cried. And remember as we got older, we got punished for things that disappointed our parents or carers? We soon learned what made our parents happy with us and what made them unhappy didn't we? This unconsciously taught us what to value and what to have rules about. These principles continue as we grow up into adulthood, and we, in turn do the same to our offsprings.

As we develop our value systems, we also develop our beliefs. In order for us to decide how these values will be met, we then need to develop our self-imposed laws or rules. Throughout our life we keep adding new personal rules to the repertoire that we already have. This is why to-day we have so many rules already in our subconscious which then act as a short-cut to our brain so that we can make rapid decisions when necessary. Albeit that this process occurs on a subconscious level.

We come unstuck when we have too many rules; we put a lot of constraints on us which make our lives difficult by putting lots of obstacles in our own way. The more self-imposed laws or rules we decide to make the more chances we have in restricting our life. When we have too many rules, we are forever trying to keep up with them and our life becomes incredibly difficult. We are so restricted by all sorts of rules that we have imposed upon ourselves, that making decision become a major drama, and our life becomes very complicated by having to adhere to all these rules, which are probably unreasonable in the first place.

Happiness becomes unclear when we have too many rules. Sadly instead of these self-imposed rules leading us to pleasure, they contribute to drive us in a downward spiral towards pain.

However, because our brain generalizes, distorts and deletes information as a working principle, we can develop rules that conflict with each other as well. This can cause us a lot of grief, confusion and pain in our relationships with others.

If we had a difficult childhood and hold a lot of resentment about the way we were brought up by our parents or carers, we may choose to do things completely differently when it's our turn to become parents. Therefore we make new rules which guide us on how we bring up our children. Often we do this because we want to give our children a better childhood than we've had; others do it out of bitterness, not to have anything to do with what their parents did. This is a conscious rule that we make, as adults, in order to avoid the mistakes our parents committed in our childhood.

It is important to know what rules control our actions and behaviours, as they may no longer be appropriate for the person we have become today. Like our belief and value system, these rules might have been appropriate in the past, but we may have moved on since then and the same rules may no longer apply.

As previously stated these rules are a short-cut to our brain, so that we can make quick decisions if need be.

For instance: We don't have to think: *Do I believe that it is wrong to steal? What are the reasons why I think that stealing is wrong? Is it applicable in this situation? Or is stealing wrong under all circumstances, or is it okay on this one occasion? Are there exceptions? What will be the consequences if I steal from someone? Is it okay if no one notices? Is stealing from someone wealthy less of an offence than stealing from someone who doesn't have much? Is stealing something small less of an offence than stealing something big?*

No! We don't have to do that! We have already got it sorted by our self-imposed set of rules. We know that we have a rule that says that ALL stealing is wrong under any circumstance. This rule short-cut to the brain makes our life a lot easier and stops us from being overloaded and bombarded with too many thoughts, before we can make a decision.

So whatever the circumstance, stealing is plain wrong! It is a complete No! No! We haven't wasted valuable time to have a great debate with ourselves to get the answer that will guide our actions. This rule guides us very quickly to a decision in a nano second. We are certain of our rule and about the consequences of our actions as it already forms part of our repertoire of rules, which we sorted out a long time ago.

Some people can make their life very difficult by having too many inflexible rules, especially those who see things either in black or white. They can set themselves up to fail every time; they very soon realize that they can never win whatever they do, but most of all confusion reigns! This can lead to learned helplessness. As they are not aware that the main reason for their demise is that it is because of their own personal set of rules, they then blame it on someone else or on the circumstances. They have set themselves unyielding and unreasonable rules based on their past, which stops them from getting ahead in the present. That is the way to pain.

Learned helplessness limits people in what they do because of their unfortunate past life experiences. Research shows that it is one of the main causes of depression, procrastination, and other self-defeating behaviours.

Another important Life's secret to keep in mind:

> *When things go wrong in your life, don't start by looking at others or at your circumstances: look inside. The answer is inside you.*

Look inside at what you did to get the results you got.

Exercise To Help You Know Yourself

When you need to change the results in your life:

Be honest with yourself and ask yourself the following questions. Write down your answers in your journal:

- What did I do to contribute to the results that I have in my life to-day?
- What consistent actions and choices did I take to get the results that I have in my life to-day?
- What is it that I do time after time to get the outcome that I keep getting?
- What part did I personally play in getting these results?
- What values and beliefs do I have which are contributing to the results that I keep getting?
- What are these personal self-imposed rules that I have that negatively or positively keep impacting my life?
- What values and beliefs do I possess that are limiting my potential?
- Are my rules empowering or disempowering? Are they too inflexible? How can I be more flexible?
- What do I need to do to get a different outcome?
- How can I change the results that I am getting?
- What actions do I need to take now to work towards what I want to achieve? In that case what do I need to believe and what do I need to value to get the results that I want?
- How do I need to react in order to get what I want?
- Now make a plan of action to go forward.

Look to yourself, not to others or circumstances. Don't make excuses! The only person you would be fooling is you. Time to stop being a victim is now. Time to stop living in denial is now too. You won't be able to move on and improve until you do. Look at all the facts face on; warts and all.

The good news on the other hand, is that the future is looking much better and brighter, if you choose to be honest with yourself.

You can take better actions that drive you forwards instead of keeping you caught in the same trap that you have been in all these years, because you believed that your bad fortune was due to bad luck or to other people's doing you down or to your circumstances and never looking at what role you played in your circumstances. The buck stops here!

That's the stuff for victims, not for you! Deep down you know that this is an escape! It is just a defence mechanism that you chose because you didn't know any better, so that you can pretend to yourself that you had nothing to do with anything. You have got used to say: It's not my fault! It's my bad luck!

Bad luck does not just come out of nowhere just to select you. It doesn't pick more on you anymore than on others. Everybody gets their turn. You can think that way when you are being a victim; but you no longer are one now!

Bad things happen to good people all the time; you are not especially chosen to be doomed! Remember, life is not supposed to be fair.

> *It is how we react to things that matter more than what happens to us.*

The brave thing to do is to own whatever problem or issue that belongs to us and take action towards it. Then we are ready to succeed. Things can now begin to change. We can proudly say: Come on Life, I'm ready for you!

Of course, now that you know better, you can do better and you can have better!

Look, I know this is not an easy thing to admit, but trust me this is what you have to do to change the status quo. And you know what? Even your best friend may not tell you! People close to you won't tell you how it is because they are scared to offend you and lose you as a friend. But, trust me, they will be thinking it! On the other hand, I can tell you as my aim is to be as honest as possible with you and help you to change what is not working for you; so learn!

Be brave, be honest with yourself. It changes everything in your life, and you will never look back. It will raise your self-esteem and you will feel good and confident about being you.

Have you ever watched programs like the X Factor or Australia has got talent? Some candidates come onto the stage and they make such a fool of themselves that it makes you cringe and you end up feeling really sorry for them because they are so bad! ... (In the talent department, they score a huge X ... Anyway not for doing what they do on television; they probably have a lot of well hidden talents, somewhere! Yet, they don't get it! The judges make fun of them and still they still don't get it! They sometimes even push their luck by trying to sing another song!!! The problem is that they can't hold a tune and are tone-deaf; worse still is that they have absolutely no insight!!!! I don't want you to be one of those candidates in the game of life! I want you to get it! To truly have insight in your behaviour; into what's working for you and what is not!

If you are making a fool of yourself in some area of your life and you don't know it, I want you to get it! The catch is that you can only get it when you no longer behave as a victim or pretend to yourself by living in denial. That's what happens to these people on those reality shows: they live in denial! You need to be "brutally" honest with yourself, so that you stand a chance of getting it! That's the only way that your life is really going to change.

And do not even think about a pity party! Do not go there! Self-pity is not your buddy!

Exercise for you to 'get it'

- First thing first: own your problem or issue.
- Recognize that we are all responsible for where we are at to-day.
- Recognizing your role in any problem is perhaps the first step in finding the solution you are searching for.
- Describe your problem in simple terms as it is, and write it down in your journal.
- Now look inside and reach out to your own resource pool—List all the solutions one by one. I mean everything.
- Now check the solutions one by one to see which one is the most realistic and suitable.

I repeat: *You have all the resources you need inside you.*

For us to be successful in life, we need self-imposed rules that empower us, not disempower us.

Take a close look at the rules you have, whether in your relationships, in your home, in your work situation, in your health and fitness, in your finances, socially, in fact in every area of your life. If these rules do not empower you, dump them fast for rules that do empower you. They will help you move on and succeed.

Are Your Self-Imposed Rules Working For You Or Against You?

In other words are they empowering you or disempowering you?

If your personal rules are complex and difficult for you to achieve, then they are not working for you; they are disempowering you. For example: you have a personal rule that says that I can't live anywhere where my neighbours do not like me, otherwise I will be unhappy.

Now, what is the problem with that personal rule?

The fact is that you increase your chances of being unhappy. Whether your neighbours like you or not is not within your control. You can be as nice as you like, but your neighbour's response to you is not down to you. If this is your rule, then you are setting yourself up to be hurt, because on the law of average there's bound to be someone somewhere who won't like you or may be horrible to you. Not everybody is duty bound to like you! It doesn't come with the job description of being a good neighbour! There is no clause in the Real Estate's contract that says that *you must love thy neighbour as thyself.*

However the reality is that some neighbours may well dislike you, as you too may dislike them too! All you need to have is a neighbourly relationship or may be not even that, just a civil one will do. They can just choose to keep themselves to themselves. There is no proper protocol on how to be a neighbour, just our own social etiquette. Though, it is much more pleasant if you can have pleasant exchanges as neighbours, without living in each other's pockets. Sometimes many neighbours can end up being best friends, as proximity can encourage friendships. We are indeed blessed when we have good neighbours.

On the other hand, if you changed this rule for I will make every effort to have a good relationship with my neighbours; now this is within your control! Then you will be empowering yourself, as it will not matter whether they like you or not, but you will have a rule that will empower you to achieve a good relationship with your neighbours, which in fact is desirable. As long as you can be polite towards one another, that's all that matters.

To recap:

> *If a rule isn't within your control: it is disempowering. If a rule is complicated, inflexible, upsets you easily, and is tricky in making you happy: it is disempowering.*

You need to make sure that your personal set of laws or personal rules are:

- Achievable
- Within your control.
- Simple and flexible
- Have lots of ways to give you pleasure.
- Not many ways of causing you pain.

There Are Always Exceptions To The Rule:

> *A rule that causes us pain can sometimes be the catalyst to help us change our life.*

The pain that we feel can be the wake-up call that we need to get us to do something that we wouldn't otherwise have done but desperately needed to do. That pain can give us the determination we need to make the change.

For example: if we hear that our best friend who smokes, just like we do, has just been diagnosed with lung cancer, it may well be enough to drive us to quit smoking.

We can get to such a point where we think: This is it! I have had enough! I am no longer prepared to go through this again. I will no longer put up with rubbish in my life! I have to do something to change! It is like the last straw! Enough is enough! The pain of being where we do not want to be because of one of our rules, may be the very reason why we can move forward and are able to take the necessary action to make things better. In this case a disempowering rule becomes empowering.

We need to make sure that most of the time, our rules lead us towards pleasure not pain and towards making us happy and empowered on a regular basis.

When we consistently feel happy or good in ourselves, it shows in our attitude towards others. When people are happy in themselves they easily show love to others and are more forgiving towards others. They want to engage with people, and this in turn helps to spread a little happiness in the world.

You can choose to be the one to influence others and empower them; and they, in turn, can continue to spread the happiness that you started to other people.

When people are unhappy they are reluctant to engage with other people and look for the worst in others. Someone who is constantly looking for conflict in others and is unforgiving as if they have never done anything wrong themselves, is not a happy person. When you feel bad you are much more reluctant to interact with other people or you only notice what is wrong and completely overlook all that is right.

Bad feelings and negativity are very contagious.

Negative or unhappy people pass on their negative feelings to other people like a virus; who in turn pass them on to yet more people, equally spreading their unhappy epidemic into the world too.

Come on! Let's spread a little happiness! Not unhappiness! Why not look on the bright side of life?

It's amazing how feelings have a snowballing effect! If you smile at someone in the street, they more than likely will smile back at you; they will then give that smile to someone else, who will smile back and the smile you started is passed on and on, spreading good feelings all around. Try it! Then that night you can safely go to bed knowing that you have spread a little happiness to a lot of people that day. How good would that feel?

Every time you smile at someone, it is an action of love, a gift to that person, a beautiful thing.
—*Mother Theresa*

Good feelings and positivity are contagious too.

I believe there is such a thing as a National Smile day. Maybe we could have an International Smile day? If it doesn't already exist, it should! Imagine the happiness that this one day can create in the world, if on one specific day of the year everyone makes a huge effort to smile to other people all day long! What about a HUG day? . . . . Am I pushing my luck???

A Tribute To Two Lovely Old Friends

I have always had a conscience about the homeless. I used to enjoy nights when it would pour with rain, and I would lie cosily in my bed listening to the rain, feeling safe and warm; then I would have a terrible attack of conscience, because I would think of all the people on the streets, who would have no shelter and would be wet and freezing in the rain, their poor feet would be so cold and wet!! How can anyone sleep with cold, wet feet? Not even having a partner to warm them on! I would feel very bad for them, and wanted to give them all shelter, blankets and food. I would try and imagine what it would feel like to try and go to sleep when your feet are soaking wet or when your clothes are damp or wet or if you were freezing cold! Especially if your tummy was empty!!!!

I remember one time, after I had finished facilitating one of my Postnatal Depression groups, when two *gentlemen of the road* approached me to ask me for some money. Of course, I felt very sorry for them and gave them some money; but when I returned to my car, I saw that I had a bag of apples on my passenger seat. So I ran to them happy to offer them my bag of apples. The two of them eagerly took the bag, and when they looked inside and saw *apples!* They started to screech with side-splitting laughter, holding on to their stomachs and pointing at me, like I was a funny-looking alien. Each time they lifted up their heads and saw me they would squeal even louder and louder with laughter! By now other people are looking at us wondering what was happening! I looked as puzzled as them! They were having what you would call a great *belly laugh*, and couldn't stop laughing; which also contaminated me and I started to laugh with them; initially for no reason, then immediately understood why, they thought it SOOOO funny for me to have offered them a bag of apples!

As I looked up at them, one of the gentlemen of the road had one remaining tooth on the right side of his mouth and the other had also one remaining tooth on the left side of his mouth! Their hearty laugh continued for what seemed a very long time, until they were both crying with laughter, including me! Anyway, that day, they spread their happiness to me and we could all see the funny side of this situation.

The next Sunday morning when I went to church, the same two gentlemen of the road were now sitting on the door step of the church; they both immediately recognized me, and started to point at me and the side-splitting contagious laughter started all over again! They made lots of other people attending church laugh with them too, without realizing why they were laughing so much. They made my day, that day, again! For all their bad luck and the difficult situations they were in, they had retained their amazing sense of humour, and could still see the funny side of life; and in their own way, they spread a little happiness by being able to laugh at themselves.

Their contagious laughter spread to lots and lots of people that day. The fact is that I have never forgotten that story which happened a very long time ago; and when I think of my two old friends, I can't help but smile again, and again and again. They didn't only spread a little happiness on those two days, but they have spread their happiness on very many occasions throughout the years as I told and retold this story as I fondly remember my two old friends; and no doubt for as long as my memory will continue to serve me well, including to-day when I write about them. I salute you, my two old friends! I never knew them really, but their positivity in their negative situation was admirable. Their sense of humour about themselves was contagious. They clearly had a rule that said: *Whatever our situation, we will keep our sense of humour.* Good on them! God bless them!

Now, if they can laugh about themselves bearing in mind their dire situation, why can't you?

Is your situation as grim as my two old friends? If not, find some reasons to be happy and spread some happiness around you. There are a lot of people in much worse situations than you are, and still manage to smile and be grateful.

Find the good in everything. If you search, you will find!

If you want to find out what rules you have about your values or beliefs, you need to know:

What do you believe needs to happen in order for you to feel . . . . e.g. happy, loved, successful etc.?

Many of our rules are not within our radar of conscious awareness, so it is important for us to try and understand these unconscious set of laws that have such power over us so that we can have a happy and successful life.

When we get offended or disappointed with someone or something, it is because one of our personal laws or rules has been broken. These rules can be very profound and inconspicuous, or it can even be that we have infringed our own rules.

> *A violation of our personal rules by us or by others is responsible for all our emotional upheavals.*

If you have an important rule that says: *You must never lie, under any circumstances*, when you catch someone lying to you, you feel outraged, because that person has violated one of your important rules. Therefore you will be much more shocked and appalled, than someone who doesn't have this rule. Those who are inflexible and do not make allowance for a little white lie, would even get offended if you lied and told them that their bum didn't look fat in their dress; they wouldn't even recognize that the white lie was said to protect their feelings.

People, who have a history about others lying to them, tend to have rigid rules about lies and very often overreact to a situation where someone is caught out in a white lie. The problem is that they do not realize that they are reacting way over the top, and believe that they are well within their right to react this way as their rule says that it is plain wrong to lie whatever the circumstances. Now, no one is saying that lying is right but getting so upset for a white lie and never ever speaking to someone close to you for years and years may be a little over reacting. Maybe they were trying to spare your feelings. Maybe seeing the position that this other person found themselves in, may have brought some compassion or allowed that person to accept that they were wrong and should not have told a lie, but maybe they were trying not to offend anyone.

One of my clients was adopted as a child, and was eventually told that the people he thought were his mum and dad were in fact the people who adopted him. He realized then that he had been lied to. To him this lie was completely, understandably, unforgiveable. He now has an inflexible personal rule that says: *You do not lie under any circumstance*! Even if he is told a very small white lie, he tends to react way over the top for what the lie was.

On the other hand, this shows us that our personal set of laws or our personal rules are very powerful and they govern and affect our lives, most of the time unconsciously. They affect how we behave and how we react to our experiences.

> *Happiness blooms in the presence of self-respect and the absence of ego. Love yourself. Love everyone around you. Love everyone in the whole world. Know that your own life is of infinite importance, as is every other life.*
>
> *—Jonathan Lockwood Huie*

As much as our beliefs and values affect our personal rules and vice versa, the rules we live our life by, also have an effect on our attitude of approach to life; and they all in turn affect the relationships we have with ourselves and with others.

Now let's talk about some **relationships secrets**!

Notes: What have you learnt?

CHAPTER TEN

Some Secrets About Our Relationships

Call a plant beautiful, and it becomes a flower. Call it ugly and it becomes a weed.
—Jonathan L Huie

Any relationship can be challenging at the best of times; whether we are talking about family relationships, friendships, working relationships or the relationship we all treasure the most, which is our own personal intimate relationship. This includes the relationship we have with ourselves. It is amazing how incredibly easy it is for things to get complicated. Relationships are open to conflict, to misunderstanding and much more.

Most relationships can experience a treacherous road on which to travel. For some finding a satisfying relationship can prove to be an enigma in itself. Any relationship, however good they are have their ups and downs; nevertheless, what really matters is how we navigate the course of that relationship, whether we have staying power or whether we choose to give up and move on, or stay but suffer years and years of unhappiness in an unsatisfactory relationship.

How we feel in any given moment is very important to every one of us. The basic fact is that none of us enjoy feeling bad; we just want to get out of pain into pleasure whenever we can. If we are feeling uncomfortable or bad, we just can't wait to get out of that state. We just need to feel better. However, there is nothing better than when everything is flowing in our relationship to make us feel like we are floating wonderfully on top of the world. When we hit obstacles in our relationships, we are plain unhappy! Unfortunately being unhappy in our relationships can very often easily spill in other areas of our lives.

Nothing is as important to us as to how we feel at any given moment. Whatever is going on, we hate feeling awful or unhappy. If we don't feel happy or comfortable in our relationships, nothing else seems to work. We are plain miserable! When all is said and done, all we want is to feel comfortable or to feel happy. We have a need to get out of pain into pleasure. The feeling we experience is very significant to us. When it comes to our personal or intimate relationships, this feeling takes on enormous proportions. If we are not happy in our intimate relationship, this feeling tends to dominate our lives; everything else pales into insignificance.

For us to feel good and have emotional equilibrium, we need to feel good in all areas of our lives;
something that many of us struggle with, a lot of the time.

Communication in Relationships

Poor communication with ourselves and others can lead to numerous misunderstandings which in turn can catapult us at the speed of light straight in the direction of pain. The quality of the relationships we have with ourselves and especially with our partners and with others is one of the most important areas of our life which affects our levels of happiness even if other things are going well for us.

Be a good communicator

> *For our relationships to flourish, we need to be good communicators. Success in any relationship depends on the quality of its communication.*

The key to any relationship, whether with ourselves or with others is to be able to clearly state what we want and what we need and to understand what others want and what others need.

In our intimate relationship we need to have a clear understanding of what we want and need as well as a good understanding of what our partner wants and needs too. The problem arises when the initial infatuation dies down. Initially when we first meet the person we love, we can easily live on love and fresh air; whatever, they do or whatever they say is wonderful! However, when the honeymoon period comes to an end and we settle into a more mature love, we may then realize that we perhaps know very little about this person that we are sharing our life with, because we have failed to communicate effectively what our needs are and have no clue as to their needs. In this situation neither needs are being met.

I met my husband when I was nineteen years old, and yes, it was literally, love and fresh air! I was pretty green in those days! We had no idea about each others' needs or anything about relationships or communication skills! However, we got lucky as we learned together to mature in the same direction and we pretty much wanted the same things in life; but this doesn't always happen to everybody.

Good communication is essential.

Good communication skills are an indispensable requirement if we want to be happy in our relationships. As they say, charity begins at home: the first person we need to be able to communicate with is *yours truly*! in other words ourselves.

We need to be unambiguous and clear in our thinking and know what it is we want and desire; this includes treating ourselves with good self-esteem and high self-respect and self-worth.

When we communicate, it is imperative that the messages that we are giving and receiving are exactly what we mean so that we do not have or create any misunderstandings by what we are saying and by misinterpreting what is being said to us.

Remember: nothing has any meaning until we give it meaning.

Misinterpretations are a by-product of miscommunications which can drive us again straight in the path of pain! If we misinterpret something because of our own filters or because we weren't listening properly, it can lead to a lot of complicated issues and even alter the course of our path.

So it is vital that the meaning we give to any experience or event is an empowering one, not one that will lead us towards feeling hurt and upset.

Poor communication can happen in a nano second. It is often quoted as being the main culprit for misunderstandings. This includes verbal as well as non-verbal communications. We need to make sure that we do not misinterpret any body language associated with a verbal communication. The result of which can have dire consequences, which can last, weeks, months or sometimes even years.

So when you are unsure of what something means, take the time to clarify it; check it out and understand it better, so that you do not suffer from any painful and unnecessary negative consequences.

If in doubt, give it the benefit of the doubt! Assume the positive, instead of assuming the negative. You have more to gain this way.

When we communicate something to others, our job is not just to say the words and hope that the other person gets it.

Our job is to make sure that the other person has truly understood the message that we are conveying to them.

If we are not sure that they have understood us properly, we need to clarify it with them. It is not up to them to second guess what they think we said. That's our responsibility.

> **Good communications produce good relationships.**

Being a good communicator goes a long way towards enhancing all our relationships; work-wise, friendships-wise and especially the intimate relationship we have with our partner.

For relationships to flourish, it is important to be honest with ourselves first, and have a healthy self-esteem. Looking for a special relationship is one of our basic emotional needs. Everyone needs that *special somebody*. We are programmed this way!

Some people choose to have a relationship for what they need and what they can get out of it, because they want certain things in life; for example: to have someone to love them and vice versa or a better lifestyle, or to have children or to have someone to take care of them, or for status or money. These things may happen anyway as a result of the relationship; however, the main reason why we have an intimate relationship is to share, to develop and to make the most of our own potential. In order to be able to do that, we need to be able to give first. We shouldn't go into a relationship for what we can take or for what we can get. That is not the stuff that a quality relationship is based on.

We have to be able to give love first in order to receive love. That's the law of life.

Unfortunately when love is not the overriding factor in a relationship, we start being mean and watch what each other does instead of being freely giving. If we start by thinking, I did this, this and this so he must do that, that and that, then we must prepare for conflict! This is a very low-level relationship, when we watch what we do or give and vice versa.

This attitude in an intimate relationship is a recipe for disaster.

If this is how your relationship works, then I am sure that you are fairly consistently in conflict and in pain. If you want it to improve you need to change this attitude. When you behave this way, you are putting nails in the coffin of your relationship already! When you watch tit for tat like that, you do not have a relationship where you can both be happy. That's not a giving attitude! It's a mean attitude, even though you may think that you do more than your partner. Discuss it with your partner and express your needs but do not be mean. It won't help you enjoy a quality relationship. If you have this attitude you find that it will not take your partner long before he or she decides to reciprocate back with the same attitude. Your relationship is then on a downward slope as there is no give and take, and a mean spirit is your master.

> *In a quality relationship, you want to give, out of love.*

On the other hand, if you are unhappy because you are in fact doing everything, and your partner is doing nothing, then you need to have a serious conversation and convey your unhappiness to your partner and renegotiate your relationship. That is a different scenario to the meanness of attitude. When it is this way, the imbalance makes you feel hard done by. It is not right for one partner to do it all, and the other doing nothing. Good communication can overcome this problem; however your partner needs to be willing to meet you half way. If not, you have a big decision to make. You need to express your needs and wants clearly.

> *Like with everything else in life, in a relationship you get back what you give out.*

Whenever you're in conflict with someone, there is one factor that can make the difference between damaging your relationship and deepening it. The factor is attitude.
—*William James*

The attitude with which you treat your relationship will decide whether it is successful or not. You need to be loving, open and generous, if you want to have a quality relationship.

If you are able to do something regardless whether it is your turn or not, just do it anyway, out of love. If you do this you are setting the tone for your relationship. If you are in a relationship, love comes first.

Love becomes reciprocal in your relationship depending on what attitude you have. Your partner wants to do things for you out of love. The balance of giving and receiving then is right.

Do not watch who does what, when and where, or who gives what or who pays for what; if you find yourself able to do something, then you just do it! You will get it back tenfold!

It is true: there is more pleasure in giving than in receiving.

It is important to be able to share, and do things when we can without being too conscious of whose turn it is to do what.

Your generosity becomes contagious and you benefit from its results.

When you love someone and want a quality relationship, you need to go there with a giving attitude. Regularly, ask yourself this one question that you must keep in your mind: How can I help my partner to enjoy today and improve his or her life experience? By having a genuine and giving relationship with your partner you are doing what you can to enhance the relationship and your relationship flourishes.

When your attitude to your partner is giving and wanting them to enjoy the experience of being in a relationship with you, you are a winner!

If you are mean and watch what you give, by the law of reciprocity, your partner will do the same, even if they were not like this to begin with. And you become the biggest loser! This is a formula for constant conflict and meanness in the relationship with resulting unhappiness.

The problem is that if your parents' relationship was this way, you may be emulating them without even realizing it, as they were your first couple relationship role models and you had no other. If they are now divorced, you may understand why! So if you do not want to head the same way, you need to do different.

> *The attitude with which you go into a relationship will determine whether you are happy or not, or whether you will stay together or not.*

The old saying: You reap what you sow, is still very popular because there's a lot of truth in it.

If you are giving, your partner will reciprocate; if you are mean, you will not enjoy the fruits of your relationship. You will suffer meanness too, and before too long there is a competition about who can be the Worst Meany! And before you know it, it's all over! Be aware that this attitude can be a form of control.

If you are controlling you are doomed for a rough ride, and so is your partner. So having a relationship does not start with looking at what you can get from your partner, it starts with you being able to give, and to have a willing attitude to make it grow and develop into a healthy relationship.

Often, you get what you think you deserve.

Every good relationship especially an intimate one should be based on mutual respect. If it isn't based on respect, whatever else you have that's good will not last.

> *A lack of respect for your partner is usually the kiss of death to a quality relationship.*

If you have good self-esteem, you expect reciprocal love and mutual respect and if you have low self-worth, you have low expectations of what your relationship can bring you; and still you may not be satisfied in your relationship whatever it's like.

Remember, in a relationship you are both on the same side; on the same team; in the same camp! You do not have to fight someone from the enemy camp.

If you feel hurt, go with the presupposition that your partner isn't primarily trying to hurt you, but only trying to meet their own needs. If you understand and keep this in mind that one simple fact, your attitude towards each other will improve tremendously. As you belong to the same team, if you attack your partner, you are attacking yourself. You are attacking your own side.

Remember that you did choose each other freely in the first place! No one forced you!

If you do not like something that your partner does, find an appropriate time to discuss it; choose what you want to say and how you say it. Do not just blurt it out and start by blaming your partner as you trample all over their feelings. If you do that, whether he or she is right or wrong, they feel obliged to defend themselves if you are accusing or blaming them for something.

Whenever you blame or criticize someone, they feel under attack, therefore they are then forced to defend themselves.

Sometimes, it may be good to choose to discuss your problem (depending of what the issue is) over dinner if you are in a public place. It reminds you both to keep your cool and not embarrass yourselves in public. It can stop an escalation of a minor disagreement turning into world war three, which can easily happen when no one else is watching, in the privacy of your own home, after a long day at work. Otherwise, all you can think of is that you feel hurt. The last thing you want to do is hurt back to get your revenge. That is very destructive and can escalade something small into something monumental.

If you are entering a relationship after having been hurt in previous relationships, be aware that you now have baggage! It is very important not to bring your past emotional baggage into a new relationship. If you do that, your relationship is doomed before it starts. If someone has said something to you in a previous relationship that really hurt and upset the hell out of you, please be aware that if your new relationship has the bad luck of mentioning something similar, try not to react to your past. Take a deep breath and react to the moment now, not to your past.

React to your present in this relationship with this person, not to your last relationship with your previous partner. Don't bring this emotional baggage into your new relationship. Your past relationship ended clearly because things weren't right. If you want this one to succeed you need to treat your present relationship on its own merits and do something different.

Expressing how you feel is more important than blaming each other.

Expressing what you would like instead is essential, as believe it or not your partner hasn't been to mind-reading classes! (Unless I'm wrong of course!)

Often we have unrealistic expectations or just expect them to know what we want. The reality is that we need to make it clear otherwise they honestly do not have a clue! Sometimes people say He/she knows how I feel! NO! Unless you tell them, they don't really know how you really feel! They just make assumptions, which may actually be very wrong; and then you feel hurt . . . again!

Being a willing partner and having the right attitude is what matters most for a relationship to flourish.

If you have not received love yourself as a child, it may be very difficult for you to give love.

This is an area that will require some work. You need to be able to love yourself first in order to be able to show love to someone else.

Love is saying "I feel differently" instead of "you're wrong"

—*Anonymous*

Exercise To Help You Love Yourself:

Mirror work is very helpful, (although you may feel a little ridiculous doing it at first; but do it anyway! Seriously, no one is watching!)

When you wake up and before you go to bed, smile in the mirror, look at yourself in the eyes, smile, speak your name and say: Mary . . . . Jane . . . . John, (whoever) . . . . *I love you* and try and be really sincere (even though you may feel really silly at first; it will make you smile; after a while, you will do it naturally and think nothing of it). Okay, I know! It can be difficult to do, but try it anyway and it will change how you feel about yourself, even if you don't believe it at first! Especially if you don't believe it! After a while, it will become easier, you will naturally wake up and go to the mirror and Say . . . Jane, remember, I love you and feel good about it.

Do this as a routine every single morning when you wake up before you do anything else, even when you are late, even when you are really busy, even when you don't feel well or feeling particularly loving, until it becomes a habit.

If you don't know how to love yourself, and can't do it alone, get professional help or be prepared to work on yourself everyday to be able to love yourself. It is only when you feel love for yourself that you can give love to others.

You may not believe it to start with, but you will after a while if you persevere with this exercise.

What your eyes take in from the mirror will reach your subconscious. What your ears hear will also be heard by your subconscious. How you are feeling is also felt by the subconscious. Be genuine so that it can really believe you.

Writing positive affirmations about you is also helpful. For example: I love myself; I deserve to be loved; I choose to love and be loved; I am worth it.

Write a journal and find all the good things that you do in the day and write them down in detail.

Enhance your self-esteem by repeatedly reminding yourself of all the amazing qualities, gifts and talents that you possess. Write them down on a flashcard and memorize them.

Look at some of the events in your life since you were young, and write down the resources that you have used in the past, to deal with different events in your life. Write in as much details as you can. Write them on a flashcard and memorize them.

Fights And Arguments

If you are having an argument, make sure that you fight fair. Try and let your anger calm down a little before going into an argument if at all possible. It is so easy to let ourselves be hyped up by anger and say things that we will regret later. Try and have some rules about arguing, such as not talking over each other and taking turns in speaking. Keep your voice at a reasonable level. Do not say things, just because you feel hurt and you want to hurt back. It achieves nothing constructive but can be very destructive. Try hard not to say things just to be vindictive. Express how you are feeling. Do not accuse; do not criticize; explain the facts. Explain how you feel and what you want.

The children

Having strong arguments and fighting in front of the children is very distressing especially to the children; it always make them anxious, worrying whether their parents are heading for the divorce courts, or if the verbal abuse will escalate into something more physical. Children tend to think that it's their fault if their parents fight.

> *If these fights are regular and significant, they are a form of child abuse.*

Your job as a parent is to love, nurture and keep your child safe and secure. Every child who has ever been born has the right to feel loved, safe and secure. In my practice, I see many adult clients, who suffer with anxiety and panic attacks, as a result of their parents' regular fights when they were children. Not knowing if the fights will deteriorate into a violent one and harm a parent or the child, can be very traumatic for the child and can be the beginning of long-term anxiety states and the resulting panic attacks in adulthood.

> **If you do this to your children, do it with the knowledge that you are condemning your children to emotional problems when they are adults.**

If a husband or wife does not support their partner or openly criticizes them in front of their children and others, the relationship turns sour into one of bitterness, anger and resentment, with cascades of tears in the process.

The trust is non-existent in that relationship but the resentment runs deep.

What is worse is that the children from this relationship may as a result learn to have no respect for their parents and will go on to reproduce this vicious cycle, as small eyes and small ears watch, observe and listen (especially what you don't want them to!); and they copy, unconsciously copy . . . . and copy particularly when they become adults. They go on to replicate what they saw and learnt in their childhood. They repeat what they lived. They go for the familiar as this is the norm for them. This works for good as well as for bad. One day they go to marry someone with whom they can fight just as well as their parents did when they were children. Hence, duplicating this cycle of abuse to their own children.

You are not bringing up children, you are bringing up adults. You are preparing them for adulthood.

> *Children are little adults in training. It is up to us to give them the best training we can as children, for optimal results when they graduate as adults in the future.*

If a wife feels abused, she often behaves as a victim, which again encourages any covert underlying bullying behaviour to continue. This works the same the other way round too:

If a husband feels bullied and abused, he too ends up acting as a victim.

Using your children to get leverage against your partner is despicable; you certainly won't have your children's best interest at heart if you do that.

If you do this, it is only to fulfil your own selfish needs, without thinking about the harm caused to your children. It only serves to confuse and upset them. It increases their anxieties, as they go on to become the next generation of dysfunctional adults.

Name-calling

Do not kid yourself: consistent name-calling is no joke! It is abuse!

Do you call your partner some derogatory name to put them down and when caught out, you say: *Only joking*!? No, you're not and you know it! Especially if this is a recurrent issue in your relationship, it is no joke! It is abuse, which damages the core of the person who is victim of this contemptible and very unkind habit. After all, name-calling at school is a well-known form of bullying; nowadays, many teenagers have committed suicide because of name-calling and cyber bullying. If that is you: STOP IT NOW!

If a father doesn't take his rightful place in the family and does not lead his family as he should, this family becomes dysfunctional.

That is not to say that the father needs to dominate his wife and that the wife needs to be submissive to her husband. Absolutely not! It just means that a father has a role to play and he needs to take his role seriously, and do the best he can for his family. He needs to treat his partner and children with the love and respect that they deserve, protect them and be an example of leading his family.

If a man chooses to opt out of his role and do just what he wants to do only, without being a good leader of his family, chaos is never far away in that family, resulting in pain, conflict and very little chance of happiness for everyone.

The sad thing is that the children become caught up in this emotional lifetrap, and reproduce the problems of their childhood later on in life. They may be drawn to partners who will repeat what they suffered as a child or what their mothers suffered, or they may go on to be the next lot of abusers.

The children will go for the familiar, unaware that there are other ways of relating.

This situation works both ways.

> **Of course if a woman doesn't take her rightful place in the family, the family becomes dysfunctional too, and equally the children become the casualties of this unhealthy relationship.**

A mother too has her role to play in a household, if she doesn't take that role seriously, that family too becomes dysfunctional and everyone suffers the consequences. As they have no other life experiences, these children repeat what they have lived in their childhood as they grow up. The actions of a mother who turns her children against their father is just as inexcusable. Whatever your relationship with your children's father is like, he is still their father and they love him and do not need to hear detrimental comments about him. If you love your children you won't do that, as you will be hurting them and damaging them.

In general, girls tend to follow what their mothers do (but not always, some may do the opposite out of rebellion) and boys tend to copy their fathers, as parents are their first role models. Research shows that if a father smokes, his son is more likely to smoke too. This is replicated in other behaviours too.

Using the Children

Some parents sometimes try to be popular with their children by taking their sides against the other parent. They selfishly do this to increase added weight to their own side, not so much because it is for the good of the child or necessarily because they believe that it is the right thing to do; but because they are misguidedly meeting their own self-centred needs. They are recruiting the child to be on their side to put more pressure on the other partner for whatever their self-seeking reason is.

On any level this is very wrong and very destructive for the relationship and extremely damaging to the children and the partner. Of course it works the same if the wife doesn't support her husband and uses her children to turn them against her husband. The children will never thank either of them in the end. The children may play along with it for a while so that they can have what they want when they want it. Children are born-manipulators; they are psychologically programmed to meet their own needs. They will use any dysfunctional situation to their advantage, but that doesn't mean that you are not damaging them.

> **If you poison your children against your partner, they will find it difficult to forgive you later on, when they themselves become parents or when they mature enough.**

It is a very dysfunctional, selfish and manipulative thing to do, and you will not have a hope in hell of having a continuing good relationship with your partner or your children. You would not earn your children's respect even if they happen to be on your "side" then. As they grow up, they will see it that it is your business together and you had no right dragging them into it.

Young children should not be involved in parents' business. That includes not discussing adult business or financial pressures with them or treating them like a "little friend" to acquire their support.

> *Your children have enough friends, they need parents.*

If you have issues between you, sort it out between you without having to use your children as pawns in the middle. In the end it turns against you when the children grow up and start to understand what dynamics went on in their household.

Children may play this game for a while to take advantage of the situation and get what they want by favouring one parent who is willing to give them what they want. A partner may do this, not because it is good for the child but because it is used as a weapon against their partner.

Children are brilliant at playing one parent against the other, if it means they can have their own way; go out when they want to or stay out late at night; or they may choose to fall in with it to gain some favours by being reinforced that they are right and that the other parent is in the wrong. But are these children happy? Absolutely not! Do they feel loved? Absolutely not!

> **When you do not have clear boundaries for a child, the child becomes insecure.**

When you allow a child to do what he wants and there are no repercussions if they come in late or for any other misbehaviour, the child does not respect you and doesn't feel loved. They see it that you couldn't care less about them so long as *you* have a quiet life.

Those who choose to behave like this eventually feel very miserable and often wallow in self-pity trying to justify themselves that they are a good parent; but when they are alone and silent, they know that what they are doing is not right. When these children mature enough to understand what went on in their childhood, they will feel resentment towards that parent or parents.

Parents should never use their children to get leverage against their partner.

This is a covert form of controlling, bullying and of ostracizing their partner.

Parenting Role Models

The sad thing about this is that these parents are the only parenting and couple role models of these children. They know no other way of how people behave as a couple or as parents. The likelihood of them repeating what they experienced as a child when they become adults themselves is very high; hence, the vicious cycle of dysfunctional parenting continues.

It is better for children to come from a broken home with two separated happy parents than for children to live in a dysfunctional home together with two warring parents.

It is far better to be healthy on your own than to be unwell in an unhealthy, harmful or dysfunctional relationship.

> *Ay, yes, divorce . . . . from the Latin word meaning to rip out a man's genital's through his wallet.*
> —*Robin Williams*

Your job as a husband or partner is to support and love your wife and to protect her. You never allow anyone, be it your children or anyone else to gang up against her. Your job as a wife or partner is to do the same. If you can't do this, you have no business being together.

Move on and find the right partner for you, where you can show each other love first and foremost, instead of destroying your partner's self-esteem, self-worth and self-respect by making their existence a living hell. That's the stuff that disease is made of!

If the reason that you are turning your children against your partner is because you have your own personal issues, then you need to address these and not make your innocent partner and children pay for your personal inadequacies. Get some professional help if you can't do it alone.

Your job as a husband or partner is to teach your children from the very beginning to love and respect their mother. Your job as a wife or partner is to teach your children to love and respect their father from the very beginning too.

If you haven't done this or are not doing it, then you have not done your job and have no business being together. Even if you part company, you have no business saying bad things to the children against their mother or father.

Are You A Victim?

If as a result of poor treatment by your partner, you behave as a victim because you feel justified, then you have to know that it is a choice that you are making. You do this because you feel hurt and think that the partner bullying you will see the error of their ways and hope that they will put things right.

The problem is that a bully never sees the error of their ways. They are always right and other people are always wrong. They are so full of their own conviction of being *right!* They sure would rather die being right than live being happy.

As much as some people with low-self-esteem apologize at the drop of a hat, the bully, (albeit that sometimes that the bullying is done covertly) can never apologize as they can see everyone else's faults but their own.

When you behave as a victim, you get treated as one.

The world responds to you *as you treat yourself*.

As Dr Phil Mc Graw often reminds us that: **You teach people how to treat you**. If you teach people that you are the victim in life, they will honour this by treating you that same way.

When you behave as a victim, you give away all your power and you become a door mat. Nobody but nobody will thank you or respect you for all your *sacrifices*. So, don't winge! Instead they walk all over you and become irritated by your self-pity and your constant winging, nagging or complaining.

> *Reacting as a victim stops you from taking action and moving on. Acting as a victim can paralyze you into depression and inaction.*

The people close to you may find it very difficult to tell you anything about what you are doing, because they don't want to hurt you or upset you any further. They may be scared of losing your friendship. Others may not care enough to tell you; and yet others may get irritated by your continuous winging of the bad things that constantly happen to you and your inability to do anything that is ever suggested.

If you find yourself waiting to find any willing ears to listen to you and hear you winge about your sad story, and how done by you are, and still in disbelief about what happened, this is for you:

Listen: Your time is now! Take action!

The time has now come for you to stop living in denial and to look at things as they are. Stop pretending! If this is you: acknowledge it! Things can only get better when you get real with your situation.

> *Self-pity is an addictive drug which is not a healing remedy.*

The tragic thing is that I may be saying these things for you, but you can be so far in denial, that the penny does not drop with you. You may read this and think about your friend, Mary, Jane or Ashley, whoever! But it never occurs to you that I am actually talking about **YOU! . . . . YES! YOU!**

Think: **Can this really be you?**

Now! Listen Good: take off your pink coloured glasses and examine exactly what is going on in your life! Be truthful with yourself for once. It is only then that you can change things, otherwise nothing will change!

Winging doesn't help you to sort things out, plus it irritates other people. Behaving as a victim stops you from improving your situation, let alone encouraging others to continue to mistreat you. Looking at life from a victim's point of view disempowers you. Self-pity drags you further down in the depths of depression. The only way is to be honest with yourself. I mean dead honest! Recognizing what your role is and what you can do to move on. No glossing things over and making excuses for yourself. No! The stark cold, honest truth about who you are and how you behave! Now, look for the solution for you.

If you were your best friend, what advice would you give her? Then, take it yourself!

When a relationship breaks down, each of you had a role to play. It's never only one person's fault. It does take two to tango! Recognize what role you played so that you can move forwards. Yes, you have been through a lot. Yes, you did put up with a lot! Yes, he/she probably is a bully! Yes, he/she probably is a b . . . . d! Nevertheless did you allow it? Maybe you maintained it or brought it on? Come on, we are being honest now! Get real! This relationship didn't become dysfunctional by itself! Yes, you became a victim and felt sorry for yourself! Yes, you behaved as a victim! And put up with it. Alright! Okay, you didn't know what to do, you felt trapped and had no money, but you are the one who made the choice to stay in a dysfunctional relationship for all this time. Now you can stop being a victim and now that you have that insight, life can start looking up! It is only when you can be one hundred percent honest with yourself that you can move on and get better.

So come one now! Take back your power. Be empowered! You are nobody's victim! Show them instead that you respect yourself and do not come from a place of self-pity.

Self-pity is for losers. Nothing constructive ever comes out of self-pity.

You are strong and willing to change and lead a quality life. When you make a decision like this, good things start to come into your life. Providence moves to help you. Be amazed! Be very amazed!

Or maybe you are the abusive one? Be honest, now: are you the controlling one? It is only when you are prepared to look at life squarely in the face, and glare at the horrid truth, and admit what and who you are, then, you can move on and do something about it. All the time you live in denial, nothing will change for you.

If you move on to another relationship, then you are bound to repeat the same mistakes you did before, if you do nothing about it and keep putting the blame on your partner instead. Remember? It does take two to tango! If your previous relationship failed because of the way you behaved, then you are predicting the future of the next relationship.

If you are true with yourself, the paralysis will leave you and you will be able to take action to make your life better. At least then you stand a chance of happiness and have enough insight not to repeat it again even if this relationship is over.

> *You can use your experience to grow and develop; it is not about being right or wrong:*
> *It is about being happy and living the best life that you can!*

There are many dynamics that go on in relationships, but not many are as soul destroying and destructive as **Sulking**!

Sulking in Relationships

The reason why I have included talking about sulking is that I think that it is far too common in the relationships of some of my clients.

> *Sulking like neediness is an unattractive trait.*

Sulking is a very selfish, upsetting, and a very negative way to behave in any relationship. It is a controlling and an immature behaviour; however, it is widespread! It is often done in private and *under cover*. Sadly they count on their partner to collaborate with them not to disclose it to anyone, if only out of shame and embarrassment.

Sulking can be a learnt behaviour from our first couple relationship role model, our parents or carers. You may have observed your mother, or father sulk to manipulate, to get their own way, whilst you were growing up. As they were the only couple role model you had, you then automatically copy that behaviour in your own relationship as a way to control your partner and get what you want.

> *Whatever you observed when you were growing up, you replicate many years later as a matter of course, without even having to engage your conscious mind. It becomes automatic.*

Sadly, one of your parents may have put up with it, but your partner now is not your mother or father and may not put up with such dysfunctional behaviour. You may soon find yourself on single-street again! People who sulk carry on sulking because to some degree that destructive behaviour is working for them; whether it is because they are getting some sort of wicked satisfaction out of it or whether their partner unknowingly is enabling them by their victim-like attitude, or they may have learned that if they carry on sulking, they will get what they want in the end; or it may be because they may enjoy punishing their partner. The sulk stops only when they think that their partner has been punished enough.

Some may sulk as a way to get their revenge on someone else. Whatever the reason is behind your sulk, it is not healthy in a relationship. Under any *sulk*, there is always anger and bitterness or resentment lurking not too far behind.

You sulk because deep down you believe that you're *right* and the other person has wronged you; however what you do not realize is that your *right* is often more than likely *wrong*, but your mind is not open enough to take it in.

At times when some *sulkers* decides to sulk, they take to their bed; in fact what they do is that *they put themselves in a place where they can really indulge in their negative thoughts without any interruptions.* They churn the same repetitive negative thoughts over and over again in their mind in a continual loop, deciding that they are right and the other person is wrong, and they are the ones who have been hard done by, and some may even plan their revenge.

So, as I'm right! That gives me the right to wallow in my very own self-pity! And I will!

Actually, No! You're not! And you have absolutely no right to wallow in self-pity if your actions have repercussions on others.

When you do this, you reinforce to yourself how you are the victim of what someone else has said or done to you. Sulkers persist in this behaviour because to some extent there is something in it for them. It reinforces their selfish ways of proving to themselves that they are right, and others are wrong and that *they* are the ones who have been wronged here; they are the victim here!

That's manipulating and controlling!

Some people sulk to express their displeasure, disappointment, frustration, anger or anxiety about something. If they find that sulking meets their needs they continue to do so, until they learn a more effective way to communicate their needs, especially if the other partner tolerates or naively maintains their behaviour by their own victim attitude.

If this is you, and sulking has worked or is working for you, I am telling you now, loud and clear that: Sulking is not ok! Sulking is dysfunctional. You have to find a better way to express your displeasure. Try, talking or discussing.

> *Sulking is a form of abuse; only this abuse does not leave visible scars. They are emotional scars! But nevertheless scars! These scars bleed; only you can't see the blood; they cut deeply into your partner's and your children's souls, only you can't see the wounds; but they are there nevertheless!*

These scars can cause untold damage to your relationships with your partner and with your children. The upshot of it is that nobody in the household is happy or having a good experience of life.

If you want to change something or express your displeasure with your partner, there are always *words*. Use them! Your partner is not telepathic. If uttering the words are too painful, try putting them down on paper. It may be the start of a communication.

You can rehearse what you have to say, so that it does not come out all wrong and inflame the situation. Write it down first if you have to; but tell your partner what is troubling you in a way that is acceptable to you both.

Remember: **Love Cures All and Conquers All**

Show Love first

Instead of sulking and feeling sorry for yourself, if you can show love and understanding and demonstrate it by your attitude and your behaviour, your relationship can be mended quicker and easier. Even if you feel hurt, you can express your love for your partner in some way, it goes a long way towards finding a compromise.

If you can show love, whatever is wrong in your relationship, can get sorted out; but if when things go wrong, you feel and show anger, hatred, resentment, bitterness or some other negative emotion towards your partner, it is a lot harder to repair or patch your relationship afterwards.

Remember, in all things, if you do not know what to do:

> *If you show love first and foremost, you cannot be wrong.*

Apologize, Apologize, Apologize

Choose to be the one to say sorry first; you can stop a fight escalating into all out war if you can say sorry. Not sorry, that you're wrong, but sorry that you're fighting; however, if you do realize that you are out of line, now is the time to say so. Your partner will more than likely meet you half way, if you do that; and you will see the magic that those five little letters produce!

Often, it is something that some men and some women find really hard to do, as they think that they will be the *loser*; some can't bear the thought of admitting being in the wrong even though they realize that they are. This comes from low-self-esteem and low self-worth.

This is for you if you find it hard to say sorry:

> ***It is not weak to apologize! It is big and strong and shows good self-esteem to be the first one to say sorry.***

What matters is for you and your partner to feel better.

It shows that you want to stop the argument and you may indeed be able to turn it into a discussion instead. Even if you are right, you will be appreciated for being the first to apologize. Your partner will more than likely help you and take their share of responsibility. This way, you can reach a compromise quicker and you would have easily averted World War Three . . . . just by yourself! You can safely put away all your planned missiles!

A lot of resentment is built up against partners who can **never** say **sorry**, whether they are right or wrong. And believe it or not, your partner never forgets that you can never say sorry . . . . maybe that's because you think you are never wrong? . . . Think again! Women especially have memories like elephants where that sort of thing is concerned. They can remember, what you did . . . . in . . . 1990 . . . and the rest! . . . . building up resentment more and more!

You may not apologize that you were wrong but you can say sorry that you are arguing, thereby bringing an end to an argument straight away as you will without a doubt be very appreciated if you do that. It will show your willingness to make things better and it becomes easier to come to a compromise.

Yet, when you know that your partner *historically* can never say *sorry*, you are more *hyped up* towards them in any argument, if only for *that* fact, which has nothing to do with this argument anyway. *It becomes cumulative.*

On the other hand, if you are one who willingly say sorry and acknowledge when you are wrong, then, your partner will have less anger towards you, and may be more willing to compromise as they do not have the hyped up feeling *of course, you're never wrong, are you?* to increase their anger towards you. Their anger is directed solely at the reason why you are fighting, without that *baggage* to make them even angrier.

I know from my own clients that some men do find it extremely difficult to apologize, but I am telling you: If you want to win Brownies points, be the first one to stop an argument deteriorating into all out battle by saying this very small word that brings huge, massive, results: **SORRY!**

You can something like: Look, *I'm sorry that we're fighting; can we start again and see how we can resolve this without upsetting each other so much?* It will go a long way towards a resolution.

Sorry is a magical five letter word that can heal most rifts. You will be surprised! It is one of the most healing words on earth. It is not admitting defeat but it is acknowledging the pain that your partner is going through when you are arguing.

Don't be so arrogant as not to be able to say sorry. If you can say *sorry*, it shows that you are the bigger person. There is nothing more unattractive and more demeaning to your partner than someone who thinks that he or she can never do anything wrong! For God's sake, we all do wrong things at some point or another! None of us is perfect . . . No! Not even you!!!! We *all* make mistakes. Believe me; I have made my fair share, but I like to think that I can say sorry!

Women, if you know how to handle your relationship, take a leaf out of the men's book, and apologize too; although sometimes saying sorry *seems* to come easier to some women but not to all.

This is not the kind of sorry that some people use in every other sentence sometimes. *Oh, sorry; sorry for absolutely everything!* That is the overuse of the word, which in the end means nothing anyway. What I am talking about is a genuine, heartfelt sorry that there is an argument and that your partner is upset.

Use "I" Statements instead of being accusing. Explain how you feel, rather than accuse your partner. The focus is not on blaming, criticizing or accusing your partner; the focus is on explaining how *you* feel.

For example:

When you do . . . . I feel . . . .

When this happens, I feel . . . .

This way, you are not accusing or blaming your partner, you are merely expressing how *you* are feeling.

> *There is nothing more damaging in a relationship than blaming, accusing, controlling, punishing, threatening or criticizing.*

If you start to say: *You did this . . . . It's your fault, you said that . . . .* You can bet your bottom dollar that your partners will be defending themselves as they are being accused. This is no way to get to the peace treaty! This way neither you, nor your partner hear each other as you are both so busy accusing and defending yourselves, and nothing gets resolved. Chances are you are both talking over each other, so nobody gets heard, but you end up with a lot of hurt, resentment, saying things you don't mean and angry feelings, as you have been trying to outdo each other's insults. In the end, you have resolved nothing because neither of you heard what each other had to say.

When you use the "I" statement, it gives each of you a chance to really hear what the other one is saying. It gives you and your partner a chance to empathize and see things from each other's point of view. In the end you sort things out quicker and you start to feel better earlier.

If when you *hear* your partner's argument and you suddenly think that they have a point, don't be too proud to go back on what you said, and *tell them* that you couldn't see before but that now you can see their point of view. Now! This is definitely the way to the peace treaty!

That too will show that you are a person with good self-esteem and fairness, not afraid to acknowledge that you are not perfect. You will be truly appreciated for it and you would have gone a long way in healing the rift. Things may well improve better than before!

But more than that, in future arguments your partner will remember that you are a fair person and that you can see other people's points of view and you would have taught them another way of fighting fair; maybe then they can decide that they can see your point of view too. You would have taught them well!

Make a Pact

If you make a pact when you are not angry with each other what you will do when these situations arise again, then it is easier to execute when you are *in it*. Whether that means making a time to meet in the *boardroom* (whatever you call your boardroom) to discuss things like adults with certain rules in place like: keeping voices at a reasonable level; taking turns in speaking; not speaking over each other; allowing the person to finish talking before jumping in; or something else that would works for you. Actively listen to what each other have to say; do not rehearse what you are going to answer back instead!

Your boardroom can be the bedroom, the den, the dining room, the lounge or the shed, or even the pub—if you can find somewhere quiet, whatever or wherever you want it to be. Making the rules when you are friends with each other is helpful. What is even more helpful is to follow the rules when you do have an argument. It stops you from focusing on your hurt feelings but helps you to work towards a solution.

If you don't do any of this and sulk instead, bad emotions just fester, and fester, and in the end if it doesn't *explode*, it *implodes* and the damage that you cause may be irreparable. When emotions and feelings implode, you end up with the nasty side effects of diseases and illnesses, such as infections, cancers, cardiovascular disease, high blood pressure, anxiety and depression, arthritis or other immune system problems such as Lupus and more.

If your partner sulks, don't get sucked into it by reacting or over reacting to it. They will get some sort of perverse satisfaction as the behaviour is working for them; if this happens, they are more likely to repeat the behaviour again and again and again.

So What Do You Do?

You need to ignore the sulking behaviour as much as possible and continue life as if you haven't noticed a thing. Hard? Hum . . . Yes, I Know! I'm not kidding though! Go out, go about your business and carry on regardless. Be happy! Go out, enjoy yourself! Don't notice anything! Speak to them as you would normally.

When the behaviour stops working for them, they will eventually have to come out of it themselves; but if you feed it, you're simply giving it more meat! And the behaviour will not only continue, but will recur as and when, it pleases them to control you.

If they think that you are suffering by their sulks then they will have found a good way of *punishing* you when the fancy takes them.

> *When you feed a behaviour, you keep it alive; when you starve it, it simply dies a natural death from your lack of attention.*

We all behave the way we do because there is something in it for us.

If we don't get anything out of it, we no longer behave in that same way. We all get a reward for continuing doing certain behaviours; that's why we continue to do them. If a behaviour is working for you, you will continue to repeat it; however, if the behaviour stops working for you, there is no point in carrying on the behaviour, as you are not getting any recompense from it. Therefore you will stop it.

For instance, if you breast feed an eight month old baby when he wakes up in the night, he will keep waking up for his night feeds; now, cut out the night feeds and you will see that the baby will sleep through, as there is no longer a reward in it for him.

The behaviour carries on all the time you are getting something out of it. The minute there is nothing in it for you, you will stop doing it. That's the way life works! That goes for all behaviours and for everyone.

If you overreact to your partner's sulking, you are feeding it and giving it power. If you continue to ignore it, it will simply give up the ghost.

It is just the same as the plants in your garden: if you tend to them, give them lots of attention, weed them, water them, talk to them, feed them, take care of them, they will flourish and thrive; however, if you stop watering them and tending to them, they will wilt and die because you neglected them.

If you neglect the sulking, the 'sulker' will not be gaining any benefits from it and the sulking will have to stop it as it will no longer be fed or be working for them as it has no effect on you.

Think about it: if you were not there to see the *sulk,* would they carry on in that same manner? If their boss walked in the room, would they still carry on with their sulk? If the Queen walked in, would they say: *Sorry, your Majesty, but I'm in the middle of a sulk*? The answer of course is: *No! . . . . Therefore it is for your benefit*. We also know that we are in charge of our emotions and that we do have the power to control them. Consequently they can control whether to sulk or not!

So, do yourself a favour and let the sulking die through your sheer lack of attention!

Often those who sulk are so convinced that they are right, and that they have been wronged, that they use it as a means *to control and to punish*. That is a very unhealthy and dysfunctional way of behaving which can only lead to painful and unhappy outcomes.

What is happening is, while they are busy sulking, is that they are also *busy in their heads*

rehashing how unfair things are for them, how badly they have been treated, etc. etc. the same negative thoughts going round and round in their heads that they can't even begin to contemplate that they may have had a share in what's gone wrong. It is a completely biased way of looking at things, but they are blinkered and cannot entertain the thought that they may have had something to do with it. They are having a *gigantic* pity-party!

Their position is: ". . . . *But, I am right!*"

They would much rather die than admit that they're at fault. They would much rather spend days being miserable than give in. They would much rather miss out on good opportunities rather than look for a solution. Their head is so crowded with their negative thoughts, that there is little room for any positive thoughts to come into their mind.

As you get more of what you focus on . . . . the negative thoughts are having a ball! Therefore no chance of seeing another's point of view . . . . at all!

Remember: Negative thoughts physically crowd your brain leaving very little room for positive thoughts to come in.

They keep their silence so as not to dilute their negative thoughts with other things that may take their attention away from their position of being *the one who is in the right here, the one who is the victim here,* and *the one whose rule has been violated here.*

They revel in their self-pity! Can anyone believe how hard done by they are?

Remember, people will continue to do what is working for them. If sulking wasn't working for them they would stop it. If you feed the destructive behaviour, your partner will continue to sulk because it is working for them. If you starve it, it will simply die off.

You feed it, by reacting to it; and you simply starve it by ignoring it and not even noticing that it is happening, and continue to live your life happily, (YES! *Happily!*) Unaffected by the sulking! There is nothing worse than being ignored! . . . . Hard? . . . Yes! But doable!

> **Sulking stems from having a self-righteous attitude, a lack of self-worth, low self-esteem and having a victim-like mentality.**

If this is you: you need to put your ego aside and learn another way of coping with your negative feelings. It's very nasty, destructive and dysfunctional!

Someone else doesn't have to pay because you feel bad!

After all, you make someone else miserable, but, for crying out loud! Who can be more miserable than you when you are sulking? Now, you tell me . . . Be honest!

For things to improve, you need to be willing to change. You do not need to carry on with this destructive behaviour. If you are not able to raise your own self-esteem, or stop sulking, you may need to seek professional help—so that you can have a quality relationship instead of a second-rate one, which goes from sulking crisis to sulking crisis or some other destructive behaviour, because you haven't learnt a better way of expressing yourself. You may have learnt these destructive behaviours from your earlier role models, like your mother or father, but please don't let a learnt behaviour which belong to others destroy your present relationship, now! And NO! That is not a good excuse, for you to continue this dysfunctional behaviour!

You need to be a person who inspires respect by respecting yourself first and by respecting your partner, by cultivating a quality and loving relationship.

Always show respect to one another.

Remember: **what you feed thrives.**

Your relationship needs to be fed daily. You have to know who you are and decide what you want in your intimate relationship. Like for any other areas of your life, it helps to have a vision of what you want.

It helps to be clear about what you want and purposefully go for it. Think about other role models who can inspire you.

You need to get back in touch with the real you, warts and all. It's no good kidding yourself. That means knowing your own strengths and weaknesses, your own values, beliefs, talents and gifts. You need to know how you normally react to what happens to you and your attitude of approach to events and experiences.

> *You only get out of this life what you put in. If you are not putting in the effort, just don't expect much out.*

By having insight, you will become aware of what you are bringing into your relationship.

> **If you bring your past baggage to your present relationship, you are not reacting to the here and now, but to your past.**

Your present partner is probably often scratching his head at some of your reactions, wondering what on earth you are thinking and why you do what you do!

There is always a very good reason not to bring the past into a present relationship. Chances are your past relationship has been unsuccessful because it is no longer alive; that's why it is past, not present!

> **If you continue to react the same way, you will repeat the same mistakes that you made in the past, and wreck your present relationship as well, before you get started.**

> *If you keep doing what you have always done, you will be getting what you have always gotten.*
> —Anthony Robbins

This phrase is well known in the coaching world, because it says it as it is. If your previous relationship failed because of how you behaved, and you repeat this same behaviour in this present relationship, guess what? . . . You will end up with the same results in this relationship as you did previously.

Einstein once defined insanity as *doing the same thing over and over and expecting a different result!*

Keep doing what you did in your past unsuccessful relationship and it will end up the same way!

> *It is insanity to expect different results when you keep doing the same thing.*

Self-Respect

If you have no self-respect, others won't treat you with any respect either. However, treat yourself with self-respect, you will find that others will follow suite; they will find it very difficult to mistreat you.

How do you treat your best friend? . . . . Great, I hope! You need to treat yourself as if you were your very own best friend. Would you mistreat and insult your best friend? Of course not! So, why do you do it to yourself? Watch for that critical little voice in your head. What is it telling you?

Become aware of your self-worth and your sense of personal value.

Work hard on to develop your self-esteem.

Aim to grow and mature emotionally.

Your self-worth is at the bottom of your success or failure in relationships as well as in every area of your life.

If you show self-respect for yourself, you will inspire others, especially your partner to treat you and treat themselves with as much self-respect. Self-respect gives you the confidence to choose what kind of relationship you are willing to settle for and not settle for mediocrity. Choose to be in control of your own life and your future whether good or bad, successful or unsuccessful is in your hands

Happiness in relationships

Understand that your happiness isn't dependent on any external factors, such as luck or someone else like your partner or others over whom you have no control over.

Happiness is any moment that makes you feel good and that is something that you can control.

Happiness or depression is a transient emotional state.

You can choose to feel happy if the sun is shining; you can choose to feel happy and delight in one of your children's smiles or you can choose to feel happy and giving and rejoice in your partner or you can choose to feel happy for no reason, just because you choose to. You can feel happy in the morning, confident by the afternoon and have a moment of depression in the evening. We all go through different emotional states throughout our day. It doesn't mean that because we are generally happy that we can't have *down* times. Having the odd *down* times, doesn't necessarily mean that we are actually unhappy.

Be bold, claim your right to have a quality and fulfilling relationship, by really understanding the real you and by treating yourself with honesty, dignity, integrity, and enormous self-respect first. If not, you can choose to experience conflict, pain, guilt, anger, frustration and confusion and you may not even understand the cause of your unhappiness.

To be able to relate to another in an intimate relationship, it is essential for us to get to know ourselves first, and then learn about our partner. The relationship then becomes a whole load easier.

> **To have a satisfying relationship, is to have one in which there is an equal partnership.**

One, where there is mutual trust, respect and the confidence to be yourself; One where you are able to lift and inspire those around you; One, in which you will be looking to be equally fulfilled.

Choosing a Partner

So making the right choice of partner for who you are today is crucial. Knowing what you want in a partner is important before you even have a partner.

> *Don't just wait and see what turns up. Don't wait and see who chooses you! No! No! You choose!*

You choose the person you believe will fulfil your mutual needs and have the qualities and attributes that you are looking for. That does mean that you need to know what these qualities and attributes are before you even decide to choose your partner.

You need to make sure that you know what qualities and attributes are absolutely essential; you need to know what are your "completely essentials" in a partner, that you are unwilling to compromise on.

In other words you need to know exactly what qualities that the person you choose *need to have* and also what you will not tolerate in a relationship; your absolute *no way, no how*!

For instance, you may choose to have someone who is reliable. When they tell you that they will be there, they are there! Any unreliability is *not* tolerated. That may mean that the first time they let you down that you give them their marching orders, no matter how cute they are. If one of your top values is hard work, you may choose someone who has good work ethics. One, who, come rain or shine, gets up and goes to work, not one that can take a *sicky* at the drop of a hat!

It may also be important for you that the person you choose is 100% honest, anything less is not tolerated; or you may not entertain a relationship with someone who has no family values. If you have thought it out thoroughly before you meet the person, you can then choose to see the one who ticks all your boxes, and reject those who don't. That way, you will have less conflict in your relationship. You do not allow yourself to be swayed by their *cuteness* factor. You do not give those who do not fit your criteria any opportunity of getting to know you better, if you know that they have undesirable traits on your absolute *No way. No how* list.

If you can know all that before you meet the right person, you will stand a much better chance at a fulfilling a long-lasting rewarding relationship.

You need to take responsibility for everything in your life. As your relationships are unique to you, you have to be responsible for the quality of the relationships that you have with anyone, including the one you have with yourself.

Relationships can be different with different people because you are only one of its kind individual, and you come with your own God-given genuine gifts and talents, not forgetting your own *baggage* but, so would others. You should not take any of your relationships least of all, your personal relationship for granted; it is life's special contribution to you. Such is the magic of life and relationships!

Cultivate the Friendship

You need to cultivate your friendship towards each other in your intimate relationship. That is your passport that will get you out of trouble when the going gets tough. If you have a solid friendship as well as love between you, you stand a better chance at making your relationship a success. Every now and again, remind yourself of your partner's many qualities and focus on them.

Warning

One word of warning though, initially there may be a lot of *lust* between you as well as personal attraction, I will warn you against jumping into bed together too soon, until at least you get to know *who* you are jumping into bed with. **They may have a very hot body, but they are a real louse otherwise!**

Often, I have clients who meet new partners and within no time, have an intimate relationship, and before you know it, the relationship is over and they wonder why??? If that was all that they wanted, they got it, thanks very much and they're off. The problem afterwards is that these same clients don't understand how come the relationship is soon over and are puzzled as to why they can't maintain a permanent relationship, as they keep doing the same thing but keep expecting different results. You need to be able *to get it!*

Above all, treat yourself with the respect that you deserve. Know what you want and don't abuse yourself because you feel you have to or because you are under pressure. Give yourself a chance of knowing if that person is suitable to you or not; that they do not possess any of your absolute *No way, no how* qualities. Remember, that if all they want to do is jump in your bed, they may well promise you the earth and many have been to charm school to get what they want! Though, the next morning you may find yourself empty with your self-esteem at rock bottom and wonder why!

As I have said, self-esteem can take a life-time to build up, but can be deflated in the blink of an eye!

Different Cultures

You also need to bear in mind that if you are going to have a relationship and marry someone from another culture different to your own, you need to know whether that will be compatible with the person that you are; so that if culture differences arise, you will be prepared to work at your relationship as you have already thought things through. You also need to know that your partner will be prepared to do the same sincerely. This has nothing to do with the colour of your skin, but this is much deeper.

> *You can take someone out of their culture, but you cannot take their culture out of them.*
> *It doesn't make one culture better than another, but it matters if the cultures are*
> *not compatible with each other.*

In some cultures, women are looked at very differently from men. So, if you choose someone from these cultures, you need to know that this is a possibility for you and if that is acceptable to you, way before problems arise. You know that these things happen, as I'm sure you would have heard it on television before. Don't think that it happens to others and it won't happen to you. These things need to be thought out well beforehand and have frank discussions about it. Then, if it is still something that you want to do, then, go ahead. However, if you are not prepared to compromise you need to be strong and make the right decision for who you are.

Some people fall in love and get married and after a while the complications of life take over, and if the couple splits up, you have to know that your child will not end up in some country far away or abducted by their own parent. You have to learn about that culture and see whether you will feel comfortable with their customs and the rest of the family or even live in their country if the need arises. Don't just be hypnotized by love and fresh air and hope for the best! If possible it would be good to learn their language too. If you want to keep your children in the same country and in close proximity, then you need to have given this some serious thoughts before marrying someone from a different country or culture to yours. I am not saying that things like that are impossible or that you shouldn't do it, but I believe that you need to think very seriously about it, and not be flippant about it and hope that love will conquer all. Some people do change after they have that ring on their finger. Sadly there are far too many narcissists in this world. They come in all shapes and sizes and from all countries. I want you to think very seriously at all the pros and cons, not just think: *We love each other, that's all that matters*; Yes, love is very important, but there are a lot of other factors to consider too.

Be also aware that when you enter a marital relationship with your partner, you are not only entering a relationship with that one person alone, you are also entering a relationship with their whole family and their culture. When you marry someone, you become part of their whole family with all their customs and traditions. A man or a woman come attached with their mothers, fathers, brothers, sisters, grandparents, cousins, aunts, uncles etc. Your status and other people's status change when you marry; you become a daughter-in-law, a son-in-law, a brother-in-law, a mother-in-law, a father-in-law, a sister-in-law, a cousin, a niece or nephew, aunty or uncle or even a step-mother or step-father, or a step-grandmother or step-grandfather. Other people's status change too. When I got married my husband immediately inherited seven sisters, a brother, a mother-in-law, a father-in-law and the rest! It would have been too tragic if he couldn't get on with them.

It is unfair to marry someone or to be in a relationship with someone and then try to isolate them from their family, because you don't like their family or their culture. If that is the case from the beginning, you have the choice to walk right away and leave the relationship, instead of causing hurt and pain to a lot of people. You should sort that out way before the relationship becomes serious and steady. It is a very dysfunctional thing to do. Families do have their traditions or their own ways of doing things. It helps if you are acquainted with each other's traditions, then things do not come as a shock, and you do not offend or feel offended if you are asked to follow certain customs. You will already know that it is expected. You need to know what you are letting yourself in for. Don't think that you can change someone else.

> **You can only make changes in you, not in others. You have control over you, but not over others**

These are things to think about way before you become crazy in love. When you are in love at the beginning, things seem so wonderful that you firmly believe that others have done these things but *no, not your lovely partner! Never!!* The problem is that these things happen; if you marry someone that you didn't really know, or wasn't aware of their family ways, this can be a source of constant conflict for years throughout your relationship.

However, if you decide to marry someone from a completely different culture to yourself, you can at least say that you went there with eyes wide open, knowing all the plus points and the minus points.

Have you seen the movie or read the book: *Not without my daughter*? In reality, in life these things happen too. It was a true story. Recently, the courts ordered 3 children to be returned back to live with their father in Italy, much to the heartbreak of the mother, the children and their Australian family. We always think that these things happen far away, somewhere, to other people, or on Television somewhere or in the movies, but the reality is that it does happen to real people, in the real world. It is as well to be prepared and have gone into things armed with knowledge, should you decide to enter in a serious relationship, with someone who has a completely different culture to you.

Go in with your eyes wide open and because you choose to, having considered everything first.

If You Are Already In A Relationship

Whatever is happening in your relationships, you have both created it together; whether good or bad things are happening. It is because you have somehow allowed it or tolerated it, by either not reacting to it or by ignoring it, or pretending it was just not happening, or by living in denial. Sometimes you may just have kept quiet for an easy life, to keep things ticking over and not to have conflict. On the other hand, you may have maintained what's happening or encouraged it knowingly or unknowingly.

What you experience in your lives now is the result of all that you have done to maintain your self-image and your way of life in the past. If you want to have the figure of your dreams, that, demands a lot of work! You need to have the way of life and the commitment to regularly eat well, exercise, play sport and do what is necessary to achieve and sustain it. If you pay lip service to being athletic, but spend your life vegetating on the sofa watching television and you scoff fast foods at each opportunity that you have, what do you think your chances are of looking like Mr. Universe or Miss World, even if you are the fairest of them all? . . . . Poor? . . . sorry! Hum . . . . Yes, very poor!! If you want to look fit and toned up, it doesn't come easy, you have to be dedicated and work hard to achieve it.

You can be as knowledgeable as you can be about nutrition, diet or exercise, but unless you put theory into practice, you will still not look like Mr. Universe or Miss World. Knowing something in your head and not putting it into action is academic. So, having all this knowledge will be academic unless you put theory into practice.

Knowledge without action equals to the status quo. It is irrelevant if you have any knowledge or not if you do not take action. Knowledge without actions is no help to anyone. Knowledge is only power when it is put into practice by taking actions.

Your lifestyle always reflects the kind of person you are.

So if you are looking for a certain type of person to enter in a relationship with, it means that you have got to look at yourself as carefully as the person you are looking for. You need to be that type of person.

Therefore if you are looking for some athletic looking man or woman, you also need to put your money where your mouth is and do the work on yourself. The reason for that is that an athletic looking person will also be looking for someone of like mind, not someone who couldn't care less what they look like.

> *The way we are, whether we are athletic, sporty or overweight, glamorous or scruffy— portrays a certain mindset which reflects our personality, our beliefs and our values which altogether form part of who we are.*

If you do not exercise, eat fast unhealthy foods, smoke, overdo alcohol, maybe dabble in a little so-called *recreational* drugs, this will be reflected in the way you look, in your values, your beliefs, in your lifestyle and behaviours and in the kind of friends you associate with and the way you lead your life.

Not only will it reflect your lifestyle, it will also reflect an associated way of thinking and your attitude towards life, including your beliefs and values. In the same way, if you want to be fit and healthy, and grow older feeling strong and fit and flexible, you need to commit to a healthy lifestyle with the associated mindset.

It is the same in your relationship, if you want to maintain a healthy and fulfilling relationship, you have to be prepared to put in the hard graft, by taking the necessary actions; by giving and taking time to emotionally feed this relationship and by choosing the lifestyle to maintain it too.

It means being prepared to consciously make time for each other every day and treat your relationship like something that you treasure, not with the attitude of *I'm too busy, haven't got time for that!*

Taking each other for granted is always a dreadful stance to take . . . . Don't even go there!

If you value your relationship you must make time for it. Relationship is about learning to give and take and getting the balance right; not one, constantly giving and the other constantly taking, and you do it all with love.

Consciously Nourish Your Relationship

If you want anything to thrive you need to take care of it; you need to feed it, nourish it and look after it. In the same way, you need to nourish your relationship positively and nurture it, as you would a precious orchid in your garden that you have invested so much in and would do anything to help it to survive and flourish.

Your relationship is precious. Treat it with love and care.

When you have a bad relationship, this too is being fed and nurtured, very often unintentionally, in a very negative way, where long-term issues stem from.

> *You feed your relationship negatively by what you accept, ignore or encourage.*

You often do not realize that by what you allow, by what you bring forth or by what you continue to accept, you are feeding your relationship and helping it to deteriorate until it's sometimes too late.

I don't think that we consciously choose the lifestyle that nurture and feed our problems; little by little they just creep upon us, without us realizing it, and before we know it we find ourselves in a situation where we want to run away from. These things often happen insidiously and we only become aware of it, when the problem is no longer a small issue.

Like any Chiropractor will tell you, by the time you feel the pain and seek help, the damage has already been done way before. It's the same in a relationship. These things creep upon us because we are not fully focused on our relationship. We have become complacent. We are busy living or making a living. We are busy being *human doings*. We let other worries in life take us over and neglect the relationship until it gets to crisis point.

The answer is that both partners need to stay constantly focused on feeding your relationship and nurture it very preciously so that it thrives daily. Do you eat everyday to feed your body? Then you need to feed your relationship everyday too. It too, needs to survive and thrive.

If you know who you really are, really know the core of you and act accordingly, you can stop problems way before they have the time to establish themselves as long-term issues. You must remain true to yourself; because if you are dysfunctional with yourself, it is impossible for you to be functional and have a healthy relationship with someone else.

If you are able to create the lifestyle and environment in which there is trust, dignity and mutual respect, you feel powerful. When there is mutual respect and dignity, you have the basis for a quality relationship.

It is important not to take things too personally. Sometimes developing a bit of a thick skin can help. We can get a little oversensitive at times. We do not have to react to every silly little thing. We can choose to let some things go and not take offence. Put it down to a bad day.

> *Everyone is entitled to a bad day every now and again. Add generosity to your values!*

Even if your partner is dysfunctional, your positive influence is bound to rub off on them. They can learn from you as a role model.

You have to know that even though some people try to control their partner, they can never truly do so. Even if they control them physically, they can't control their mind and their thoughts. They can never get into their head space and really know what's going on in there. They may be able to get their partner to do what they want out of fear or intimidation, but they can never know what the other person is truly thinking or feeling.

Controlling a partner in a relationship is very detrimental to both parties and to the relationship.

A person can never really and truly possess and control another.

You can't change your partner; it is for them to make their own changes. That's not your job. They probably are very happy the way they are. After all, they may not think that they have anything to change. You can only ever change you. Can it be that it is you that need to change rather than your partner?

You may not be able to tell your partner how to behave, but by your behaviour, you can inspire or motivate them.

If you choose to no longer fight, and start behaving in a new way, it will be very difficult for your partner to keep fighting, if there is no come-back and you have a more open attitude—unless you are in an abusive relationship! To keep fighting we need for the other person to retaliate too. If you choose not to retaliate, you may well avoid many fights. On the other hand, if you have issues to be discussed, you can set new rules for how you do that without it deteriorating into a fight.

You can decide to be brave, and take the lead in how you should behave instead. You don't have to take everything personally. When you turn everything on to yourself, it becomes very easy to feel hurt and offended, even when none was intended.

Remember, sometimes things are not really about you, it often is about someone else's requirement to meet their own needs. Controlling you may be part of trying to meet their needs.

It may not be right, but it is also not about you. It is more about them. So, there is no need to take everything personally. If you realize this you can make a plan on how you tackle this. Nevertheless do not allow another person to control you. If meeting their needs affect you negatively, then you need to bring this up and find a way to satisfy you both, where both parties can be satisfied. If you can't then, seek professional help.

Remember, that you are both on the same side. Make the presupposition that your partner's motive comes from a positive point of view. It may not be one you approve of, but nevertheless, positive in the first place.

Sometimes, you can easily fall into the trap of arguing like a two or three year old. He says something, she says something back. He says something worse; she is outraged and can't help saying something that will hurt him more, and so on and so on.

In this situation, someone needs to make a stand and realize that this kind of fighting only ever goes round in circles and doesn't ever solve anything, but end up making you both feel very upset and very miserable.

The problem with this sort of situation is that we all carry our own private emotional baggage, from which we have made certain personal set of laws or rules.

Often we do not react to what's happening but we react to what went on in our past.

The only issue with that is that our partner can't get into our head and understand how we are seeing things.

Sometimes it is as if one partner is speaking Chinese and the other Japanese, but both wanting to resolve an issue in English; both are speaking different languages and coming from different angles. What are their chances of resolving their differences???Zilch!

When it gets like that, make a point of stopping! Listen to what the other is saying! Then if they make sense, tell them! You can say something like: *I hear what you are saying; I think I can see where you are coming from!* Just that simple act, can stop an argument escalating dead in its tract! You probably will shock your partner too! But that's a good thing! The good thing is that your partner will suddenly feel *heard*, instead of both of you shouting over each other and not listening to what either is saying. Sometimes we get upset because we don't feel that the other person is listening and understood our side of things.

At times people treat their dog or strangers a lot better than they treat the one they are supposed to love! Don't let this be you! Your partner will feel a lot better just knowing that they have been *heard* and will be more inclined to make a compromise and meet you half way too.

Focus on the solution not the problem.

To fight it takes two people at least. If one partner is looking for a fight and you just refuse to play ball, but instead stay calm and behave in such a way to quiet the situation down you will get a very different outcome than if you just take the bait and react just as angrily. (I know! So, damn easy to do! But the reality can be very different; however, not impossible!) This way you can stop Vesuvius erupting, and avoid the volcanic lava of hurt spilling out into other areas of your life; as a result you may not have to walk on hot coals all week! On the other end, it could get icy! You may be sent to the North Pole for a while but even ice melts when the temperature warms up!

Why is this important?

It is important because unless you start to live with dignity, respect and integrity in your relationship, you will never have the quality relationship that you desire; this is where you start, right here, right now!

I believe that when things go wrong in a relationship, it starts first of all, with the *wrong thinking*. This is not only in our intimate relationships; this is for all relationships!

We sometimes mistakenly make the wrong assumptions. Don't just assume things; don't let two plus two make five! Clarify it with the person if you're not sure. Don't just get hurt and say nothing. This can lead to disaster.

Sometimes when things are going right in our lives, we have the luxury of spending time pontificating over some stupid little things that we think someone has done to us, caused may be through somebody's thoughtlessness rather than nastiness; and instead of just letting it go, we allow it to hurt us and we end up focusing on it and feeling really sorry for ourselves.

Often that thoughtlessness is due to someone else being overloaded by the stresses of their own lives.

What is worse is that we don't just get hurt there and then move on! No! We hang on to the hurt not only for days, but for weeks, even for months, and very often for years! We keep counting the bad things that someone may have inadvertently done to us and feel really sorry for ourselves.

Each time the hurt is recalled it gets bigger and bigger, when the original offence was only something very minor. But, no! Not us! We keep it alive and never forget how we have been *so* wronged! *How can they possibly do this to ME?*

Because of course, we are so self-righteous that we would never have done such a thing! The problem is that we forget to examine ourselves! We forget to realize that we have probably done that, and the rest, and worse to others and even may be to the same people we're upset with, but it doesn't even occur to us!

Other people's sins are always a lot bigger and more unforgiveable than ours! As far as we are concerned!

When we are whiter than white, and when we have never done anything wrong, may be then, we can allow ourselves to pontificate!

> *The thing about being human is that none of us is perfect, which literally means that we are all imperfect. In order words, we are all, may be guilty of having done something that is less than perfect to someone else at some time or another.*

Do you think that you would be wasting so much time on these stupid little things if you really had something big to worry about? Absolutely not!

If you are stressing because someone didn't acknowledge you the way you were expecting to, or over some equally petty thing, do you think that you would give this another thought if you had been given a nasty diagnosis, or if your partner had just suffered from a heart attack or if your child was involved in a major road traffic accident?

If you wouldn't even give it a second thought in those circumstances, then you should do the same now. Do not allow brainless things to come between you and your joy. If it wouldn't matter then, it truly doesn't matter now either! We really need to learn to count our blessings rather than our woes. Assume that others mean well instead of jumping straight for the worst conclusions. Allow others to be human too.

At the end of the day, if we think the worst, we are the only ones hurting, not others. Others haven't the foggiest idea that we are stressing over something that they wouldn't give a second glance to.

Choose to think the best of others. You will inspire them.

Usually things never go wrong because of some fundamental huge issue. It's usually an accumulation of trivial things. It is always the small things that end up getting to you and making you feel angry and resentful. They stay in your head and build up anger and the resentment is loud and clear. This usually occurs mainly because you are not feeling loved and respected at these times.

For example:

—Can you please wash your cup after you've finished . . . ? *I might as well do it myself; I can see that you can't be bothered to do it!*

Or: *I'll* do the dishes *again*, shall I?

. . . . *Attitude!!!!!* . . . . *not good being passive aggressive!*

Although what you are saying appears caring, but if it is said with resentment, in an aggressive tone; you are showing anything but a caring attitude or love.

Small incidents like this accumulate and before we know it, it becomes our usual attitude towards one another; then we let our imagination run riot and start believing that we are on opposing sides, and before too long we begin to treat the neighbour's dog better than the person who shares our life.

Ask yourself, would you treat your neighbour or your colleague that way? If the answer is *No*, then you better change your attitude whatever he or she may have said or done or not said and not done.

It starts first of all with the wrong thinking, which leads to a negative attitude towards the person you are supposed to care about. We have a few negative thoughts about our partner, then our imagination goes wild and we then follow a negative scenario through in our head.

When we feel negative towards our partner, we also behave negatively towards them. We then reap what we sowed by them reacting just as negatively towards us.

> *Unchecked negative imagination can have a very destructive effect on a relationship.*
> *It plays havoc with our thinking.*

Wrong thinking slowly poisons the mind! Every negative thought that we entertain, represents a poison drip, seeping slowly drop by drop into our mind, rendering it more and more toxic, until we are unable to think rationally or clearly and see things as they are. We imagine all sorts and allow that to contribute to our feelings of hurt and pain.

When we are so negative, we can bite anybody's head off for very little reason! We are not pleasant to have around. Can we then blame our partners for finding excuses not to be around us?

Research shows that negative thoughts physically take up more room in our brain than positive thoughts. The first thing we need to do is to clean up our thinking and get rid of this wrong thinking.

A good presupposition to make is:

> *Behind every action is a positive intention.*

If whatever your partner does that displeases you, you choose to believe that there was a positive intention behind what they did; you would cope a lot better and resolve conflict much quicker. Even when the other person's behaviour impacts on you, you would probably be quicker to forgive if you knew that your partner's intention started by being a positive one in the first place. It may not be what you want, but at least their intention was legitimate in the first place.

Another good presupposition to have is to:

> **Believe that you are both on the same team at all times.**

If you attack your partner, you are in fact damaging yourself.

When you have a disagreement, it is helpful to express it in a positive way.

Express how you feel, without blaming, accusing or criticizing.

Whatever you do, complain about the behaviour, but do not assassinate their character. That is difficult to repair later on.

This is where the "I" statements help again. Express what you feel without saying dreadful things about them personally. When you use the "I" statements, you are not attacking or blaming, you are merely expressing how you feel when . . . .

When you do . . . . I feel . . . .

For example:

When you ignore me when we go out and you do not show me that you care, I feel that you no longer care about me. That upsets me as I just want to feel loved by you.

Not

1a. *You are so disgusting! When we're out you couldn't care less if I was there or not. You don't care about me and completely ignore me. You've got no manners, just like your dad! You are so selfish, you can only think about yourself! Typical of your family!*

Or

When you come home late and have not phoned me, I get very scared and by the time you come in, I am frantic with worry.

Not

2a. *Where the hell have you been? What time do you call this? I bet you've been at the pub drinking with your mates again! That's typical! What about me? No thoughts for me and the children! You wouldn't care if anything happened to us!*

In the first two scenarios, 1 and 2, you simply express how you are feeling, without any accusations or blame. Whereas in the next two scenarios 1a and 2a, you do not say anything about how feel, you are just busy blaming, criticizing, accusing, complaining and insulting not only your partner but his dad and his family and making assumptions, without giving your partner a chance to explain themselves.

Remember? If you attack them, they are forced to defend themselves!

In 1 and 2 type scenarios chances are your partner will be able to apologize, explain themselves, show you love and compassion and try and make things right for the rest of the evening, as they would feel loved by your concerns.

In 1a, and 2a, their backs will be up and this situation has got a good chance to escalate into all out war by the evening, and your chances of the volcano erupting is at danger level!

A lot of the time we make the mistake of personalizing things when our partner's aim was only to meet their own needs.

Half the time, it is not about us; we just happen to get hurt because they were trying to get what they want or do what they have to do. They don't deliberately go all out to upset us!

Looking at our two scenarios again: the first one could be that he wasn't really ignoring you, but was just enjoying having a discussion with someone else and didn't even realize that you were feeling ignored; in the second one, it could be that he had an accident on the way home or that he had a lot of work on or that he stopped somewhere to get you some flowers and chocolates or that he offered to help someone in need. Okay, I agree, this may not be the everyday explanations! However, sometimes there are other perfectly simple explanations that we just overlook because worry, resentment, hurt and anger take over.

However, there are also not such nice explanations as well. For instance, they may well be playing away from home or stop at the pub on a regular basis before getting home. Still, this wouldn't be the only clue that you got; if that is the case, don't beat about the bush and tackle it head on by asking the appropriate questions, without living in denial or doubt or just picking a fight, with no intentions to face things afterwards.

> **If you want honest answers, you need to ask honest questions and be prepared for the answers.**

Be aware that if that is the case that you would have to take some actions if the answers are not what you want to hear. But that is better rather than to continue to live in denial.

Often people choose to believe all sorts of myths about relationships, which clearly have no place in a healthy and harmonious relationship. These can lead to misunderstandings, which can lead to disastrous outcomes. Not being on the same wave length encourages conflict.

> **Challenging your wrong thinking can change your negative attitude and your negative behaviours towards your partner.**

Decide what you want in your relationship and how you want it. If you choose to understand your partner better, you will make better connections.

> **You need to make a commitment to want to improve your relationship on a daily basis and be disciplined to work at it.**

Solution

If you want to find the solution to any problem, you must first be able to identify and define exactly what the problem really is and how each of you sees the problem. You more than likely may have different perspective on the same issue.

Sometimes instead of reacting to what is happening you react to some other past baggage that you carry with you emotionally. This tends to blur your thinking and stop you from identifying the real issues at hand.

Discuss things when you are not angry with each other, where you can both identify what part you have played positively or negatively to put your relationship where it is to-day.

> *You don't have to be right; it is more important to be happy.*

Try to really put yourself into your partner's shoes and really understand how they feel and why they behaved the way they did; this is always very helpful, and helps you to see your partner's perspective better. Demonstrate love.

You can never do the wrong thing if you come from a position of love. Loves solves a lot of problems. Show compassion and generosity.

> *Know that by what you accept in your relationship and by your behaviour past and present, that you are teaching your partner how to behave towards you.*

Whatever happens in your relationship and whatever continues to happen is because in some way you allow it to happen, encourage it or maintain it. You do this by the way you communicate with your partner and by the way you behave and by what you accept in your relationship.

Never Try To Control Your Partner.

Your partner is a living, thinking human being, who has their own mind and free will to think for themselves, to make their own decisions and behave the way they choose to. If you try to control your partner, you are heading for a miserable dysfunctional relationship. The only person you can control is yourself. The only behaviour you can control is yours. The more you try to control your partner, the more unhappiness you spread. So examine what exactly is going on and what behaviour you allow, encourage or maintain.

> *Criticizing, blaming, complaining or nagging have no place in a great relationship. Worse still is punishing, threatening or even bribing so that you can keep controlling the other person. Instead cultivate trust, encouragement, and respect.*

Be accepting and become a great listener. Be supportive. Chances are if you set the tone in your relationship, your partner will learn and develop those skills too. Treat your partner as you would love to be treated.

An important thing to do is to decide that you do not use bad language or obscenities towards each other. The "F" or "B" words are a complete no, no! When you do that you are not respecting your partner.

Use Humour

All too often we forget to laugh enough in our relationships. Laugh as much as possible. It is said that we should laugh at least 20 times a day. Humour very often can dissolve conflict and stop you from seeing things in a negative way. Use it! Even abuse it! Remember, how you used to laugh at his or her jokes when you first met? Go there again!

If for example, you accept that your partner spends most of his evenings in the pub or on his computer; then one day after you decide to have an addition to the family, you now decide that this behaviour is no longer acceptable. This now becomes a cause of conflict in your relationship. Your partner learnt by the way you previously responded that this behaviour was entirely acceptable. *What's wrong with you? Why have you changed?* Will be their thinking! They have no idea where you are coming from as you have previously never expressed any dissatisfaction with this behaviour.

> *You need to express your feelings clearly and renegotiate what is acceptable behaviour and what is not for you at all times, for the person you are today.*

You may have dropped your standards, or given in to him or her. If you keep quiet for peace sake, you teach your partner that everything will be alright because you won't give them a hard time as you will just put up with anything. When you do this, your partner will keep taking more and more advantage of your placidity.

By the feedback and the way you respond to your partner, you are constantly negotiating your relationship into shaping it the way it is to-day.

So if you are not happy with certain aspects of your relationship, talk openly and express yourself, as your partner doesn't know what you've got on your mind, unless you say so. May be you say: *They know how I feel.* No! Why should they just *know*? You need to put your feelings into words.

As you gather, men and women see life very differently! We are different species! We are wired completely differently. (*We even, I think, come from different planets! Does Venus or Mars mean anything to you?*)

> **When you have a disagreement, it is important to aim for a win/win outcome.**

Don't aim to make your partner lose so you can feel good. If that's what you want you will lose even if you think you've won.

Fighting to win makes the other person the loser. It is not helpful in any relationship. We should aim to do what works for us, not to prove that we're right. When we win and the other person is the loser, we have also lost.

Learning *to agree to disagree* is an important skill to add to your talent list. Decide to be happy rather than right.

Sometimes it is hard to see things from our partner's point of view, because we all come from different backgrounds, education, and influences. We are genetically different; we are physically, physiologically, emotionally and psychologically different. We come from different parents with different upbringings and very often different parts of the world; we often come from different cultures; have had different teachers, different education and even levels of education. We have different peer group influences; have different jobs and media influences upon us. It is no wonder that our values and beliefs sometimes vary greatly. Our brains are physically wired up differently, which is why we can't see things the same way. We have different filters and boundaries due to our different life experiences.

Isn't it inevitable that couples have fights and disagreements? It is to be expected. What is important is our attitude towards each other and how we react to those arguments. We need to fight in a fair way.

We can let our arguments deteriorate into major fights or we can simply agree to disagree, or we can fight fairly by expressing our view point and not take things personally by attacking their character. It is vital to allow each other to take turn in expressing ourselves. This way we can have emotional closure. That's the healthy way to have a disagreement.

Always look for a win/win solution.

If there is no emotional closure at the end of an argument, we accumulate negative feelings, which then make us react in a snowballing manner to future arguments, as by then we are ruminating on our resentment towards our partner. Those accumulative feelings occur because we failed to get proper emotional closure in previous arguments. We harbour all that resentment.

If we controlled ourselves so much in previous confrontations, that we chose to bite our tongue, we would have kept a lot of very negative feelings inside us. The problem with that is that we become like a pressure cooker waiting to sssssssssss . . . . EXPLODE! And it doesn't take much to let our steam burst out from our heads, ears and mouth! We then end up saying things we regret!

These feelings often are fuelled by anger, resentment, bitterness, hurt, jealousy, self-pity or some other unprocessed emotions. These emotions all carry very harmful energies. When we have such an accumulative reaction, we end up exploding over some trivial issue, which leaves our partner flabbergasted at our overreaction; this leads us to (especially if you are a woman) being accused of being completely hysterical or insane! (I can bet that many of you can recognize what I am talking about, right? Hum! Yes!)

We can choose to let our partner dictate our behaviour and we can choose to be a door mat; or better still we can choose to be our own person with our own thoughts and attitudes, and deal with the consequences of life as necessary and lead a quality life instead of one of turmoil.

In relationships as well as other areas of our life, we always have a choice. How we react to any situation is always our choice.

We can only control ourselves, not our partner; and that goes for our partners too, we are only in charge of our own happiness, not theirs.

We alone create and live the experience of our life, including our own happiness. That doesn't mean that we don't have to be pleasant or create a welcoming atmosphere for our partner, and do what we can to help them enjoy being in a relationship with us. However, their happiness isn't our job!

Our job is to do what we can to enhance their happiness, but it is not our responsibility to *make them feel happy*.

When we start a relationship, we have to negotiate what we think is acceptable behaviour and what is not. If we accept a destructive or toxic, or unhealthy behaviour because we are hypnotized by love at the time; and if after a while we find this behaviour unacceptable and we haven't said anything but feel resentful, this can become a source of constant inner conflict and deep resentment.

By accepting it at first, we taught our partner that this behaviour was acceptable; he or she is now completely amazed that we've changed our mind, as we never spoke up in the first place. As our situation changes we need to continually renegotiate the rules of our relationship. We are both accountable for our relationship because we are both responsible for where it is at, at any one time.

It is the decisions and actions that we took together that created the kind of relationship we enjoy (or not) to-day. The fact is we got where we are to-day, *together*; good or bad.

If we act like a martyr or a victim, it is a choice that we make. If we choose to be a doormat, remember, that too is a choice. It is an attitude that we have towards our relationship, and it is up to us to change it into a healthy one.

For our relationship to flourish, we need to respect each other's rights and encourage each other to grow and develop at our own rate.

In an ideal world, there are some things however, we should never argue about. For instance: we should never argue about money (in an ideal world).

> *If you find that you have regular arguments about your alcohol consumption, then, stop living in denial and get real, because you DO have a problem. If you do have a problem, you need to look at it from a solution-focused approach, rather than blaming each other. If you can't sort it out, you need to go to see a man (or woman) who can.*

One partner should not be able to keep the other partner from doing anything that he or she feels she should or would like to do, especially if it is something that our conscience is telling us to do or not do.

We are all free agents. We were all born with our own free will. If our partner stops us from doing what we feel we need to do, it breeds a lot of resentment and anger, and can end up being very disastrous for the relationship. Bottom line is that you end up very unhappy and *splitzville* isn't far.

If a partner tries to isolate you from your family and friends, never, ever allow it, as you will find yourself cut off, lonely and extremely unhappy, controlled and downtrodden. By cutting you off from your support system, they hold the power over you and can control you. Let this ring major alarm bells for you!

Be warned! No one has a right to impose their will upon another human being, without them agreeing freely to it.

> *Don't settle for a relationship that won't let you be yourself.*
>
> *—Oprah Winfrey*

> *Never ever stop working on your relationship and never take each other for granted however long you have been together.*

Stop all the criticizing, all the blaming, all the complaining or nagging or even the threatening or punishing ways you may have fallen into. That is for people who do not deserve a quality relationship and who choose to be unhappy.

Choose to demonstrate love, caring, compassion, listen, support, encourage and accept your partner as they are. Cultivate mutual trust and respect. Choose to negotiate your differences.

> *Life's greatest happiness is to be convinced we are loved.*
>
> *—Victor Hugo*

Things To Remember:

- Tell your partner that they are loved every day.
- Be the first to say sorry.
- Do small things just to please your partner or to give them pleasure. Do things because you want to and because you choose to.
- Do not watch what others do; do what you can because you want to, and you will be much appreciated; you will see that it will become reciprocal too.
- Put respect and trust high on your relationship's list of priorities.
- Do not use bad language towards each other.
- Never argue about money.
- If you are arguing about the quantity of your alcohol intake, you DO have a problem. Get help.

- Never let your partner isolate you from your family and friends.
- If there is abuse, end the relationship. Never stay there for the sake of the children. The children will never thank you.
- Never behave as a victim or doormat.
- Banish criticism, encourage kindness, love, caring and support for each other.
- Concentrate on your friendship at all times.
- Cultivate humour in your relationship.
- Concentrate on your partner's qualities rather than their less fortunate ways or habits.
- Put yourself in your partner's shoes and try and see things from their point of view. Remember, we all come from different points and our views of the world are influenced by our filters.
- Think every day what you can do to make your partner's experience of life better and more enjoyable, remembering that it is not your job to make them happy.
- Practice compassion in your relationship.
- Practice forgiveness. Get used to forgive the little things; it will become easier to forgive the more serious misdemeanours. Your partner will do the same. We are all human and we too make mistakes. It is not weak to acknowledge our mistakes. It's the right thing to do and your partner appreciates it. Mistakes are blessings in disguise to help us learn.

In any relationship, whether intimate or not, the practice of forgiveness is essential to be able to move on, develop, flourish and live the rich life that we deserve.

Now you know many of the secrets of a happy relationship!

Part of the happiness of life consists not in fighting battles, but in avoiding them. A masterly retreat is in itself a victory.

—Norman Vincent Peale

Notes: What have you learnt?

CHAPTER ELEVEN

Secrets About Forgiveness

Forgiving is not a gift to someone else. Forgiving is your gift to yourself—a great gift—the gift of happiness.
—*Jonathan L. Huie*

The inability to forgive ourselves or those who have wronged us is often at the base of a lot of people's pain, misery and ill health. Where there is unforgiveness, there is always pain, resentment, hurt and anger lurking not very far away.

We can sometimes beat ourselves up so much and be very unforgiving to ourselves for something we wish we hadn't said or done or something we should have said or done. We can sometimes commit some acts of omission as we can also carry out some sins of commission.

Tragically, many of us find that the person we are most unable to forgive can be ourselves. If we can't forgive ourselves, why should others forgive us? Is it any wonder that we find it hard to forgive others?

It is essential to be able to forgive ourselves and others if we want to feel free, emotionally relieved and experience happiness. We need to choose to release our past and forgive everyone, especially ourselves. How on earth do we expect to forgive others if we are such ruthless judges of ourselves?

The life of inner peace, being harmonious and without stress is the easiest type of existence.
—*Norman Vincent Peale*

On the other hand, when we decide to forgive, we experience relief, like a heavy load has been lifted off our back or shoulders, and we feel light again as if we can literally walk on air. It is only then, that we can freely smile, have inner peace and enjoy life.

Forgive those who have injured you—not because they deserve your forgiveness, but because you can never be happy until you release your anger and grant forgiveness.
—*Jonathan L. Huie*

Some may find it very hard and difficult to forgive their enemies or they may not know how to; but if they are at least willing to consider it, then they stand a chance to heal their wounds. It is essential to make a *decision and commit* to forgive yourself or anyone else you need to. Don't delay; do it now. There is no time like the present. You have nothing to gain by keeping unforgiveness on the boil.

Ask yourself:

Am I willing to consider forgiving or am I going to continue to keep this anger or hatred festering inside me? Who is it hurting the most?

The person with whom you are angry or whom you hate may be unaware of all the mental torture that you are giving yourself on a daily basis on their behalf. If they were aware, would they care? As you are giving yourself such grief, you become even more resentful towards the person you hate, because you now blame them for all the mental pain and anguish that you are self-inflicting.

Ask yourself:

- Is unforgiveness worth it?
- What am I gaining from keeping this hurt alive; from keeping this anger or hatred festering in my heart?
- What am I missing out on whilst I stay with this anger, hurt or hatred?
- What kind of person does that make me to harbour such grudges? What has it done to me, personally, mentally, emotionally, psychologically or physically?
- What kind of a person is it turning me into?
- Am I proud of what it has done to me?
- What about all the happiness I am missing out on because my main focus is on anger and hate?
- What will I gain if I am willing to forgive?
- What would it feel like to be relieved of this heavy load?
- What is the ultimate price I am willing to pay for unforgiveness?
- What would it feel to be free from such emotional burden?
- What would my life look like to be finally free of unforgiveness?
- What can I achieve when I am finally free?
- What would it feel like to have peace of mind and peace in my heart?
- What would real peace feel like?
- What would my life look like?
- How positively will forgiving affect my mental, physical and psychological health?
- Am I ready to get out of the fog and start feeling alive and live again?

> *Unforgiveness makes us bitter, resentful, and miserable; it robs us of our joy and peace of mind.*

We cannot be truly happy and at peace if we hold on to unforgiveness, even if we can kid ourselves for a while. We can pretend, but when we are in our own head space, we know that this unforgiveness is eating at us. We have no peace of mind because of it.

Unforgiveness robs us of who we really are or of who we should really be. Our husband or wife or our children or our family cannot get the best of who we really are or could be if we harbour unforgiveness in our hearts.

We can never be happy and healthy until we release these unhealthy feelings from our heart. It is a real choice that we do have. It is within our power to forgive or not to forgive. We all have this freedom of choice.

> *Forgiveness is a choice we make.*

We can say: *They've done me harm, so they have to pay for it by me hating them* or *they don't deserve to be forgiven but I can choose to set myself free.*

Think: Have you never done anything wrong? Have others forgiven you? Do we not all make mistakes at times or behave in a way that we are not too proud of sometimes?

So long as we can go back apologize or forgive we can move on. If we can't, we then are stuck and become unable to get on with our life, because what is in our hearts is reflected in our outside world.

> *If our heart is dark, so will our world be. If our heart is light, that too will be reflected in the world around us.*

If you have never ever done anything wrong, then you may not be able to understand the need for forgiveness; but if you are like every other mere mortal like me, I know that I have done the wrong things sometimes and that I needed to be forgiven. You will then, understand that forgiving is essential to live a quality life. You can never be happy until you have peace in your heart and in your mind.

Forgiveness means freedom to the person who is forgiven but it especially liberates the person who chooses to forgive.

Some people behave like humongous idiots on the road if someone *cuts* in front of them. They behave like a psycho who has never ever made an error on the road, swearing and maybe chasing the other car, and are not happy until they have satisfied their rage. Do they never make any errors when they are on the road? .... What?? Never????? Get real! Everyone has!

We, most of the time don't mean to do it, but we are all human and make mistakes at times. So, for heaven's sake! Choose to forgive other people's mistakes.

Okay! Someone did something you didn't like on the road, choose to let it go! Choose to be gracious! Bless them on their way! Remember, you make mistakes too! It's a lot healthier for you to adopt this attitude. The other way, you have a huge rise in your blood pressure; you suffer all the negative physiological reaction that stress and anger bring; worst of all you feel really ghastly, especially if it ends up in an accident! Just not worth the hassle!

Choose forgiveness, even in the little things in life; especially in the little things in life.

So, next time someone cuts in front of you on the road, relax, and choose to forgive. When we get used to practice forgiveness in the little things in life, it becomes easier to forgive when more serious things happen to us in life as we have been exercising the muscle of forgiveness regularly. We can choose to let go.

If you hold on to grudges or choose an unforgiving attitude, which of course you can, you will never be able to achieve a quality life and fulfil your full potential, because it will always hold you back. Wouldn't you like others to forgive you too?

After all, who on this earth is perfect? Forgiving is about using our free will.

What you have to do is to make that _decision_ to forgive. It is your choice. It isn't something that you are completely incapable of. You don't have to know how to, you just need to want to. It is within your control. You can choose to.

Forgiving doesn't mean that you have to go to the person and say: I forgive you as if you were a priest in a confessional box! No! Forgiving just means letting go; it means releasing any ill feelings from us.

It means that you choose to let go of all your negative feelings towards the people you are angry with including yourself. You are just releasing your past and moving on, instead of being trapped in this phase of bitterness, anger or hatred.

Try it! You will feel liberated, lighter and more joyful and you will feel physically more relaxed, happier and healthier. Your friends will notice something different about you. The result will show in your face, in your demeanour, in your speech and how you interact with others.

You will be able to breathe freely. You will be able to live again the life that you were meant to live. And what's more is that your soul will feel soothed and healed. The amazing thing is that you will find that whatever health issues you were having suddenly starts to improve miraculously.

> **_Forgiving doesn't mean that you necessarily have to have that person back in your life either or that you have to like them or have to associate with them._**

You cannot be forced to like someone or have them in your life if you don't want to. You more than probably won't be able to like somebody on order. However, you can love someone without liking them.

The Bible says: _Love one another_ and again _Love thy neighbour as thyself._ This assumes that we do in fact love ourselves; if we love ourselves it means that we must also forgive ourselves; and forgive our neighbour and love them too. You can love someone without necessarily having to associate with them.

Love here means that you want the best for the other person and not harbour bad feelings towards them. Our neighbour here, does not literally mean the people who live next door to us, it means everyone.

You can decide to forgive someone, without making them your friend. Forgiving doesn't mean that you should be a door mat either.

NO! It means that you choose to release the past, but you don't have to put up with any old rubbish either. It is choosing to let go of all the hurt and pain. It's choosing to set yourself free! It's getting to a place where you can actually think about what that person has done without any negative feelings towards them. It's getting to a point where we can actually wish the best for that person and mean it, instead of having any ill-feelings towards them.

It is certainly not a license for those who do not like you to do you harm because they know that you will forgive them; or for you to accept it and put up with it either! Absolutely not! If the person whom you need to forgive is toxic in their behaviour, then this is the sort of person that you forgive, want the best for them, but keep them out of your life and move on. You can be quietly assertive and stand up for yourself. For us to be able to heal and move on, we just need to get rid of any unforgiving feelings that we have and forgive everyone.

> *We forgive for our sake not for anyone else's benefit!*

> *If you hate a person, you hate something in him that is part of yourself. What isn't part of ourselves doesn't disturb us.*
>
> —*Herman Hesse*

Think about this quote and you may find some revelation in it.

Affirmations

Affirmations tend to work very well in helping us forgive. However, we must repeat our affirmations with discipline, intention and attention. If you do believe in a higher power, pray so that you can fully forgive.

Research shows that prayers do work miracles.

> *Affirmation without discipline is the beginning of delusion. Affirmation with discipline creates miracles.*
>
> —*Anthony Robbins*

Practice these affirmations:

I release (name the person) and I forgive her/him.
I forgive (name the person) and let her/him free
I forgive (name the person) and let myself free
I forgive myself, and set myself free.

Write these affirmations down and any others you choose to formulate and add to them.

Repeat them with intent and with discipline each day as many times as you can. It will go into your subconscious and you will find it easier to forgive.

Through repetition the message reprograms you. You end up by really believing that you do forgive your enemies and release your past and you are on your way to healing and to freedom, even if you had found it hard to forgive them in the first place. However, you need to be genuine and want to believe what you are saying and know that the end result will be that you will be free and renewed.

Affirmations are sentences that we repeat many times during the day and at night too, if we're awake! These repeated sentences sink into our subconscious mind, and has the power to materialize those words and phrases that we repeat, into our external world.

This really doesn't mean that whatever we say to ourselves will materialize into our world. For affirmations to work well, and for our subconscious to be triggered into action, we need to be authentic and say them with feelings.

Our brain is like an extremely sophisticated supercomputer. Whatever we ask of it, our subconscious finds a way to give us an answer if asked in the right way.

When something happens that we have been thinking about, and we think: *What a coincidence! I was just thinking about that.* It's not really a coincidence; it's our subconscious working for us. It is just like buying something that you hadn't previously noticed its existence before, suddenly wherever we turn there it is. Our subconscious is now sensitized to it and points it out to us whenever we come across it. It was always there, but we never noticed it until it meant something to us.

So to get positive results, affirmations have to be phrased in positive words and in the present tense. Our subconscious doesn't recognize the negatives. It does not recognize words like, *no* or *not*, or *don't*. Never put any negatives in an affirmation or you may get the negative results you fear.

The problem is that we often think more about what we don't want rather than what we do want. Often I ask my clients: *What do you want*? To this question, they often tell me everything they don't want. They often find it more difficult to put into words what they actually do want, however what they don't want comes readily. But that's okay as if they turn it around then they will know what you do want.

For example:
I don't want to fail
The affirmation is:
I want to succeed or *I choose to succeed.*

It may not seem like much difference because it is the same result that we are after; however the first sentence accentuates the fear of failing in our mind, whereas the second affirmation immediately conjures up a mental picture of success.

Or, for instance:
I don't want to be fat.

The affirmation is:
I choose to be slim and fit.

Or

I don't want to live with anger anymore.
The affirmation is:
I choose to forgive and set myself free.

You can't just say the affirmation a few times and then say that it is not working. The problem is that we often want instant gratification. We have to be patient, committed and consistent and affirm with attention and positive intention, and with strong desire and persistence, daily.

Believe that whatever you are repeating on a consistent basis is going to work.

Don't just hope it will work, as this shows that you have doubts.

Expect it to work because you are focused and committed.

Keep doing it until it works.

Believe you will attract it into your life. Believe your subconscious will find a way.

Don't worry about *how* this will happen; you do not need to know the *ins* and *outs* but just believe that it will.

Timing

Just because you don't get instant results doesn't mean that you won't get what you want. At times God's delays are appropriate or may be even deliberate, but they are not denials; maybe the timing is wrong or you have something in life you need to learn first.

> **At times if you don't get what you want when you ask for it, something better comes along later. Learn to be patient and believe that when the time is right you will have what you want.**

Everything happens in its own time. Sometimes that may be much longer than you hope for; but you must never give up. If you keep at it, you will see that your patience and persistence will eventually be rewarded. There is definitely a time for everything. If you are not getting what you want yet, it may just be that the time is not yet right for it to happen.

Sometimes we don't get what we want when we ask for it, but then get better than we expected because of the delay in getting what we wanted.

Maybe we have valuable life's lessons to learn first before we can get what we want. Maybe something else needs to take place before we get what we are asking for.

It is sometimes difficult to see things the way they are or should be until we can see the *bigger picture.*

It's important to choose the right affirmation for the specific situation, or we may get something we didn't want. We have to be careful that what we ask for is really what we really do desire.

Use your imagination

Using visualization with our affirmations makes them more powerful. We can choose to vividly see in our mind's eye, what we are wanting in our affirmations.

See it as if you've already got what you wish for. Before you get what you want, you need to visualize the end result vividly, as if you already have it. See what it would be like when you do have it; hear what you hear when you have what you want; and feel what it would be like to really have what you want.

The words we use are very powerful and our subconscious is on duty twenty-four hours a day listening to what we say to ourselves, and working to find a way to bring us what it thinks we desire. So we must watch the words that our internal voice is using when we talk to ourselves. We must not indulge in negative thoughts and think that they don't matter because we haven't said them out loud or to anyone. We have *the spy within* listening in on our conversation with ourselves!

Control Your Thoughts

Sometimes, try as you may to get rid of some repetitive thoughts, the same old thoughts keep coming back to haunt you and you find yourself giving up and following your negative thoughts or scenario through, which result in increased anxiety.

They may be repetitive thoughts about the person you want to forgive, such as: *I feel silly being the first to initiate contact* or *If I contact her, it is like admitting that I'm guilty* or *If I get in touch with him, he will be laughing at me and get one over me.*

When this happens, relax; don't fight your thoughts anymore; accept them; for instance you can say to yourself: *This is the story that my mind is telling me but now I choose to think that being free from all these negative emotions will free me from feeling so bad, and I will be able to move on.* Let the second part of this sentence (*being free . . .*) become the new repetitive thought.

Now dream about what it would be like when you get what you want; what it would feel like to be free from guilt, anger, hatred; and at the end of this dream, include a positive or happy past experience; whenever these thoughts recur, tag this happy positive experience at the end. Since you end with a positive experience you are able to be left with positive feelings.

If you can't think of any happy positive experience, make one up that you wish for. Imagine what it would be like to achieve what you want and imagine a happy scenario to follow. Let your imagination of the happy thoughts go wild. Dream big and dream vividly. Let these happy feelings and thoughts linger on; as soon as your negative thoughts return, go back to your happy scenario and thoughts at the end. So your negative feelings always end up with positive happy thoughts and feelings.

The brain cannot distinguish between something that has been vividly imagined and something that is real. The positive thoughts are the thoughts you are left with to ponder over.

Put your focus on adding some positive thoughts in, instead of focusing on getting rid of your negative thoughts. It will make controlling your thoughts easier.

You can write some empowering words about you want on a card as a reminder . . . . on your desk . . . . in your handbag or in your car to keep reminding yourself that you are sticking to being positive and that you choose to forgive, whatever happens.

When you can control your thoughts, you can control what happens in your life. Your life will change if you consciously and consistently do this.

When you are deliberately taking care of putting positive thoughts in your brain, you are leaving little room for negativity to come in. It stops the habit of negative thoughts overpopulating your brain.

Negativity Is Just That: A Horrible Habit!

One that is very easily acquired and difficult to get rid of. It means that you need to intentionally work at ridding yourself of negativity. If you do this you will begin to see changes, and you will be creating new situations and circumstances around you.

Your Internal Voice

Is your internal voice on your side or is it working against you? Is it your friend or your enemy? If that little voice which is in your head or sits on your shoulder or your chest isn't very friendly or kind to you, and is telling you that you must not forgive and to remember what bad things have been done to you, you need to give it its marching orders! Pronto!

If that voice is telling you things like: *You surely aren't going to forgive her, after all she has done to you!* That voice is not your friend and doesn't want what's best for you! If you need to point the finger at someone or something to blame for the results that you are having in your life to-day, then your finger should be firmly directed towards that critical voice.

Realize this! Find a more supportive voice, one that will allow you to set yourself free and look forward to a bright future ahead of you, where you can enjoy peace of mind.

> *Nothing feels as good as peace of mind.*

Your inner voice is very powerful; it can be either your enemy or your friend; it can be the voice of an angel or the voice of the devil or that of your mother or teacher.

It can enhance your life or destroy it. It can help you create a great life or it can nag you to death, telling you that you are not good enough or that you're not worth it, then again that you don't deserve to be loved. But, you know what? You really, and honestly, don't have to listen to it! You CAN just dump it! You CAN choose to have a voice that is positive and constructive instead.

If it keeps telling you negative things about yourself, you sure know that it is not your friend; and what do you do with someone who is your enemy? You get rid of them and you ignore them.

Instead choose the voice of a good friend who has your best interests at heart.

Exercise To Get Rid Of Your Negative Voice

- If you find it hard to get rid of your unhelpful voice: go somewhere quiet and close your eyes. Listen! And hear what that voice is telling you.
- Concentrate where you hear that voice is situated in your body; give it a shape and a colour. With your mental powers, move the shape and colour that you have chosen up and down for a little while; then push it away from your body at least 12 feet away from you. Now watch it gently fade away into the wall, or in the distance.
- If after that, you can still hear that negative voice. Then hear what that voice is telling you in Mickey Mouse's or Donald duck's or Bugs Bunny's voice (*What's up Doc! You wanna forgive?*)
- When you do that it will seem ludicrous and you will no longer believe it. Instead it will make you laugh at it and its ridiculous suggestions.
- You can now move on to your friendly voice. It can be the voice of an angel or you can choose for it to have the voice you decide on, but a friendly voice nonetheless. Now listen carefully!

What we are not aware of, is that we spend all of our life listening to that voice. We can't escape it! It's in our head! On our shoulders, in our stomach! When it says something, it better be good!

That Voice Is Your Inner Critic.

Sometimes that voice is the voice of an authoritarian or abusive parent, or one that constantly puts you down or a teacher's voice who repeatedly tells you that you won't ever amount to anything.

The minute you become aware of it, say *NO! I'm not listening to this* anymore! And consciously find your *chosen* voice to counteract what you previously said to yourself and listen to what your friendly voice has to say.

> *If you hear a voice within you say "you cannot paint", then by all means paint and that voice will be silenced.*
>
> —Vincent Van Gogh

> **Forgiveness doesn't mean that you condone what the person has done.**

It just means that you made a decision to let it go and liberate yourself from the toxic feelings that unforgiveness brings. If you find it really hard to forgive someone, then, know that, that person is the most important person that you must forgive.

You do not need to know how to forgive, you just need to be willing to forgive and decide to forgive and just let go. The rest will take care of itself.

We need to remember not to behave the way we would have done when we were unforgiving. This too is a habit that we must break. We can't just pretend to forgive, we need to truly forgive, body and soul. Our words need to match how we feel inside. We need to genuinely let go and not harbour negative thoughts towards the person we wish to forgive. The rest takes care of itself.

If we remember that under all human behaviour there is a positive intent, then it can help us to understand a little about other people's behaviour.

Maybe the person you need to forgive was just only trying to cater to their own needs, and you happen to be a casualty in the process? Isn't that a possibility?

An Important Life's Secret to Remember:

> *We all do the best we can with the resources that we have at the time.*

If we happen to have great resources at the time, the outcome is far better than if our resources were depleted.

Maybe that person was in a bad place at the time and didn't have the resources that they needed then. They didn't know any better. They can only do better when they know better.

If they don't know better, believe that they still did the best with the little they had at the time. It wasn't good enough but they still did their best with what they had.

Another thing that can help us to forgive is if we understand that: The people who hurt us may more than likely have been in pain too, and did what they could with the internal resources they had at the time to make themselves feel better. They may not have been adequate, but they couldn't do better as they didn't know any better. It is after all a matter of individual perception and what meaning we choose to give to our reality.

Choose to believe that behind every behaviour there is a positive intent, then forgiveness becomes easier.

The positive intent may have been for them, but we got hurt as a result.

If we comprehend that they were doing the best they could with the understanding, knowledge and awareness they had at the time, we will find it easier to be able to forgive. Maybe they didn't have what it takes? Maybe if they had they would have done better? Maybe they thought that they were doing the right thing?

Even if we decide that they did know better and still did what they did, it is not our place to judge others as we can never really know what is going on internally in another human being, what made them do what at a certain time in their life. After all, are we perfect?

It is never our place to judge other people whatever they do and whatever they're like.

One of the main reasons to forgive is to realize that we are wasting precious time in our own lives. While we are wasting our life feeling hateful and unforgiving, we have to know that we can never relive those days, weeks, months, and years again. Ever! That time is gone forever! And our lives are shortened by those same days, weeks, months or years spent in unforgiveness. We often hear that life is short; but somehow we never realize this until a tragedy happens to someone we know that we weren't speaking to because we couldn't forgive them. Then it may be too late!

> **Forgive while you can still do it, even tomorrow may be too late.**

Unforgiveness cheats you of who you really are. Your nearest and dearest are being cheated by not getting the best of you. You are cheating yourself, by not allowing yourself to reach your full potential.

Unforgiving days turn into weeks, then into months and before we know it we are torturing ourselves for years unnecessarily. We have our chance to live our days the best way we can; it is futile to waste them in bitterness, anger and unforgiveness. There will never ever be another chance of living *these same days* ever again in a better way, with better feelings and emotions.

If this is you and you are a child who hasn't spoken to your parents, call them now; if you are a parent who hasn't spoken to your child, don't waste another minute, get to the phone! If calling is too hard, writing is a good start. But do it and do it fast! There is no time to waste!

Don't waste energy on feeling silly, embarrassed or uncomfortable or worrying about whose fault it was. Who cares? If there is anyone you need to forgive, now, is as good a time as ever, don't delay, free yourself from that burden and you will be so much lighter! Let all that negative energy float away from you and you will be able to concentrate this energy more positively in your family or on other things that you hold dear to you.

If after all your efforts, the other person isn't willing to meet you half way, then you must let them go out of your life, but forgive them all the same. It doesn't mean that because you are willing to forgive that others will fall at your feet with gratitude. You can only control you, not others. Others have the freedom of how they choose to react. Either way, choose forgiveness and set yourself free.

> **We can never relive to-day or yesterday again. They're gone! All we have is now.**
> **We don't even have the future! To-morrow is a gift, not an entitlement!**

Even the future is uncertain. We are blessed that every day is a treasured gift granted to us, and no one (unless you're God of course) can promise us that we will be here to enjoy to-morrow. Many do not realize the beauty of the gift we have in life until we no longer have it. It is not something that belongs to us; or something that we should have.

We are all here but for the grace of God! It is not our due!

So, let's appreciate it and be grateful for it! Let's not take something as precious as life for granted. Let's make it good; great! Fantastic! Magnificent! Spectacular! Brilliant! Let's aim to make to-morrow better than to-day, much better than yesterday and the day before, and very much better than the day before that.

Do you realize that with every single day that we live, our lifespan is shortened by that one day? Isn't it a bit of a revelation when you realize that you have lived more days than you have left to live? I know I have!

There are more than likely fewer days left for me to live than the days that I have already enjoyed. This isn't only relevant to the older person; it is relevant to all of us, young and old, because none of us know how much longer we have left on this planet irrespective of age.

So it is crucial to make the most of every day that we have here on earth and make our experience a great one; one where we grow and contribute to others, and allow our loved ones to have the best of who we are, not one full of unforgiveness, bitterness, resentment and anger.

If our heart isn't candid, no one can have the best of us, even when we do our best to pretend. If love isn't in our hearts, our body will betray us.

Living with unforgiveness in your heart is very destructive, first and foremost to you; not forgiving can have life-lasting repercussions, because it can be too late if that person dies, and you have to live with the consequences. When someone dies it is too late to make amends! You can't go back and say what you wanted to say or that you would have forgiven them. It is over then. End of story. Nothing else to say!

Think, if there is someone you need to forgive, do it now; do it sooner rather than later. It's not always the older person who dies first. It can happen to anyone at any time.

None of us knows when our time will be up. So don't take anything for granted. Let it go, however old you are, knowing that if they died you are going to be comfortable with your conscience. Give yourself that gift!

Beware of living years and years and years in resentment because of something that happened a century ago. For a start your recollection of what may have happened may not even be your own. Don't let someone else's contaminated judgment by their own personal baggage, keep you locked in an unforgiving prison. You may have heard it said so often that you may have taken their word for it and their reality has now become your reality. When truly, none of it is what in fact really happened. Remember, there is no reality, only perception. So don't waste your life this way!

Exercise: *Should I Forgive Or Not?*
Ask yourself:

- Was this person's behaviour typical of their character?
- Where is the evidence?
- Doesn't everyone deserve the benefit of the doubt?
- Doesn't everyone deserve a second chance?
- Did they really want to harm me or were they doing what they thought was best for them?
- What about me? What role did I play in this situation?
- How did I contribute to the outcome?
- Whatever it is, I choose to forgive to set myself free.

Even if the person is guilty as charged, rise above it, practice truly forgiving them, not for their sakes but for yours; so that you can be free! You can live life without anger, hatred or bitterness.

Research shows that your health is certain to benefit from forgiveness.

Harbouring years of resentment will inevitably land you in great strife. It eventually turns on you. This is the stuff that cancers, heart disease or auto-immune diseases are made of. And, horror of horrors, for those of you who like to stay youthful: there is nothing like fermented unforgiveness in your heart to add years to your face! Those deep wrinkles are a dead give-away! If only for that, isn't it worth considering forgiveness? There is nothing like nasty, resentful, bitter or angry feelings to give your face a harsh, lined and older appearance.

> *A bitter person's face tells a whole story without even having to utter a word!*

More importantly, bitterness and resentment stifles your personal growth, your personality and your true happiness. You are forever on the lookout for people who you think are out to do you harm. You can never be truly happy when you entertain such negative and destructive feelings, however you dress it up!

The problem is that sometimes, some people have absolutely no insight about themselves, they can see what they don't like in other people's behaviour and have no qualms telling them about it; but they cannot see that their own behaviour may be far worst. They become so self-righteous about putting other people right, without realizing that they themselves have far more unpleasant traits. They are genuine in how they see things; that is indeed their perception. However, no one can let them into the secret that the way that they see things may be completely warped, as they can be very unpleasant and are not scared of any negative consequences or of hurting anyone.

This of course is an attitude of entitlement that their opinion matters more than others and that of course, they are right and everyone else is wrong. This is the kind of thing that can lead to deep-rooted resentment, unless someone is big enough to be the hero and rise above their pettiness and forgive. As they have no insight, sadly, this, they interpret this as confirmation of their rightful stance. On the other hand, if no one decides to be the hero, then this behaviour can create years of bitterness, resentment, aggression, alienation and pain to both parties.

But, check their faces and it is written all over them. They firmly believe that they are so clever and can fool the world. They do not give others the credit for their intelligence. Remember? You only get back what you give out! Still they carry on life by being always right and others are the ones who persecute them and cause them aggravation wherever they go.

They believe that they are so smart, but do not work out why these things continually happen to them. They have no insight that others are not so silly; they are probably kinder and clever enough to rise above it and choose to forgive instead of carrying on grudges. If you choose to forgive, you are the bigger person! Don't ever think that they have won; you are the winner as you liberate yourself by forgiving and moving on. They may think in their self-righteous way that they won, but still winning doesn't bring them happiness either. If you, on the other hand choose forgiveness, you will have peace in your heart and will be happy.

Choose Forgiveness

The answer to all of this is forgiveness. Forgive! Forgive! Forgive! You have nothing to lose but everything to gain!

> *Forgiveness brings healing and peace of mind; it is the best thing you can do to relieve unnecessary stress in your life.*

Holding grudges can bring their own problems. It may be difficult to mix in certain company or you may find it awkward to attend some social situations. You may have to avoid certain places or some people, which can really complicate matters. Choose to be free to see anyone you want and go where you want to go at anytime you want to.

When you genuinely forgive others, albeit in your heart, you do not find these situations difficult, because your conscience is clear and you are free as the wind to go wherever your heart takes you. It shows on your face and in your body language. You are transparent.

You know that you have truly forgiven if you come across the person that you forgive and no longer feel any hurt or pain.

You do not need to have this person back in your life; you just need to emotionally release them and wish the best for them. That really means not having any bad feelings towards them and truly wanting good things for them.

Forgiving is by no means condoning what they did; it is choosing to let go of any ill feelings you have against another person.

Silence Is Priceless

Take time to be still. Silence is good for the soul and for healing. Appreciate being happy in silence with yourself. Pray, meditate and practice relaxation, whatever gives you comfort and helps you to forgive.

> *You are never alone, if you like the person you are alone with.*
>
> —*Eleanor Roosevelt*

The helping professions

People who have a social conscience, like nurses, teachers, social workers or doctors or those who have a service mentality always are more prepared to forgive because their natural *penchant* is to do good for others. These people tend to be more giving and do better.

Remember the Law of attraction and the Law of reciprocity?

> *You get what you give out. If you forgive, others will forgive you too.*

Live in the moment. Forgive and move on, and don't worry about what other people would say. Quite honestly? . . . . It's none of anybody else's business!

Living in a negative past only brings grief, unhappiness and disease. If you choose this path, be prepared for pain. Choose to live calmly and freely in life. Don't take yourself so seriously. Learn to be able to laugh at yourself. Cultivate your sense of humour.

Self-Acceptance

In Emotional Freedom Technique (EFT), we use a statement of acceptance such as *I deeply and completely love and accept myself,* because EFT believes that deep down we don't truly and deeply love and accept ourselves as we are.

When we begin to really love and accept ourselves *exactly as we are*, everything else falls into place, and our experience of life improves. We are good enough! We don't have to be perfect; in fact perfection is only a mere illusion. Good enough is good enough! Let's embrace that!

When we forgive we feel happier, healthier, our relationships thrives. We attract good things in our lives, if we learn to accept ourselves just as we are. We are more open towards other people and we do get back what we practice.

On the other hand if you see the world as dark and everyone is out to get you; subsequently, you live in constant fear of *someone getting one over you* or wanting to cause you harm; everyone is a potential enemy. Life becomes very difficult as only your nearest and dearest are your only friends, if that! The rest of the world is foe. Nevertheless, it's a big world out there! That's a lot of fears to have to battle with each day!

If this is the norm for you, your perception may be very distorted. It's an extremely sad and worrisome world for you! Life is a real struggle! It is not easy as you spend a lot of valuable energy on things that may never happen! You may yet come to the realization that it is only this way, because your perception of the world has been distorted by your past experience.

Can you change it? Absolutely! But you must really want to change it and make a decision to trust and do different. If you want different results in your life, you need to do different to what you have always done; otherwise you will continue to get the same results that you don't want in your life.

If you see the world as basically good, although you acknowledge that evil does exist, your experience of the world is very much happier and much more relaxed. You will not feel the need of being on your guard and guard against people doing you harm.

Remember: You get more of what you focus on.

> *Self-acceptance and self-approval underpin positive change in all areas of our lives, including the ability to forgive.*

If we feel happy in ourselves, we find it a lot easier to forgive, and we relate better to others. If we are happy we look for the good in others, not the bad and we find it easier to accept that other people have their faults the same as we do, and forgive them as we like to be forgiven too. We need to live and let live, and abolish the spirit of criticism if someone doesn't think like we do or do the things that we do.

If we believe that everyone we meet is a potential enemy, our experience of life is very much more complicated. Sadly, some always find someone else to blame instead of looking at what role they played in the situation or experience.

If you look for answers to your problems by blaming others, you will never find the solution that you are looking for. You are looking in the wrong place! You need to look inside yourself!

The answer is always within!

> ***Any fool can criticize, condemn and complain and most fools do.***
>
> —*Benjamin Franklin*

Criticism

If we love something or someone we never look for the bad in them or criticize them. We expect to see the good in them and only see the good. So, if you love yourself, you need to start with not criticizing yourself in any way. None of that stuff like: *I look fat; My bum's too big; I don't like my nose; I'm not worth it; I'm not good enough etc. etc.*

You Are A Work Of Art! Period!

You were made especially by your Creator to be just who you are; just as you are! Warts and all! No one but no one is ever exactly like you or has ever been or even looked exactly like you in centuries and centuries and never will in future centuries either. That makes you very special!

> ***You are you! A unique human being with unique qualities, talents, gifts and attributes!***
> ***No matter what you look like! You are precious!***

There may be someone else carrying your name, but there will never be anyone with your finger prints or your footprints. You are indeed truly unique! How wonderful! If it wasn't to cramp our style so much, we are so unique that we could be put in a museum, as we are such priceless pieces of artwork! If only for that we should love ourselves just as we are! Never mind what we look like, we are all special!

People with good self-esteem, love themselves never criticize themselves, their bodies or other people. They search look for the positive in themselves and in others. Others in return show them the respect that they show to themselves.

> ***Criticizing others is a nasty habit that sticks and gets worse as you get older.***

People who criticize themselves or others are usually very negative people who look for the bad instead of the good. Quite frankly, it's an indulgence in self-bashing and people-bashing! It is such a habit that you no longer realize how unkind you are being to your fellow man, woman or child. The problem is that it is contagious! Yes! Just like an epidemic! You contaminate the people that you are in close contact with and you pass this nasty critical habit down the generations. An awful legacy to leave behind and to be remembered by!

Choose to be an example by seeing the good first and giving no attention to the bad, just as if you haven't noticed.

Practice, and practice and practice doing this! If you feel your usual critical spirit creeping up, stifle it and swallow your words; do not allow them to pass your lips.

Keep doing this for seven days, when the time the eighth day comes along, you would be in the practice of noticing the good first and the negative would gradually fade away. . . . Negative? . . . . What negative? . . . . You've now got the positive habit! Yes!!!

Exercise To Express Self-Love
Mirror Work

- Look into the mirror deep into your own eyes.
- Smile in your own eyes and express love and love what you see.
- Give thanks for the face, body and mind that you have, whatever it looks like; your body which is fully functional or partly functional for some. Give thanks all the same.
- Be thankful for all the parts of your body and love what you see, whatever it is like. Write it down in your gratitude journal.
- Now, count the blessings in your life. Even if you are going through a bad time, you can still find a lot of good, if you look for it.

It doesn't mean looking in the mirror and seeing that *your skin is pimply* or that *your hips are far too large* and that *you have saddle bags on your hips!* NO! It means loving your body warts and all and not a hint of a criticism in sight. Use it to express gratitude. Accept yourself, just as you are. You are perfect. Practice seeing all the good things first and stop seeing what is not so perfect. Show love to yourself and fully accept who and what you are.

When you criticize your body, remember: your subconscious is listening! Your subconscious is always there 24 hours a day with you and it is listening to what you are saying to yourself. Negative thinking poisons your brain, and gives you the result that you fear.

> *Be aware if you get into the habit of criticizing, it becomes a pattern, a way of life for some.*

When some people look at someone instead of admiring that person's beautiful smile or cheerful soul, or charming personality, all they can see is what isn't so good about them; when they do that, then they are doing themselves harm. It is a very negative habit that keeps you locked into a negative spiral, from which you have greater and greater difficulty to escape.

The problem is that these habits can be passed on to your children and their children. This is the very thing that you need to watch out for. When you catch yourself doing this, try to reverse it and find something positive to say about that person, and mean it! Think if someone was thinking or saying these things about you, would you like it? If you wouldn't then, others won't either.

Treat others as you wish to be treated.

Next time, choose to only say the positive and banish the criticism.

If you keep looking for the best in others, that too, becomes your new habit, which becomes your pattern after a while. This too can be an example that gets passed from generation to generation and gives such liberation that you are unable to believe unless you experience it. Try finding the good in everything and forgive the little things. You will be an inspiration to others.

If you are thinking of coming out with a negative comment, practice turning this around by making a positive one. If you keep doing this for seven days, you will already be on your way of acquiring a new habit. It will help you shed your, perhaps inherited critical spirit. The wonder of it is that you will pass this positive habit from generation to generation, and stop the vicious cycle you were born in. The world becomes a far happier place to live in.

Being critical often stems from our upbringing as we grow up copying our first role models when we are children; we react like our caregivers without engaging our brain for ourselves first.

> *A child, who lives with criticism, learns to condemn but a child who lives with happiness will find love and beauty in the world.*
>
> —*Ronald Russell*

Do not underestimate the powerful long-lasting effects of our childhood values over our life and behaviour, good or bad. Become fully aware of what kind of example you are for your children.

Now that you know better, it is time to get rid of the nasty criticism habit. You, more than likely will influence and inspire others around you to look for the good in everything too. This can have a snowballing effect as you spread more joy in the world.

When we are accustomed to thinking negatively, it is easy to jump to the wrong conclusion and get angry and hurt over some inconsequential thing or event. We get so hurt and upset that we then find it hard to forgive and are quick to blame others for our pain. These negative feelings can keep us unnecessarily in an unforgiving mood for a very long time.

Understanding ourselves and treating ourselves with respect, love and gentleness help us to move out of our negative pattern of thinking and behaving. It also helps us in forgiving those who we think have wronged us and helps us to forgive ourselves easier.

Remember though, that other people's criticism cannot harm us, unless we allow it.

No one can make you feel inferior, without your consent.

—*Eleanor Roosevelt*

We only feel hurt if we somehow deep down believe that there may be some truth in the criticism and allow it to get under our skin. If you criticize someone and say something like: *The talk you gave could have been a lot better!* Now, if that person felt confident about how their presentation went, and has been receiving good feedback, they could represent this to themselves as *Oh, well, can't win them all!* However, if that person suffers with self-doubt, and lacks confidence in their abilities, they may represent it to themselves as: *Oh, my God! I must have been really awful!* This may make them feel very negative towards the person who criticized them and increase their lack of confidence in themselves.

On the other hand, if the person has good self-esteem, and realizes that maybe they could have done better, they could see it as an opportunity to work on their presentation and do better in the future. In that case the critic may have rendered a great service to that person. This can be seen as constructive criticism, which is positive.

> **We must welcome constructive criticism. It is a way of improving ourselves.**

Again it is the meaning you put on something that makes you feel good or bad; your perception, which makes it your reality. So, when you hear something said about you that you are not happy with, ask yourself, if there is another explanation for what you heard. Keep asking until you find a more positive truth acceptable to you. If you need to improve, then do what you have to; you may need to master certain skills to do that. Go and learn and practice till you've mastered that skill. This goes a long way to improve not only your skills, but your self-esteem and self-confidence.

Conversely, it is not just the spoken words that matter in giving criticism; it is also expressed by the tone of voice and the way and the mannerism in which the criticism is delivered, that matter.

So when we are criticized we can take a moment to see how we are representing this to ourselves. We can check if we are reacting to our past or our present; or if some of the criticism is justified. If so, we can do something about it, by improving ourselves. However, if it isn't justified we can choose to see it as one person's point of view and that they are entitled to their opinion, and not take it personally and move on.

If the criticism is unfair and incorrect, it helps to realize that the problem lies, not with you, but with the person dishing out the criticism, especially if it was delivered in an unkind manner or in a sarcastic tone of voice.

That's when you make a conscious effort to rise above and choose to be gracious and forgive the unenlightened and move on. This demonstrates that you have compassion, you have good self-esteem and that you can rise above pettiness.

If evil be spoken of you and it be true, correct yourself; if it be a lie laugh at it.

—*Epictetus*

When you know who you really are, you are able to do this as your self-esteem is healthy enough for you not to be affected by someone's unfair, unkind or incorrect comment. If we do this, we are less likely to react negatively or childishly to other people's criticisms. We may even teach others something.

Remember, no one can make you feel inferior, without your consent!

A criticism can be a blessing in disguise; it can help us turn what could be a weakness into a strength. We all need constructive criticism to help us grow and improve. Though, it is how we deliver the constructive criticism that matters. If it is done with kindness and empathy, it is bound to be well received.

People, who give constructive criticism in a humane and constructive manner, are truly our friends.

Anyone who wants to enhance our life is indeed our friend; anyone who wants us stuck in bad and destructive habits may appear to be our friends, but in reality they are our enemies.

Some may hold lifelong grudges against their childhood teachers or their parents, as they may have thrown comments like: "You will never get anywhere in life" or "you are so stupid, who would want to employ you?" I must admit that these are absolutely disgraceful comments and that these people who hold a position of power should know better! Nevertheless, you can choose to allow such disparaging comments to crush you and destroy you or you can just decide to show them what you're made of. Often these sorts of comments are precisely the reason why some people do well in life, out of rebellion.

If you do well but you still hang on to a grudge in your heart, your self-esteem can never recover. On the other hand, if you choose to let go of anger and resentment towards those who offended you and to see it that their comments have in fact been beneficial to you despite their own inadequacy, you can feel gratitude towards them as you wouldn't be where you are to-day, had you not had a point to prove. You can then be proud of yourself as you wouldn't have suffered in vain.

If you are one of those who have allowed shocking comments like these to scar your soul, now is the time for you to move on and prove to yourself first of all, that you are better than that; that you will no longer let some nasty comments from unkind people who do not deserve your energy or time to bother you. As we have said before: Life's too short! We don't get to go back and do it again.

If you show compassion to your critics, you will impress them. You can set the example by showing them understanding, and that you have inner peace and confidence in yourself. You will be teaching your critic a good life lesson.

You cannot be hurt by other people's words, without your consent—if you are in control of your thoughts, if you are in charge of your emotions and if you are in control of your reaction to any event.

Your emotions are the by-product of your thoughts and you have the power to reject disturbing thoughts that cause you to feel or behave in a negative manner.

In NLP, we are taught that we are in control of our behaviour, emotions, speech and thoughts.

These are our 4 personal powers.

Behaviour
Emotions
Speech
Thoughts

No one can make us behave in a way that we don't want to. Equally no one can make us feel any kind of emotions unless we choose to. No one can put words in our mouths and make us spit them out. Finally no one can make us think anything that we do not choose to.

We have that control! We have that power over our behaviour, emotions, speech and thoughts.

Never forget this! From now on, you can no longer cop out by saying: *Look what you made me do!* or *Look what you made me say!* No one can make you do or say anything without your choosing to.

It is essential to forgive yourself and others if you want good health, inner peace and harmony. You cannot forgive others completely until you have forgiven yourself first.

It is worth repeating that, research has shown that unforgiveness, resentment, anger, aggression, and criticism of others are the root cause of many illnesses, from cardiovascular disease, stomach ulcers, depression and anxiety, cancers and arthritis, Lupus to name but a few. The effects of these negative emotions directly impact our immune system leaving it vulnerable to disease and infections.

The following poem should be studied by all parents to help them realize that our precious children are our future adults in training who through the lessons, experiences and examples that we give them in life will become the kind of adults that they will be to-morrow. We have the power now to influence who the next generation will be to-morrow.

We can choose to stop passing on the unresourceful habit and pattern of unforgiveness, negativity and criticism down the generations. Instead, we need to teach them love, compassion, forgiveness, kindness, caring, praise, encouragement and support and ensure that their safety is paramount.

> *Every child is entitled to be loved, to be nurtured and to feel safe in the world.*

LESSONS FROM LIFE

A Child that lives with Ridicule learns to be Timid.
A Child that lives with Criticism learns to Condemn.
A Child that lives with Distrust learns to be Deceitful.
A Child that lives with Antagonism learns to be Hostile.
A Child that lives with Affection learns to Love.
A Child that lives with Encouragement learns Confidence.
A Child that lives with Truth learns Justice.
A Child that lives with Praise learns to Appreciate.
A Child that lives with Sharing learns to be Considerate.
A Child that lives with Knowledge learns Wisdom.
A Child that lives with Patience learns to be Tolerant.
A Child that lives with Happiness will find Love and Beauty.

—Ronald Russell

Don't think for one minute that you are doing someone else a favour or that you are doing an amazing selfless act when you forgive someone.

> *Forgiving is a selfish act. You forgive for YOU. You forgive so that YOU can feel better; you do not forgive because you want the person you forgive to feel better!*

You release the past and forgive those who have wronged you because YOU wish to be free from the pain of the hurt and the hatred and the bitterness, resentment and the anger.

As hard as it is to understand, that you would want the best for your enemy, you can if you really want to. Again it starts with: Making a decision. *Decide that you choose to.* You can work on yourself as many times as you have to. If you can't manage it by yourself, get professional help; but it is essential for you to be able to forgive for your sake.

Repeat your affirmations, and believe them. Say them with love and forgiveness in your heart and wish the same for the one you wish to forgive. You will surprise yourself and feel better and feel much lighter emotionally, like a load has been taken off your shoulders.

You will know when you've forgiven someone, because you will no longer feel pain at the sound of their voice or when you see them or if someone says something good about them; you will feel no resentment or feel yourself tightening up inside. You will be at peace and feel nothing but positivity.

However, if you can still feel anger rising in you when someone tells you something good about the person who has wronged you, cheated you or defrauded you, then you have not forgiven and the hatred and anger are still playing havoc inside you. You must continue to work on yourself. Emotional Freedom Technique (EFT) is very helpful for this type of issue. Find an EFT practitioner to get help.

When you can remember what happened but can no longer feel the pain, the hurt, the anger, that kept you prisoner for so long, then you will know that you have released your past and have truly forgiven. You will then be able to talk about it without welling up or without any negative feelings, almost like it happened to someone else or something that happened in another life, a very long time ago. But it no longer has any emotional impact on you. Then, you will know that you have your power back!

You need to forgive mentally, emotionally, psychologically and spiritually. You need to genuinely forgive on all levels. Otherwise you will be simply deceiving yourself. You will just be pretending and you will find no release or healing.

I am not asking you to like the person who has wronged you; to be their friend or even to talk to them.

All I'm saying is that you need to fully release and forgive anyone who you believe has done you harm, for your sake so that you can have a quality life and be the person you are meant to be.

Your family will not get the best of who you really are until your heart is cleared of these negative and destructive feelings. You can go through the motions, but that is not living the best life you can and not achieving peace of mind.

You can stop blaming other people for all that is wrong in your life. The buck stops here with you.

And Yes! You can! And No! You are not a victim!

You are better than that! You are a winner! To be a winner you need to be able to have forgiveness in your heart. Pray about it, meditate about it, do relaxation, talk to a friend, get professional help, do what works for you but do it. Do not entertain thoughts of unforgiveness; it only comes back to bite you in the end; if it's not through a negative event in your life, your health may end up suffering instead.

We all create our own experience of life. If it's good, it is down to us; however, if our experience of life is not so good, there is no one else to blame.

By realizing this, you will also realize that your life is your own, no one else's; whatever results you enjoy or not have been your choices; you have to own your life and owning your life means that you have to take responsibility for it and for where it is at to-day.

You own your behaviour, your emotions, your speech, your reactions and your thoughts; and this helped you to create the experience of the life you now have.

All you can control is yourself; you are not in control of anyone or of any external factors. It's a cop out if you act the victim and blame external factors or someone else for all that is wrong in your life. It's a stupid game to play to believe that by some bad luck, dreadful things just keep happening especially to you. There is no such thing as being *jinxed*. You make your luck.

You may say things like: *Just my luck; it's one thing after another; I knew things wouldn't work out for me; Friends always let me down or take advantage of me* . . . . No! They don't! These things happen to everybody sometime! You're not anymore special than anyone else! It is up to you what meaning you choose to put on these events and it is certainly up to you to do what you can to make things better.

You are where you are to-day, because of the actions you took following the decisions you made, based on those thoughts that you chose to entertain in the past.

Although you have no control over external factors, you can choose to make intelligent, informed choices to avoid getting yourself in difficult situations time and again.

Accept Your Own Responsibility.

Don't look elsewhere for something or someone else to blame, if you don't like what you see and how you feel. It is only then that you can make things better. Give yourself a chance to improve things. You can only do this when you stop kidding yourself and playing the victim.

Even if you choose to live in denial, your subconscious knows *what's what*—the problem is you're not listening!

The answer is: Listen!

> *Every thought we think is creating our future.*
>
> —*Louise L Hay*

Thoughts Are Powerful

You have to understand that thoughts are not just anything innocuous that are around and that they do not matter because you can't see them.

> **Thoughts are things that can materialize themselves in our world.**

Our thoughts produce the life we are living to-day. Our thoughts produce the experiences we have to-day.

Thoughts are powerful; because whatever results we have in our life to date first started with our thoughts.

Before we can create anything, we have to have an idea. Before an idea is acted upon, it is but a thought to start with. Thoughts are constantly travelling through our subconscious like stars in the Milky Way. Some just pass through without leaving any impressions; others come, drop in for a while, often unexpectedly, like some unwanted guest; some loiter around a bit longer, mess things up a little in our heads then fade away in the background after a while, leaving room for other thoughts to travel through.

Many thoughts however are persistent and repetitive and remain in there much longer; they can often gain momentum and become powerful, affecting the life of the person having these thoughts. Most of the time if these lingering thoughts are positive, the person feels great and empowered, enjoying positive results in life. Unfortunately, often these lingering thoughts can be negative, even toxic, with disastrous emotional consequences.

Depression can be the result of people allowing their predominant thoughts of worry, anxiety, fear, anger, hurt, unhappiness or unforgiveness to invade their minds most of the time. They rehearse negative situations, events, actions or catastrophic outcomes in their mind in a feedback loop resulting in a debilitating state of mind.

For example:

If you have a fear of flying and constantly rehearse in your mind that the plane is going to crash, the plane is going to crash; the plane is going to crash on and on; at the same time visualizing the plane crashing, the passengers in panic mode or dead, luggage scattered everywhere etc. etc. You get the picture? . . . . I think, even though I do not have a fear of flying, it will be enough to give me a panic attack, if that is what goes on in my mind prior to taking an airplane!

If you want to feel better about flying, you need to rehearse thoughts of a peaceful and relaxing flight instead, visualize yourself lying back and enjoying the movie or the food and you will have the corresponding emotions in your body when you are in the plane. Use EFT, deep breathing exercises or relaxation; it helps. Prepare yourself mentally first.

You have to understand that whatever you are rehearsing in your mind affects your subconscious mind, making it accept and take seriously the thoughts that you have expressed in your internal conversation.

If you do have a fear of flying and you have to take a plane, prepare for it. As when you are scared of flying you are rehearsing a catastrophic flight, you must condition yourself in your mind to a peaceful and enjoyable flight. Do some relaxation exercises, and using the movies of your mind, visualize the flight to go the way you want it to. Condition yourself to a wonderful flight, so that when you take the plane, your mind is prepared for a relaxing and peaceful flight. If you know how to do some tapping, please tap away as it is excellent to change your emotional states. Do it throughout the flight too. It will help!

Thought is action in rehearsal.

—*Sigmund Freud*

Your decisions and actions are the results of those very same thoughts, which give you the corresponding results and emotions in your life, and ultimately shape your future.

I repeat again, that the mind cannot distinguish between something that has been vividly imagined and reality. If you vividly rehearse catastrophic outcomes, your brain will believe that it is happening, therefore increase your fear and panic. So watch what you say to yourself. Never ever think that what you are saying to yourself does not matter as it is personal and not outwardly verbalized. It is very important.

What you say again and again to yourself stays in your subconscious. Your subconscious believes what you say without judgment; therefore it finds a way of getting you what it thinks you want good or bad.

Repeated thoughts get stronger the more times you repeat them; the more you do it, the more they gather momentum. They get into your subconscious and affect your actions and behaviour. These thoughts affect your reactions too and result in where you're at in life. That's why affirmations work, but this time in a positive way.

> **Your subconscious takes you seriously and doesn't have any sense of humour. It is not in the business of guessing what it thinks you mean. It aligns your words and thoughts with reality.**

For instance, if you keep thinking that you are poor and think of lack all the time, that you can't afford things, you can't go there because you don't have enough money, your subconscious will take you seriously and will put obstacles in your way and stop you having the money that you yearn for. The right opportunities will not present themselves to you in order to make more money because your subconscious will keep you in line with your spirit of scarcity and poverty, as it truly believes that you do want to be poor.

You may be thinking: *I don't want to be poor*, but as your subconscious doesn't understand the negatives, it hears: *I want to be poor*, and therefore does all it can to keep you poor.

Conversely, if you think abundantly, and think rich and you keep telling yourself that you are rich, it will find ways and opportunities to get you what you want too.

So practice thinking that you are richly abundant! You deserve it!

Affirmations:

- I have all I need.
- I feel abundant.
- My needs are regularly met.
- I choose to forgive.

Someone once wrote:

Watch your thoughts, they become words.
Watch your words they become actions.
Watch your actions, they become your habits.
Watch your habits, they become your character.
Watch your character, they become your destiny!
(*Picked up from the net*)

True!

Your destiny depends on the quality of the words you put in your thoughts and the actions you take on a consistent basis. Everything starts as a thought.

> *The words that come out of our mouths are an extension of what our thoughts are,*
> *and what's in our hearts.*

If our hearts are full of unforgiveness, we show the effects of these negative feelings in our body too, especially in our facial expressions.

Observe someone who you think is bitter, and who finds it hard to forgive any silly little misdemeanour! Watch their facial expression! What do they look like? It is pretty plain for anyone to see what their thoughts are. Right? Even if you don't know what they're thinking, you know whatever the thoughts are they are not good. Can you see these lines of deep bitterness on their face? They couldn't raise the corners of their mouth to smile if you were giving them the world on a platter! As far as they are concerned it would be too little too late!

Now, look at a lovely smiling, happy go-lucky person, who easily forgives anything that happens to them! What do they look like? Isn't that written on their face too? Their easy smile says it all! Not a frown or bitter line in sight! Most of all their eyes are expressive and smile.

For as a man thinketh in his heart, so is he.

—Proverbs 23:7

What we think and what words we utter, influence the appropriate actions we take to support our thoughts.

Remember how powerful your thoughts are and that you do have control over your thoughts, not the other way round. Choose thoughts of forgiveness, love and compassion. Others will do so towards you as well. Your thoughts are powerful, but you have power and control over them and over the words you say.

> *Forgiveness is the finishing of old business that allows us to experience the present, free of contamination from the past. Forgiveness is not always easy. At times it feels more painful than the wound we suffered to forgive the one that inflicted it. And yet there is no peace without forgiveness.*
>
> *—Marianne Williamson*

Now let's look at how **the power of our words** can affect our life and ultimately our destiny.

Notes: What have you learnt?

CHAPTER TWELVE

Secrets About The Power of Words

Enthusiasm is the most beautiful word in the world.
—Christian Morgenstern

Stick and stones can break my bones but words can never hurt me! How many times have we said or heard this slogan as a child? We say these words in the hope that they can help us cope and feel better when someone says something nasty about us. But do we really believe these words? Can words never hurt us? Or do we feel the pain just the same when we are uttering these words?

Some words can cut right down to the bone and break us! They may not break our bones but they sure can break our spirits! Ask any child or adult for that matter, who has had the misfortune of being bullied, what they think! Some adults are still tormented years later by words that were spoken to them when they were children.

Each time I have a teenager or adult walk through my office due to bullying incidents, I become more and more conscious of how powerful, nasty, horrible and bullying words can be and how they can affect a human being's life for months or years to come, way after the original bullying stopped. The teenagers hear the words that cut them so deeply; now they often see them too on social media via cyber bullying which can pretty much destroy a lot of them. Teenage years are an especially vulnerable time, where negative events can adversely affect them in a most powerful way well into adulthood.

Words can be the reason why so many adults life are messed up to-day. Many adults to-day are still suffering from low self-esteem, low self-worth, and low-self image because of some words, repeated to them, in anger or out of pure nastiness or even out of ignorance while they were growing up. Many others are using destructive behaviours because they were verbally abused or bullied as a child. Somebody I know told me that his teacher had him stand in the front of the class once to tell him that *he didn't have an inferiority complex. He WAS inferior!* These kinds of words negatively affect people's lives for very many years, if not forever!

Many adults and their children still suffer in diverse ways to-day because they were verbally and emotionally mistreated as a child, either by their parents or carers, or by their siblings or their (so called) school friends. Others take drugs, smoke or abuse alcohol to numb the pain.

We repeat in our adult life what we have lived as children. Our parents and carers taught us everything we know about how to be a parent. Hence, the cycle of abuse is perpetuated for some.

> *As thoughts are powerful, words are equally as powerful.*

Words communicate meaning. Use the correct words and you convey the correct meaning; but words can also be the reason of many misunderstandings. Our inner thoughts are articulated through our words.

Our words can trigger emotions in us as well as in others. They can make us feel good or they can make you feel bad. They can create heaven on earth or they can create hell on earth. Words have the power of biologically altering our hormones in our blood and changing our blood chemistry. Words can affect our mind and body's reactions. Words also affect our actions and behaviours.

Now would you say that words are powerful or what?

Words are an extension of our thoughts which communicate meaning and feelings. They influence our memory including the movies of our minds, which are represented by mental imagery and symbols.

Words can make us fall out with our friends or they can make us friends. Words can produce war, hatred or can demonstrate love.

Our words underpin all our decisions and our influences.

Words can in fact change our life; by changing words there may also be a change in meaning consequently a change in perception, resulting in a change in how we feel and consequently in the course of actions taken.

If words can change our perception, they can also change our beliefs and our values. They can make us buy or reject things as anyone in marketing will know. They can decide what job we do and where we live. Words can also dictate what we like and what we dislike.

Words can equally get us in trouble as they can out of trouble.

> *If we have a way with words, we also have the gift of influencing and of persuasion. If we have the gift of influencing or of persuasion, we can be very influential and powerful.*

In Ireland, visitors to Blarney Castle, go through dreadful contortions facing a huge fall of hundreds of feet from the castle in order to kiss the Blarney stone; as legend would have it, if you kiss the Blarney stone, you will get "the gift of the gab!" (One of my sisters couldn't resist it! But she shouldn't have bothered, she already had it!) Having "the gift of the gab" can get us out of a lot of trouble and make things work in our favour instead.

Being able to persuade others can be very influential and can lead to amazing outcomes, personally or in business. Words can help us get jobs or promotions; give us confidence in a social setting or make new friends. They can influence others in seeing things our way, which can be an asset in business and make us socially popular; words can save our life when we are in danger, to name but a few.

In the penal system, it isn't the innocent person who is found not guilty; it's the cleverest barrister who has the gift of the gab or who has kissed the Blarney stone that manages to plead a good case by manipulating his words to his client's advantage that gets him acquitted. The one, who has the power over words and has the power of persuasion, is the one who comes out triumphant, not necessarily the innocent person. Doesn't seem fair does it?

Words can trigger fights, start battles, wars, revolutions, even mutiny or create peace, in politics as in our private lives. Words can turn man against man, country against country or bond them as allies.

If you heard someone speaking in a foreign language, unless you were familiar with that language, it wouldn't mean a great deal to you. They would be just words with a different sound to what you are used to. They are only sounds because they actually have absolutely no meaning for you, unless you understood that language. It would not matter how profound these words were, you would not be able to take them into your brain and give them any meaning.

The meaning we give to our words depends on our understanding and is crucial to the actions that we choose to take as a consequence.

Language and words are actually how we figure out meaning. When we can manipulate language we can give empowering meanings to our life events, if we have the words to describe how we feel.

When we control language and meaning we can also control thought.

As you remember, with every thought there is a physiological reaction; which means that the language and the words we choose to talk to ourselves or to others with, will determine how we feel at any given moment. This can work for the best or it can be for the worst, depending on what we are thinking, writing, reading, watching or listening to. Anxiety and depression can follow very negative and destructive words used in our thoughts.

> **Equally reading or watching toxic materials can put excessive fear and lasting anxiety into impressionable minds by the meaning that the words and imagery convey.**

So, if Zombie movies or dark movies disturb you, please do not expose yourself to them anymore. You are causing a lot of damage to your impressionable minds. All too often young people are not aware of the damage that they can do to themselves and their subconscious by exposing themselves to dark movies or literature. It is often the cause of many being haunted by dark desperate thoughts of anxiety and depression and even suicide.

We represent words as symbols and images in our minds. If we are told not to think about something, we still will represent it by its symbol in our mind. If I say: *Think of the number 10;* you will immediately see ten as a symbol in your mind, but if I said: *Do not think of the number 10,* you will still ten as a symbol in your mind.

Every day new things are being discovered and we give them a new name, which soon becomes part of our language, and within no time at all they form part of our vocabulary as if they had always existed.

This is done deliberately because it impresses us that new knowledge, new technology is constantly being discovered, and we are keen to be amongst the first to be able to say we've got it, can work it and are familiar with it. We very soon begin to use these words in our everyday vocabulary to keep with it; and of course we then need to buy the latest technology that these words convey, contributing to the riches of technological companies.

If, you are like me, who has another mother tongue other than English, you may have some difficulty in keeping up with those new technological words in your own language, because words have evolved since you left. My mother-tongue is French and I have lived in an English-speaking country since I was eighteen years old. Even though I pride myself that my French is still very good, I have to make an effort to keep up with new words or fashionable phrases as language evolves—however, many of the new words often amaze me as many of them are made up of English words. The funny thing is that my French friends tell me about these new words as if they are something new to me, not realizing that they are based in the English language, which have now been incorporated into the French language.

Wouldn't it be easier if we could all learn a universal language where we could all understand each other and keep our own mother tongue for those who understand us?

Have you noticed how teenagers have their own language, as if they form part of some special in-group, where others who do not understand their *lingo* are excluded? One of the reasons may be so that their parents do not understand their secret code. That would not be cool! What about texting and Twitter? You sometimes need a special dictionary to be able to decipher some of the words. Is it any wonder that there is conflict between the generations? All this does nothing to help bridge the generation gap.

The same words used by different generations can have very different meanings to the people involved. They demonstrate the power of words and the scope for misunderstandings. Poor vocabulary and the inability to understand each other's *jargon*, often lead to conflict and widens the gap between the generations.

Sometimes we use old words and give them new meanings. For instance, when I was growing up, if you were gay, you were joyful and happy, to-day it has an entirely new meaning. New generations may not even realise that to be gay is to be joyful. Words like *Fabulous* now means *like a fable* or *fantastic* meaning *like a fantasy. L.O.L* now means "laugh out loud". Previously it was an abbreviation for *lots of love*. I still live in the past on this one and use it in my texts and I believe that the recipients of my texts get it! It's almost like a code for an in-group to talk to each other, without others understanding what they are saying, like a secret language. Some find it a bonding exercise that they understand each other's language putting them on the same wave length.

I expect it's the same sort of satisfaction you get if you want to say something privately in another language and the person you are communicating with is the only one who can understand what you are talking about.

Words can carry and elicit emotion in us and in others.

How do we feel when someone swears at us or is rude to us? Movies are censored by society because of abusive language which we describe as not suitable for children.

Controlling or emotive words are enough to control people or change them.

How do you feel when you hear the four letter words? Is it offensive to you? Or is it the norm for you? It will depend upon your up-bringing and the social circle in which you spend most of your time in. Some of us would be horrified whereas others would not understand why we should feel offended.

Using emotive words like: furious, livid, or revolting, can hype up our emotions.

Other words like: calm, peaceful, harmony, inner peace, relaxation, create a picture of being comfortable and at ease with oneself.

The value of what the content of your words are, is what ultimately matters, right? However, we must not underestimate the power of words combined with relevant visual cues to be able to carry a message across. For example: in movies and especially in commercials.

When words are accompanied by visual cues and auditory cues, the impact on us is even greater.

For example: We are easily influenced by movies and commercials that we see. The words that we see or hear are so subtle that we are not aware that we are being influenced. Yet these influences may end up forming part of our belief and value systems, without us even realizing where they came from.

Have you ever been to a football match or to a racing circuit or watched one on television, where the names of different companies are being advertised all around the field or circuit? Often we are not even aware that we are consciously noticing what we are actually seeing. Yet, sublimally, our subconscious has taken it all in. The next time we need to buy a camera, need batteries or tyres, you go straight for Kodak, Duracell, or Dunlop. What happened is that, your eyes unconsciously took in the pictures and symbols, and they influenced our subconscious mind, which came up trumps when it was needed.

Remember, our subconscious never sleeps; it is listening and watching twenty-four hours a day to give you what it thinks you want! It takes in everything, including the things that our conscious mind is unaware of. Remember though that our subconscious doesn't understand negatives. Now add in a catchy jingle or a popular piece of music and we are hooked without even realizing it!

It is vital for parents or teachers to pay special attention to the words they employ with children as they are programming them for adulthood. If critical words are repeatedly used, the child grows up with low self-esteem and learns to condemn.

If positive words or empowering words are utilized, the child is well-adjusted and has a healthy self-esteem. Some of us, all too often speak words to our children without engaging our brain first, not realizing that our words may be negatively influencing their childhood. These same unhelpful words can adversely affect the child and can leave them with long-lasting issues even in their adult life.

It is important to use positive words when we talk to ourselves. If we want to bring happiness and success into our everyday life, we must make a conscious effort to feed our minds positively, in order to change any negative programming we may have had earlier.

We need to feed our bodies with the correct nutrition to keep healthy; equally, we need to feed our minds with the correct thoughts to have a healthy thought life. It is not only our minds and our bodies that need to be fed appropriately, but we also need to feed our spirits with inspiring spiritual thoughts and words to have a healthy spiritual life. Research shows that there is a great mind-body-and-spirit connection.

When we make use of positive affirmations, we employ positive words about a desired outcome, event, habit or goal. When these affirmations are repeated often and in a certain way, they eventually take root in the subconscious mind and influence it to act accordingly.

These affirmations are words that have to be repeated in faith, sincerity, concentration and discipline to change the programming in our subconscious and alter the way we think, our habits, attitudes and improve our skills. They help us to create a better experience of life and attract new opportunities in our lives.

You get what you repeatedly think and say.

A man is what he thinks all day long.

—*Wayne Dyer*

Your experience of life depends on the words that you speak to yourself with all day long, including your thoughts and feelings. You neither need nor deserve a critical inner voice. Choose to speak to yourself with an empowering one instead.

If you constantly think of success, you will achieve success. Equally if you continually think you will fail, you will never succeed.

Your words of failure all day long are programming your subconscious to fail. It becomes a self-fulfilling prophesy. Your mind believes that you wish to fail and helps you to do just that. Do not expect any other result if that is what is going on in your mind.

Every affirmation is said in the present tense and in the positive for a very good reason. Say what you want, not what you don't want.

For example:

I am successful.

Not

I don't want to fail.

If you find it difficult to think positively, affirmations are a good start to change your thinking. It is crucial to be willing to change. Affirmations are powerful to change unresourceful thinking pattern. You can repeat your positive affirmations to change your thinking when you get an attack of negative thinking; even before, as soon as you become aware of your pessimism.

If you don't know what affirmations to say, just think about what you do not want. Now, write down the exact opposite, and you will know what you do want.

For example:

I don't want someone who lets me down constantly.

Instead you can say:

I want someone reliable in my life.

We are all blessed with this most magnificent, sophisticated human brain that can think and imagine what doesn't yet exist and understand complex concepts.

If you can easily assume the worst; it is proof that you also have the ability to imagine the best.

Therefore, you can change negative statements and mental imagery for constructive ones.

For example instead of:

We don't have any money! We can't afford to do anything.

Turn this into:

I am abundant and I accept prosperity in my life

I can do anything I choose to.

You may not have much money but it is free to take a romantic walk on the beach and enjoy a wonderful sunset. Look and search for all the positives in life.

Think affluently and wealth will seek you out.

Words that have repeatedly been used during an individual's developing years can produce a state of learned helplessness and program some individuals to be a negative person as an adult. This negative programming can affect all areas of their life including, health, relationships, work, finance, friendships and socially; unfortunately resulting in a life of mediocrity full of regular conflict.

Words are the body of thought

—Carlyle

The Importance Of Having A Good Vocabulary

Research tells us that there is a direct correlation between vocabulary size and strength and how successful we are in life. The more successful and confident people are in life, the bigger and better vocabulary and verbal intelligence they have, than their counterparts, whether it is in their work, in their social life or in their personal life or studies.

We rule men with words

—Napoleon

Why are words important?

Words have incredible power. If you have the art of manipulating words, and have great verbal intelligence, you have the edge and you can benefit from the power to persuade, to inspire, to motivate, to captivate others, win arguments, and to influence others, not to mention success in your career.

For instance: In a discussion, the one who has the ability with words and who can express himself elegantly and articulately, without losing his cool has the advantage; whereas the one who does not have this ability can become dumbstruck, frustrated or even aggressive as he cannot fully express what he wants to say. This inability with words puts the latter at a disadvantage. Some people suffer from verbal dyslexia.

Verbal intelligence is extraordinarily important because without words our world would be in complete chaos as no one would be able to understand the other.

Consider being dumb and not being able to express what you want or express how you feel or try to do your work and explain a difficult concept to someone else or explain what you think about philosophy, anthropology, technology or politics, without words? So spare a thought for those who are unable to speak for whatever reason; be compassionate if verbally dyslexic people get frustrated and angry. They may be having a hard time expressing what they want to say.

Imagine going to work and being unable to use the appropriate words or using unsuitable words to communicate with your colleagues! As you know every work place tends to have their own *jargon* or *in language,* or *specialized vocabulary,* its own specialized terminologies and expressions. This jargon is the link that keeps all of you connected and in the same *club.*

Research shows that those who speak the *in* language are more successful at work. It shows that the top ten percent successful workers in an organization make use of their specialized vocabulary.

In Coaching we often say, if you want to achieve a goal, *act as if.* Basically, you act *as if* you already have what you want, and eventually you won't need to act as it will become part of you. So if you want to be in the top ten percent, act like you are already there by using your work's jargons and expressions. If you keep it up, you will soon find that you will no longer be acting as the jargon will just come naturally and will form part of your vocabulary.

> *Language is the armoury of the human mind*
>
> —*Cooleridge*

Verbal Intelligence

Verbal intelligence is one of the varied intelligences we benefit from; for example, the Intelligent Quotient (IQ) deals with the Academic side, the Emotional Intelligence deals with your emotions or Social intelligence, which deals with our social ability.

Exercise To Improve Your Verbal Intelligence

- If you want to improve your verbal intelligence, listen up for new and unusual words, as you go about your daily business: from your colleagues, from the television, the media, or anyone you happen to interact with. This exercise improves your listening skills as well as your verbal skills as you can't help but actively listen to others. A good listener has an incredible attractiveness to others, because you will be giving them your full attention; and of course, learning all the new words will enlarge your vocabulary and increase your verbal intelligence.

- Get a small notebook, especially for your new words. Then when you learn a new word, look it up; find out what it means; make a point of using it as many times as you can in the following seven days, so that it becomes really embedded into your memory.
- When you read the newspapers, magazines, books, surf the net, instead of ignoring words that you do not understand as you may have done previously, make a point of jotting them down in your notebook.
- Look up their meaning in the dictionary, and over the next few days, practice using those words as many times as you can. Keep them at the forefront of your mind. This will make you an attractive and more confident communicator.

You need to invest in a good dictionary and a good notebook!

Research tells us that the larger the vocabulary, the more skilful one is at using words, the richer the emotional life and generally the more successful one is in life.

Suzuki was a Japanese teacher, musician and instrument maker who discovered that every normal baby's brain's ability is so great, that they have the capabilities of learning millions of potential languages. The younger you learn a language the better; the more advantage you can take from this gift.

In ancient Egypt, the priests were the *keepers of the word*; they tried to keep it secret as they realized the power that words gave them, helped them to keep the population fearful and superstitious. They realized that they were better able to manipulate them and keep themselves superior to the people. Their power with words not only kept them mystifying and powerful, but they discovered that it gave them the power of persuasion, the power to inspire, to hypnotize, to control, to influence and lead others.

> *Our words are a reflection of what we think and what's in our hearts.*

We are shocked at times, by some words that escape out of our mouths without our conscious awareness; we say things that we have been thinking about, but did not want them to go through our lips. The reason for that is that whatever is in our hearts unconsciously spills over into our world by the words we utter.

> *You can speak well if your tongue can deliver the message of your heart.*
>
> —*John Ford*

Most of the powerful speeches from History came from the heart, the excellent ones and the dreadful ones. Winston Churchill, the British Prime Minister during the Second World War and his sworn enemy Adolf Hitler are both repeatedly quoted as examples of eloquent speakers. They both had incredible skills in manipulating the spoken word and influencing their respective nations. Churchill words influenced the British nation for good, whereas Hitler chose to manipulate his words to the German nation for his own personal psychopathic wicked ends.

Churchill's moving supernatural gift with words motivated the British nation to support their country and execute unbelievable acts of bravery beyond belief. His inspirational words made them proud to be British, encouraged heroism and stirred up patriotism. Churchill's famous words led his people to win the war even in the face of certain defeat. His awe-inspiring words helped them to visualize victory over the enemy. He prepared his fight in the minds of his nation way before they ever fought the battles.

Churchill's very famous speech calling the British to never surrender convinced his fellow-countrymen to understand that their country needed them and that with their help they would win the war; He single-handedly turned what could have been Britain's worst calamity into its finest hour by the power of his words. Not only did his immortal words inspire the British public but his famous words influenced the rest of the world too in supporting good to triumph over evil.

> *History will be kind to me as I intend to write it*
>
> *—Winston Churchill*

On the other side of England, Churchill's sworn adversary, Adolf Hitler was also a brilliant speaker, but he used his talent with words adroitly to manipulate and persuade his nation to do nauseating acts of violence and cruelty never previously encountered in the history of the world. His words too came from his heart, as his dark thoughts revealed his psychosis and his unlimited degree for abysmal evil.

The influence of his words was so powerful that he hypnotized the German nation to commit horrific acts of unspeakable brutality, which we pray will never ever be repeated ever again. His skill of persuasion was such and his aptitude with words was equally as remarkable that he managed to convince his countrymen to join his crazy pursuit for world domination.

As fate would have it that, we had two exceedingly gifted leaders with words living during the same historical period, being at war opposing each other with very different ideals and philosophies. That's the kind of stuff movies are made of! Winston Churchill had the edge over Hitler, as he represented what was good. His speeches contained powerful words and messages that reached and persuaded the allies to join him against Hitler. Had Hitler gotten his wicked ways, we could all be speaking German to-day; but he made the mistake of underestimating Winston Churchill.

I hasten to add that the German people are no worse than any other nations who have had charismatic malevolent leaders who are clever with words to misguide them, for instance in countries like Romania, Serbia, Croatia, Iraq, Iran, Uganda, Libya, Egypt, and many more besides.

Hitler confirmed his understanding of the power of his words when he uttered these words:

> *If you tell a big enough lie and tell it frequently enough; it will be believed.*

Adolf Hitler was a very evil man, with an enormous perceptive and knowledge of the power of words on man's subconscious mind when he said this next quote:

> *By the skilful and sustained use of propaganda, one can make a people see even heaven as hell or an extremely wretched life as paradise.*

Throughout history we see other great leaders who were also masterful with words that inspired their people. General de Gaulle instilled in his people the patriotism that they needed to keep resisting their invaders during the Second World War, despite the fact that he required the help of the allies to win the war.

De Gaulle realized the power of the words of the media when he told us:

I might have had trouble in saving France in 1946—I didn't have television then.

Could Napoleon Bonaparte have controlled and persuaded his men to fight and invade other countries if he didn't have the power of an extensive vocabulary, the power to influence and the power of persuasion through his use of words? Napoleon, like de Gaulle, comprehended the immense power of the media to manipulate words, when he expressed the following opinion:

Four hostile newspapers are to be feared more than a thousand bayonets.

In the last century, the likes of Margaret Thatcher, Ronald Reagan and Bill Clinton, amongst others were all masters of their trades when it came to using powerful, influential and persuasive words in their address to get their people to support their policies and vote for them.

Words create the history of the world. As words can start wars, they can equally bring peace or love. Imagine what would the Bible or the History books be like if we had no words to express what these books wanted to say or if they had a limited vocabulary?

Words have the power to affect the human brain for better or for worse. Words have the power to produce emotions. They have the power to affect our behaviour, our decisions and our actions. Words also give us the power to show love, to fight, to forgive and to pray.

By using appropriate words, we can control our thoughts and ultimately our destiny. The words that emerge out of our mouths reveal what we are thinking and what's in our hearts. Our thoughts divulge what we have in our hearts.

We create our world with the words which express our thoughts. We bring forth the things we think about and what's in our hearts into being by the actions that follow the words that we utter.

> **What we do on a consistent basis conditions us.**

We have to be conscious of what words we use to speak to ourselves with, as these words are conditioning us to a good or bad experience of life. To make the most of our power over words or of our verbal intelligence, it is important to be congruent. In other words, it is important for our body language to match our words.

If we don't mean what we say, our subconscious will betray us and we will not be congruent.

For example: you cannot say *yes* in word, but shake your head (indicating No). You will not be congruent; therefore you will not be believable. People won't trust you, because they will read your body language and will not believe the words they hear as you are not congruent.

Words form part of our belief system and of the movies we create in our minds.

The way we interpret our words and the meaning we give them affect how we feel at any given moment.

> *Words affect our perception, our attitude including our behaviour.*
> *They generate emotions and feelings.*

If you wake up and see that it is a rainy day, you can interpret it as: *Oh! What an awful day!* Or you could exclaim: *It is raining! Great for the garden! I won't have to water the plants to-day!*

If you choose to say: *What an awful day!* you immediately have the corresponding feeling in your body and start to feel miserable about that awful wet day, and sure as sure can be, you will have an awful day. The problem is that you carry that miserable feeling with you in whatever else you're doing throughout your day; the world will respond to your attitude and before you know it your day becomes a self-fulfilling prophecy: your day is awful! And it all started because of the *words* you used to yourself to interpret that it was raining.

However, if you belong to the second category of people who believe that rain is a blessing from heaven for the garden; you would also have the corresponding emotional feeling to go with it. Your attitude is completely different and the world responds to you accordingly. All of a sudden your day is an absolute victory; all because of the *words* you use in your interpretation of a rainy day!

You may have been spurred on that your plants were being well-watered by the rain, which is good for them and looked forward to your day, and you didn't allow a bit of wet to ruin your day! It isn't an awful or a wonderful day! It is just a rainy day.

Depending upon the words we choose to interpret the event of the rain falling, we either feel good or bad; hence we program ourselves accordingly for the day. Isn't it far better to feel good and look forward to having a great day? We can do program ourselves to a great day every single day of the year as we wake up. It is up to us! We have that power!

Words are the dress of thought.

—*Chesterfield*

> *If we want to feel wonderful, great or amazing, we have to have the corresponding thoughts.*
> *Whatever we send out, we will receive the same back, just like a boomerang!*

The game of life is the game of boomerangs. Our thoughts, deeds and words return to us sooner or later, with astounding accuracy.

—*Florence Scovel Shinn*

You Are The Power In Your World.

You get in your external world whatever you say to yourself in your internal world. So, it is vital that the words you choose to converse with yourself in your internal world are positive.

Successful People

Successful people never ever entertain or wallow in negative self-talk. They don't waste their time this way.

Successful people instead actively search and eagerly look for positive and winning self-talk. They visualize themselves as successful at what they want to achieve. They rehearse success over and over again in their mind. The thought of failure doesn't even enter their heads. They know that the words that come out of their mouths are vitally important to their success. They know that their words are influenced by the feelings that those words produce in their hearts, and this in turn influence what actions they take. The actions they take get them the results they want.

Successful people never allow themselves to consider discouraging or humiliating self-talk. They are optimists and cultivate their enthusiasm.

Add Optimism And Enthusiasm To Your Values.

Successful people invest in winning self-talk.

Successful people don't just hope for the best or don't think about it and think whatever will be, will be. They set their mind up to thinking positively; they indulge their time in being enthusiastic and cultivate being optimistic by the thoughts that they choose and the words they allow to infiltrate their mind.

Any negative thought is rejected first-hand; negative words have no place in their world.

Successful people know that being positive will make them take the correct actions for them to be successful; being negative won't get them there.

On the other hand, unsuccessful people have not worked out this life secret!

Now that you know their life's secret, copy them! Just do it! Make it happen! Become one of the successful people that life is proud to boast about!

Unsuccessful People

On the other hand unsuccessful or negative people continually rehash negative self-talk and are indulgent in self-pity, under the pretext that they are *Realists*. They prepare themselves for defeat, *just in case. Poor me, they say, things are always against me; just my luck!*

> *There are only two possibilities: 50% right or 50% wrong. The odds are the same! So why not influence it to go the right way? Why not hope for the best instead of the worst?*

Remember: your words and your thoughts are powerful and bring into your life what you are continually thinking. You will get more of what you focus on. Use the power of your words and your thoughts to bring you successful outcomes not the other way round.

> *Self-pity is our worst enemy and if we yield to it, we can never do anything wise in this world.*
> —*Helen Keller*

Negative People

Negative people bring defeat into their world, by the *thoughts* that they have cultivated and rehearsed; by the *words* that have continually been swirling in their minds and have used, to make it their reality, followed by their consequent *negative actions*.

.... And you know what? These very same people will dismiss what I am saying as garbage. And do you know what else? ... That is because they just don't *get it*. They just cannot believe that it is as simple as that. However, if they try they will see that is exactly how it works. No big mystery here! Think good, you get good; think bad, guess what you'll get?

Negative people picture *defeat* in their mind over and over again, long before it happens; and sure as sure can be they get what they have been rehearsing; just as the winner would have been rehearsing their positive outcomes and rejoice in the results they benefit from.

> *With negative thoughts, come fear and the accompanying pessimistic emotions and feelings, to make the negative person edge towards anxiety and depression.*

So, consider positive words in your self-talk and thoughts; visualize yourself as successful and you will be successful.

If you choose negative words in your self-talk and thoughts and visualize yourself as a failure, you will be anxious, maybe depressed, or a failure as a result. It is that simple!

Just because you've had some heartbreaking experience and you believe that anyone else would feel just the way you do, it doesn't mean you *have* to allow yourself to wallow in negative thoughts. You can show the world what you are made of! You can choose to be resilient and get up, dust yourself up and hold your head up high and search for a positive solution instead of giving in to despair or melancholy. When you are clouded in depression you cannot see any opportunities.

And what if it's happened to you before? .... You didn't know any better then, but now you do! Didn't you read anything I said about resilience and being persistent??? You clean yourself all the same and see that this is a new occasion with a new positive outcome instead. However similar a previous situation, it's never exactly the same. Search for the positive and treat each situation on its own merits.

Another secret to remember:

> *Our words design our future, therefore determine our destiny.*

When we are able to control our words, especially those we speak to ourselves with, we are able to control our life.

Exercise

- If you find it hard: make it a habit everyday to write down what your thoughts are in your journal; then if you don't like what you read, rephrase what you wrote in a more positive way (even if you don't truly believe it at first). Rephrase it in a more positive truth for you. Rehearse the positive version in your mind. If you finish with the positive version, that will be the last thing that your subconscious will hang on to.
- Write down what life lessons you can learn from your experiences.

> *Anxiety in the heart of man causes depression, but a good word makes it glad.*
> —*Proverbs 12: 25*

If you catch yourself thinking or verbalizing your negative thoughts, STOP! There and then! You can make a physical gesture, like snapping your fingers or tapping a table top and say STOP! You can either drop the thought completely or rephrase it in a positive way.

> *Words are the most powerful drug used by mankind*
> —*Kipling*

The words we choose, create the experience we call our life. They can lift us up or they can poison our mind and ruin our experience, including the relationship we have with ourselves and others.

How Do The Negative Words That You Inherited From Your Childhood Affect You?

You had no control over your birth circumstances but it is up to you to choose your reactions to what happened to you as a child, when you are adults. Don't waste valuable time in self-pity. You can choose to be a victim and let self-pity choke you or you can do better and use your experiences to grow and develop and make a difference. You can let them ruin your life, live in resentment, bitterness, anger or hatred for the rest of your lives; or you can choose to language what happened to you in a positive way, using empowering words and give empowering meaning to those circumstances and events. You can turn your life around and reach your full potential, and be who you were meant to be!

Don't forget what we discussed about Forgiveness! When you choose to forgive, you can move on with your life.

Jon's Story

Clients come to see me for solutions to a range of issues. One client, whom we will call Jon, came to see me at the age of 62 years old. He was having a difficult time emotionally because he had been physically abused as a child by his alcoholic father. His father had died 12 years previously. Amazingly, Jon managed to live for 50 years with pure hatred in his heart for his father. To that day, the abuse was still troubling him, causing his dark moods and depression.

If you carry hatred in your heart, you can never be happy no matter what wonderful things happen to you. Part of you will still feel wretched!

On exploring how he felt, and what had happened to him, I was pleasantly surprised to find out that he had married a wonderful woman, and had 4 fantastic sons who had all done very well. The family is a close-knit family. He is a very good father unlike his own, and he loves his wife and has a good marriage. He is a very successful business man, has achieved his goals in business and is well respected in the sports arena. Financially, he has done extremely well. He has four investment properties and is financially very sound. In fact, he has everything to be happy. He has great friends and is very proud of his family and his sports achievements. At 62years old, Jon looks years younger, is physically very fit, tanned and toned. This man should have been on top of the world! But he was awfully unhappy. He was very troubled by the words and thoughts that kept coming into his head regarding his father: *Why*?

He was so miserable because he hadn't changed his internal dialogue for years, whilst growing up, during his adult life, into his middle years; it had become a habit. He used the same words and the same language to describe to himself how hard done by he had been as a child. He saw himself as the *victim* and *self-pity* engulfed him.

With this self-pity, came a lot of feelings of sadness for himself, resentment, anger, bitterness and hateful feelings towards his father. He felt sorry for this poor little boy, who was the *victim* of an alcoholic bullying father. He had continued to nurture these same thoughts and visions throughout all these years, despite all the success that he managed to achieve in life. Is it any wonder that he felt unhappy? He made little of his successes but managed to language his childhood in such depressive and hateful words to himself that they made him feel physically unwell.

Jon had hated his father for so long that words of revenge dominated his thinking; however that wasn't possible, because his father was no longer here.

Jon never realized that how he was feeling was of his own doing; it was not his father's fault. His father had long done. It was the way that he was thinking; the words and language he used to talk to himself that made him feel so bad.

His father wasn't making him unhappy or sick! His father was dead! The abuse stopped physically 50 years ago. The one person who was abusing him mentally was himself. He was torturing himself by his very own words.

He found it very hard to admit that he wasn't a victim and was addicted to feeling sorry for himself. He truly believed that he *was the victim* and it was appalling to him to even think of questioning that. After all didn't his alcoholic father abuse him and mistreat him? He may have been once when he was a little boy; but 50 years had now passed and no one had abused him in that time.

Jon never understood that just because it was understandable that he had cause to feel upset then, that he had a *choice* now, not to stay in self-pity; that he could be proactive in turning the bad in his life into good.

Instead of feeling gratitude, that *despite* his abuse, he is one of life's successes. Instead of mentally wording his internal conversation something like: "Despite, all the terrible things that my father did to me, look at me now! I managed to achieve what my own father never could by being a good father to my 4 children. I managed to show them the love that I never got when I was young; I have brought them up the way I wish I had been brought up as a child, and I have succeeded. I have achieved beyond my wildest dreams! I have a wonderful wife who loves and supports me in everything that I do and I love her; I love my family more than anything and everything is going really well for us! I have a very successful business and am very successful in my sport; in fact I am successful in all areas of life. I am very proud of all my achievements, in spite of my poor beginnings! I did it all myself, regardless of my dreadful childhood and abusive father. I am a good husband to my wife, which is more than my dad was for my mother. I am proud of who I am!"

Well! These should have been the words that Jon should have been saying to himself. Unfortunately, the reality was far from this!

Instead, Jon's mind was bitter with years of repeating the same negative, hateful, resentful and bitter words that he grew up with. He never changed the words. In fact, he became a good father to his children, to be the exact opposite to what his own father had been. At least that was a good by-product, even if he did it out of rebellion! In a way, he felt cheated that his father had died, because he could no longer get his revenge. The words and language he used to talk to himself were so destructive and full of hate, that Jon was feeling the repercussions of these negative thoughts by the way he was feeling, suffering from dark moods and depression, without even understanding their origin, and of course blaming his father for his depression and dark moods.

Remember: with every thought, there is a physiological reaction.

When you think good thoughts, you feel good; when you think bad thoughts you become prey to dark moods and depression.

There were a whole lot of bad thoughts going on there! Thoughts, composed with unconstructive and unresourceful words.

Unfortunately Jon was reaping what he had sown all these years and what he was still sowing; hence he was reaping a harvest of dark moods and depression. Worst still, if he carries on, he will fall prey to diseases such as cardiovascular disease, arthritis, cancer, autoimmune diseases and the rest.

His belief was that he was the victim! However, the words that he used in his internal conversation were something like: "My father ruined my childhood and my life. I am 62 years old and he is still bugging me, because of all the nasty things he did to me! I hate him! He is dead but he is still upsetting me! I have done okay in life, but what could I have been and what could I have achieved if he hadn't abused me when I was young? Who knows what I could have been if he hadn't done this to me? Maybe I could have been someone rich and famous!"

Now, this tape played those words over and over in a continual loop, for years and years in his head! Is it any wonder that he felt terrible and depressed and overwhelmed by his dark thoughts?

He was reaping in his mind and body what he had sown in his mind all these years.

He had got so used to hating his father that he couldn't bear to stop. It had become a habit. It gave him some kind of personal satisfaction and revenge by hating him. In fact he had kept himself in a mental prison of his own making for most of his life. In reality what was worst was that he continued to abuse himself way after the abuse by his father had stopped.

It was understandable and comprehensible for him to feel compassion for himself because he was the one who was harmed. However, that it was very destructive to himself to live in self-pity and hatred. As much as it is sometimes obvious that certain situations convey some clear negative feelings, it is not helpful to stay in this dark place.

You may feel you have the right to react negatively because of something that happened to you which wasn't your fault; nevertheless, it is unconstructive to stay in self-pity and to react as a victim.

> *We always have a choice on how we react to any event. It is not what happens to us that matter most, it how we react to what happens to us.*

Jon felt cheated because his father was dead and he couldn't put things right the way *he* wanted to. Hating him gave him some sort of morbid satisfaction. It almost felt good to hate him so much. It was his kind of *revenge*. He had repeatedly told himself that *he* was the *victim*; it was a shock for him to hear that he has in fact been very successful regardless of his difficult childhood, which made him far from being a victim.

His bitterness and resentment stopped any feelings of gratitude and enjoyment that he could have had for all that he had achieved and for what he has in his life, because in his head he focused on *what else could he have achieved had he not been abused by his father as a child*. He missed out on all the joy that his achievements could have brought him and the many blessings that life gave him. Instead he cultivated hatred and anger towards his father, who had stopped abusing him over 50 years ago, and who had been dead for over 12 years!

He made very little of his successes but spent much time on the negative in his life, wondering if he could have done better. Jon did not realize that those difficult beginnings may have been the catalyst to help him make a success of his life as he had something to prove. Had he not had difficult beginnings, he could have gone off the rails and not been motivated to succeed as much as he had. His circumstances gave him the focus to become successful in his own life. Yet, he did not appreciate his successes but amplified his negative past.

His focus was on the wrong things! Had he changed his habitual words to himself, he would have changed the way he felt. To-day instead of having his dark moods, he would have been a very happy man.

His negative self-talk never changed; he never had any appreciation for the positives in his life. The more he achieved, the more he felt he could have been someone even better, *had he not been abused as a child.* As a true victim, he allocated all the blame onto his abusive childhood.

> *Where there is no gratitude anger and misery are never very far away!*

He had spent years and years building his own internal mental prison, brick by brick! Now the walls were solid, and he was unwilling to unlock the door.

Jon's dark moods and depression were only a reflection of the power of the words that he chose to focus on and of the dark thoughts that he was harbouring in his heart. He missed out on the enjoyment of all his successes because of his *distorted thinking.*

All his sufferings were due to the result of the words he was using in his internal conversation. The way he was feeling was the result of the emotions triggered by words, such as *hatred, anger, bitterness, resentment, revenge, and unforgiveness.* Examine these words and see whether you would be able to feel happy experiencing the emotions that these words emanate.

Jon's case is typical of what happens to you when there is no spirit of gratitude and when feelings of hatred, bitterness, anger and resentment are *cultivated.* They eventually erode your spirit and bring disease.

> *Where there is no gratitude, there can be no happiness.*

Where there is hatred, anger, bitterness and resentment, there is no inner peace and contentment.

We can keep wishing that our childhood had been different or that our families should be this way or that way—unfortunately, if the reality is different, and if your family is far from being like the one in *The Little House On The Prairie,* then stop kidding yourself and acknowledge that you wish it were different, but the reality is otherwise for you. Don't kid yourself about what you have in your head that families *should be like.* Accept the one you've got as a fact of life, not what you think your idea of what family should be like. Choose to accept the family you have, just as they are, warts and all.

Get real; see things as they are. Use positive words in your internal conversation. Make a decision that you will use the lessons of your past to make your future happier. Do not let your past wreck your future.

Don't live in a fairy tale and say *that's what family is supposed to be like.* Yes, of course, that's how it should be! But if it is not like that for you, stop living in cloud cuckoo land, because every time, you set yourself up for more and more pain. You have expectations that are never going to be met, which can lead to huge disappointments every time. The time has come to accept things as they are and make your experience now much better and more realistic.

Accept your reality, not one that doesn't exist!

Make a decision that from now on, you will accept your family as they are with all the good that they come with and all the bad too. When you do that you avoid pain. When you choose to pretend, you inevitably get hurt; because each time they do something that you were not expecting you set yourself up for pain and drama.

If your family has been dysfunctional all your life, why would you think that things will be any different now, just because you want it to? Do not expect anyone of them to behave like 'you' think they should.

Accept your reality, just as it is, whatever it is like. Even embrace it and language it to yourself in positive words that will help you to have a quality life and enjoy the good that your family offers. Do not set yourself up for regrets, disappointments, pain and bitterness, where you can't appreciate all the good that happens to you, like Jon.

Be aware that no matter how nice your family is, no matter how much that you have a similar way of thinking, they are not you! They may well make decisions that you will frown upon, or act in a way that you disapprove. But remember that they have that right; you can just love them even though you don't approve of something they do or say. We are not going to like everything that our family members do or say; just like they may not like everything that we do or say. Our job is to love them and forgive if we need to.

When you are brought up with negative words, they can tend to stick in your brain; such words as: *You're stupid! You're useless; You will never achieve anything in life*; if these words have been repeated to you over and over again you can by now believe that you really are stupid, useless etc. This has now become a limiting belief for you.

Time has come to remove the old program; remove the old software and reprogram your brain with new software by using the right words in your new program. Understanding how these things work can liberate you and make you change your thinking and what you say to yourself, ultimately change your life.

Affirmations

Use affirmations to help you reprogram your brain. Select the words you wish to reprogram your brain with. Empower yourself instead with a new belief and develop an attitude of gratitude, such as:

I can do handle anything that life gives me.

I can do anything that I put my mind to.

I accept my family just as it is.

I am stronger because of/despite my upbringing.

Because of my upbringing, I can achieve anything I put my mind to.

I am thankful for my life experiences.

I believe in myself.

I am thankful for what I am.

I am grateful for who I am.

I am thankful for my family.

I choose to be joyful.

I choose gratitude.

I am abundant.

I attract wealth to me.

I give thanks for my body.

I give thanks for my health.

I give thanks for everything in my life, good or bad.

I give thanks for my relationships.

I give thanks for my work.

I give thanks for my gifts and talents.

By using positive affirmations and continually repeating them to yourself, you can counteract your negative programming, and re-program yourself into the positive. Now add some relevant to you.

Your Words Rule!

Words, that you keep thinking about and talking to yourself with, can bring into your world the very thing that you fear. If for instance, like another client of mine, who repeatedly accused her partner of cheating, and believed that *sooner or later he will end up cheating on her anyway."* Her behaviour and the way she acted were congruent with how she talked to herself: *Sooner or later, he will cheat on me.* These words spilled out of her mouth, as they reflected what she had in her heart.

> **Your words do end up manifesting themselves into your external world through your thoughts.**

Well? . . . . He did! . . . . He did end up cheating on her, with someone far too close to her. Self-fulfilling prophecy!

What happens is that your partner is repeatedly accused of cheating when he didn't. Eventually, what ends up happening is that the partner cheats, therefore fulfilling the prophecy! If he gets accused again, then at least it is true! And he feels that at least if he gets the grief then, it is for something he did rather than for something he didn't do! So now the accusations are justified!

It may all have started with you using the wrong words in your head to start with. So, as you have seen, words are powerful! Not just powerful, but very influential. They have the ability of manifesting what you say to yourself.

> *Negative words that were said to us as children can still have a powerful effect on us as adults.*

This is not to say that we can't shed them if we work on ourselves. Many times we promise ourselves that when we have children, we would never say some of the things that our mothers may have said to us . . . . but when we become adults and eventually have our own children, we wake up one day and . . . . there it's happened! . . . . the words have come straight out of our mouths before we even had time to engage our brains! . . . . and then suddenly our mothers words are ringing in our ears! *The old programming is alive and well!*

Now that you know better it is up to you to consciously stop this vicious cycle.

Reframe

Decide to change the words, the language you use to talk to yourself with. When you change words, you also can change the meanings that you had previously given to some things. Let it be for the better! Consciously use positive words to rephrase whatever negative thoughts enter your thinking. It is vital to think right and reframe the negative meaning and empower yourself instead.

> *Don't use words lightly.*

If your words are not helpful, if you think of yourself as a victim, you will never have a happy life and fulfill your full potential.

If you do not forgive; if you keep revenge and resentment in your heart; you will be old and still be tortured by your resentful and vengeful thoughts (like Jon). You will keep yourself frozen in an internal prison of your own making—a prison you have the power to bring down the walls bit by bit.

On the other hand, you can choose to forgive and be compassionate; choose to be your best friend and choose positive words to have the right dialogue with yourself. Use positive words and positive language to yourself. Your words have undeniable authority over your life.

The Movies Of Your Mind

Words help you to represent experiences and events in your mind; if you can't language it in your mind, you can't represent them; and if you can't represent them in your mind, you can't experience them.

If you can see events in your mind, without having the words for it, you are unable to articulate them and give them substance and make them real, and experience the feelings good or bad. If you do not have words to describe an event, you can't experience the array of feelings that you could be able to.

Have you ever been lost for words to explain something and couldn't find the right words to describe what you wanted to say? Did you feel frustrated with yourself? . . . . hum, Yep!

But imagine never using certain words that incite or pain for us! If we never articulate things that provoke pain for us, we cannot experience the pain associated with the negative emotions involved, right? True, that is right! Absolutely true! Because if we stopped ourselves from using certain words, we would also stop ourselves from seeing the mental images, the movies and mental pictures that they conjure up, as well as feeling the corresponding physiological reactions in our body.

Imagine if words like anxiety or depression didn't exist, therefore you could never say: *I feel anxious or depressed.* This would also mean that you would find it hard to experience feelings of anxiety or depression emotionally and physiologically! That in fact would be great! So why don't we pretend that we do not know these words and avoid using them? Therefore we would be unable to experience these feelings.

We can use other words to describe these negative feelings by saying words like: *overwhelmed, overloaded, fed up, frustrated, sad or concerned*—immediately by substituting those words for anxiety or depression, the intensity of our negative feelings is reduced. Some words hype us up; others bring down the intensity of feelings.

We can change our words for other unresourceful states too. Instead of being angry, furious, or livid, miserable, we can choose to be annoyed, frustrated, irritated, puzzled, confused, unhappy or uncomfortable. Again that brings down the intensity of our feelings. We are no longer ready to punch someone lights out as when we were angry, furious or livid.

Choosing our words wisely is crucial for a balanced life. Our words carry a lot of influence. The words that we use can, not only produce emotions, but they can hype us up or chill us down. Choose to chill!

Words can create what we do and control the direction our life takes by the decisions we make; some, we may regret for a long time; some we may rejoice in for a long time too! We end up enjoying or regretting the results that is our life to-day, by our actions and their consequences.

Saying hateful or angry words to someone to vent our anger or frustration may end up keeping us living in guilt for a very long time, especially if that person is no longer there for us to make amends to or they may have dire consequences like losing our job.

Choose your words and choose to demonstrate love daily.

Appreciate your life every day. All too often life can change in the blink of an eye.

Show love and appreciation to the people in your life; if they have faults, do your best to pass on them; you're not perfect either! You never know when you will be able to see them again.

Life is a God-given gift to be appreciated every day! It isn't something that we are entitled to. We have no control over when it's our turn to depart this earth. We do not get another chance. It is then too late to make amends or do better next time.

So choose your words carefully, they channel your actions.

Words Have Serious Consequences

Imagine, you say to yourself that you are *Furious! Livid!* at what someone did to you, so much so that you punch him in the mouth. It could end up being, one of those *king-punch* that kills someone. The police are called. You now have to deal with the consequences of that action for a long time to come, as a result of *one fit of temper*, because you acted before engaging your brain into gear. You are arrested, attend court, and have to suffer the punishment dealt to you by the law. This, now has serious repercussions all round; in your private life as well as in your working life. You may lose your relationships, your family, your job, go to jail; you now have a criminal record; you are judged by family, colleagues, friends and enemies; neighbours point the finger at you when you walk down the street; you become a *persona non-grata* if you apply for a visa for another country as you have killed somebody (you're now a killer!) and the list goes on, not to mention the psychological devastation that all this cause; not only to you but to the victim himself, to his loved ones, and to your own family. It all started with hyping your feelings by the poor choice of words you initially used to yourself. Those poor choices of words resulted in hyping your feelings much more than if you had used a milder version of those words.

Instead had you told yourself that, this person was *irritating* or *annoying*, chances are you wouldn't have punched him and would have had none of the above consequences to deal with. You would have had a very different outcome.

> *Before you act, think about the consequences of your actions, and who they can affect.*

Before you take action, be conscious of what words you are using to language what is happening to you.

Please do not think that I exaggerate, that has happened to some people. It's real! Had the person calmed themselves down with a few calming words, a huge disaster could have been avoided.

If you are in the habit of using negative words, you may be used to saying words like: *I hate* instead of *I prefer something else* and have to deal with the consequences of your words. For example: *I hate my work; I hate my body; I hate Mondays; I hate my mum; I hate my colleague; I hate my boss; I hate my dad; I hate my sister or brother; I hate my nose.*

The word *hate* heightens the intensity of your feelings and spurs you on to do things or say words that you may regret.

Saying: *I prefer if my nose wasn't so long* makes it more acceptable, and lessens the intensity of feeling that you totally dislike your nose. It becomes more tolerable. *I'm not keen on my job* is more tolerable than *I hate my job* . . . . So, reframe the negative words that you employ; it will have a huge effect on how you feel.

> *Using emotionally charged words can transform your emotional state as well as other people's.*

Politicians are well aware of this fact and deliberately *use words to trigger emotions* when they want people to vote for them. Remember President Obama: *Yes! We can!* indicating to his voters that he is a man of action and Yes, as a nation we can do anything together! We can achieve great things together, unlike the opposition. He managed to involve his voters' emotions who then got behind him. Julia Gillard tried to show emotions to involve the Australian people's emotions with her carbon tax; but was she successful at showing her softer side?

Adolf Hitler used emotive words to involve his nation's emotions to get Germany behind him to declare war against other nations.

> *The German people are no warlike nation. It is a soldierly one, which means it does not want a war but does not fear it. It loves peace but it also loves its honour and freedom.*
>
> *—Adolf Hitler*

Hitler, like Napoleon, Churchill, Regan or Clinton not only knew that they had the power to influence with their words, but they also knew how to manipulate their words to affect their audiences' emotions. Once they knew that they had influenced their countrymen's emotions, they knew that the people would be eating out of their hands, they would then do anything to back up their leaders.

John Kennedy's famous words stirred up the American people's emotions when he told them:

> *Ask not what your country can do for you, but what you can do for your country.*

A poor selection of words to describe an event can devastate us leaving us to deal with their consequences. However, choosing an effective selection of words can do the complete opposite and can be very uplifting. They can leave us feeling empowered, excited, charged up and heighten our emotions in a positive way, cultivate enthusiasm and positivity.

The words we use about ourselves matter.

> **By the words we use to speak about ourselves, we confirm to ourselves and to others what we say we are and who we think we are.**

So, make a decision right now never to use any self—depreciating or apologetic language when you refer to yourself. This kind of language only serves to batter your self-esteem and keep you feeling inferior. It sets you up to fail in whatever you try to do, and serves absolutely no purpose other than to keep you down, victim-like and feeling sorry, very sorry for yourself and wallowing in self-pity. Well! NO MORE!

For example you may be used to saying things like:

- Just my luck!
- Knowing my luck it's bound to go wrong!
- I'm only a housewife . . . .

- I'm not clever like . . . .
- I don't have the qualifications . . . .
- I can't cope like the others . . . .
- I'm not very good at this kind of thing . . . .
- You know me! I don't enjoy learning . . . .
- That's the way I am; I can't help it!
- I never win at anything . . . .
- I'll forget my head if it wasn't attached to my shoulders . . . .
- I've got a memory like a sieve . . . . (If that is your belief, how can you ever expect to remember anything?)
- I never try new things. What if I can't do them?
- Trust me, I can't get anything right!
- I always get it wrong . . . . I'm hopeless! It always goes wrong for me.

Can you imagine President Obama or Kevin Rudd saying things like that? . . . . then, why do you?

I firmly believe that if we are wrong, that we should apologize and say sorry. However, some live their lives saying *sorry*; they constantly apologize especially when it isn't their fault. They assume that whatever is wrong is their fault.

- Sorry, it's all my fault . . . . (Can imagine the likes of Julia Gillard or Angelina Jolie saying this . . . then, why do you?)
- Sorry I shouldn't have done this . . . .
- Sorry, sorry, sorry . . . . (*For breathing!*)

Do you recognize anyone here?

When you find negative words like the above, coming easily out of your mouth, it means that you have been playing these negative tapes over and over in your mind maybe since you were a child; you are so familiar with it that it is now second nature to you; you no longer have to think; these words are easily available to you from your subconscious. They come rushing out of your mouth to confirm to you who you believe you are and they stop you from improving your life.

When you constantly apologize for things that you haven't done, you're revealing your low self-esteem to the world. You are encouraging others to squash you as you don't matter, others are much better than you! On the other hand, as I have previously said:

> *Sorry is a magical five-letter word that can also put many wrongs to right when used appropriately.*

There is another side to this coin! There are those who can never say *sorry*, even, and especially, when they are wrong. This is a mixture of arrogance, entitlement attitude and poor self-esteem mixed in. It is very destructive especially if that is the way you are with your significant other. That kind of thing breeds deep resentment! It is very important to own your faults and sincerely offer an apology if you are wrong. If you have good self-esteem, you will have no problem with this. The simple fact is that we are all human; and as a human being we make mistakes; which definitely makes us wrong sometimes! So what's wrong with saying sorry when you don't get it right? What's the big deal?

Some feel that they can't say sorry because the other person will have *one on them* or that they would *lose face* or that they would feel *less than*. I am telling you now: it is much worse for you when you can't recognize that you were wrong and offer a sincere apology. It demonstrates your poor self-esteem and your arrogance very well.

If you can say a genuine sorry, people, (especially your partner), would respect you and hold you in higher regard.

Having the ability to apologize, when we are wrong, depicts a healthy self-esteem. Never being able to apologize when we are in the wrong, feeds anger and resentment. Saying sorry for no reason is not credible and smacks of low self-worth.

Using self-depreciating words is a very powerful and effective way to reinforce unresourceful ways of thinking and seeing yourself, even though you may not be consciously aware of it. It knocks your self-esteem, your self-image and your self-worth and helps you to believe that you are a poor hard-done by victim. It is a very efficient way of keeping your life at an inferior level. You are negatively programming and reinforcing your mind.

If you continue this harmful habit you will never be successful as your mind will not believe that you can be. You will be trapped and unable to move on in life, all because of your choice of words towards yourself.

Positive affirmation works well because it uses positive words to reinforce what you choose to feed your subconscious with. When you use self-depreciating words, you are programming your subconscious with very negative information and it works equally as well; however, very negatively.

Using self-depreciating or apologetic words keeps you emotionally deprived and in a failure lifetrap as it stops you from succeeding. It is a very dodgy practice; so stop it! Stop it now!

You need to reprogram what you think about yourself by rehearsing a new tape which uses positive and empowering words about yourself. Studies have shown that people, who are brought up to like and feel good about themselves become happier, more successful, kinder and nicer as adults. It is vital for you to give up any self-depreciating words, as research proves how harmful they can be.

Instead Use Positive Affirmations, Such As:

- I choose to treat myself with respect.
- Harmony reigns in my life.
- I choose how react to anything.
- I enjoy good relationships with people I care about.

- I honour and respect myself and others.
- I am a beautiful, loveable and a deserving human being.
- I deserve the best.
- I am worth it.
- I am as good as anyone else.
- I can manage anything that comes my way.
- I am resourceful.
- I am successful
- I have a good brain.
- I can achieve what I want to.
- I give thanks for my gifts and talents.

The trouble is that most of us are not taught to make a *conscious choice* in the words that we use. We tend to say whatever comes into our heads at any given time. Our choice of words is mainly unconscious. The words we often utilize are usually the words that we have been using when we talk to ourselves, probably for years; many of those were learnt from our past, which are almost certainly no longer relevant for where we are at to-day. Nonetheless, these same words may have serious consequences.

The words we use to communicate with ourselves and the choice of words we choose to speak with others have the powerful repercussions on how others treat us.

Our words exert power on our actions and ultimately on our life.

Choose empowering words in your internal conversation and with others when you are referring to yourself.

Never ever put yourself down unless you want others to put you down too.

Words Affect How We Feel.

So the more words we have to describe how we feel, the more positive emotions we can experience.

If you can't describe something you cannot feel it. Therefore it is important to have a rich vocabulary, because the words we use give us our emotional experiences.

If we do not have empowering words to describe how we feel we cannot experience empowering feelings. The smaller our vocabulary is, the smaller our emotional experiences are. So we must choose words that will make us feel joyous, cheerful, passionate, happy, inspirational, exceptional, sensational, ecstatic, charged up, charismatic, hyped up with excitement, energetic, optimistic, creative, blissful, magnetic, plentiful, enthusiastic, empowered, abundant, positive and much more.

Since words affect the way we feel, we want as many words as we can to make us experience amazingly good feelings and minimize our language to very few words that can make us experience bad feelings.

People with an abundant vocabulary, not only create enriching and empowering emotions for themselves, but experiencing these emotions also creates opportunities for them, which sooner or later enhance their life's journey.

Not everyone is good with words. But if you are not good with words, consciously choose to learn and improve!

Exercise To Improve Your Knowledge Of Words:

- Read, and keep a small book with new words that you have learnt. Look up their definition and keep using them until they become familiar to you.
- Make it fun and practice using them with friends and let them know that you are learning to enlarge your vocabulary.
- You can learn other words from friends who try to impress you with their knowledge. Let it be just another fun way to add to your learning and enlarging your vocabulary! Encourage a bit of a competition.

By just changing one key word, sometimes it can alter how we communicate with other people. This simple act can change how you, and how others feel and how you live. Instead of saying: *That's good*, you can say: *That's awesome; That's spectacular;* or *That's sensational!* When you say these words you also have to have the expression on your face and the tonality to go with these words. Your experience is enhanced and it empowers you. You suddenly feel more energized.

We tend to never give a thought to our every day words or question ourselves whether our words are empowering us or not.

Observe yourself and watch what you say, whether your words are positive or negative or whether your vocabulary is limited or not.

You may be using negative words naively which in fact may not reflect what you want to say at all. Some people use swear words a lot which emphasize what they say. When you add a swear word to your sentence, it has the power to make it that much more forceful, when this may not be the case at all. It can easily change the meaning of what you want to say but worse still it changes the emotions behind what you mean.

The problem is that swearing is a normal way of communicating for some. Take away the swear words and their vocabulary shrinks to nothing.

This reminds me of a little story: my niece is a social worker; she was working with some prisoners at one point for a justice department. One assignment she had was to help one of the prisoners. Of his own accord, he told her that he was working on himself to stop swearing, as it was impossible for him to say a word in court, if it wasn't accompanied by the "F" word or worse. So she did some work with him, whatever that was! After a few days she went back to see him again. He greeted her and after a while she asked him how he was getting on with reducing his swearing? His reply was: "F . . . ing good!"

The problem is that if he didn't use any swear words, he needed to learn some new words to replace them. That man was clearly so used to swearing that he really didn't have a vocabulary if you withdrew the swear words from his language. He was unable to talk or express himself. Swear words were the extent of his vocabulary, but they also probably hyped up his negative emotions enough to get him in trouble to find himself in court and in jail; it probably was all he ever heard growing up. He spoke the only way he knew how! The swearing was probably the legacy he got from his early role models. One wonders what difference it could have made to him, if he had come from a background where profanities were not the norm? Maybe he may not have found himself in court or in jail?

When we use negative or degrading words we have the corresponding emotions which give us a negative life experience. When we add strong adjectives to qualify our words, they intensify the emotions that those words carry. Who knows how many people could escape prison if they had a better choice of words and a better vocabulary?

> **When we change our everyday words, we also change our everyday emotional patterns.**

Exercise To Develop An Awareness Of Your Vocabulary:

- Change your habitual words and develop an awareness of the words you use to describe everything you experience on a daily basis, in order to experience better-quality emotions.
- Write down in your journal the new words that you are using to add to your vocabulary.
- Describe the difference that you feel when you use different words to express how you are feeling. Score yourself for both on a scale of 0-10. (0 being low and 10 being high)

If we use the same words to describe our experiences, we will not have a variety of emotional experiences. If we use words like *frustrated, stress, angry* or *depressed*, we feel the corresponding negative emotions each time we utter these words. This is not a recipe for happiness.

I know! I know! It's a habit! .... But you can stop it!

You can choose your words more carefully, and make a decision to expand on your choice of words, as you have now been enlightened of the extraordinary power that words exert over us!

Words Affect Our Belief And Value Systems

Words are at the basis of our belief system and of our value system too, including our personal rules. The words we choose determine how we feel; and the actions we take and our consequent behaviour reflect our beliefs and our values. The decisions that we make reflect the personal rules that guide our lives. All of these depend on our choice of words to ourselves.

> *Words are the fabric from which all questions are cut*
>
> —*Anthony Robbins*

Questions

The answers to the questions we ask ourselves on a regular basis establish the paths we choose to take. We use words to put together the questions we ask ourselves daily. The answers to these questions produce the outcome we have today. Therefore it is important to ask empowering questions so that we can have empowering answers, as they result in the actions we decide to take.

The only questions that really matter are the ones you ask yourself.

—*Ursula K. Le Guin*

Our Words Exert Their Power Over Us In Every Area Of Our Lives.

Our words have a great influence on our personal set of laws or rules by which we live our lives; they are the foundation of what we say to ourselves; they influence our belief and value systems; they are the essence of how we put our questions and answers together. Other people's choice of words has the power of influence and persuasion over us and vice versa.

Exercise To Change How You Feel By Changing Your Words:

- Use someone who is a master of words as a role model and copy them; you may then start to experience the emotions that your role model experience.
- Commit to consistently using empowering words like enthusiasm, awesome, commitment, passion, incredible, amazing, fascinating, wonderful, positive, spectacular, magnificent, exquisite, optimism or confidence amongst others; if you change nothing else but change your vocabulary to more empowering words, you can transform your experience for the better.

Change how you feel: When you change your words, you also change how you feel. If your mood is inclined to be down, you can immediately alter it by changing the kind of words you use throughout the day.

Words can do a lot of good, but they can also create anxiety and confusion and can have dire consequences. It is crucial to be able to communicate clearly and unambiguously if you belong to certain professions more than others. This is when you realize the power that words can carry, because they can save you, condemn or kill you, put you in jail or give you your freedom.

Imagine a doctor or a lawyer expressing themselves in very poor vague language; the result of which may be that the nurse gets the wrong end of the stick, doesn't give the right treatment and the patient suffers unnecessary pain or dies as a result. Or the client can misunderstand instructions from his lawyer and do something that he is not supposed to and finish up in greater strife, thinking that he was following his lawyer's instructions.

So, now that you understand how very powerful words are, take control of your life and have the insights that words and their consequences can have on you.

Develop a passion for words. It can be a lot of fun!

Words can make you feel great or miserable. Let's choose to feel great! Spectacular even! Or sensational! It is just a matter of the power of words!

What's great about it is that we can manipulate it for better or for worse; but it's up to us! The power of words forms part of the rich tapestry of life which is part of life's lessons.

Life is a succession of lessons which must be lived and understood.

—*Helen keller*

The ability to have power over our words can change us for the better and give us great.... ***CONFIDENCE.***

Notes: What have you learnt?

CHAPTER THIRTEEN

Secrets About Gorgeousness And Confidence

Who are you to be gorgeous, talented, fabulous? Actually, who are you not to be?
—*Nelson Mandela*

Confident people are seen as gorgeous people and vice versa. No matter what they look like! Look at Seal! He is hardly the stereo-typical gorgeous male, but a lot of people fall in love with him and his music. Gorgeous people seem to exude an enviable confidence. Seal has it. People who enjoy confidence have an air of easiness about them and of being comfortable in their own skin; they do not appear anxious or troubled; they don't have something to prove; they freely smile, are well presented and are pleasant to have around. Charm is their middle name! Other people are inclined to get pleasure from their company. They lift our spirits and energize us. Gorgeous or confident people don't worry about what others think of them; they do not make the assumption that others may not like them or criticize them. What matters to them is what they themselves think of who they are.

Who Do We See As Gorgeous?

When you think of someone who is gorgeous, does it remind you of someone famous, like an actor, or a friend or does it remind you of your mother or perhaps your grandmother, or maybe your children? Maybe you think that you are the gorgeous one? Who comes to your mind when you are thinking of someone who is gorgeous? Miranda Kerr? Jennifer Aniston? Orlando Bloom? Keith Urban? George Clooney? Richard Branson? Prince William or Prince Harry? What about the Duchess of Cambridge? Oprah Winfrey? Or maybe Nelson Mandela himself? What about Joel Madden?

> *Beauty is in the eye of the beholder and so is gorgeousness.*

This is not a trick question; the answer is anyone can be gorgeous! You are! I am! It is available to all of us to claim that right! Gorgeousness is not rationed to a privileged few. We can all be gorgeous! The planet is big enough to accommodate every single one of us as gorgeous!

Nelson Mandela says it best: "Actually who are you not to be?"

To be gorgeous and confident, you don't have to be good-looking and have a physique to kill for; you do not need to have a lot of money; you do not need to fit with what the media professes gorgeousness is.

You just need to cultivate being gorgeous and thrive on the confidence that it gives you. You can choose the kind of gorgeous human being you want to portray to the world.

Recipe For Gorgeousness And Confidence:

The first thing you need to do is to **believe** that you are indeed gorgeous in your mind. **Gorgeousness starts in your head first.**

The desired ingredients being:

- A good pinch of self-belief, mixed with a healthy self-esteem and self-worth
- Gently toss in a bowlful of charm and confidence
- Followed by a good helping of being happy in your own skin
- Add handfuls of charm and respect for yourself and others
- Finally, add a good cupful of kindness and compassion
- Finish with putting it all in a well-groomed recipient.
- Blend all ingredients together and throw in bunches of humour and the result is a happy, confident and gorgeous human being! Et Voila!

> *Treat yourself as gorgeous and you will be seen as gorgeous. Others will treat you the way you treat yourself and reinforce that feeling of confidence and gorgeousness.*

To be gorgeous is at the heart of who we are; it is how we choose to present ourselves to the world, our personality, our character and how we interact with others.

We are unique works of art, whatever we look like! We deserve to show appreciation for that exclusive gift.

As I said before no one is exactly like us in every way, this century or the last or the ones before that. Not now, not before and not ever! It doesn't matter how like someone else we think we are in hundreds of different ways, they can never ever be *exactly* like us. They will never have our fingerprints or our footprints. That is incredible! That makes everyone of us very, very special!

As a human being we are extremely valuable, in fact we are very precious! Let's treat ourselves as such! As with most things that I have talked about in this book, everything starts in the mind.

> *Confidence and gorgeousness start with our thoughts, our beliefs and our values.*

It begins with how we feel about ourselves; what we value and who we believe we are, including what we repeatedly say to ourselves about us in our mind.

You cannot be gorgeous or feel gorgeous, if you don't first of all *believe* that you are gorgeous. You need to really and truly emotionally believe: *I am Gorgeous!* And No! It isn't being arrogant! It shows a healthy self-esteem and self-worth. How can you expect others to see you as gorgeous if you don't believe that you are gorgeous?

By the way that you treat yourself, you teach others how to treat you.

So you have to treat yourself as gorgeous, and thoroughly believe it. It has to be genuine.

You need to behave in a gorgeous manner, when you speak about yourself and others, so that others are convinced that you are who and what you say you are. Others will not fail to notice as they will believe that you are in fact gorgeous and will treat you accordingly, because you will naturally emanate *gorgeousness*.

The way the world responds to you depends on how much you believe that you are gorgeous and confident.

There are many beautiful women, successful singers, models and actresses, whose looks most women would see as gorgeous and yet they do not have this appeal, because they do not have the self-worth, character, self-respect, self-acceptance and self-confidence or behaviour that is required to be gorgeous.

Low self-worth leads many of them to ruin their lives with drugs and alcohol and some finish up in rehab at best or dead. Who wouldn't have thought that Marilyn Monroe wasn't gorgeous? But did she think so? The fact is that to be gorgeous doesn't only depend on how you look. If that was the case she would have ticked all the right boxes; but to be gorgeous is to be much more than the way you look.

The media treats Cameron Diaz as gorgeous and yet would you say that she is particularly good-looking? However, her smile lights up the cinema screen and those watching her. Whenever you see her on screen, you have no doubt that *she* believes that she is gorgeous. Look at Oprah Winfrey! One wouldn't say that she has conventional beautiful looks or figure for that matter, and yet the world adores her and thinks that she is gorgeous. They revere her as a queen of television. She has thousands and thousands of fans all over the world. It wasn't always like that for her; she wasn't born with a silver spoon in her mouth, but she has worked very hard on herself to be the gorgeous woman that she is to-day. These women woo us by their confidence, charm, warmth and intelligence, their sense of humour and their own self-worth and self-respect.

Gorgeousness has nothing to do with the classic, slimline beauties who could do with a good steak inside them; but it has a lot to do with character, warmth, self-respect, humour, manners, sex-appeal, charm, self-confidence and the belief you have in yourself that altogether make you act in a gorgeous manner. Since these people exude gorgeousness, none of us would ever dream to question them as such; we all believe them and see them just as they choose to portray themselves to the world: *Gorgeous and confident!*

All these qualities stem from very deep inside. These qualities may not have been there since childhood, but gorgeous or confident people realize that no matter what their childhood was like, they choose to language it to themselves in a positive fashion. They choose to learn all they can about how the world works and how to respond to the world. Unlike what Lady Gaga tells us, most of us are *not born this way*; we learn to become that way when we work hard on ourselves.

If we have unconditional love from our parents since we are babies, we grow up loving ourselves, having good self-worth and self-respect and feeling equal to anyone without having to prove ourselves to feel accepted.

Sadly, the reality is that many people have had very troubled childhoods, with the result that as adults they choose destructive ways to compensate for their low self-esteem and self-worth. As such they send out negative vibes, cues and messages to the world. The world in return treats them in a reciprocal manner, which confirms to them their low self-worth. It is once again a self-fulfilling prophecy.

The important fact is that just because you've had a difficult childhood, it doesn't necessarily mean that you have low self-worth and self-esteem. It is never too late to learn and experience what you didn't get in your childhood and work on yourself to acquire it. For instance, Oprah had a dreadfully abusive childhood, but she has managed to overcome all the obstacles that were in her way to become the amazing icon that she is to-day; instead she uses her experience and privileged position to help other underprivileged children.

Anything is possible if you want it enough and put your mind to it.

The only limits in our life are those we impose on ourselves.

—*Bob Proctor*

So How Do You See Yourself?

Do you see yourself as beautiful and gorgeous, assertive and enjoy being confident or do you see yourself as useless or fat and ugly, or lacking confidence and self-worth? Something in-between? Do you love yourself or hate yourself?

Some clients tell me that they see themselves as fat and ugly and not very attractive, even when they look the most divine creatures on earth. This belief has nothing to do with how they in fact look physically. Equally gorgeousness has not much to do with what your physical attributes are like.

Whatever you've got, make the most of it. You can't just say that as you are not very pretty, it's no point trying to be. To be gorgeous and confident, it is important to make the most of what you have been given. That is all part of your self-esteem.

> *Whatever you look like, you are always first-class, as you were created that way for a special reason.*

Remember, that you are a unique work of art, never seen before or ever likely to be seen again, even after you leave this earth! So, honour your Creator and look after what you have been given in the best way you can, take care of it, present it well and be proud of who you are.

If you do suffer from a low self-esteem, remember that it is just a state of mind, a limiting belief that you are entertaining, and negative thoughts; and Yes! You can change it.

Your self-esteem is all about the thoughts that you choose to entertain about yourself.

Affirmations:

- I appreciate that I am attractive.
- I appreciate my natural beauty.
- I appreciate that I am a unique human being.
- I appreciate my gifts and talents.
- I believe that I am gorgeous and act as such.
- I love and accept myself, just as I am.
- I radiate confidence.
- I radiate energy
- I believe in the good in others.
- I approve and love my body.
- I am comfortable and relaxed in the presence of other people.
- I want the best for me and for others.
- I am fit and healthy.

Use these affirmations daily, and add some of your own.

You are reprogramming your subconscious to love and accept and approve the new gorgeous you.

You have to remove the negative programming and put in the new positive programming in your brain. Remember that beauty is in the eye of the beholder.

It is imperative for you to be gorgeous, that you first convince yourself that you are. You must truly believe in your mind that you are gorgeous.

Affirmations repeated with intention, commitment and discipline are very effective. Write the affirmations that resonate with you on a flashcard and keep looking at it and repeating them throughout your day.

Your subconscious will not argue with you. It simply acts on the instructions that you give it and finds a way to give you what it thinks you want. It is the "spy within"; it is listening 24/7 to what you are saying to yourself about you.

If you say to yourself and believe that you are fat and ugly, it will believe you and act accordingly by keeping you fat and ugly. If you say and believe that you are beautiful, talented, gorgeous and fabulous, it will certainly believe you too. So the main person you need to convince is *you*. Use the affirmations with conviction on a consistent basis, and you will do a pretty good job.

It's up to you to select the software that you want to program your computer (brain) with. You have that power!

Whenever I visit one of my local shops, the sales assistant always welcomes me as: *Hello gorgeous lady*; this simple remark has the delightful way of lifting my spirits and making me smile. I think that she is a gorgeous lady who naturally knows how to lift her customers' spirits, and create magic if only for a moment. I'm sure she doesn't only say this to me, but in that moment, you truly believe that she really means it just for you and means what she says. These three uplifting words help her customers to feel good about themselves and reinforce a belief that they really are gorgeous! (*But of course, if you really feel gorgeous, you may well want to buy one of her dresses to prove it! clever lady!*) If you are already gorgeous, will whatever clothes you try on you be anything other than more gorgeous? This is one very shrewd psychologically aware sales lady, and I admire her and really think that she is truly gorgeous as she is sincere and congruent when she speaks to her clients. In fact, she inspired me to write this chapter on confidence and gorgeousness.

So, if you start to believe that you are truly gorgeous, other people, with whom you come into contact with, will reinforce it too; you will feel uplifted, confident and it will enhance your mood and ultimately your life. The more you treat yourself as gorgeous, the more confident you will be and the more others will join in confirming your new belief.

The more you can see yourself as attractive, the better you will look and feel, and the world will corroborate it too. You may suddenly discover that people who didn't notice you before suddenly come out of the wood works and start to compliment you on how much better you look, how much younger, how much slimmer, on your hair, what beautiful colours that you are wearing etc. All this serve to reinforce and support your beliefs about yourself.

If you present yourself to the world and you look a mess; you feel a mess, you believe you are a mess; you will not have any reinforcement from anyone to help you believe that you are gorgeous. If you don't believe it why would others believe you?

Make no mistake, when we are stressed others can read our state of mind as the stress lines and tautness of our face do a good job in betraying us, without us having to utter even one word; equally when we are relaxed and enjoying life that too shows on our face; and there's nothing more attractive than bright eyes and relaxed facial muscles to make you look sunnier and younger; your facial lines tend to fade away and make you look younger and even more beautiful as you easily smile.

> *Our face is the mirror that reflects to the world what is going on the inside of us.*

Now, that you know how to control your thoughts and make yourself gorgeous on the inside, let's turn our attention to the outside.

> *The way we present ourselves to the world also gives a message to the outside world about who we think we are.*

The world will be confronting what's on the outside of you first before they get to discover your magical personality and get to enjoy your many wonderful talents and attributes.

Some may say that it doesn't matter what you look like; what matters is what's inside. What's inside is vitally important, but, I am telling you that:

What you choose to present to the outside world does matter as first impression always counts and they are difficult to shake off.

How you choose to present yourself to the outside world is key. When someone doesn't know you at all the only thing that they have to judge who you are is by the way you present yourself.

Like it or not we all form an opinion within the first few minutes of meeting someone.

If you look gorgeous and behave in a gorgeous manner, the world forms the view that you are indeed gorgeous and confident; however, if you look like a tramp, they also see you as a tramp, and that is the judgment they will keep of you.

First impressions do count and do last.

If you value who you are, you would want to present the best of yourself. You need to go out looking the best you can, not once in a while but consistently, every day, whether it is going to work, shopping or going to meet friends or when you socialize in the evenings.

Let's say that you are looking for a life partner; you could meet him or her at any time, when you least expect it. Wouldn't it be a shame to let an opportunity pass just because they formed the wrong opinion of who you are?—Because when they met you, you didn't fit the image of what they have in mind for their life partner, all because you were too lazy to be bothered?

To look your best, you need to be well groomed and put in an effort on your personal appearance. Then you will be walking your walk and talking your talk, and letting anyone who has the pleasure of casting their eyes on you, know that you do take pride in yourself, because you are worth it.

> *What makes you gorgeous and confident isn't only what is on the inside or what is on the outside; it is the whole package that makes you truly gorgeous and confident! It starts with healthy positive thoughts and finishes with what others can see.*

There are many people who really do not take care about how they present themselves to the outside world, and never put in any effort in their appearance. Each time you see them, they look like they have just rolled out of bed! Often they pretend that they are far too busy or superior to take time for such frivolity or else they play the victim who looks after everyone else's needs but there's absolutely no time in their generous charitable schedule for their very own bighearted selves. In fact what that is saying is that you do not value yourself and have low self-esteem and low self-worth.

On the other hand some of these people often try to make those who have enough self-worth and self-respect, feel bad by assuming that they clearly don't have much to do if they do find time for such trivia. Their *far too-busy* selves could never find time for such indulgence! They say things like: *You make me feel so bad; you look so beautiful; look at me! I look dreadful, but I'm just so busy!* This is definitely not a compliment! Or *Gosh, I am far too busy looking after my children to have time for such luxuries!* This statement makes the assumption that if you do have children, you clearly don't spend the time taking care of your children, but spend the time on yourself—which one could assume makes you a *selfish bad mother!*

Well! I have news for them: with a bit better organizational skills, you can have time for both!

These words show that they do not treat themselves with self-worth and self-respect, and do not believe that they are worth it; but somewhere inside they do feel ashamed about the face they choose to present to the world, otherwise they wouldn't feel bad when they see someone else who has made the effort.

I find it amazing that people will look at someone who has clearly made the effort to take care of themselves and say: *they* make *them feel bad*!!! Do they mean that this person took good care of presenting herself well to the world, in order to show them up? Why? . . . . Because that person did her best and treated herself with respect! What an incredible concept!

The answer is, if you don't want to feel bad when you see someone looking good, make the effort to look after yourself before you leave the house, but please don't come up with such absurdity!! It smacks of low self-esteem.

> *Look in the mirror before you leave the house! If you're happy with your reflection, walk out the door; if you're not, now is your chance to do something about it!*

Thankfully, usually the well-groomed person's self-esteem is able to withstand such negative comment graciously—part of their attractiveness and gorgeousness!!

When you take good care of yourself, you are saying:

I'm worth it! I deserve it!

On the other hand, when you do not take care of yourself, you are saying:

Don't worry about me, I don't really matter! I'm not worth it! I don't deserve it.

The answer is:

Very few of us are born with perfect features and perfect complexion. If you are blessed with both, then wonderful! Lucky you! If you look great in a garbage bag, this is not for you! But most of us may need a little help. So take care of yourself. Watch what you look like before you leave the house. Don't be afraid to use a little enhanced help; wear a little make-up if you need it; have a smart haircut if need be; take care of your nails. This small tip goes a long way towards enhancing your confidence and gorgeousness.

Make sure that you are happy with the clothes you are wearing. Check your shoes. Enjoy wearing some of your jewellery if you have some and a little smelly wouldn't go amiss either. I promise, you will feel great about yourself. Just try it!

If you do this regularly, it will become your new habit and will go a long way to help you raise your self-esteem and give you confidence. It will influence how others treat you. You will discover new found respect.

Your inner beauty is vitally important, but your outer beauty matters too. It doesn't matter how pretty or handsome you are what matters is that you do the best with what you have been given.

> To look gorgeous and confident means: "the whole package, inside and out."

Looking gorgeous has nothing to do with being good-looking. It is making the best of what your Creator gave you, and having and demonstrating good self-worth and self-esteem.

Exercise to promote good mental health and good self-esteem.

- Add exercise as part of your routine of looking after your body. Research has repeatedly shown that exercise is great at promoting good mental health; it can lift depression and improve anxiety.
- Walking is an excellent all round exercise. 30 minutes to an hour each day is a good start. Otherwise join a gym. It may also be a good place to enlarge your social circle. If you are a woman and don't enjoy mixed gym, you may prefer a women only gym, which cater only for women's health needs.
- Be conscious of what you wear and how you present yourself to the world.
- Pay attention to your clothes; *choose* what to wear daily; don't wear any old thing that happens to be practical! It is as important as what you nourish your body with. You are nourishing your self-esteem.
- Enhance your best assets. Draw attention to your good points and minimize the bad.
- Wear clothes that make you feel good in. They do not have to be expensive or trendy.
- Use colours. Colours are uplifting and have a beneficial effect on yourself and others. People are uplifted by colours. If you do have a tendency to feel down, try wearing bright blue, orange, yellow, green, purple or pink and you will see the difference it will make to your moods and to others.
- Please don't wear something just because it's *handy* and *comfy* or because you can't be bothered. *Comfy* in every day terms usually translates into *scruffy*; can even be literally translated into *grubby old track suit*; something that is always handy to slip into when you can't be bothered, right? . . . .

Hum! If you have these types of scruffy-comfy-type clothes, *get rid of them*! If you want to relax, be happy in the comfortable clothes you choose to relax in. Comfy clothes you won't be embarrassed to be seen in.

- Never let me hear that you took the children to school in your pyjamas! Or that you went to the shops in your slippers!

Make sure you're happy with the way you look, each time you leave the house. You never know who you might meet to-day! It could well be the man or woman of your dreams! Wouldn't that be a pity if they saw you at your worst?

Check your reflection in the mirror and ask yourself: *Would I feel good if I met someone important, when I'm out?* If the answer is *yes*, leave the house with confidence. If you were to meet your partner with their boss would they be proud of you?

There are very few natural beauties; if you are not one of them, do use some make-up to make you look and feel better. There is absolutely nothing wrong with enhancing yourself with a little help. These days, it is very easy with mineral make-up. You don't need to do much and it takes a minimal amount of time, however, the difference is amazing. It just shows that you feel you are worth the effort. It all helps to complete your gorgeousness.

Pay attention to your hair; present your hair in its best light. If your hair is one of your main assets, then use it. Don't display *the just rolled out of bed* look!

If you do this you will feel and look gorgeous to you and the world will respond to you accordingly.

When you feel gorgeous, your attitude towards the world changes for the better. Your self-esteem rises. In return the world reacts to you in a reciprocal manner. All of a sudden things start looking up! More than anything else, it will increase your self-confidence as you get amazing feedback from people you will come into contact with. If you are inclined to have low moods, your world will suddenly change for the better. Things will look sunnier. The constant positive feedback you get does wonders for your self-esteem and your self-confidence.

Always be a first-rate version of yourself, instead of a second-rate version of somebody else.
—*Judy Garland*

What Is Confidence?

- Confident people love themselves and take pride in who they are and what they do.
- Confident people understand themselves and make an effort to continuously learn, grow and develop throughout their life.
- Confident people are not hesitant people; they know what they want.
- Confident people plan their lives. They write down their goals and plan their future. They don't leave their future at the mercy of others. They know that if they do not make a plan others will do it for them, and it is bound not to be what they want.

- Confident people are positive thinkers and know that every problem has a solution.
- Confident people know that if they break any problem in smaller chunks they will be able to solve the puzzle. They are optimistic and creative about problem-solving. Their positive energy attracts other people.
- Confident people are open, generous and gracious towards others.
- Confident people are skilful, and can adjust their attitudes and behaviours to accommodate varying situations.
- Confident people respect themselves and other people and treat them as an equal.
- Confident people use their positive feedbacks to support their confidence.
- Confident people never put others down to give themselves more power or importance. They are fair and inspire trust from others. People seek them out and enjoy their company as they are open and genuine. They make others feel secure and know where they stand with them. This in turn reinforces their self-confidence. They inspire others to improve themselves too.
- Confident people value confidence and encourage it in others as confidence is a value they enjoy themselves and hold close to their hearts.
- Confident people are not defensive as they accept that they may be wrong sometimes and are willing to recognize their weaknesses and work on them. They know that nobody's perfect, so understand that people make mistakes. They understand that making mistakes is part of life's learning process and they are willing to learn from their mistakes.
- Confident people are relaxed and don't feel the need to shout the loudest and prove themselves or compete.
- Confident people smile easily, making others feel easily at ease.
- Confident people know that bad times do not last forever. They know that life has its ups and downs; they know that everyone has a bad time sometime, but that they do get over it; and that things do get better again after a while and that the good times are only around the corner.
- Confident people are not scared about being embarrassed sometimes, as they know that it is momentary and that they will soon feel better. Being embarrassed sometimes is part of life's journey. Everyone goes through it at times. They also know that they would have learned something as a result and that no one has ever died of embarrassment. This attitude soon helps them to recover from their embarrassment and before long they continue to enjoy life.
- Confident people do not waste valuable energy on negative thinking and outcomes. They never waste their time on self-depreciating talk. Their goal is to concentrate on positive results. They use positive words in their internal dialogue.
- Confident people have a winning attitude in life. Their stand in life is positive. They rehearse positive outcomes and manifest them into their physical world.

Confident people have good manners.

Part of their charm is the fact that they are never rude, but are generally charming. Good manners add to their natural charm. When you treat people with good manners, you are treating them with respect, kindness and showing love. Love is not unkind or rude, neither are confident people.

We have all seen people whose manners have horrified us, including children. People with bad manners are seen as rude, ignorant, and arrogant, depicting a complete lack of gratitude and decorum. On the other hand when we are treated with good manners, we are impressed by their charisma, humanity, thoughtfulness, and caring and we are left with a much happier experience.

Good Manners
To develop your confidence and improve your good manners, here are some tips:

Please and thank you: First of all basic courtesy demands that we say *Please and thank you*, even if that person is not important in our eyes.

Never forget to add *please* at the end of a request and a *thank you* when you get what you asked for.

If you are given a gift, the least you can do is to thank the person graciously (even if you don't like the gift!), and show them that you are pleased. After all they took the time to look for that gift and think about what will please you. You will be a good role model for your children and they will not take things for granted, like far too many people do, and grow up with an attitude of entitlement. If it is your custom to give a hug and a kiss, please do so, especially if it is the custom of the person offering the gift.

Writing a Thank you note to show your appreciation is a nice touch. People never fail to notice when you are gracious, courteous or respectful towards them. You create a really good impression.

So, whatever else, you don't do, never forget your please and thank you. That is just basic good manners.

Hold that door! If you are going through a door and you have others following you, rather than let the door slam behind you, take a couple of seconds and hold it for the next person. If they smile and say *thank you,* great! If they don't you may have taught them some good manners; failing that, understand that the problem is not yours here!

Conversation manners! During a conversation, avoid interrupting the other person or *speak over* the other person, when they are talking, or even finishing the other person's sentence or story for them. THAT IS VERY RUDE! And definitely not gorgeous! When you are doing that, you are not listening! Instead it demonstrates your insecurity and low self-esteem, as you do this because you need to be the one who competes for everyone's constant attention to yourself. Practice becoming a good listener instead. *Listen* to what is being said instead of rehearsing what you want to say next. When you do that, you have not listened to the person you are speaking with, and are showing them serious disrespect.

Good listeners are attractive. People like nothing better than to be heard. So, learn to take turns in conversations and wait for the other person to finish before you can say what you have to say.

Do not be the one hijacking the conversation! Be aware that there are some of you, who, wherever you go, tend to takeover the conversation. In case anyone hadn't noticed, it's all about you! Some people *looove* the sound of their own voice! No one else get to say anything as you are the one who has the most to say but do not allow anyone else to offer their opinion, whether it is socially, on a course, or in a meeting. This shows insecurity and selfishness. **Become Present**; in the here and now!! Realize what you are doing and observe how others are feeling listening to your monologue! Stop thinking just about you! Be here now! Use your ability of stepping back and observing your own behaviour. Become aware of your behaviour. If you find that you hijack all the conversations, wherever you go, or that you are seriously competing with others for what you have to say, please, stop living in denial! Get real with yourself. Do not kid yourself and think that the others were fascinated by what you had to say! Or that they were even interested! No! They probably were irritated that you were the only one who got the chance to say anything or voice your opinion! Be aware that all anyone can hear is your voice.

If you are in the habit of doing this, watch the bored expressions on other people's faces; notice if they are not frustrated or about to kill you! (You may not have realized it as you were too busy talking!) They may even be angry or fighting the strong urge to stuff a plug in your mouth to shut you up! BUT YOU STILL DIDN'T GET IT! The reason for this is that you are insecure and selfish, only thinking about yourself; your ability to read people is way off the radar! So, don't live in denial, be honest with yourself and be present and observe your behaviour and most of all, CHANGE it!

Now! If you suspect that this could be you:—(NO! NO! This is not about Tom, Dick or Harry! It's really about you!)—Re-read what I have just written; digest it and get real with yourself. Dig deep inside and choose to change this part of you as this is not the road to gorgeousness and to enhance your life. It only feeds your selfish needs and your insecurity. It may just be a very bad habit that you inherited somewhere. Time has come to shake it off!

For God's sake, for your sake and especially for the sake of other people listening to all your rhetoric— Try hard to have some insight in your behaviour! But most of all: GET IT!

Let this be your moment of realization! Be honest with yourself! But please just get it! Then, you can do something about it. Unless you are 100% honest with yourself, you will never be able to change your behaviour.

Don't read this and think of other people. Read this and get real! Ask yourself the question: *Is this how I am?* Ask other people what they think; if they are honest and a good friend they'll tell you the truth. Some may even be really glad that the penny has finally dropped for you!

Allow other people to have a go; realize that there aren't just you. Other people have as much right as you do to express themselves and contribute to any conversation. It may be difficult at first, but keep reminding yourself that the world doesn't revolve around just you, allow others to have a go too. That way, you will stop them talking about you behind your back. Every time you stifle the urge to take over any conversation, give yourself a huge pat over the back and reward yourself in some small way. Tell yourself how brilliant you are that you are able to control this dominating urge to control the conversation. You may be surprised that, as your listening skills improve that you may learn quite a lot by listening to others, which you completely missed before when you were the one doing all the talking. You may find that suddenly your popularity rating gets better and better. Your "likeability" improves. Others will find you far more attractive and courteous and would seek you out instead of avoiding you. In fact, ask them what they think about . . . . You are now on your way to gorgeousness.

Now look at several different situations that you have been in, who did most of the talking? . . . Who demanded most attention from others? If that is you, then it is time to change and concentrate on your listening skills instead. Observe your behaviour as if you were an observer in the room. Practice taking turns in conversations. Wait for the other person to stop talking before you jump in.

Travel manners! When travelling or in a public place, be courteous towards other members of society who may be weaker than you, like the pregnant woman, the older person or the frail and infirm. If you have a seat and they don't, and you are able to, be really gorgeous and offer them your seat. You may have paid for your seat just the same, but I promise if you can offer your seat to someone less fortunate than you, you will feel GOOD! And definitely gorgeous!

Be a good sport. Be competitive but always congratulate the winner. Be a great winner but be an even better loser. Congratulate people if they have done something worthy of praise and mean it.

On the road, be a courteous driver. Being courteous on the road is more than having just good manners. It is a matter of safety. It prevents road rage incidents and accidents. Do not behave as a bully by tailgating others. It is rude and dangerous. Be patient, and allow for mistakes on the road, as none of us are perfect. Remember to forgive the little things. There is absolutely no need to insult other drivers; and YES! Indecent gestures are definitely not gorgeous! Learn to be gracious on the road.

Greetings! It is important to get it sorted out how we greet different people. Different cultures have got different ways of greeting each other. Young people too have their own little idiosyncrasy! They have their special hugs and convoluted handshakes. When you do not know how to greet people appropriately, you can be seen you as *rude, gauche, ignorant or insulting.*

Greeting rituals are important. If you have people from different cultures in your circle of friends and acquaintances, it may be wise to get to know what their custom is. There are different ways of greeting different people. You would not greet the Prime Minister or the Queen with a *Hey, How's it going*? Using appropriate greetings and gestures with different people is important. Wherever appropriate, you may need to bow, nod, or offer a handshake, Hi five, knuckles, a hug or a kiss. Get it straight in your head once and for all and you will not be caught unawares and feel awkward when you are least expecting it. If it isn't your practice to kiss or hug, please be gracious and accept it gracefully and forget about feeling award! Get over it! Others do . . . everyday! Don't let it become an issue for you. There are far more important things for you to worry about than that!

I do realize that there are some people who have had difficult experiences who cannot abide being hugged or kissed. If that is the case then you need to find a way of greeting people that will not be offensive to you or to them. Only if that is the only way, then let it be known in a polite way that you prefer to . . . . Just say hello . . . . Hi 5 . . . . Or something else (instead of being hugged or kissed).

Name etiquette: Call people by the name that they introduced themselves to you by. Don't give them a shortened version or a nickname. That is not gorgeous or polite! Give good eye contact and do remember their name. If you forget a name, it is like saying that they are so insignificant that you can't even remember their name!

Groom yourself appropriately. We discussed that one before, didn't we?

Dinning manners! If you are invited as a guest to someone else's house, it doesn't hurt to ask what you can do to help, especially if you can see that the host or hostess is stressing to get everything done by themselves. It's also kind to see if you can help clean up afterwards rather than let one person do everything, whilst you sit down, relax, enjoy your glass of wine not caring about your host or hostess or what needs to be done. If you help then you can all relax sooner and enjoy that glass of wine "together". If you help you are more than likely going to be asked more often than if you don't. People notice these things! They may refuse the help but that's okay; however, you showed caring and good manners.

Never chew gum especially with your mouth open when you are talking with someone, particularly if you are invited to dinner!

At the table: Remember, this is not a race! You do not get a prize if you finish first. Do not chew with your mouth open; worse still do not chew noisily and stuff as much as you can in that oral cavity! It is very offensive and off-putting and definitely bad manners. (I remember being invited to lunch once, and the person I was with reminded me of a turkey who was being forced-fed! Extremely off-putting!!) Put just enough on your fork for a small mouthful, and chew quietly. And, NO! It is not a competition to see who finishes first!

Whether you are a child or a grown-up, you have to say *Excuse me* if you have to leave the table. Teach your children good table manners as soon as they are old enough to understand. It will help them socially as they grow up. Good table manners start in childhood and we acquire them from our parents. People loathe children with poor table manners.

Remember this: Wait for everyone to be served before you start to eat. It is important to wait for everyone to be served at the table before you can start eating. Preferably this is done when the hostess is ready and wishes everyone *Bon appétit* or gives you the signal that you can start to eat.

You do not attack your dinner the minute it is in front of you, never mind if others have been served or not. That is bad manners and definitely not gorgeous! If others are still eating, you should not leave the table. Children should not be running around the minute they have decided they no longer want to eat anymore. Good manners requests that they stay in their seats. If young children want to leave the table, they need to learn to say: *Please, may I leave the table*? And, I am sorry, but if the answer is *NO*, then they need to learn the discipline of being able to sit on their chairs until they are allowed to leave the table.

Definitely no elbows at the table and unquestionably no singing at the table either!

If you are invited to dinner: please make a point of saying thank you for the invitation to the host or hostess and how wonderful the meal looks and tastes throughout the meal. And never forget to thank the hosts again before you leave, repeating how exceptional dinner was. You can even flatter them by asking for the recipe. There is nothing worse than to have slaved over a hot oven all day to find that it was not appreciated, or that your guests leave without any mention of dinner. That is rude and absolutely not gorgeous!

Formal and informal settings: Teach yourself to manage formal and informal settings. If you don't know which implements to use for what, a simple rule is: start by using the knives and forks or anything else from the outside first and work your way towards your plate. If you still can't remember, watch what others do first . . . . And copy! Hold your knives and forks appropriately. Your fork is not a shovel! And your knife is not a pick axe! You do not need to dig and shovel as fast as you can! If you don't know how to, then look at someone who looks comfortable with their knives and forks and copy! Look at what people who seem to know what to do and do the same thing with your knives and forks. You'll get the hang of it . . . . eventually! Take your time and chew . . . . quietly! With your mouth closed!

When you have finished eating put both your knives and forks together on the left side of your plate to indicate that you have finished.

Mobile Phone manners! When you are speaking on the phone, there is absolutely no need to shout, unless you are talking to someone who is really hard of hearing! No one is interested in your conversation! Speak loud enough for the person you're talking to, to hear. Speak politely and keep the volume down! Be aware of your language when you are in public. No dirty jokes, no swear words, no rude topics! And definitely no bodily functions, please! People who do not know you do not find these things funny! It does not add to your charm, charisma or personality; on the contrary, they take away a lot! You are seen as rude and crude! That is definitely not gorgeousness! Whenever we get dirty looks from other people, when we use our mobile phone, we get it, don't we? That this is not the place to be talking on a mobile phone, don't you think so? No one wants to hear someone else's loud conversation on a mobile phone, whether we are in a restaurant, in a public restroom, in a meeting, on the train or the plane or when we are buying something, or when we are in the cinema or in church—especially not at a wedding! If you have to make a call, be discreet and keep your voice low, and go somewhere where you won't bother others. Be conscious where you use your mobile phone and be aware not to disturb others. Choose to be mobile phone courteous!

Three-way conversations: Do not have a three-way conversation when you are on the phone to someone. That is not the time to discuss something irrelevant with your little darlings! Finish your conversation then concentrate on your little treasures! It teaches them that they sometimes have to share Mummy's attention—and that's a good thing!

Timing: As a rule, it is rude to phone or text someone too early or too late. The 8 o'clock rule is good. Not before 8am and not after 8pm.

If you know that the person that you are ringing have certain commitments, like young children or elderly parents, avoid their crucial busy times, as a matter of courtesy.

Answering the phone: Decide on a polite way of answering your phone: *Hello, it's . . . . how can I help you?* Or something else but in a polite and suitably gorgeous manner; not shouting down the phone: *Who's that?*

Texting: It is however, very impolite to write long texts to other people or have a long conversation on the phone when you are with friends or other people, unless it's a matter of life and death. If you are out to dinner with a friend, please do not spend half your evening texting or speaking with someone else on the phone. It is very rude and do not be surprised if you never hear from that friend again! Unless it is urgent, the text or phone conversation can wait until you are free to do it. If someone rings you, keep it short or ask if you can ring them back later.

Be conscious of other people's feelings: When you phone someone just because you have some free time and feel like it or because it doesn't cost you anything, don't spend hours and hours on the phone. The person you are phoning may have a busy life. If you are phoning someone in a different time zone, you may be feeling nice and fresh in the morning, but they may be getting ready for bed after a hard day. Or they may just be very tired as it may well be the end of the day for them. As much as people love to hear from you and love to chat to their family and friends, remember that you do not know what may be happening for them in their lives. It may become a stress for them. You may be talking to them about everyday things but it may be a real stress for them to stay on the phone for a very long time. They have their own pressures of life. Twenty minutes chat may be a pleasure; two hours chat may become a stress. Be aware of how the other person may be feeling. If you find that they want to cut the conversation short, be understanding and end it! If they sound great and want to chat then by all means stay on the phone, but sensitive to how they are feeling.

Use humour but stay polite. There is no such thing as being too polite in the world of the gorgeous. Use good manners with your nearest and dearest, your parents and grandparents. Don't make the mistake of thinking that you don't have to make the effort with them. They taught you all you know! Of course, you need to make the effort! First of all, you will make them proud! Secondly they will congratulate themselves that they did a good job on you! But if you make no effort with them, they will be despairing that they failed you.

Children learn what they see: If you want your children to be confident and gorgeous in every way then you need to be a good role model for them. In fact you are their first role model. Often children naturally copy what their parents did when they become adults. They will treat you the way you treat your parents. If you do not show much regard for your elderly parents, do not be surprised that your now loving little prince or your beautiful little princess become selfish or heartless bullies towards you as they and you get older, and treat you much the same way as you treated your own parents. If you showed your parents selfishness and had no time for them, and did not value them, that will get back to you multiplied. You would have taught them well. However, if the opposite is true, you will also get that back multiplied too. We all reap what we sow.

Children do not have to be formally taught; their powers of observation last a lifetime! Even when they are the adults and you are now the elderly parents! Remember that they choose what happens to you when you get older! How do you show your older parents that you care about them? Do you give them the time that they deserve? Are you kind to them or do you see them as a nuisance now that they're old and no longer fun? Your children will treat you much the same way. You reap what you sow. Whatever you are doing now, you will harvest later in your old age. On the other hand if you are doing the right thing, you will also reap what you have sown. It typifies the saying *what goes around comes around.* Generosity and kindness are essential attributes of gorgeousness and confidence.

Instilling good manners in our children: stand them in good stead later on in life. They learn gratitude by your example. As they grow up, they have *savoir faire* and that gives them the edge socially and in the workplace. On top of which they would be showing respect, love, compassion and kindness to others, which will not fail to make them popular! All thanks to you and your gorgeousness!

People with good manners are attractive people. They never fail to impress. People with bad manners are often associated with being inferior and of poor character.

Elevators, Train or Bus! It is good manners to let people come out of the elevator, train or bus before going in. Barging in whilst people are still trying to get out is of poor taste and definitely not gorgeous! Wait until they are out, and then take your turn in going in.

Treat others as you wish to be treated: with respect. Keep a smile not far from your lips. **Smiles are contagious and they spread happiness**. Confident and gorgeous people smile easily and genuinely. Smile, to your family, friends, colleagues, neighbours and others. Never leave somewhere without saying good bye to the people there. Smile and say a good word. It is catching.

Most of all treat yourself and everyone you meet, whatever their status, with good manners and respect.

Aren't these enough reasons why we should aim to be gorgeous and confident?

Many clients come to see me to work on their confidence. They may lack confidence in their work because they may not believe that they're up to the job; but most often, it is a lack of confidence in the Self; a lack of confidence that often originates from their earlier programming. As a result their internal dialogue is very negative, including the thoughts that they repeatedly run through their subconscious.

People who lack self-confidence often feel lonely and isolated. They are awkward around other people and feel embarrassed about silly things. They worry about their embarrassment as if it is a matter of life and death. They feel powerless and are easily frightened. In certain situations, the anxiety can be so strong that they physically feel sick and tense. Some may suffer from panic attacks, depending on the degree of anxiety.

People who lack confidence are the total opposite to the confident ones. They feel insignificant; feel less than others, worthless and useless. They feel guilty very easily and are ready to blame themselves or others. To some the word *sorry* is so familiar to them because it is part of their habitual vocabulary; others may react aggressively to cover-up their lack of self-confidence.

People who lack confidence are often pessimists and rationalize this by telling themselves and others that they are *realists.* They frequently don't try things because they believe that they would *realistically* be unsuccessful anyway.

People who lack confidence feel misunderstood and feel that life is passing them by and time and again feel let down. They feel that life isn't fair, not realizing that maybe life isn't supposed to be fair. They suffer resentment and bitterness as a consequence. They are easily hurt and angry. Their thin-skin can lead them to fall out with a lot of people around them.

At times depression and apathy may fill their life. These symptoms may be obvious in some but there are others who regularly conceal how they feel under the pretence of apparent over-confidence and success. They pretend to be cool by laughing to overcome their lack of self-confidence. Others are scared of being seen as over confident and of being called *bossy and arrogant;* this is reflected in their attitude. This belief springs from ignorance.

> *Confidence has nothing to do with being bossy and arrogant, or being too big for your boots, or getting above your station.*

To be confident is to be comfortable with who you really are; to love and value yourself; to have good self-belief and to have good self-esteem and self-worth. To be confident is to feel comfortable with anyone and to believe that everyone has the right to be an equal to others. It's about having strength of character, kindness and compassion. It is about believing the best in others. It is not about feeling superior. It is about being comfortable in your own skin.

So How Do You Become More Confident?

- As with most things to increase your self-confidence, you start with the **belief** that you are able to change and become more confident.
- You understand the need to change and choose to change.
- You have to to be motivated to be confident and visualize the benefits that confidence will bring you.

- You must understand yourself and what you are doing and how increased confidence will change your life.
- It is important to set realistic goals; otherwise you will be setting yourself up to fail.
- You must seek support for that change from the right people.
- Reward yourself regularly, as lacking confidence is punishment in itself.
- Cultivate positive thoughts, as it is the basis of self-confidence.
- Practice looking, acting and being self-confident on a daily basis.

Self-confidence comes from self-love and self-knowledge.

You need to love and cherish yourself, before you can love and cherish another. You have to improve your self-esteem by watching that your internal conversation is positive. It is important to take care of what happens in your internal world as well as in your external world, by choosing your thoughts and by taking care of your body and your appearance. Watch how you interact with others.

Respect your feelings as they don't lie.

Don't make your feelings wrong or ignore them; if you are feeling a certain emotion, there is a reason for it. As previously stated, every emotion carries a message; so pay attention to what message your emotions are trying to convey to you and act appropriately on them.

Find appropriate ways of expressing your emotions. Be creative. If you are used to shouting and raving and ranting, go for a long walk in the fresh air or do some exercise like jogging or skipping. When you've skipped or jogged for about 5 minutes, you will no longer feel like raving and ranting. If you still do, skip or jog for ten minutes; keep making the time longer until the feeling passes. Pent up emotions drain your energy and cause you distress and pain. You need to find a way of releasing them; if not they build up stress hormones in your body.

Exercise increases self-confidence and enhances good mental health.

It may be necessary to alter your lifestyle to increase your self-confidence. You do this by living your values and the values you want to acquire, by having the right work-life balance and by choosing the relationships you desire in your life.

Confident people are assertive people.

They have an ease about them. They feel comfortable with themselves. They don't worry about what other people will think and say. It is what they think and believe that matter.

Confident people benefit from assertiveness. On the other hand, people who lack self-confidence tend to suffer from a lack of assertiveness. Many use passive-aggressive behaviours when they think they are being assertive. For example:

I'll cook dinner AGAIN then, shall I?

Many make the mistake of taking assertiveness for aggressiveness. Being assertive has nothing to do with being aggressive even if you do it passively.

Assertiveness helps self-confidence. To be assertive is to aim to have a win/win situation. That means respecting your rights and those of others and meeting your needs without putting the other person down.

ASSERTIVENESS RIGHTS

1. The right to ask for what we want (realizing that the other person has the right to say "NO").
2. The right to have an opinion, feelings and emotions and to express them appropriately.
3. The right to make statements which have no logical basis, and which we do not have to justify.
4. The right to make our own decisions and cope with the consequences.
5. The right to choose whether or not to get involved with the problems of someone else.
6. The right not to know about something, or to understand.
7. The right to make mistakes.
8. The right to be successful.
9. The right to change our minds.
10. The right to privacy.
11. The right to be alone and independent.
12. The right to change ourselves and be assertive people.

N.B The assertive person is not just concerned about his or her own rights but always encourages and promotes assertiveness in others.

—(as cited in Gael Lindenfield Assert Yourself, 1992)

It's perfectly Okay to Say No

Some people have great difficulties saying no. Having self-confidence helps you to stand up for yourself when you need to. It is perfectly okay to say no, if it's not convenient for you. If you choose to do something for someone else because you can and you want to, that's wonderful; however there are situations, where it is really difficult for you to fulfill someone else's needs and it is often at your own expense, even if it is only emotional. Then it is perfectly okay to say No.

When it is inconvenient for you, or if you choose not to fulfill someone else's request, practice saying NO and feel fine about it. You don't have to be sorry, rude or pad your NO with lots of excuses. You can be polite but all the same just state that you are not available on that day at that time, for instance.

It is important not to let others use you, as you will end up resenting them. Remember, you are not being horrible when you say NO. You are just looking after your own emotional and physical needs, which is your God-given right.

To have good assertiveness skills, it helps to have good communication skills.

Confident people are good communicators

Good communication skills are an essential component of self-confidence. Some are so good at it that they have turned it into an art form. Therefore, if we improve the art of conversation, we are able to communicate effortlessly with others.

The ability of being able to communicate seamlessly increases our self-confidence. Nevertheless, it requires practice on a daily basis in our interaction with anyone we come into contact with. It is not really what we say as such that matters most, but it's the way that we say it. When we are unsure of ourselves and stutter over our words, we tend to lose confidence.

Communication is barely only about the words that are being said. It involves our tone of voice, the speed of the delivery, our facial expression and other non-verbal cues. And, yes! This is the time to start making use of those new words you learnt. And remember:

Practice does make perfect.

Small Talk with a Big Purpose

Confident people have an ease about them and are good at small talk.

Have you ever noticed how some people are ace at the skill of small talk? They can keep going and going, and finding more and more things to talk about when they've only just met someone they know nothing about, whilst others really struggle. The fact is there are an awful lot of safe subjects to use in small talk without bringing in anything personal. That makes it safe to talk to anyone.

Small talk serves a great purpose in the knack of communicating well. When you do not know someone well, you do not want to go into deep conversation about their lives or yours, small talk is the perfect thing to fill that gap. Many of my business clients are really good at what they do; but for some, you could say that small talk is hardly their area of expertise. Unless they are talking about business in which they are very competent in they are very comfortable, otherwise they find small talk a struggle. Some believe that small talk is irrelevant providing that the executives are good at their job.

> **Small talk is the beginning of any relationship and as such is very important.**

The initial step towards having any relationship creates the impression that others will have of you. Other clients such as teachers, managers, sales people, real estate or anyone in the medical field value information on communication including small talk and body language. They understand that these are fundamental to their jobs in order to be really good at what they do. Some find situations where they do not know anyone really challenging for them; for example in meetings, training courses or especially at social gatherings. They awkwardly answer other people's questions instead of finding their own topic of small talk in these situations.

> **It is not the most intelligent person or the unintelligent person who does better at small talk. Small talk has nothing to do with intelligence.**

While for some of us this kind of small talk can be a bit of fun, it can be sheer misery for others. To be able to hold conversations with other people are crucial life skills.

To be articulate gives you an edge. Verbal dyslexia is a clear disadvantage.

Being verbally dyslexic can cause untold misunderstandings. That is not to say that if you are verbally dyslexic you can't do anything about it. It requires working on yourself and constantly being aware of how you communicate, and practice on a consistent basis so that you can improve. It has equally to do with having confidence and a comprehensible vocabulary.

The standard of our conversations affects all our personal and public relationships. In fact the way we relate with ourselves and with others affects the quality of our lives. Before we get to know anyone, small talk is a good means of breaking the ice. We use communication skills in our personal relationships, in our work place, in interviews, to exchange information, to inform, to negotiate, to express our views, to discuss, to relate, to persuade, to dissuade, to educate and to influence others. In fact there is little we can do in life without having to communicate in some way with others, unless we are a complete recluse.

Some people boast that they are not much good at small talk as if it is too beneath them to participate in such trivialities. They say it with pride and wear it as a badge, as if it is of an additional benefit because they are so far above this pathetic practice, as they have far more important things to think about!

There is absolutely no correlation between high intelligence or academic achievements and the ability to hold conversations.

Small talk performs a very important function in how we interact with others. It helps us to get to know other people and get to observe the behaviour of the people we are talking with, without being intrusive. Sometimes small talk serves in calming an anxious, distressed or irate person down. Most small talk is safe as it is non-threatening, and it usually isn't personal.

When we talk to a stranger, we try to find a common point to be able to continue our conversation. Finding common ground helps us to decide if we want to develop the relationship further or not. Small talk fulfils that function. Sometimes chitchat can be useful as we can acquire bits of information which make other things fall into place and suddenly you can piece a puzzle together. It helps us realize what really is going on.

I am not suggesting to you however, for you to become gossipers; but there are gossips and "*gossips*"! Nasty gossips which are out there to destroy someone's reputation is despicable and do not deserve any attention; however, informative gossip about your work or organization may be quite useful, especially if you are concerned about a colleague or if you want to make an internal move. Through small talk you can become aware that a position that you have been after for a while has now become vacant. It can give you an opportunity to apply and get the job you really want. Sometimes you are able to understand or help somebody because you heard something through the grape vine. For example if you've heard that Mary's moodiness may be due to her imminent divorce or to the loss of her father, it will help you to be more understanding and compassionate towards Mary, instead of getting upset and calling her a *moody so and so*. Use your judgment and do not jump to easy conclusions either; you may be completely on the wrong tract.

Nonetheless, these small talks during coffee time, morning tea, in meetings or socially, can help us to build our personal and professional relationships. Having initially broken down some barriers through small talk with someone makes it easier and more relaxed and comfortable the next time you come across them again, as you now know a little bit about that person. This can help especially in the work place or socially.

If you're not much good at this kind of thing, learn a few tricks of the trade. For instance, you can discuss about how you got to where you are meeting, whether by plane, train or automobile; there is a whole lot to be said about any kind of transport; or if all else fails the *weather*, is a wonderful fall back. Isn't there always so much to say about the weather? It's too hot, too cold, too rainy, too stormy, too snowy or too much hail, or too wonderful! Ten, twenty years ago we didn't have all this . . . . this could lead to a discussion on climate change . . . You could do a thesis or a documentary on how different the weather can be! It would keep you talking for hours, especially when you start to compare it with what it is like in other countries at this time of the year, and see how lucky we all are, and how much worse it could be!!!!! After all, we rarely get tornados like in America! And what about those floods? These poor people . . . . Now how dreadful was this earthquake in Christchurch and what about the tsunami in Japan? Imagine the threat of radioactivity? So you can go from talking confidently about the weather to the effects caused by the inclement weather, and this can easily lead you elsewhere if you choose to or you can start a story about when you were on holiday somewhere and discuss what the weather was like then; this can lead you to talking about the places you travelled to, and exchanging stories. . . . . This can keep you busy chatting for hours and hours!

What about talking about what happened on the way to your destination? What about the *traffic*? . . . . What a fascinating subject of conversation we can make it or . . . . May be milk it! You can have some mileage out of that one.

. . . . You really wouldn't believe this, but to-day, on my way to the city, I witnessed two people stopped in the two middle lanes of the freeway and one man was beating the hell out of the other in such a shocking manner! Both cars had stopped for whatever reason . . . in the two middle lanes of the freeway! The cars carrying on either side of them! Can you just credit it? One was almost killing the other! And do you know what? Not a soul stopped to help this poor man! Not even me! (I have to admit, they scared me! Apart from the fact that it may have caused an accident!) What kind of world do we live in? Can you really believe this? It is so shocking . . . . That actually really happened to me on my way to a meeting.

Can you imagine if you wanted to discuss this and make small talk how much mileage you would get out of that? Another way would be: *My goodness, I was stuck in such heavy traffic getting here! Did you come by car too or did you take the train?* Hopefully you'll get a conversation going with this opening.

Or

Did you hear about the Icelandic Volcano, how it affected all the European flights? Isn't that scary? Can you even pronounce the name of that volcano? and of course, now there is the Chilean volcano to add to your small talk; this can lead you talking about volcanoes or even the movies you once saw with volcanoes in . . . .

Or

Making small talk about exercising is often another subject that can keep you busy chatting for a while: *When I went to the gym this week . . . . Do you belong to a gym? . . .* this can lead on to talking about health and fitness . . . . Please do choose who you talk to about exercise! Approach this subject with someone whom you can see from their appearance that they do exercise. If you come out with this subject to someone who is morbidly obese and doesn't know the difference between their dumbbell and their rowing machine, they may well think that you are being rude or sarcastic.

When you meet someone for the first time, it is good to find a common denominator. For instance: children, work, sports etc. By offering small talk subjects to those who find it harder, you are encouraging others to perfect their art of small talk too. They may want to share in this interaction, by expanding on what you talked about and then finding their own subjects and share them, and in the meantime, you gradually get to know them and start to feel comfortable in their company. You can both relax and enjoy the company.

This way you and others feel safe as nothing personal has to be disclosed or divulged.

This kind of small talk helps you to make a connection with other people; but more than that it tends to create a bond. If you find it difficult: collect small stories or jokes; keep snippets of current news that you've heard to discuss and keep the conversation flowing, instead of feeling it's like pulling teeth talking with you. Relax and don't put pressure on yourself.

I have a small book of *Freaky Facts* which is quite interesting as you can have such mileage out of it for small talk. It gives you weird and wonderful facts, which are really quite interesting but wouldn't be common knowledge. For example, did you know that there is a name for every kind of phobia? For example: Philophobia for the fear of falling in love to Tonsurophobia for the fear of haircuts, to Vestiphobia for the fear of clothing or Syngenesophobia for the fear of relatives. These are bits of pretty useless information but all the same, they are amusing, fascinating, fun and easy subjects of conversation and they are entertaining and safe for small talk.

How Can We Improve Our Small Talk Skills?

- To become excellent at the art of conversation, you need to be genuinely interested in the person with whom you're talking.
- You must use active listening and show a genuine interest in the person you're talking to. People love a good listener, especially when they are talking about themselves.

- You have to be able to ask open questions like *how do you feel about exercise*? Instead of the closed question: *do you exercise*? An open question gives you more information than a closed question. With a closed question, it only gives you a *yes* or *no* answer. It is wise to choose a safe and non-threatening topic; avoid politics and religion.
- Practice your listening skills with your family and friends. Try to listen more rather than talk, then try concisely repeating back what you've heard in the conversation to check whether you got it right. All too often people do not listen properly they are too busy rehearsing what they will say next instead of listening to what is being said. If this is you STOP it! You miss out a lot by doing this. Learn to really listen to others, and when you have something to say it will be worthwhile, instant of pointless constant chatter. Other people will find you very attractive as everyone loves to be listened to.
- Be positive. There's nothing worse than chatting to someone who is full of doom and gloom and you are left depleted of any energy you had! Many avoid these people when they see them coming.
- Use humour. A good story teller is always popular, (like my husband). Jokes always help to break the ice; however, keep them clean and politically correct if you don't know who your listeners are!
- Don't be late! Whether it is at a social gathering or a meeting or any other occasion, get there early, so that you can make the acquaintance of people as they turn up first; it makes it easier to intermingle later. It helps you to feel confident as you would have been one of the first faces they saw when they arrived. They too, would be looking for a friendly face; someone they can strike a conversation with. Be sure to say hello and smile! Smile! Smile! It helps to make you feel relaxed and approachable.
- Arriving late can often make you lose confidence, as it can make you feel awkward like the new girl or boy; by then everyone has met everybody.
- Be open and give good eye contact when you speak or when others are speaking. Be genuine and sincere. Be authentic. It increases your confidence.

Smile easily and often and have a good laugh when appropriate. Others will respond to you in a similar vein. It helps to relax you, and when you are relaxed, you feel more confident. Remember: when you smile you build up good hormones in your body. It all goes a long way towards feeling good and building your confidence.

Body Language

85% of communication is non verbal, communicated in gestures, facial expression and tone of voice. Non-verbal signals may contradict a verbal message or alter its meaning. It is important to be congruent to be credible. This means that our body language needs to match what we are saying.

Another study carried in varied occupational backgrounds showed that 70% of their waking moments were spent in communication. Writing took 9%, reading 16%, talking accounted for 30% and listening 45%.

The average person does not communicate well. To be confident in your communication, good eye contact is essential. This is as important when you are talking as when you are listening.

John Kennedy and later on, Bill Clinton had a special eye contact technique. They developed a way of being able to look at an individual and flick their eyes from one eye of the person they were talking to, to his or her other eye in succession. When they did this, they created the impression that they really cared about what made their subject tick, and that they really cared about them. They both did this in a television broadcast which then, convinced the whole American nation that their President really cared about them. And guess what? They both got elected Presidents! President Reagan was also known to be another great communicator who managed to communicate well with his public by making use of his body language when using powerful and forceful words in his speeches, and in so doing managed to convince the American people to elect him too.

You may never be like John Kennedy, Bill Clinton or Ronald Reagan; but you are now more aware about the importance of being able to communicate effectively. The use of listening skills, the power of words, the facial expressions as well as the tonality of our voice including our hand gestures all form part of our communication tools that, if handled well can lead to greater confidence and successful relationships in our private life as in our working life.

Compliments

Confident people find it easy to compliment others if they have done well. There is nothing nicer than to receive a genuine compliment from someone. Giving and receiving compliments is a wonderful skill that makes us feel good; we enjoy it and it is one of the small pleasures of life. However, when you lack confidence, you may find giving and receiving compliments quite a difficult thing to do. Some people become extremely embarrassed, and mumble or even refute a compliment or throw it back at the person—which incidentally is very rude.

For example: *What! This old thing? I found it in the back of the wardrobe! I've had it for years!*

Okay, so now you've told the kind person who offered you a lovely compliment on your dress that they love outdated old rubbish that has been stuck in the back of the wardrobe for years! Not only do they have bad taste to like that, but are also way out of date!

The assertive and confident person has learned the art of giving and receiving compliments gracefully and the unassertive one remains mystified and can't work out how to do it. To give a genuine compliment can be inspiring and can become contagious. Like everything in life you get back what you put in. The more you do it, the more you get back and the more polished you become. Practice does make perfect. As a result you benefit from a raised self-esteem.

When you choose to give genuine compliments to others, it takes away any spirit of criticism that you may have had.

Giving Compliments:

- When you give a compliment, be sincere; relax; make sure that the time and the place are appropriate.
- Keep good eye contact.

- Be specific about the compliment. Rather than say: You look nice, you could try: *This yellow dress really suits you. It sure complements your blond hair.* If you go over the top, it can embarrass the person; people don't like to be put so high because it puts them under pressure, however a simple genuine compliment is appreciated.
- Never include any put downs for either you or the other person.

For example: *You're such a great cook. I'm useless in the kitchen* or *Well done, you've finished at last. It's about time!* The first shows poor self-esteem and the second demonstrates feelings of resentment or bitterness; it's a back-handed compliment! It would have been better to say nothing!

> *Back-handed compliments are no compliments at all. Best to say nothing!*

Receiving compliments

- When you receive a compliment, it is good to be gracious and smile nicely. Don't spoil it by an embarrassed giggle or by belittling it! Enjoy someone boosting your self-esteem for you. Appreciate the spirit in which it is given.
- Listen without interrupting with some silly explanation, and maintain good eye contact.
- Don't respond by putting yourself down. For example: *Oh, no! I didn't really do well; that's just a fluke!* It's quite rude to dismiss a compliment and you embarrass the other person. It's like telling the person that you are so stupid as to think that you could have done well!
- Do not do any tit for tat or smother the compliment either! *Oh, but you look lovely too and much better than me!*
- You can clarify what the person has said by asking questions, and then you can smile and assertively appreciate the compliment by saying *thank you* or you could add: *It's very kind of you to say so,* or *I really appreciate that, thank you.*
- Of course saying the appropriate affirmations to gain confidence is always helpful. If you are not naturally a gorgeous, confident or assertive person, you must work at it to gain better skills. You must continue to practice these skills, as practice does make perfect, if not immediately, sooner or later if you keep at it.

In fact lack of practice does make you imperfect.

Knowledge is a treasure, but practice is key to it.

—*Thomas Fuller*

Now, that you have learnt many secrets about how to be gorgeous and confident, let's look at the secrets of **Faith versus Fear.**

Another sunrise, another new beginning.

—*Jonathan Lockwood Huie*

Notes: What have you learnt?

CHAPTER FOURTEEN

One Last Secret: Faith Versus fear Take a Leap of Faith

Lord grant that I might not so much seek to be loved as to love.

—St Francis of Assissi

Many people who do not put their faith in anything are convinced that relying on faith is stupid or a waste of time. Yet, it is coincidental that these same people who think that it's stupid to have blind faith are often the very ones struggling. Those who put their trust in their faith, tend to fare much better altogether, whilst the doubting Thomases constantly prepare themselves for the worst case scenario *just in case.* Those who put their trust in their faith on the other hand, pray for good outcomes and expect them; consequently have a better experience of life.

Expecting the worst case scenario or preparing yourself for a bad outcome just in case, puts you in a fearful and debilitating state which leaves you wide open to a lot of negativity to enter your world.

> **You bring about what you fear.**

To have faith you have to be able to trust. Frequently this feeling of lack of faith springs from thoughts of fear and the inability to trust. Fearful thoughts and lack of trust breed scepticism.

Thoughts are things; things that can materialize themselves into our world. We can bring into our physical life the very things that we fear, simply, because we get more of what we focus on.

What we focus on affect our emotions and our actions. When we fear something, our focus ends up stuck on it. We can't relax as it constantly gnaws at us.

What we focus on grows and gathers momentum.

So thinking the worst brings on the worst. That same negative continual loop of negative thoughts that you are constantly playing in your head is what you are unconsciously focusing on. Those same negative thoughts are all fear-based.

As a rule our subconscious finds a way of getting us what it thinks we want. As I have previously said, the difficulty is that it doesn't understand the negatives; so *I don't want to do badly in my test*, becomes *I want to do badly in my test*; and sure enough you will! Whereas the one who does not suffer from negative thoughts, will focus on *I want to succeed in my test*; and sure enough he will too.

Remember, that with every thought that enters your mind, you have the corresponding physiological feelings in your body; these affect your emotions and your moods. So thoughts of fear will bring down your mood, and can bring on feelings of panic making you feel physically sick, if you keep rehearsing disastrous outcomes every time you come across a problem. That's the stuff that panic attacks are made of.

Fear Is The Opposite Of Faith.

The other side of this coin is that if you trust and demonstrate your feelings of faith, the result is that you feel more positive; your physiological reactions too are positive; your emotions are affected in a similar vein and your mood is lifted. This gives you peace of mind and you bring on into your physical world more positive outcomes, which ultimately shapes your character and your future.

> ### Your Subconscious Is Always Faithful To You.
When you think: *I don't want to lose my job,* your subconscious hears: *I want to lose my job;* and it becomes *un fait accompli* (a done job!). After which you say: *See, I was right, I lost my job.* Of course you are right! Your subconscious was trying to get you what it thought you wanted! The only problem it read your thoughts and the words *don't* just never registered. If you believe that you did have faith and asked not to lose your job, that's where you went wrong. Your subconscious did not understand that. You need to put your requests in the positive, like *I choose to keep my job.*

> *Having faith means really but really trusting in the invisible before it becomes visible.*
> *No question of letting the devil doubt in!*

All the time you entertain *any* doubt, you are not showing faith. If you don't have faith, you have fear. You know that you are not demonstrating faith by the way that you are feeling. If you have butterflies in your tummy and feel shaky because you're scared, or have this feeling of impending doom, you are not trusting in your faith.

You don't get what you want when you doubt. You don't show faith when you doubt.

And, yes, I know, it is hard! That's when you need to trust more in a Higher power, and believe that things happen for your greater good.

On the other hand, sometimes we can demonstrate faith and not get what we want. On these occasions, when we do not get what we want it may be because we can't see the bigger picture. What we want may not be the best for us. We may not get something that we think we want because there may be something much better waiting for us further down the line only we can't see it yet. Or else, it may be that life has a lesson to teach us, that we need to learn for us to grow and develop. It may well be that what we want isn't actually good for us and would end up causing us more trouble in the long run.

So when you don't get something that you want, there may be very good reasons for it. This may help how you react to not getting what you desire.

Adopt the belief that things always happen for a good reason, and you may not know what that reason is for a very long time; if ever, sometimes.

Have you ever said to yourself: *"If "…." hadn't happened, "…." wouldn't have happened, and I wouldn't be where I am to-day"*? Sometimes we have to go through bad times to get to the other side where we are meant to be; only problem, it is hard to see it at the time.

So, if you don't get what you want, don't despair as the best may yet be on its way to you.

For example: It is hard to go through a divorce when a marriage is at an end, even if it is something that you both want. It still is a bereavement; the death of your relationship. But maybe years down the line you meet the perfect partner for you, marry and live happily ever after! When you were going through the hard times of the divorce, it would have been impossible for you to see that it was essential to go through the bad times because in the *bigger picture* happiness was waiting for you; but it couldn't happen until you had gone through the bad times and came out the other end.

Those who have faith in a Higher Power tend to manage much better in life and often enjoy more success in all areas of life. Faith gives you confidence and peace of mind. One thing is certain that people who can trust feel much happier, calmer, more relaxed and have more enjoyment in life. They reap all the benefits of their positive thinking and their trust.

There is nothing like mistrust to make you anxious, resentful or unhappy.

Faith, according to the Collins Dictionary means assurance, confidence, conviction, credence, credit, dependence, reliance, trust; and there are other explanations as well. Somehow people tend to think that faith is something that you either *have* or *don't have* or something that you are born with or something that comes in families. Or that you can *catch it* like the flu! Some think that it is something to avoid, as if you have a faith, your life may have to change in a way that may cramp your lifestyle. It is far cosier to have a lay in on Sunday morning than to have to get up early to go to church.

No! It isn't a virus; many of you however, do have faith without knowing that you do. You have faith that you know how to brush your teeth or know your way to work. You maybe also do *have faith* that somehow *bad things always happen to you* or you may have faith that *things always turn out well for you.*

What can happen sometimes is that we put our faith in the wrong things or the wrong belief; in that situation it doesn't empower you or enhance your life; in fact it can lead you to a life of misery. When you put your faith in negative things, it doesn't help if you want good things to happen to you; they won't.

When you say: *Just my luck, things always go wrong for me*! you are showing faith in your negativity. This is just the type of thing when you need the angel doubt to creep in!

What about all the times when things did go right for you?

Yes, it does matter which household you are born in. If you are brought up in a household where both your parents demonstrate that they do have faith and trust God and the world, the same as with your belief and value system, it is bound to rub off on you too; your outlook in life is more positive and does give you an advantage. They pass on their value and belief systems onto you as well as their faith. Now, you can choose to rebel against them or keep your faith, values and beliefs. Whatever you choose will be the results you will get in your life.

> **Faith is an act of will.**

It is a *decision* that you make at some point in your life. You choose what to believe and what to put your trust in.

If you are a Christian, you choose to make the decision to accept Christian values and to believe in Christianity. Equally if you are a Muslim or a Jew you also make a choice in what you choose to believe in and put your faith in. If you are an atheist, that is also a choice and a decision; you make a choice and decision to believe *in not believing*.

People who have no spiritual beliefs find life harder when things go wrong; they have no Higher Power to turn to.

> **After all, it is well known, that we are Mind-Body and Spirit. We feed our Mind and Body appropriately; it is equally as important to feed our Spirit well too.**

If you believe that you are on this planet for a little while, go through your trials and tribulations and then one day you die, like everyone one else; you get burnt or else buried and that is it! End of story! It is very difficult to live with purpose and feel that there is hope, or may be to develop a moral compass.

When things go wrong, anxiety is heightened as there is no trust or faith to comfort you and no one to turn to. You can hope for the best if you are a very positive person but, all things being equal! You are more likely to think of the worst case scenario, which incidentally does nothing to bring you hope or happiness.

People of faith, whatever their faith, can, however to turn to God and ask for help, which can offer them comfort, hope and peace of mind. They believe and trust that their prayers will be answered. This gives them an anticipation that things will work out and a reassurance that they are loved. Through faith, they find support. Their mindset is more positive and they expect positive results.

> **Research does back the belief that prayers do work. In a recent research of 269 doctors, 99% of doctors believed that prayers heal and that miracles do happen.**

When you *take a leap of faith*, you, at that moment make a decision to believe and to trust. You may make a decision in what to put your faith in, or you may choose not to put your faith in anything; it's up to you.

When you're making a choice not to choose faith, by default you make a choice to choose fear instead.

You either have faith that things will work out for you, or you are fearful that thing won't work out for you. Faith is what grounds you and helps you to believe in the positive and gives you hope. One of our life's secrets is that we get more of what we focus on. We manifest into our physical world what we focus on.

> *Our prayers are more likely to be answered when we demonstrate our faith.*

Fear is what unsettles you and scares you in believing in disastrous outcomes and lose hope. When you do not have faith, you focus on the negative that you fear, therefore helping the negative outcome to enter your world too, as that's where your focus is.

All of it is a matter for you to choose and decide on. It is that simple!

When you do something very well, you absolutely know that you can do it efficiently. You have developed a conviction about it. It means that you have faith that you can do it well. It is the same with having faith, when you have faith; you have a complete conviction about something. Sometimes you do have faith but it may not be exactly in the area you would like to. It is now a matter of what you put your belief in.

For example when you choose to be a Christian, you are choosing to put your faith in God and in Jesus. When you choose to be an Atheist, you are choosing not to believe in God.

What you choose to put your faith in or not can have repercussions on the quality of your life.

Take a look at the average person who has faith in their life and at one who has no faith! What's the difference? Is the person who has faith a lot calmer, more relaxed and coping with life a lot better? What does the other person who doesn't put their faith in anything look like? Does that person suffer more from worry or anxiety? Is he or she insecure? Constantly worrying about a lot of things? Maybe complaining and fearful that bad things follow them or that they are unlucky in life? They find decisions hard to make? Even depressed?

The one who chooses faith often can relax more as they believe that they can turn to a Higher Power for all their needs including for love and help in anything.

The belief and reassurance that you are loved and that your needs are being taken care of and provided for is enough to remove a huge stress from them, unlike those who choose fear. That doesn't mean to say that those who choose faith have no anxiety, stress, worry or depression or do not suffer from mental illness. This is a generalised broad view. Having a belief in God doesn't exclude you from life's issues but it helps.

Even when the people who have faith don't get what they want, they believe that there is a good reason for it, and their hope remains alive. Acceptance becomes easier.

Those who choose faith worry less because they believe that things happen for their higher good. They do not need to see something to believe that it is possible.

> *When you choose fear, peace of mind, hope and faith are far away.*

You focus on what can go wrong, and often it does; not because bad things follow you, but because your thoughts are things that can make things happen, and because you get more of what you focus on.

Fear is pervasive and unfortunately, it is like an infectious disease; it spreads! It can, not only contaminate us but also those who are in close proximity too.

Imagine if fear was as visible and looked like the measles! if fear looked like measles, what would you look like? Would you be covered in an itchy red rash depending on its severity? Well, fear does the same thing to you emotionally; only there are no obvious spots or rash to see, however, its invisible spots make you unwell, stressed, panicky and unhappy; the severity of those will depend on the extent of your fear. The result is the same; you don't feel well and you don't feel happy and you feel scared. In fact you feel down outright miserable, just like with the measles; the Latin word for measles being 'misery'.

Fear is one of the most incapacitating and debilitating emotions anyone can be afflicted with.

Fear can keep you frozen, stuck and unable to move on with your life; and sadly, most of the time it is self-generated.

Can you believe that when you are feeling doubtful, scared, having feelings of impending doom, sick feelings in your stomach, worrying over a dreadful outcome, that you are doing all of it to yourself? These are the symptoms of your fear.

If you have faith, you can actually give your troubles away to a Higher Power, and take a break by feeling peaceful, knowing that you are being watched over, provided for, cared for and loved and that everything will work out for the best. Even if there is nothing you can do, there is always acceptance.

The absence of faith increases suspicion, doubt, fear, anxiety and insecurity.

When you choose anxiety and insecurity over faith, you are making, albeit an unconscious choice not to put faith in your life.

> *Insecurity heightens stress, anxiety and fear.*

When you fear something, you become insecure; you search for evidence to support what you're scared of. You find ways of justifying your fears. You concentrate on the negatives that support your theory, and ignore all the positives that don't. When you can't find the evidence you need, you hallucinate and make them up. You can talk anything up or you can talk anything down.

This, very often results in believing false evidence, but which to you appears real.

However, it is most often a pure invention of the mind. Your imagination takes over and goes wild.

Remember: The mind cannot distinguish between something that is real and something that has been vividly imagined. As far as your mind is concerned, what you vividly imagine is your reality.

Note: Not reality itself, but <u>your</u> reality.

Function of Fear

Fear, per se, is not altogether a bad thing. There is healthy fear and toxic fear. It is rather the question whether you choose fear over faith and whether your fears are actually serving you or not.

Healthy fear does exist for a purpose; it is there to protect us.

For instance, I often go walking near the nature reserve close to where I live. If I was to hear a hissing noise in the bush; would I be wise to ignore it and take no notice? It would be pretty foolish, no? The fear I would feel is very useful as it is telling me to be careful and be prepared to take action as there may be a snake or some imminent danger lurking around, which could do me harm. And guaranteed! You would not see me for dust! I know all about my fight or flight response! Fear in this case is healthy and serves a good purpose in that it helps me to get ready for action to get me out of a potentially dangerous situation.

Still, sometimes your senses can be on edge and respond inappropriately to some internal stimuli. When you are gripped by irrational fear, you can ask yourself: *what's the worst that can happen? Will anyone die? Or that you may be made a fool of? That you'll be rejected? Or found out to be inadequate? Or you may be in physical or moral danger?* Whatever it is, you can get prepared.

> *All too often the fear you feel is unfounded. It is the result of wild imagination and of unhealthy or toxic thoughts.*

Whatever it is that's keeping you stuck in fear, the first step is to own it, be honest with yourself and acknowledge it to yourself.

Unless you own your feelings and accept things as they are, you will never be able to change them. Be brave, you have nothing to lose! Look at it squarely in the face. Remember how dangerous it can be to live in denial?

Unless you own your fears, they have a shocking habit of mastering you instead. Fear can overwhelm you and engulf your life into inaction.

Your fears become in charge of you, and you dance according to whatever tune your fears dictate. You do not want fear to be boss in your life and allow it to direct your life. You need to be at helm in your life. So be brave!

> *The very act of owning and acknowledging your fears is an act of courage. Recognize what price you are paying for letting your fears run your life—or rather ruin your life.*

What Is The Price Of Fear?

Even if there is no guarantee of success, step outside your comfort zone; you will be proud that you dared to try; you will no longer be a prisoner of your fear and living a life dominated by fear. You will feel liberated.

> *Continuous fear tends to lead to a panic state; and when we panic, our imagination goes crazy.*

It gets our brain thinking all sorts of appalling scenarios, which we play and replay in our minds; this has the disastrous effect of escalating our fears. It is precisely that kind of thinking that exacerbates worry, anxiety, panic attacks and depression and results in an inferior unhappy life.

Continuous negative thinking very quickly becomes habit forming.

This habit of listening to long term wild imagination can lead us to becoming irrational, anxious and neurotic.

Your nervous system is on constant high alert and your nerves are continuously on edge, making you act irrationally. Others around you are baffled by your actions and reactions.

When you are in a neurotic state, it regularly leads you to overreact to even the smallest everyday problems and helps you create mountains out of mole hills. Drama becomes your best friend. Family and friends find this exhausting and very tiresome. *Not again!* they say, as they see you coming.

As we have seen previously, the brain can generalize, distort or delete information if it suits. Neurosis and crazy wild imagination distort your ability to think clearly and affect your quality of life. They cause poor life experiences and result in a lot of distress, worry and unhappiness, not only for you but also for those close to you. The only hitch is that you probably do not have enough insight to realize what's going on.

The problem is that this can have a snowballing effect as the danger is that neurosis is only a stone throw away from psychosis. Another way of describing psychosis is insanity. Madness! Lunacy! When you are psychotic, you are no longer in touch with reality and can no longer function as a rational, able human being.

Prolonged constant untreated irrational fear can lead to a psychotic episode.

This is a possibility if you choose fear. Instead take a leap of faith.

Choose faith.

Choose faith and reject fear. Faith lifts your spirits and soothes your soul. A soothed soul enjoys peace of mind and confidence.

Your outlook on life becomes much brighter, more hopeful and positive. It gives you hope to have faith in knowing that everything will work out for the best and hope that your needs will be provided for. Even if it isn't what you wanted, you will have faith that there is a very good reason for it, even if you don't know what it is yet. More than that you will feel loved and supported. You will no longer carry your burdens on your own. You may find a heavy load has been removed from your shoulders. You can share your problems with your Creator. As the saying goes: *A problem shared is a problem halved.* The result is that you feel very much better.

If, for instance, you choose to believe that all's going to work out, and that you will always be provided for, it will immediately go a long way towards your battle on fear. You can make a choice for this to become your new belief.

You always get more of what you focus on. It is up to you what you choose to put your faith in. It is up to you to do your own soul-searching and find God.

Those who enjoy the benefit of faith have a very different outlook on life. When you have someone to turn to, it gives you peace of mind and confidence.

> *Peace of mind and confidence leads to feelings of security. When you feel secure, fear disappears and you are more relaxed.*

All of a sudden, your meaning of life changes to one that you can enjoy. Feeling secure allows you to breathe normally and unwind. Security promotes relaxation.

Relaxation gives you, what we all look for, a sense of balance to life.

When you go through life feeling secure, and relaxed, it raises your confidence, your self-esteem and your chances of success; your experience of life is altogether enhanced as you achieve a sense of balance. Others also reinforce these feelings in you by the positive feedback that you get.

When you have balance in your life you have inner peace. When you have peace of mind you can think clearly. With clarity of mind comes a sound mind.

When we have a sound mind, we are sane. We have good mental health. This all stems from making the decision to choose faith and to reject fear.

To choose faith is to exercise your free will.

It is up to you what and who you choose to believe in; it isn't something you either have or don't have or can or can't do or something you *catch*. It is a decision for you to make or not make; to believe or not to believe. It's your choice!

You are born with a free will. Exercise this free will to enhance your life, not to bring it down.

> *Choose faith; reject fear, as faith is far mightier than fear.*

Fear

Fear is the mother of all disasters. It creates catastrophic thinking, depression, anxiety attacks and leads you to make wrong decisions.

> *Fear stops you from finding resourceful solutions to your problems.*

Fear keeps you locked away in a self-made prison. Your, out of control fearful thoughts built this prison brick by brick, until you become a powerless hostage within its grip.

Fear produces confusion, frustration, inner conflict, tension and stops you from doing what you need to do or what you want to do. It immobilizes you.

Fear produces apathy, demotivates you and reduces the quality of your life. It negatively impacts all your relationships. Fear makes you worry about all sorts of things that might (never) happen! As human beings our behaviours are influenced by the thoughts we create and by our belief and value systems. It is vitally important to have the right beliefs for you, and cultivate quality thoughts and avoid fear.

When we have faith we are helped by our belief and when we have fear we are hindered by its effects.

Active fear is produced by false and limiting beliefs. Active faith is produced by correct beliefs.

To recap:

- We get more of what we focus on.
- What we focus on, we create in our life.
- By our fearful thoughts we generate into our physical world all that we actively fear.
- By having faith we bring into being what we want in our life.
- What we continually actively fear ultimately manifests itself into our life.

So, it is essential to cultivate the right thoughts and starve yourself of negative thoughts. Don't say that you can't do it. Everyone can! You have the power to be in control of your thoughts.

Choose to entertain your positive thoughts and deliberately block out the negative ones; either by using your affirmations or by just accepting that's what your mind is telling you, but now you are thinking . . . . then add a positive statement or think of a positive event. This positive statement or event becomes linked to your negative thought; and every time that negative thought comes back to your mind the positive thought and event is tagged to it at the end. You are then able to end on a positive.

If you find that you are your own worst enemy, get professional help.

Faith

Faith is the mother of inner peace and harmony. It is up to you to do your own soul-searching to discover what you want to put your faith in and what the right beliefs are for you. When you have active faith, it leads you to believing the right way, which in turn helps you to be close to your Creator. Active faith positively impacts your life.

> *The right beliefs bring hope, relaxation, balance, security, confidence and harmony, peace of mind, sanity and happiness.*

You generate into your physical world, all that you have actively focused on and hoped for. Therefore it is essential to choose to cultivate the right thinking and beliefs.

As we discussed previously: When you plant flowers, you expect to get—Flowers. When you plant weeds, you expect to get—Weeds. When you plant nothing you also get—Weeds!

So, plant the good seeds of faith in the garden of your mind with your positive thoughts and pull out any negative weeds that threaten to destroy your garden. Don't be despondent if you do not see immediate results. Sometimes, it takes a while for the seeds to come to the surface, but it doesn't mean that nothing is happening underneath. We can't see what work is actually going on under the surface.

Good things happen to those who have the patience to wait.

If your mind is idle because you have not sown any seeds, weeds will grow by default. It is essential to cultivate the right kind of thoughts in the garden of your mind, so that you do not become overwhelmed by the weeds (fearful thoughts).

Every thought represents a seed that you have to reap later on. Let it be a good harvest, not one that brings you grief.

What do you have to gain if you believe the right way?

Faith yields an array of positive by-products. It results in gratitude and blessings. It leaves no room for negativity to flourish. Good things happen because you are only open to good things. You manifest into your physical life the products of your right thinking and you get what you do want. All manner of opportunities open themselves to you as your focus is positive and of course Providence moves to help you too.

What do you have to lose if your beliefs spread pernicious fear in your life?

As much as we reap positive by-products from faith, fear is also prolific in its own harmful by-products. As a result fear can bring misery, anxiety, panic attacks, insecurity, depression and possibly neurosis, and at worst psychosis.

Even if you do not suffer from the full by-products of fear, it can leave you feeling very low, with constant anxiety or worry and keep you in a lower level life. We can manifest in our physical life the products of our wrong thinking and end up getting what we fear. No opportunities present themselves to us as they are blocked by our distorted thinking.

What happens if you plant nothing in the garden of your mind and believe any old way or whatever happens to be the trend at the time?

You get the same as you would if your thinking was wrong, just like not planting anything in your garden; *weeds* still come through. As you are not actively cultivating the right thoughts of faith, negative fearful thoughts infiltrate your brain by default.

When you turn the spotlight on your fears, and concentrate on what isn't working for you, you strengthen the fear. You give it power. It is like switching on the *fear switch*. Fear gathers momentum and becomes more powerful.

When fear is powerful, it shuts down any opportunity for finding resourceful solutions for any problems, which leads to distress, disappointment and misery.

Fear claims your attention on all the bad stuff in your life; you can't even begin to imagine that anything good can happen. It has you locked into negativity and you can only perceive obstacles as opportunities escape you.

What do you have to gain when you think this way?

Nothing! Or worse still: disease! If you expect bad, what do you think you'll get? Of course, you'll get bad! Your subconscious never fails to disappoint. It faithfully works hard to give you what it thinks you want.

Fear holds people down and prevents them from reaching for the stars. If you can overcome your fears, you can reach your full potential and reclaim your own power.

When you focus on fear you feed it and give it oxygen; thereby giving away all your power.

Often you are not consciously aware that by going with the flow and not stopping long enough to correct your thinking, that you are cultivating that spirit of fear; you are giving away your power to your fear and blocking all your resourcefulness. Any opportunities that could have come your way are lost forever.

Don't kid yourself! Fear only thrives on the thoughts that you choose to allow in your mind. You need to make a conscious effort to be deliberately attentive to what thoughts you choose to tolerate in your mind. If they don't serve you well, get rid of them!

Whatever you concentrate all your focus on, gathers momentum. Choose to concentrate your focus on faith instead of fear. Reclaim your power, now.

You need to get real and look inside and ask yourself, if your fears are real or imagined or false evidence which to you appear real; whether they are based on facts or based on irrational thoughts? If so, where is the evidence?

Are your fears real, based on true facts?

Do you have a genuine reason to be fearful?

Or has your imagination become overactive?

Is your fear based on focusing on things you are scared of experiencing?

Very often the things you are scared of are only figments of your imagination. The reality is never half as bad! Having faith, helps you to focus on things that you do want to experience in your life, not on what you fear.

Sometimes we do complicate our lives by looking at things in a difficult and complex way, instead of looking at a simple solution.

> *Fear defeats more people than any other one thing in the world.*
>
> —*Ralph Waldo Emerson*

The secret is to look at things simply. Do not make things more complicated than what they actually are, by choosing to believe the wrong way. Keep it simple! It's always a good principle!

Make a conscious choice, take a leap of faith, to swing your thinking in the direction you want to go, and you will get there. You will bring into your world the positive things that you are focusing on. Let this be just the thing you needed to put you back on the right track.

So, as you wake up and want a joyful productive day, start the day by believing the right way. Plant the right seeds in the garden of your mind before you leap out of bed and the rest will follow. We always reap what we sow; what we send out comes back to us (multiplied) like a boomerang. This is a recognized universal law. No one escapes. It affects us all the same.

Some people think that they don't *have* faith because they weren't *born* with it. This is nonsense. You don't have to be 'born' with it or come from a family who enjoyed faith.

You can be who you want to be, when you decide to, no matter what others are doing around you, whether your family had any beliefs or not. You are your own person, with your unique gifts and talents, with your own free will and spirit.

In fact you can decide to be anything you choose to be! If your family enjoyed having faith, then that's great; if not why can't you be your own person and decide for yourself? You can choose who or what to put your faith in.

Don't worry about what other people would say, especially if you were previously very critical of others who were not scared of showing their faith before. Anyone has the right to change their mind according to their own growth and development.

This is your life! You are the only one who get to choose how you live it! Others don't get to choose! It is not about others and what they think. It is about you doing what's right for you.

Everyone has faith in something. We believe that the sun rises in the East and sets in the West. In fact we believe that this happens everywhere. We believe that if we eat right, exercise right, sleep right, have adequate rest, don't abuse drugs or alcohol, and don't smoke that we will be healthy and fit. We have faith in Education; in Medicine, in the Laws of science; we have faith that if we press a switch that the light will come on. What's even greater is that we don't even have to understand the laws of electricity to know that if we flick that switch we will no longer be in darkness! We don't need to understand the laws of the universe to know that the sun will rise to-morrow; however, we do have faith that it will.

We don't need to know the intricate details of the *how* or *why*, the sun rises in the East and sets in the West or how electricity works; we just believe it! Therefore we have faith in it! So why do we need to know the intricate details of faith? With faith, we do not need to know some intricate details of how and why; we just have to believe what makes more sense to us, just like the sun and like the light switch. We just *know* it. That is what faith is! We can just choose to decide to believe or make a leap of faith to. This is a matter of choice for you to decide.

> *Choose the life you desire with faith or choose the life you're afraid of with fear.*

Even when you do not have the results that you truly wish for in your life, it is vital that you keep faith that things will turn around for you and that you will get what you desire when the time is right for you. The only difference is when you have faith, the process is smoother, calmer, you feel more relaxed and supported. Your faith supports the belief that things will work out for you.

If you look at the results you have and decide that you are *realistic* and that nothing will ever change for you, believe me, things will never change for you. Having faith means believing and not giving up that things will get better, may be not in your time frame, but in God's time frame. So be patient!

Choose your thoughts wisely and encourage the ones you want and banish the ones you don't want. It will make all the difference to your experience of life.

No one else creates your experience of life but you. Faith removes limitations and creates miracles. With faith you can reach for the sky. Faith causes healing to happen and can and has moved mountains.

Miracles do happen, but not without faith! Research has repeatedly shown that prayers do work and healing does take place. How many times have some extraordinary things happened and someone has exclaimed: *That's a miracle! We never expected that in a million years!* And everyone agreed however everyone took it for granted and never gave it another thought after a little while. They think that what's happened is out of the ordinary but assumed that is just a miracle, as a catch-phrase without much thought going into it. Yet small miracles do happen all the time; we just don't spend the time to stop, to appreciate and to give thanks for them.

It is up to you to believe the right way or to believe the wrong way. Your choice! No one can make it for you. Life is for living and enjoying, and not to be feared or endured.

> *Your life is the sum total of all your choices.*
>
> —*Albert Camus*

Faith is stronger than fear. Faith leads you where you want to go; fear hinders you and stops you getting where you want to go.

Faith caused a young inexperienced black senator in his first term of office, from a Muslim background to believe that he could win the American public and become the most powerful man on earth, because he *believed that yes, he could!* He lived by faith and not by what he feared. President Obama finished what Martin Luther King began with his famous speech: "*I have a dream . . . .*" No black man had ever been the President of the United States of America before, but Barack Obama really believed he could be the first black President. He didn't let fear stop him from trying; instead he had faith that he would succeed. He had to fully believe it before it materialized itself in his external world. His faith was rewarded not only once, but twice!

> *Fear is the cheapest room in the house. I would like to see you living in better conditions.*
>
> —*Hafiz*

Your subconscious mind does not remain inactive. If you fail to plant the right seeds of faith in your mind, it will feed upon fearful thoughts which will invade it by default, as a result of your neglect; and that can be anything that may appear positive however, can be anything but!

It is your responsibility to make sure that the right positive thoughts constitute the dominating influence in your mind. If you make a habit of this, the Law of Habit will help you to stop the negative thoughts from entering your subconscious mind. As it takes seven consecutive days to form a habit, start the habit of thinking right and believing right consistently and after seven days, it will start to come naturally.

> **What you think about, you create in your life. So start creating now! The right stuff!**

As Dr Joseph Murphy states, there are two types of people: *Those who are magnetized, are full of confidence and faith. They know they are born to succeed. Others are demagnetized. They are full of fears and doubts. Their fear to go forward makes them simply stay where they are.* These people are caught in their own web and unable to move on with their life.

The thing is, you too, can be one of those magnetized people; there is nothing that says that just because you feel you have been unsuccessful, full of fears and trepidation that you need to stay there. You can change. Take a leap of faith and see what you can create.

You can choose your attitude. You too can choose what you build in your life.

Magnetized people are full of enthusiasm and attract others to them. Their energy and *joie de vivre* is contagious. Demagnetized people are energy-drainers. People avoid them if they can help it.

Aim to be one of the magnetized people; and avoid the demagnetized people as much as you can. Choose who you allow to influence you.

But most of all choose to think right and believe right.

> **Choose Faith And Reject Fear.**

Choose Faith; never mind what you said about it before and never mind what your beliefs were before. That was before, now is what you are concerned with. Live in the here and now. The past is over. The future is bursting to offer you bigger and better things.

Don't worry about what others will think and say: It's your life, not theirs! They are not asked to vote here! You are the only privileged one who can do this!

A Life Lived in Fear, is a Life Half-Lived

—*anonymous*

Go on now, take a leap of faith and live life to the full.
God bless and may you live the best life you can in faith.

Worry looks around
Sorry looks back
Faith looks up.

(Picked up from the net)

May your life be blessed and always look up!

Notes: What have you learnt?

A Reminder of All Life's Secrets and More . . . .

When life gives you lemons, make lemonade.
—Anonymous

To finish our journey together, I would like to remind you that life is like a tapestry; the front of the tapestry may look magnificent, but the inside can look rather confusing and difficult to understand. Sometimes it can even be a mess. In the same way to the outside world, our life can look glossy, wonderful and enviable, but on the inside it can be a very different story.

Even though it can look messy on the wrong side at times, there are plenty you can do to make things better and you have the power to do that, if you have the key to the secrets of life. You just need to be willing and make a decision and a commitment to do so.

I do hope that the secrets of how life works revealed in this book will help the tapestry of your life to look magnificent inside and out, so that you can live your life with no regrets and that you can reach for the stars, and enjoy the journey.

Here are some of the secrets that are worth remembering to help you along the bumpy road of life. Please bear with me if I repeat myself, as I am a firm believer that repetition is the mother of all skills. That's how we learn, by hearing or seeing things again and again.

I chose to give you reminders at the end of the book as they will be easily available should you be looking for them; and if they are the last things you read, it is hoped that they will stay in your memory and come to your help when you need them.

Points to Remember

Chapter One: <u>Some secrets revealed to help you change your life</u>.
Life's Too Short

The first secret to learn is to learn to respect time and respect life. Use both well. Life is too short to waste it and not live it well. Before you know where you are it can be all over.

Plan and create your life.

Never stop learning as you go through life.

The pain and pleasure principle

All of us are slaves to the Pain and Pleasure philosophy. We either do things because we get pleasure from them or we avoid doing them to keep away from the pain that could follow. We are programmed to avoid pain and seek pleasure.

This means that we have to do our best to associate as much pleasure as we can with what we want to achieve in life and connect as much pain as possible with the things that sabotage us, or with things that are detrimental to us.

Really bad health problems happen to people who take risks with their lives. You do not know when the bad news can hit you. But whenever it does, I can assure you, you are never ready for it. Don't kid yourself that it happens to other people or older people and not you! That is called denial!

We are here on this planet to learn from life and to grow and to develop.

People who love to learn have more fun and lead a more satisfying life. They are more successful than those who choose not to learn. This learning doesn't even need to be formal. You just need to want to grow and develop. Associate a lot of pleasure with gaining knowledge, as knowledge is power if you use it to take action.

The secret to maintaining any changes we make is to keep reinforcing it, starting straight away.

You have to keep practicing your new behaviour to condition yourself to it and to the associated behaviours. Practice does make perfect.

Our perception is our reality, not reality itself.

A change in perception is all that is needed for a story to change its meaning.

To change the meaning of an event or experience we need to give a different significance to that event or experience; in other words we need to change how we perceive this event or experience by changing the meaning we gave it.

There is no such thing as reality, there is only perception.

Each one of us sees the world through our own unique filters.

The way we see the world colours what interpretation we put on an event or an experience.

When we change our perception of something, not only we no longer see it as we used to, but we also change how we feel.

Nothing has any meaning until "we" decide what meaning we want to give it.

To change our perception, we need to change what meaning we give to things.

The meaning we choose to give to anything can put us in a resourceful or unresourceful state. It is our choice. What meaning we give to things will determine whether we are happy or not.

Most people do not deliberately try to hurt us, most of the time they are just trying to meet their own needs. We sometimes just get caught up in their way and become a casualty. Often, the intention isn't to hurt us but to do what's best for them, although we may actually get hurt through their need of getting what they want.

People do what they can with the resources they have at the time.
   If you understand this life's secret, it becomes easier to forgive others and yourself.

Whether our perception is real or imagined, it is made up of the meaning we choose to give it.
   Whatever you do consistently for seven days, will become a habit after that.

Chapter Two teaches us about the
Well-Known Secrets About The Magic Of Our Brain
   The Human Mind generalizes, deletes and distorts as a learning principle.
   Bear this in mind when you find that you or others exaggerate, delete or distort the truth.
   Having a little understanding of how our brain functions helps us to understand how we can change our emotional state and control our thoughts.
   Our brain responds to our environment and to novel experiences by growing new brain cells.
   Our personality is lodged in the frontal region of our brain. This area can become affected by trauma, drugs and disease.
   The conscious mind helps us on a daily basis to make decisions.
   It creates the meaning we give to things and the awareness of our world.
   The subconscious mind deals mainly with repetitions and learnt behaviours.
   It is always working for you; it never sleeps and listens to what you say to yourself to get you what it thinks you want; it is the "spy within"!
   The subconscious uses the association of our habits to help us do things quickly. It is our shortcut.
   The mind cannot distinguish between something that is real and something that has been vividly imagined.

Whatever you rehash over and over again in your mind is conditioning you.
   Whatever you focus on, will be what you are programming your mind with.
   The way we feel affects what we do.
   Our emotions and our behaviour are closely interlinked. One affects the other.
   Whatever you sow in the garden of your mind, you will reap in your body and in your environment and it will create the results you experience in your life.
   You always reap what you sow.
   Every seed you sow, you will harvest later on.
   You get back in life what you put in.
   If you put in a lot, you get a lot back. Equally, if you make little effort, you get very little back. It depends on you only.

You get more of what you focus on. Whatever you focus on grows. Whatever you focus on takes on more importance.

Focus on positive, you will get positive, focus on negative, you will have more of that too.

An understandable excuse is no justification for continuing to indulge in negative or toxic thinking. This is the stuff of self-pity that keeps you stuck and reacting as a victim.

You have been through bad times before, and you got over it.

This time too, won't last forever and better times are ahead.

Trying to find a positive in any situation helps you to feel empowered and gets you out of the troubled spot you find yourself in.

In all things we do have a choice on how we behave or how we react. All of our choices have consequences.

Choose the thoughts you want to concentrate on. Write them down as a reminder.

Whatever problem you have, break the problem down in small pieces and it will be easier to find the solution.

Concentrate on what you do want.

Choose your behaviour; choose your attitude.

You have the power to choose your behaviour; you have the power to choose your attitude; and you can choose how you react to what is happening to you.

Thoughts

Thoughts are not reality and they do not accurately reflect reality either.

We have the power to control our thoughts.

Our thoughts have power over us only if we let them. We can choose what thoughts to entertain in our mind.

The power our thoughts have over us depends on the degree of importance that we choose to give them.

Every thought has a corresponding electrochemical reaction in our body, and consequently a physiological reaction in the body.

The brain produces different types of chemicals depending on what kind of emotions we are experiencing.

There is absolutely no doubt that what we think affects our emotional state.

Think good thoughts and you feel good; think bad thoughts and you feel bad.

It is very important to control our thoughts to be able to lead an emotionally happy and physically balanced and healthy lifestyle.

The more focused and aware of our thinking we are, the stronger the memory we build.

Toxic wastes build up through negative thoughts; they diminish the quality of our stored memories.

This is when we do not remember things accurately and our memories become distorted. When neurons work properly, they build healthy memory instead of toxic distorted memory.

Focusing helps us to live in the here and now and improves our memory.

Concentration gives us focus; focus gives us power and power gives us an edge.

Learn to just *be*—

It helps to repeat *Be present now* to bring us back to what we want to focus on.

Set aside a worry time.

Worry at that time only and refuse to worry at any other time, as you know you can concentrate fully on your worries at your appointed time. If you can make this secret work for you, it will change your life and you won't look back. Many may find this challenging, but if you can do this, brilliant!

Chapter Three: <u>Secrets About Attitude</u>

The world always reacts to us, the way we treat ourselves and others.

Jealous attitude: Jealousy is toxic, whichever way you look at it! There isn't any good side to it.

Jealousy has nothing to do with love.

Jea*lousy* is very *lousy* and extremely selfish!

With jealousy there is always control. The jealous person controls what you do, where you go, even where you work sometimes.

Do not allow anyone to abuse you whatever their excuse.

Do not allow anyone to control you either. We are free spirits, born with our own free will, to make our own decisions and choices.

You can do and achieve anything you want to do if you put your mind to it (within reason! . . . . not if you suddenly decide to become the Queen of England or the Chancellor of the Exchequer, without the right credentials!).

There is always a way. Search and you will find it.

If you need to leave a destructive relationship, leave sooner rather than later.

When there is no trust or respect in a relationship, then there is nothing else.

Jealousy is a deadly disease. It damages your personality and who you are.

We all create our own experience of life good or bad.

By our own attitude, by our own behaviour, our actions and our thoughts, we create the results we have in our life to-day.

It isn't weak to ask for help; it is the smart and sensible thing to do.

In life we get back what we put in. You are getting back now what you put in.

A serious change of attitude can work magic.

Time doesn't change anything; what creates the change is what we do with that time.

Think: five years from now, who and where will you be?

Whenever you focus on the negative, you become a magnet for attracting negative events and experiences in your life.

Successful people never waste their valuable time focusing on negative outcomes.

Learn to be enthusiastic. Cultivate optimism.

Make a commitment and stick to it.

We all do the best we can with the resources we have at the time.

You do have a choice on how you react to any circumstance in life.

Sometimes mistakes are blessings in disguise; they are there to teach us valuable lessons in life, if we are prepared to learn from them.

All the time that you believe that you are a victim of other people's actions, you can never be happy or live a quality life, as you have no control over other people.

Victims repeat the same mistakes over and over again and create conflict around them; however, the sad thing is that they do not work out that they are the common denominator.

The way you react to the world is the way that the world responds to you. You get back what you put in.

If you want to know the answer to your problems, look inside not outside of you. If you look outside you will not find the answers.

Always look inside of you and you will get the answers you need.

It is not *normal* to fall out with lots of people *all the time* and believe that everyone is dreadful except for you.

Face things so that you can do something about it and live a quality life.

You will never be able to change if you do not admit your reality first.

Self-pity is a horrible place to hide in. It ruins not only the person's life, but affects the lives of those around you.

If you do not come clean with yourself, you cannot change anything. You are not serious about changing.

Learn to be self-reliant.

You have all the resources you need inside of you. All you need to do is to reach out to them.

When you behave as a victim, and let others use and abuse you, you give away your power.

Please do not prescribe to martyrdom!

When you behave like a victim, you get treated as one.

But treat yourself with respect and become self-reliant and others will follow your cue.

No one else is responsible for where you are at but you. It is pointless blaming others or your circumstances.

Take action, there is no time like the present.

In relationships as well as in other areas of your life, the attitude with which you approach things is as important as to what you actually do.

Your attitude can escalade something small into something enormous or your attitude can instantly dissolve conflict by the way you handle it.

Develop an attitude of gratitude.

By being grateful you can change a negative attitude into a positive one.

We do not have to win every argument we have.

It is important to know when to stand your ground and when not to.

Compromise, Cooperation and Collaboration are our allies.

Gratitude overcomes every negative feeling if you really mean it.

Gratitude is a natural gift that you can easily give your children. It costs nothing and your children will reap the benefits all their lives. In fact it is your duty to do so!

Your children are little adults in training. It is work in progress.

When you concentrate on good things, other good things start to happen in your life that you never expected.

Avoid the word *should*.

Research has shown that smiling and laughter have great health benefits and can even ease pain.

Chapter Four: <u>Secrets About Emotions</u>

Every emotion is a direct result of the thoughts we entertain.

Emotions give us a message that we need to take some action; every emotion has a direct effect on our body. Every emotion results in an attitude and a behaviour.

Our emotional state is basically the mood that we are experiencing at any given moment. When we repeat the same thoughts and behaviour, we strengthen these corresponding neural pathways, and they become easier to be repeated.

The way we feel affects our actions, therefore what we do, what actions and choices we take. Our emotional state is important not only because of how we feel but also because it affects what we do.

Fear can be our friend as it can be our worst enemy. All negative emotions are created by fear.

Toxic feelings produce toxic emotions which produce toxic attitudes, which in turn produce toxic behaviours and toxic physiological reactions, which is no recipe for a happy and stress-free life.

Emotions are contagious, good or bad. Toxic emotions spread very quickly in abundance. It is our job to keep our emotions in check.

The state that our body is in, affects how we react emotionally and it affects our experience of life.

Our emotional states guide our attitudes, decisions and behaviours. How we feel have consequences on the actions we decide to take and on the behaviours we choose at the time.

Our emotional state affects what meaning we give to any experience or event.

These internal representations are unique to us. Therefore it is only our reality, our perception—not that of reality itself or anyone else's.

How we feel in our body has a direct effect on the state of our conscious and subconscious mind, including our emotions.

The way we feel at any time is the direct result of how we are using our body.

The symbols, pictures and sounds as well as the movies we make in our mind, including our internal voice all contribute to influence our emotional state.

We have a choice of how we react to any given situation.

We all see the world through different filters, influenced by our past.

Our posture, our breathing or muscle tension all influence how we feel; in other words they affect our emotional state.

How we feel have consequences on the actions we decide to take and the resulting behaviours.

Our thoughts can alter the chemistry of our brain.

Silence is golden. Use silence to listen to what your emotions are telling you.

Our emotions are part of our intelligence.

Every emotion carries a message for us—

It is up to us to find out what message they want to give us.

We often react to our past experiences.

We respond to memories or usual thought patterns we have been having, instead of reacting to the present.

Chapter Five: <u>Secrets About Our Belief System</u>

It is our belief in ourselves which determine whether we can or can't do something.

You self-sabotage because you have a belief that you are incapable of doing something. If you have a belief that you are able to do something, then you will do it.

Limiting beliefs rob you of the person you were intended to be. Who could you be if you got rid of the beliefs that are limiting you?

You have the power to do anything you want to do; you need to be willing and to believe that you can.

If you never try anything new, you will never succeed at anything in life.

There is no such thing as failure, there are only results.

Once you make a commitment, new opportunities suddenly open up to you.

It is the way we represent not being successful in our mind to ourselves that matters.

The first person we need to learn to trust in life is ourselves.

If we don't believe in ourselves, why should others believe in us?

Our purpose here on planet Earth is to learn, to grow and to develop.

If you believe something, your subconscious works to prove you right.

Whatever you say to yourself, your subconscious will work to make it happen.

Watch what you believe about yourself and what you say to yourself. The way you think about yourself decides if you are successful or not. If you have no belief in yourself, you are unable to achieve what you wish for in life.

Your subconscious is always listening 24/7.

When something is said repeatedly we end up believing it, even though it is not true; and even if we didn't agree with it in the first place.

Nothing in life has any meaning until you decide what meaning you want to give it.

You have the power to give empowering meaning to your beliefs as you have the power to give them disastrous meaning.

Practice makes perfect.

You have the power to choose what meaning you give to any experience you have in life. You can choose to be positive as you can choose to be negative.

You can use your negative experiences to achieve positive outcomes for others.

If you start to doubt anything long enough, you will sooner or later not believe it.

Limiting beliefs can have social or career consequences.

Whatever you avoid becomes bigger and bigger in your mind. Avoidance can lead to the development of phobias. People who avoid being with other people can develop a social phobia.

The more you avoid things you don't like to do, the bigger they become in your head and in your body.

The more stubborn you become about them, the worse things get for you. Exercise the muscle of trying things you think you can't do.

Life is a lot happier for those who are flexible, relaxed and happy to go with the flow, providing you are not going against any of your beliefs and are not restricted by the limiting ones.

Make a plan or plan to fail.

Adopt a new belief:

There is nothing that I can't do; or I can manage anything that comes my way.

However bad a situation is, we always have the choice of how we react to any experience.

We can choose to react as a victim or we can choose to dust ourselves up and take positive action.

When things are tough and you don't know where to turn: think of others and do something for someone else, who is worse off than you.

Confront your fears instead of avoiding the situation. Don't give up until you have conquered your fears.

Anything and anyone that puts limits on you is not good and things only get worse with time.

I repeat: The mind cannot distinguish between something that has been vividly imagined and something that is real.

The mind's primary role is to prove itself right, because it needs to stay consistent.

The mind cannot cope with two conflicting beliefs, so it will try to prove itself right so that it can stay consistent with what you believe in.

How you feel about yourself will affect how other people will feel about you and how they will treat you.

If you do not show respect for yourself, why should others treat you with respect?

Do not give in to your fears.

Self-pity is not your friend! Do not indulge in it. It can become very addictive.

Self-pity robs you of your power, and stops you being who you are, who you can be or who you could have been.

Even the worst amongst us have some things to be grateful for; if you look you will find.

Chapter Six: <u>Schhhh .... A Few Secrets About Friends .... Persistence ... And More ...</u>

We are all judged by the company we keep, rightly or wrongly; that's how life works.

Our friends can be the making of us or they can be our biggest downfall. They can make us winners or they can make us losers.

If you make friends with people who have dubious values and character, you will be judged by their standards and you will be tarred with the same brush.

You can have many acquaintances, but you must choose wisely who you pick as friends.

You can't choose your family, but you can choose your friends—wisely.

Show love to your family but be careful who you choose to associate with as friends.

Friends have a huge influence on us.

People do rub off on each other whether we like to think so or not.

If you are trying to improve your life and live the life you deserve, you need to move more towards people who have the values and beliefs you have or wish you had; those whom you admire, not those with dubious characters, beliefs, values and low standards.

The most important thing is to live in the here and now and to be fully conscious and aware what influences you; to make healthy positive choices, and also be aware of who and what you choose to influence you.

You do not need to compare yourself to others. When you do this and you do not make the grade, you are indulging in self-pity and cultivating low self-esteem.

Your self-esteem and self-worth are a lot harder to rebuild than to bring down.

Self-esteem can be very hard to build up and can be squashed in an instant.

We are all responsible for our own life, and we are creating the experience we are having now, by the thoughts, decisions, and behaviours we choose to take.

We have all the resources we need inside of us to help us cope with whatever life throws at us. It is time to realize this and go get it!

The problem with to-day's society, is that it is a NOW society and a ME society. We want instant gratification; and when do we want it? NOW! Of course! And who is it about? ME! Of course!

Persistence is the essential value you need to have.

Believe first that you can and your mind will find a way.

Assertiveness

When people feel that they have been heard and that you have considered their feelings, they are more likely to listen to you and are more prepared to negotiate with you.

It's okay to say No.

Chapter Seven: <u>Secrets About Our Value System And Its Importance</u>

It is the decisions that we make consistently which give us the results that we have in our life to-day.

We can't live by our values if we don't know what our values are.

Anything that means a lot to you is a value.

As we are all unique individuals, our values are unique to us.

Our values need to be updated regularly to make sure that we are living what we truly believe in.

When couples or friends regularly clash it is often because they have conflicting values.

If we change our values, our life changes too.

Chapter Eight: <u>Some Secrets About Our Self-Image</u>

When you speak, your words represent who and what you believe you are. Your self-image is reflected in whatever you do and in whatever you believe in.

Your outer world reflects your inner world.

When you have a poor self-image, you highlight the negatives and make little of the positives.

Your behaviour is always in sync with your self-image.

How we think about ourselves affects how other people think about us and treat us.

If we don't believe what we say, our body language will betray us.

Research tells us that criticism is the main cause of low self-image.

If you want good self-esteem, it takes practice. Start with loving yourself for who you are. Look to yourself to improve your self-esteem, not to others.

Chapter Nine: <u>**Secrets About Our Own Personal Set Of Laws Or Rules**</u>

Our reality is experienced by each of us individually; however, our reality is influenced by our beliefs and values, which control our experience of life from which we make our own personal rules or set of laws which control our life.

We are in charge of our happiness.

No one else controls whether we are happy or sad, angry or bitter. That's our choice.

Our happiness is our job! If we are unhappy, that's our responsibility.

Our happiness depends on us and the rules we have about what makes us happy. We are the only one responsible; no one else! Happiness is a factor inside of us.

When things go wrong in your life, don't look at others or at your circumstances; look inside. The answer is inside you.

Look inside to see what you did to get the results you got.

Always look to yourself, not to others or circumstances. Don't make excuses. The only person you would be fooling would be you.

Time to stop being a victim, is NOW! Time to stop living in denial is NOW too. Time to take action is NOW also! You won't be able to move on until you do.

Look at all the facts, face on; warts and all!

Bad things happen to good people all the time; you are not especially chosen out of the human race, to be a "jinx" person! Remember, life is not supposed to be fair. Sometimes bad things happen so that we can benefit from some serious learning about the game of life. Sometimes, we don't get what we want because there is a good reason for it, only we can't see the bigger picture.

It is how we react to things that matter, not really what happens to us.

You have all the resources you need inside of you.

For us to be successful in life, we need our own self-imposed laws or rules to empower us, not disempower us.

If you have difficulty achieving your own rules, then they are disempowering you.

If one of your rules depends on something that isn't within your control, you need to ditch it, as it is disempowering.

Look for the good in everything; if you search, you will find.

A break of our personal rules by us or by others is the guilty party behind all our emotional upheavals.

Chapter Ten: <u>**Secrets About Relationships**</u>

To be successful in our relationships, we need to be good communicators. Remember: nothing has any meaning until we give it meaning. Misinterpretations can drive us straight into the path of pain!

Good communications produce good relationships.

We have to be able to love first before we can receive love. That's the law of life.

Like with everything else in life, we get back what we give out. If you are in a relationship, love comes first.

It is true; there is more pleasure in giving than in receiving.

The attitude with which you go into a relationship will determine whether you are happy or not or whether you stay together or not.

The old saying: You reap what you sow, is still popular, because there's a lot of truth in it.

Put in a lot and you will get a lot back. Put in little? Well, don't expect much back! Because in life you get back what you put in! You often get what you think you deserve.

Every relationship, especially an intimate one, should be based on mutual respect.

A lack of respect for your partner is usually the kiss of death to a happy relationship.

Remember when you are in a relationship you are both on the same side. Your partner doesn't belong to the enemy camp.

Whenever you blame or criticize someone, they feel under attack, therefore they are forced to defend themselves.

If fighting in front of the children is regular and significant, that is a form of child abuse.

If you regularly fight in front of your children, do this with the knowledge that you are condemning them to emotional problems when they are adults.

Children are little adults in training. It is up to us to give them good role modelling and the best training we can as a child, for optimal results in the future.

If a father doesn't take his rightful place in the family and does not lead his family as he should, this family becomes dysfunctional.

If a wife doesn't take her rightful place in the family, the family becomes dysfunctional too and the children become the casualty of this unhealthy relationship.

Parents should never use their children to get leverage against their partner.

It is better to be healthy on your own, than to be unwell in an unhealthy, harmful relationship.

If a behaviour is working for you, you will continue to repeat it. However if the behaviour stops working for you, there is no point in carrying on the behaviour, as you are not getting anything from it. Therefore you will stop it. We do all things because there is something in it for us; when there is nothing in it for us, we stop doing it.

If you keep doing what you have always done, you will get more of what you always got.

Never, ever, poison your children against your partner. You will eventually suffer the consequences and ruin your children's lives at the same time.

Your job as a husband or partner is to love and support your wife and protect her. You never allow anyone, be it your children or anyone else to gang up against her. Your job as a wife or partner is to do the same. If you join in with your children to go against your partner, this constitutes a form of bullying. It is very dysfunctional, and the result is that you are all unhappy.

Your job as a husband or partner is to teach your children from the very beginning, to love, honour and respect their mother. Your job as a wife or partner is to teach your children to love, honour and respect their father from the beginning too. If you can't do this, you have no business being together. Even if you part company you have no business saying detrimental things to the children about each other or use them to get inside information about each other.

The problem is that a bully never sees the error of their ways.

When you behave as victim, you get treated as one.

The world responds to you *as you treat yourself*; you do teach others how you to treat you.

When you behave as a victim, you give away all your power.

Being a victim can paralyze you into depression and inaction.

You have absolutely no right to wallow in self-pity especially if your actions have repercussions on others.

Sulking is not okay. Sulking is dysfunctional and is a form of mental and emotional abuse.

If you want to change something or express your displeasure with your partner, there are always words; use them! Your partner is not telepathic!

Instead of sulking and feeling sorry for yourself, remember to show love and understanding and demonstrate it by your attitude and your behaviour.

If you show love first and foremost, you cannot go wrong! Your partner will meet you halfway.

Choose to be the one to say *sorry* first; you can stop a fight escalating if you can say sorry. Not sorry, that you're wrong, but sorry that you're fighting.

Sorry is a five letter word that can heal most rifts. It is the most healing word on planet Earth!

Use "I" statements instead of being accusing.

You need to ignore the sulking behaviour as much as possible and carry on with life.

When you feed a behaviour you keep it alive. When you cut off its oxygen, it dies a natural death from your neglect.

If a behaviour is working for you, you will continue to repeat it.

Negative thoughts physically overpower your brain leaving very little room for positive thoughts to come in.

There is nothing worse than being ignored.

What you feed thrives.

You only get out of this life what you put in. If you're not putting in the effort, just don't expect much out of life.

It is insanity to expect different results when you keep doing the same things.

Happiness is any moment that makes you feel good.

Happiness or depression is not a permanent emotional state.

To have a satisfying relationship is to have one in which there is an equal partnership.

When choosing a partner, don't just wait and see what turns up; No! You choose! Check their credentials from the very beginning to see if that person is someone desirable to be in your life; someone you can be proud of; someone who has potential and someone you will be happy to introduce to your family and friends. You need to do this, way before you get caught in the web of love. By then, it can be too late.

You have to know that this person has your absolute "Must have" and you need to know that this person does not have any of your absolute "Must not have" as qualities. This means knowing exactly what you are looking for. Some things can be accepted or worked on, but if there are traits in this person that you absolutely hate, but keep going with the relationship, it is a recipe for future conflict in the relationship. Things do not get better as we age, they get worse.

What you experience in your life now is the product of all that you have created to maintain your sense of self and your way of life in the past.

Knowledge without taking actions is a waste of time. Knowledge is only power when it is put in practice by taking actions.

Your lifestyle always reflects your character and the kind of person you are. It also reflects an associated psychology, your attitude including your beliefs and values.

If you value your relationship, then you must make time for it. Consciously feed your relationship.

Relationship is about learning to give and take and getting the balance right.

When there is mutual respect and dignity, you have the basis for a quality relationship.

A person can never really and truly possess and control another.

You may not be able to tell your partner how to behave, but by your behaviour, you can inspire and motivate them.

Always remember that you are both on the same side.

Focus on the solution instead of the problem.

Unchecked negative imagination can have a very destructive effect on any relationship. It can play havoc with your thinking.

Wrong thinking slowly poisons the mind!

Every negative thought that we choose to entertain, is like a poison drip, seeping slowly drip by drip into our mind, rendering it toxic, until we are unable to think clearly or rationally.

Behind every action is a positive intention.

Most of the time it isn't about us. Sometimes we get hurt, through someone trying to fulfil their own needs. On the whole people do not do things deliberately to hurt others.

Men and women see life very differently. We are different species! We are indeed wired differently.

In an argument it is important to aim for a win/win outcome.

Choose to be happy rather than right.

How you react to any situation is always your choice. You have the power to choose how to react.

It is not our responsibility to make our partner happy, although we can work on enhancing their happiness and improving the relationship. We are responsible for our own happiness.

The fact is you got where you are to-day "together".

Never ever allow a partner to cut you off from your family and friends. This is the tactics of bullies and abusers.

You need to make a commitment to want to improve your relationship on a daily basis and be disciplined to work at it.

When you hit trouble in your relationship, you need to identify exactly what the problem is, and how each of you sees the problem.

Discuss things when you are not angry and really try to put yourself in your partner's shoes.

By what you accept in your relationship and by your behaviour, past and present you teach your partner what is acceptable and what is not. This teaches them how to treat you.

Whatever has been happening in your relationship and whatever continues to happen is because in some way you are allowing it to happen, you are enabling it or maintaining it by what you do.

Never ever stop working on your relationship, even if you have been married or been together for many years; and never take each other for granted.

If you are in a rut and you're not happy with it, it is up to you to change that.

Remember to tell your partner every day that they are loved.

Attitude is everything. It is the small thing that makes an enormous difference.

Chapter Eleven: <u>Secrets About Forgiveness</u>

What is necessary is to make a decision and commit to forgive yourself or anyone else you need to, for your peace of mind.

Peace of mind is priceless. Forgiveness brings peace of mind.

It is within your power to forgive or not to forgive. Absolutely everyone has this choice.

If our heart is dark, so will our world be. If our heart is light, that too, will be reflected in the world around us.

Forgiveness not only liberates the person who is forgiven, but it especially frees the person who chooses to forgive.

Forgiving is about using your free will.

Choose forgiveness even in the little things in life.

Forgiving means letting go . . . letting go of hurt, hatred, resentment and much more negative feelings.

Forgiving doesn't mean that you necessarily have to have to go to that person or that you have to have that person back in your life either or be a push-over; or that you have to like them, approve of them or associate with them.

You can decide to forgive someone without making them your friend or part of your life.

We forgive for our sake, not for anyone else's benefit.

Forgiving is choosing to let go of all the hurt and pain. It is choosing to set yourself free.

Negativity is just that: a habit! A persistent nasty one!

Have faith that whatever you are repeating on a consistent basis is going to work. Expect it to work. Keep doing it until it works. You will attract it into your life.

When you find it difficult to get rid of your negative thoughts, focus on adding some new positive thoughts in.

The focus is on adding new positive thoughts, not on the getting rid of negative thoughts. It makes controlling your thoughts easier.

Forgiveness doesn't mean that you condone what the person has done.

We all do the best we can with the resources we have at the time. When we acquire new resources we can do better.

Is your internal voice on your side or is it working against you? It can be the voice of an angel or it can be the voice of the devil.

If you find it hard to forgive someone, then, know that this person is the most important person that you must forgive.

If you want to feel emotionally light, forgiveness is the answer. Free yourself and shed that load.

You do not need to have this person back in your life. You just need to emotionally release them.

You do not need to know how to forgive, you just need to be willing to forgive and decide to forgive and let go. The rest will take care of itself.

It is never our place to judge other people whatever they're like.

Forgive sooner rather than later. It is not always the older person who dies first. It can just happen to anyone at any time.

A bitter person's face tells a whole story without even uttering a word.

Forgive, forgive, and forgive! You have nothing to lose but everything to gain.

Forgiving is by no means condoning what they did. Choose to live lightly and free in life. Learn to be able to laugh at yourself. Cultivate your sense of humour.

Self-acceptance and self-approval underpin positive change in all areas of our lives, including the ability to forgive.

You are a work of art, completely unique with your own qualities, talents, gifts and attributes.

Try finding the good in everything.

Be aware if you get into the habit of criticizing, it becomes a pattern; a way of life.

Remember, other people's criticism cannot harm us, unless we allow it.

We are in control of our behaviour, emotions, speech, and thoughts. These are our four personal powers.

Behaviour

Emotions

Speech

Thoughts

Forgiving is a self-centred act. You forgive for you! You forgive so you can feel better. You do not forgive because you want the person whom you are forgiving to feel better.

You release the past and forgive those who have wronged you because you wish to be free from the pain of the hurt and the hatred and the resentment and the anger.

You can stop blaming other people for all that is wrong in your life. The buck stops here with you, and YES! YOU CAN! You are not a victim!

All you can control is yourself; you are not in control of anyone or of any external factors.

You create your own experience of life. If it's good, it's down to you; however if your experience of life is not so good, then you have no one else to blame.

It is essential to forgive yourself and others if you want good health, inner peace and harmony. You cannot forgive others completely until you have forgiven yourself first.

Research shows that unforgiveness, resentment, anger, aggression and criticism of others are the root cause of many illnesses.

Thoughts

Understand that thoughts are not just anything innocuous that are around and that we can't see.

Thoughts are *things* that have the power to materialize themselves into our world.

Our thoughts work on our subconscious which brings them into existence.

Think *abundantly*; think richly.

There is plenty for everyone on this planet Earth.

Someone once wrote: (picked up from the net)

Watch your thoughts, they become words.

Watch your words, they become actions.

Watch your actions, they become your habits.

Watch your habits, they become your character.

Watch your character, they become your destiny.

Your thoughts are powerful, but you do have control over them. You can choose what you want to concentrate your thoughts on.

You are where you are to-day, because of the thoughts you chose, the actions you took following the decisions you made, based on those thoughts in the past.

Be the designer of your own thoughts and the architect of your dreams. Dream big!

Chapter Twelve: <u>Secrets About The Power Of Words</u>

As thoughts are powerful, words are just as powerful.

Words express meaning, feelings and mental images and symbols and are represented in the movies of our minds. Language and words are actually how we figure out what something means.

Words certainly can get you into trouble, but also out of trouble.

Having a way with words means that you have a gift for influencing and a gift for persuasion. That's power!

The meaning we give to our words is crucial to the actions that we choose to take as a consequence.

When we can control the words we use in our language and meaning, we can also control our thoughts and feelings.

Anxiety and depression can follow very negative and destructive words.

Equally reading or watching toxic materials can put excessive fear and lasting anxiety into impressionable minds by the meaning that the words and imagery convey.

Words can contain and trigger emotion in us and in others.

Controlling our emotive words are enough to control people or change them.

It is vital for parents and teachers to be aware of the words they use with children as they are programming them for adulthood.

You get what you repeatedly think and say.

You neither need nor deserve a critical inner voice. Choose for your inner voice to use empowering words.

If you can easily assume the worst, it is proof that you have the ability to imagine the best.

Words have incredible power.

Research shows that those who speak the *in* language are more successful at work.

Words are a reflection of what we think and what's in our hearts.

Words have the power to affect the human brain for better and for worse.

The words that emerge out of our mouths reveal what we're thinking.

Words affect our perception, our attitude and our behaviour.

By your words, you are the power in your world.

Add optimism and enthusiasm to your values.

Successful people invest in successful self-talk.

Self-pity is our worst enemy.

Our words shape our present and our future; therefore they determine our destiny. Our words exert power on our actions and ultimately on our life.

When you think good thoughts, you feel good; when you think bad thoughts, you become prey to dark moods and depression.

Where there is hatred, anger, bitterness and resentment, there can be no happiness or peace.

Where there is no gratitude, there can be no happiness.

Accept the family you've got as a fact of life, not what you think your idea of family should be like.

Accept your reality, not one that doesn't exist.

Accept your family as they are, warts and all.

Your words do end up manifesting themselves into your external world through your thoughts.

Don't use words lightly.

If you do not forgive, if you keep resentment in your heart, you will be old and still be tortured by your resentful and vengeful thoughts. You keep yourself imprisoned in an internal jail of your own making.

Words have unbelievable power over your life.

Words can have serious consequences.

Before you act, think about the consequences of your actions and who they can affect.

Before you act, check what words you are using to language to yourself what you are experiencing. Words can produce emotion in us and in others.

The words that we use can, not only create emotions, but they can hype them up or chill them down.

The word *Hate* heightens the intensity of your feelings and spurs you on to do things or say words that you may later regret.

Using emotionally charged words can transform your emotional state as well as other people's.

Positive affirmations work because they are positively reinforcing to yourself what you choose to feed your subconscious with.

Words are so powerful that in law, it isn't the innocent person who is found guilty or not guilty. It is the one who can manipulate their words to persuade and influence best.

Words can trigger wars, revolutions, or create peace.

Controlling our emotive words are enough to control people or change them.

You get what you repeatedly think and say. Words affect how we feel.

It is up to us to choose our reactions to what happened to us as a child when we are adults. We have the power to choose how we react in the present, as an adult, to something that happened in the past.

If you carry hatred in your heart, you can never be free and happy, no matter what wonderful things happen to you. Part of you will still feel wretched!

Choosing our words wisely can produce amazing results.

Appreciate your life every day. Life can change in the blink of an eye. The problem is we only acknowledge this fact after a drastic event.

Show love and appreciation to the people in your life always; if they have faults, pass on them! After all, you're not perfect either! You never know when you will be able to see them again.

Life is truly a God-given gift, to be grateful for and appreciated every day.

It really isn't something we "should have" or that "we're entitled to" or that we "choose". None of us knows when it will come to an end. We have no control when it's our turn to say our grand farewell. All we have is now. It is too late to make amends then, or say the right words to our loved ones or do better the next time. So let's appreciate the here and now and live so that we don't have the regrets if we lose someone close to us or if it's our turn to say good bye.

The choice of words you use to yourself and the choice of words you choose to communicate with others have the powerful repercussions on how others will treat you.

If you're not good with words, learn! If you can't describe something, you cannot experience the emotions that go with it.

When we change our every day words, we can change our every day emotional experience; in other words how we feel at any given time.

Words affect our beliefs and values.

Be the master of your vocabulary and the controller of your words.

Chapter Thirteen: <u>Secrets About Gorgeousness And Confidence</u>

We all deserve to feel gorgeous and confident.

We are unique works of art, whatever we look like. Whatever we are like, we are always first-class, as we were created that way for a special reason.

Anything is possible if we put our mind to it.

Your self-esteem is all about the thoughts you choose to entertain about yourself.

Your subconscious does not argue with you. It simply acts on the instructions that you give it, and finds a way to give you what it thinks you want. It is the "spy within". It is listening 24/7 to what you are saying to yourself about you.

It's up to you to select the software that you want to program your computer (brain) with.

Our face is the mirror which reflects to the world what is going on the inside of us.

What you choose to present to the outside world matters as first impressions always count and they are difficult to shake off.

Like it or not, we all form an opinion within the first few minutes of meeting someone.

Be conscious of what you wear and how you present yourself to the world. First impressions do count!

When you feel gorgeous your attitude towards the world changes for the better. As a rule, the world returns the compliment.

To be confident is to be comfortable with who you really are. It is not about feeling superior; it is about being comfortable in your own skin.

Self-confidence comes from self-love and self-knowledge.

Be aware of how you interact with others.

Respect your feelings as they don't lie.

Increase your self confidence by believing that you are able to change and become more confident.

You must see the need and want to change.

You need to be motivated to be confident.

You must understand yourself, set realistic goals, seek support and get rewarded.

Confident people are assertive people.

It's ok to say no, if it's not convenient for you.

Confident people are good communicators.

Confident people have good manners.

Practice makes perfect.

Confident people have an ease about them and are good at small talk.

It is not the most intelligent person or the unintelligent person who does better at small talk. It has nothing to do with intelligence.

To be articulate gives you an edge. Verbal dyslexia is a clear disadvantage.

To be good at conversation, it is about being interested in the other person, actively listening, showing genuine interest and asking open questions.

Try to listen rather than talk. Be positive. Use humour, give good eye contact and smile easily and often.

When you give a genuine compliment, be sincere, relax, make sure that the time and the place is appropriate, give good eye contact, be specific and never include any put downs or do any *tit for tat* compliments.

Back-handed compliments are no compliments at all; best to say nothing!

Chapter Fourteen: <u>One Last Secret: Take A leap Of Faith</u>
Faith versus Fear

Faith is an act of will.

It is a decision that you make at some point in your life. You choose what to believe and what you put your trust in.

Thoughts are things that can materialize themselves into our world.

So thinking the worst brings on the worst.

Fear is the opposite of faith.

Having faith means really, but really trusting in the invisible before it becomes visible.

Fear is one of the most debilitating emotions anyone can suffer from.

You don't get what you want when you doubt.

Believe that things happen for a good reason. Sometimes we need to go through bad times to come out the other end and be where we are meant to be.

When you are making a choice not to choose faith, by default you are making a choice to choose fear instead.

Fear is one of the most incapacitating emotions anyone can suffer from.

Insecurity heightens anxiety and fear. Unless you own your fears, they have a nasty habit of owning you instead.

What is your fear costing you, in terms of health? Missed happiness? Unhappiness? Missed opportunities? Missed experiences? Friendships? Marriage? Relationships? Children? Work? Etc

Continuous fear tends to lead to a state of panic.

This habit of listening to long term wild imagination can lead us to being neurotic.

The very act of owning your fears is an act of courage.

Recognize what price that you are paying for letting your fears run your life—or rather ruin your life!

Those who have faith have a very different outlook on life. They are confident that they have a Higher Power to turn to, which in turn gives them peace of mind and confidence.

Whilst others who have no faith, suffer with fear, anxiety, feel lost and alone; those who have faith have the confidence of knowing that they can turn their worries to a Higher Power and have the hope and confidence that things will be alright.

After all it is well documented that we are body-mind-and spirit. We have to nurture our body, feed our mind, but let's not forget our spirit.

Choose faith, reject fear. Faith soothes your soul.

A soothed soul enjoys peace of mind and confidence. When you feel confident, you have security, which leads to relaxation.

Relaxation produces a sense of balance in your life. The result of having a balance in your life produces peace of mind.

Fear stops you from finding resourceful solutions to your problems. Active fear is produced by incorrect beliefs. Active faith is produced by correct beliefs.

What you actively fear will ultimately manifest itself in your life. You bring into your physical world what you actively fear.

Whatever you concentrate all your focus on becomes more powerful.

When we turn our attention on our fears, and focus on what isn't working in our lives, you strengthen the fear. You give it power. It is like switching on the "fear switch". It gathers momentum and becomes more powerful.

Having faith helps us to focus on things that we do want to experience in our life.

We reap what we sow. What we send out comes back to us multiplied. This is a recognized universal law. No one escapes. It affects all of us.

Choose the life you desire or choose the life you fear.

No one else creates your experience of life but you.

Faith removes limitations.

Remember what you think about, you create.

Choose faith and reject fear.

Take a leap of faith and live life to the full, the life you so richly deserve. Life truly is too short to mess it up. Come on! Don't worry about what others think! It's your life, not theirs!

Whatever actions you choose to take, they have consequences. You can read this book as an academic exercise or decide to use it to do something to change your life. Even if all is well, we always want more. It is a law of life that we need to grow and develop and improve; there is always something we can improve on. We can never achieve perfection as perfection itself doesn't exist, which means that there is always room for improvement.

Whatever behaviour you choose, you also choose the consequences.

Therefore the choices that you make are vital for the consequences that you will enjoy or suffer later on. The actions that you decide on now will reap benefits or misery in the future.

You can let life take you down the garden path of misery or you can take control and choose the right path for you, with the first-class consequences that you desire, instead of getting *whatever* consequences by default.

Think first before you act.

Never forget that your behaviour may have consequences which can affect other people's lives, sometimes permanently. The better your actions, the better the quality of consequences you will have. You can choose to clean up your life and choose the resulting consequences, which will bring you a lot more satisfaction and happiness—or you can choose the status quo; the consequences being that nothing will change for the better and you will continue to get more of what you always had all along, maybe continue to blame circumstances or others for them, instead of looking inwards. The answer is not out there! It is inside of you. That's where you need to look.

Now is your time! Now is the time to empower yourself. Reclaim your power! NOW!

You can decide what you want and actively work towards it. You can be self-reliant and you can be self-sufficient; and if you think right, your subconscious will find a way. Remember bad things may have happened in the past because, you constantly replayed negative thoughts in your mind; and as you thought negatively, bad things happened as a result. Now turn it all around, get into the habit of rehashing uplifting thoughts constantly, in your mind; things that you DO want for your life instead—and your subconscious will find a way!

Look at the successful people you know; I bet they never waste their time rehearsing negative thoughts, right? Successful people's thinking is always upbeat! They visualize success instead of disaster and they get success.

So go on! Reclaim your power! It is there waiting for you! Get passionate. Claim your right to a wonderful life. You deserve it. You just need to make this decision and take action to get the life you want. Get excited and don't let anything or anyone dissuade you. You know that when you decide to do something different that the negative *doom and gloomers* will put all sorts of obstacles in your way or even laugh at you.

The answer is: let them! In fact, laugh with them! But do exactly what you need to do. You are bigger than that! You can cope with this and continue with what you want to change. When you would be where you want to be, they will still be where they always were!

Claim your right to the life you deserve! It is your God-given right to be happy and live the life you wish for.

Now that you understand many of the secrets of the tapestry of life, you no longer need to live your life anxiously, feeling helpless about your circumstances and waiting for things to come to you or to go wrong. You know that you are not a victim! You don't have to be needy. You already know that neediness is a very unattractive trait. If you need something, you need to go out there and do what it takes and get it. You know nothing will happen if you sit on your butt waiting for things to come to you. You believed that before and nothing happened; you know better now!

Nothing is supposed to come to you! And if life is unfair, that's just how it is! No one ever said that it is supposed to be fair! Right?

You are in charge of you and of your destiny! You choose to win and not sit there and feel sorry for yourself and expect that somehow things will come to you. That never takes you anywhere but downhill all the way! You KNOW that! You own your life. You take charge! You decide! You go get it! Make it worthwhile. Find your way of contributing.

Find excitement, motivation, optimism and enthusiasm and be the best that you can be.

Decide that you are an optimist, and cultivate that value every day. You are the sculptor of your life, the designer of your thoughts and the achiever of your dreams. Everyone has been given their own gifts and talents. Whatever they are, let's make the best with what we have been gifted. If you don't know what yours are; FIND THEM! Look and don't stop until you find! You owe it to yourself. Visualize the end result of what you want and steadily work towards it. Let it inspire you.

You are in control of what you choose to think and say. You are in charge of your emotions. And you know by now that you are in control of your behaviour, and how you choose to react to any event in life is entirely your choice.

A final word

To conclude our time together, I want to remind you about one last secret:

It is important to have a plan for our life and for our career.

We need to plan so we don't fail.

It is much better for us to plan which direction we want our life to go, instead of leaving it to fate or to someone else to decide for us. Our career or job is a big chunk of our life, as we spend half of our waking hours there. With a plan, we have direction and something to work towards and we stand a better chance of getting where we want to be and where we want to end up, not leaving it haphazardly to fate.

Give plenty of thought to where it is you want to be. If you are doing a physical job, will you still be able to do it as you get older? If so, can it leave you with a disability? If that's the case, you need to have a plan to guide you towards something more suitable as you get older; something where you wouldn't have to rely on your physical strength to perform it. This is relevant to those who suffer from a chronic condition, like back, hip or chest problems, so that they can have other options if the need presents itself. It is also relevant to those who are asthmatic and work in an environment which is harmful to their condition. If you have given it some thought, then it won't come as a shock or you won't be so much in a quandary if you need to change directions. You would have your plan to guide you.

Sometimes it may mean getting more qualifications. If that's the case then plan what you need to do to get what you want. May be it may mean that you need to do some research first. Do you need more experience? If that's the case discuss the possibilities with your superiors. If it means that you have to change job, then you need to start searching for a new position. Or it may just mean that you just need to change the way you work or perhaps change departments or areas.

Whether you work in an office or whether you are a teacher, nurse or in the medical profession or other caring professions, you need to plan where you want to be in the next five or may be ten years from now. Is your next step to be a supervisor? A Trainer? A Manager may be? Head of department? A C.E.O?

Whatever it takes, plan and work steadily towards your future. When you have a plan, it is like having a map that you can follow to take you to your destination. Without a map, you may get lost along the way and end up where you don't want to be.

If you are bored with what you are doing, then make a decision to find a job that will stimulate you and that you can enjoy; one that can lead you in the direction of where you want to end up eventually.

Work keeps us mentally agile and young in our outlook. There is a social aspect to work that can be very beneficial. It keeps us in touch with people and with the world. Sadly a lot of people can't wait to finish work because they believe that the grass is greener on the other side. Unfortunately when they get there, they, then realize how lucky they were to have a job.

Our work presents us with a daily challenge, which stimulates us and makes us strive to do our best. Having a hierarchy in work is beneficial as it encourages respect for our superiors, colleagues and other people associated with work; it also teaches us discipline in our life. These work-related skills are an advantage in our private life too.

So, don't badmouth your bosses. They serve a purpose. Work gives us skills, like people's skills, that we can sometimes be deficient in when we don't belong to a workforce.

If you do not have a direction for your life, job or career, you will drift and be at the mercy of your environment, as you will not have a clear idea of where you're going. If you have no idea where you want to be, you could end up just about anywhere, which could be the exact place that you loathe. You must have a vision of where you would like to be in the future. You also need to know exactly where you don't want to be and take steps to avoid it.

When you make a plan, it takes conscious effort and it forces you to seriously think about your future and what you truly want for your life. Without a plan, it is easy to become despondent and apathetic. You may find yourself at the mercy of others. You are allowing others to control what happens in your life. This helps you to feel disempowered. When someone else is in charge of your life you do not make conscious informed choices, but you react to whatever comes your way.

It is never too late to start planning. Your age doesn't matter.

People, who do well in life, do it by design. It doesn't all come together by accident. Their plan is work in progress; they are flexible as they may have to change course along the way if they want to achieve a certain goal. They know where they are going. They are positive, and if they're not they *act as if* until they are where they want to be. The very act of *pretending* eventually becomes the belief that they want to have. In the end they no longer have to act as it becomes natural for them to be that way. They keep their eyes fixed on the end goal.

Whatever we do for a living has repercussions on our world, on us and at times on others. It may affect us for better or for worse. It may enhance our brain function and improve our intelligence and stimulate us or it can leave us with a permanent health problem.

What we do may have an influence on our environment which may cause pollution, for instance; or you may work in a tobacco industry and have the so-called *perks* of getting free or cheap tobacco which is responsible for causing many to suffer lung cancer, emphysema or Chronic Obstructive Pulmonary Disease. Many others have suffered from dire work-related diseases as a result of being exposed to asbestos or coal dust. Some who value money more than anything else may be seduced by the financial rewards that working in the mines may offer; however when you are away from home three to four weeks at a time, and you only have a week back home to recuperate and then the cycle starts all over again, you may be doing it at the expense of your relationships with your partner and children or putting your physical or mental health at risk.

I am not actually saying that working in the mines is wrong. No! What I am saying is that you have to weigh up the pros and cons and decide whether you can do such a job for the kind of personality that you are. It is not for everybody. If you end up with a lot of money but in a disastrous relationship, and have seriously poor mental health or cirrhosis of the liver as a consequence, you have to know that all the money in the world is not worth that huge sacrifice!

The choices you make for your career and the choices you make when you marry have their long-lasting consequences and effects on your destiny.

Give very serious thought to the path you want to take in your work or in your life. Be aware what you do for a job or who you marry may have consequences on the rest of your life. Be very conscious of the impact they have on you and on the environment.

When you make a career plan, you need to consider what the long term effects of your work would be, on you, on your environment, on your family and on our planet.

So, plan well.

It is hoped that you use the information that you have read in this book to work on and enhance your future, and that you may pass it on to others.

May you live the best life that you can as this is no dress rehearsal. You only pass this way but once. Don't waste your time on stupidities and get upset about things that do not matter. Cherish the people in your life. You only get one crack at the whip, and there is no second chance. Don't hang on to hurts that can damage you in the long run.

Live the best life you can live and most of all, be happy. If you want change in others, remember that you have to be that change that you are looking for. You can only ever change you, not anyone else.

May you live long and well to achieve your full potential and enjoy your life.

May life bring you lots of blessings, happiness, joy, success, great relationships, wonderful career, fulfilment, and no regrets.

Now, go on! Be happy and have an amazing life!

Go on! . . . . Life is really waiting for you! Go on, go for it! Give it your best shot!

You have so much to achieve, so don't waste any time!

So, from me to you, I do hope that you have understood and enjoyed reading about the Secrets of the Tapestry of Life and that they help you to live the best life that you can and achieve what you are meant to!

God bless, may you have everything in your life that you would wish for yourself and most of all be the best that you can be. Be kind, caring and compassionate to others and to yourself. Remember that your attitude of approach to life is everything; get it wrong and a lot can easily go wrong. Believe in yourself and have confidence in yourself and feel gorgeous. Have faith, keep hope alive always, be happy and share what you have learnt with others. That is my wish for you and it comes with so much love!

> *To laugh often and much;*
> *To win the respect of intelligent people and the affection of children*
> *To leave the world a better place*
> *To know even one life has breathed easier*
> *Because you have lived, this is to have succeeded.*

—*Ralph Waldo Emerson*

END

___

Notes: What have you learnt?

INDEX

BIBLIOGRAPHY

Recommended for further Reading

Dr Mc Graw, Phillip—Life strategies, Vermilion (2001)

Robbins, Anthony—Awaken The Giant Within, Pocket Books (2001)

Mc Kenna, Paul—Instant Confidence, Bantam Press (2006)

Dr Atkinson, Mark—True Happiness, Piatkus (2011)

Glasser W and Glasser C—Eight Lessons for a Happier Marriage, Harper (2007)

Dr Murphy, Joseph—The Power of Your Subconscious, Pocket Books (2006)

Marieb, Elaine, N—Human Anatomy and Physiology, Second Edition, The Benjamin/Cumings Publishing Company, Inc. (1992)

Lindenfield, Gael—Assert Yourself, Thorsons (1992)

ABOUT THE AUTHOR

Lily is a successful Life Coach, mentor and Counsellor, who is passionate about motivating, inspiring and empowering her clients, to drive them to make the necessary changes in order for them to achieve their goals and reach their full potential.

Lily specializes in clients with anxiety, depression, and relationships issues. Prior to Life Coaching, Lily worked as a qualified Health Visitor and Nurse Practitioner (UK) who has spent over 30 years in the Health industry, including being a Clinical Postnatal Depression Specialist and Manager.

Lily coaches individual clients, couples, groups or by Skype.

Lily is a keen Emotional Freedom Technique (E.F.T) Practitioner and a Master Neuro-Linguistic Programming (NLP) Practitioner. She firmly believes that these wonderful techniques make a huge difference in her clients' lives.

Lily was recently nominated Australian of The Year 2013, and is a member of the Worldwide Who's Who for Professional Women.

From Me to You the Tapestry of Life and Its Secrets is her first book.

Lily is happily married and lives with her husband Leigh in Perth, Western Australia for the last 8 years, when they came to join the rest of their extended family.

Anyone wanting to contact Lily can reach her at www.lilyfoyster.com.au

Or if you want to contact her by phone, please call (00-618(9)-0432-557-046

If you have enjoyed this book or have found it helpful,
Lily wants to hear from you.